~~Joseph P. ...~~

~~40 K of C Ladies' Auxiliary~~

~~Christmas 1950~~

J Scally

THE PURSUIT OF HAPPINESS

(IA IIAE)

A COMPANION TO THE SUMMA

A COMPANION TO THE SUMMA

VOLUME II—THE PURSUIT OF HAPPINESS

(Corresponding to the *Summa Theologica IA IIAE*)

By

WALTER FARRELL

O.P., S.T.LR., S.T.D.

Member of the Thomistic Institute

NEW YORK

SHEED & WARD

1945

IMPRIMATUR: T. S. McDERMOTT, O.P.

NIHIL OBSTAT: GEORGIUS CAN. SMITH, S.TH.D., PH.D.
CENSOR DEPUTATUS

IMPRIMATUR: LEONELLUS CAN EVANS,
VIC. GEN.

WESTMONASTERII DIE 29A MARTII 1938

Thomas Aquinas

PRINTED IN THE UNITED STATES OF AMERICA
BY THE POLYGRAPHIC COMPANY OF AMERICA, N.Y.

CONTENTS

FOREWORD

LIKE many modern books, this present volume traces its origin to a series of lectures. However, the lectures from which this work has sprung were of an oddly ambitious character. They were given in New York under the auspices of The Catholic Thought Association and were designed to cover the whole of the *Summa Theologica*, question by question, at the rate of one Part each year.

As the work progressed it seemed evident that there was a much wider field for such an ambition than was offered by the walls of a lecture hall. In fact there seemed to be a double need to be met by just such an attempt. There is first of all the ordinary Catholic's evident need of a rational defence of his faith against the atmosphere in which he is forced to live. Secondly there is the need felt by those who, having heard enough of St. Thomas to whet their appetite, suddenly discover that they cannot go directly to St. Thomas without the guidance of a professor; and for most of them the leisure days of the classroom are over for ever.

This, then, is the double purpose of this book: to furnish a rational defence of his faith for the ordinary Catholic and to open St. Thomas to the layman who has no professional philosophical or theological knowledge. It is not, then, intended only for the very learned, nor for a text-book. If it must be described in a phrase, it might best be called an easy guide-book to St. Thomas's greatest work.

Just as a guide-book to Paris can be best evaluated in the streets of Paris, so this guide-book to the *Summa* can be best appreciated in the pages of the *Summa*, by comparing the individual chapters of the book with the corresponding questions of the *Prima Secundae* (First Part of the Second Part) of St. Thomas's *Summa*, questions that are given at the head of each chapter. Any particularly striking point will be found more fully and more beautifully developed in the *Summa* itself; further proofs, explanations, and illustrations can all be had directly from St. Thomas. This guide-book is merely a shadow of the beauty of the *Summa* itself.

But it is important to remember that it is the *Summa* reduced to popular language and not merely another book about St. Thomas or about the *Summa*. In fact it is often more than that, for, particularly on difficult questions, the parallel passages in other works of St. Thomas have been freely used where the conciseness of the *Summa* might have caused some obscurity for one not wholly familiar with the thought of Thomas.

The impossibility of adequately realizing such an ambition as prompted this work is self-evident. But St. Thomas himself had such a love of "beginners" that at the height of his powers he wrote his greatest work for just that class. Surely he will be patient with any efforts made on behalf of his beloved beginners. Because he too was a member of an Order whose motto is "*Veritas*" and whose radical explanation is a burning love of truth, he will be gentle with the shortcomings of a work the end of which is to bring men into direct contact with his own great love of truth and so start them off, as Albert started him off, on the romantic pursuit that will end only with the vision of the First Truth. I wish to express my profound gratitude to my brethren and the members of the Thomistic Institute for the patience and co-operation which has made this work possible.

W.F.

CHAPTER I

(OUTLINE)

THE ESSENCE OF HAPPINESS

(Q. 1–5)

1. The key to the mystery of human life is happiness:

2. Happiness consists in the attainment of the goal of life.

3. The study of happiness must begin, not at the beginning, but at the end, the goal:
   - (*a*) There is a goal of life:
     - (1) Fact of man's goal—from his activity.
     - (2) The failure of modern philosophy.
   - (*b*) The nature of this goal:
     - (1) It is uniquely human.
     - (2) It is ultimate:
       - *a*. Each man has but one goal.
       - *b*. That goal is the source of all other desires.
       - *c*. It is the same for all men.
     - (3) It is the end of all creatures, but differently:
       - *a*. By participating an image.
       - *b*. By essential participation.

4. Objective Happiness—determination of the beatifying object:
   - (*a*) Three possible—and historical—mistakes:
     - (1) External goods: riches, honour, fame, power.
     - (2) Corporal good: the body itself, its pleasure.
     - (3) The soul of man.
   - (*b*) The true object in whose possession lies happiness is the Universal Good.

5. Subjective or Formal Happiness—the attainment of the goal:
   - (*a*) It is possible—from a comparison of man's faculties and man's goal.
   - (*b*) It is accomplished by an act of man:
     - (1) Not by any of his inferior acts.
     - (2) But by the supreme act of man—intellectual vision.
       - *a*. The essence of formal happiness.

b. Two common errors in regard to this formal happiness:

1. Cannot be had.
2. Would not give happiness if it were had.

(*c*) Characteristics of formal happiness:

(1) Once gained it can never be lost.
(2) It cannot be had by natural powers alone.
(3) It is strictly a personal accomplishment.

6. The perfection of happiness:

(*a*) The three essentials of happiness: vision, comprehension, joy.
(*b*) Role of the body in happiness.
(*c*) Role of external goods.
(*d*) Role of friends.

Conclusion :

1. Key to present or imperfect happiness—where and how happiness is to be found here and now.
2. Activity and progress as a measure of happiness.
3. Answers to the puzzles:

(*a*) Of activity.
(*b*) Of despair.
(*c*) Of boredom.

CHAPTER I

THE ESSENCE OF HAPPINESS

Q. (1–5)

THE first volume of this work is no less than an expedition through the halls of infinity. Aided by the revelations of His private life made by God Himself, St. Thomas looks as closely at God, the life of God, and the activity of God as human reason permits. In a way, that work is an immediate preparation for what is to be done in this second volume. In the first volume we saw God the exemplar of man, here we look at man the image of God; there we saw God the supreme intellect and will, in Himself, and as the principle from which all things flow, here we see man, the image, possessed of intellect and will, the principle of his own works with dominion over his acts.

Here we have, as a matter of fact, reason for the same terror that engulfs a man at the beginning of his study of God. The terrific complexity of man's life and man's activity might well seem an overpowering assignment for the limits of one volume. The scope of those activities, stretching from ocean to ocean, from pole to pole, from the earliest beginnings to the limitless future, would be far too much to touch upon, let alone plunge into, if man were not man. Because he is man, there is an element of unity that binds together the whole sweep of man's doings as closely as his nature binds the individual; there is a common harmonious note that reveals the meaning of the whole apparently discordant chorus.

That note of unity and harmony is human desire. The same force that has driven men apart, that has set nations at one another's throats, that has wiped individuals and races off the face of the earth, is at the same time the one great focal point of human agreement and harmony. All men agree on this—they want what they want. And because of this desire, men act. In the attainment of what they want we have the essential notion of happiness. It is not pleasure, not enjoyment, but the possession of the object of desire which constitutes happiness. And in this sense all men want to be happy. Happiness is the key to the mystery of human life, of human activity.

The material of our study in this volume, therefore, is human action, particularly in its culmination in happiness. It is fortunate for our feeble courage in the face of this task that the fundamental notions involved are so clear. At least most of us will agree theoretically on what a human action is; certainly all of us will agree practically in determining when a man is acting humanly. Theoretically, an act is human over which a man has control, an act that is done deliberately, i.e. on purpose, for a precise reason, to attain a definite goal. When we catch ourselves up now and then and ask in astonishment, "Why in the world did I do that?", only to find there is no answer to the "why" of that question, we are right in concluding that we need sleep, or a vacation, or a visit to the doctor. For while a human being has certainly placed an act, he has not acted humanly. Practically, we have a whole set of phrases to express the difference between a human action and one that is not human. A servant explains: "I'm sorry, I didn't mean that"; and of course the apology must be accepted, even though the coffee spilled on us is, unlike most coffee, incredibly hot. A man whose foot has been trampled in a subway crowd says what he says because he "is angry, not himself". We are "beside ourselves" with indignation, "in a trance, absent-minded, forgetful, cross, hysterical or terror-stricken", and of course our actions are not human.

For if human they are, then they must be done for some

reason, to some end, for some goal. For, after all, action has to do with the attainment of the object of desire, and the object of desire is precisely the goal or end of that particular action. The study of happiness, then, cannot begin at the beginning; it is too intimately wrapped up with the finish or goal. It is not that man's head is befuddled, but rather that man has the kind of head which makes it necessary to begin at the end. He is not living his life backward, but has that divine faculty of standing off to one side and looking at his life, or of looking ahead of his life, and so is capable of appreciating its meaning as well as its humour. And looking ahead, he will see that the goal does much more than flavour the action directed to it; it does even more than explain the existence of that action, as we shall see presently. For on the determination of the nature of that goal depends the meaning of the whole life of a man, the nature of all his activity, the very destiny of man.

From what we have seen of action that is human, we know the life of man has some end or ends, some goal or goals. The very fact that an act, to measure up to our requirements of human action, must be deliberately controlled, places it as coming from deliberate will; the act is ours and imputable to us because we have willed it. This is universally true of any act that presumes to be human; so that human activity comes from the human will and goes to the object of the human will. In other words, it is placed because of some good, some end, since it proceeds from the instrument of human desire (will) whose only object is good.

Here we come upon one of the most drastic failures of modern philosophy. Face to face with the unquestionable fact of finality—purposiveness—in human action, modern philosophy has taken refuge in the murk of vague speculation. In the face of modern contempt for any but the most empirical knowledge, modern philosophy has committed itself to the building of castles in the air. It is dangerous to attempt to classify modern ethical theories; they are so intensely flavoured by the individual philosopher's personal outlook and background that almost every man has a system of his own. But, roughly, we can split modern ethical theory into three classes: (*a*) the first tries to explain this finality of human activity in terms of the society to which man belongs, reducing ethics to positive law, to some form of public opinion, to sociology; (*b*) the second attempts the same task in terms of a necessity of the universe in which man moves, whether mechanical or animal, reducing ethics to mathematics, biology, or psychology; (*c*) the third, faced with the dilemma that reduced Aristotle's magnificent reasoning to vague muttering, makes a god out of man and talks in frankly, or insidiously, subjectivistic terms, describing its ethics as individualistic, emotional or autonomous.

The human being, in whose name all this has been done, is an intensely individual and practical being. To explain patiently that his efforts, his sufferings, his triumphs, his courage, his loyalty, his failures have no objective significance for him personally, merely exasperates him. If all his activity is only in the name of, and for the vague purposes of a very intangible, perhaps very distant, community perfection; or is only the ceaseless grinding of a giant machine, the necessary, irresistible urging of an animal, or the frail spinnings of his own mind, he will do one of two things: either he will stop all his effort, all his activity, or he will push the theorizing of philosophies into the room with the children's toys and make his own decisions. And this latter is precisely what he has done. The position and influence of philosophy in our universities to-day are adequate testimony of philosophy's failure in the field of ethical theory. The pursuit of wealth, of power, of pleasure, of food or drink, of physical perfection, or of scientific inquiry as the goal of human life, gives the other side of the picture, the failure of philosophy in the field of ethical practice.

Men and women of to-day are no more satisfied with fables than were the men and women of any other age. And if we are to get at the truth of human happiness, we cannot simply scramble human activity with every other form of action in the universe. To act for a goal of our choosing, and that means to attempt to attain happiness, is a uniquely human right. Other things, other creatures, may be propelled towards a goal by the drive of physical necessity or of animal instinct, much as an arrow is shot towards a target by the impulse and aim of the archer. But only man can direct action towards a goal, for only man is in control of his actions. Control of action involves deliberate will, the ability to see the connection between the tools used and the job to be done, between the means and the end. To envy the secluded happiness of a pampered lap-dog is a waste of energy; he cannot be happy because he cannot know what it is all about. We might, indeed we do, whip a puppy for chewing up slippers, we hope that he will remember the whipping in connection with the slippers and avoid both; but we never think of absolving him from his sins.

Aristotle, and St. Thomas after him, laid the solid foundation for the investigation of human activity by tying its goal up with the order of reality. In his treatment of God, St. Thomas triumphantly vindicates both the reality and the sublime supremacy of the divinity by first showing its connection with the very first principles of being and thought. Here, in the very beginning of his investigation of the meaning of human life, we see him laying down the same metaphysical basis for his thought, bringing out clearly the connection between that goal of human activity and the first principles of reality.

Precisely because a human action, to be human at all, must be directed to some goal, to some good, it follows that there must be some goal that is the last, the ultimate explanation of all human activity. Just as all movement must have one supreme beginning if there is to be any movement at all (as we saw in the first volume in proving the existence of God), so all human movement must have one goal, one end, if there is to be any movement at all. In concrete terms, I buy a boat-ticket to Europe, either because the supreme goal of my life is the possession of such a ticket, or because I want that ticket for some other purpose, such as to go to Europe. Whatever it is I strive for, I want that thing either for itself, or as a step to getting something else. Of course no one starts to climb a flight of stairs devoid of the conviction that the stairs go somewhere, that they have some end; for after all the whole purpose of stairs is to get us to some other place. So, no human being starts a chain of action that is going nowhere; for the whole reason of acting at all is to get somewhere, to attain some object of our desire. This is the first argument used for the existence of God, but taken from the order of efficient cause and put to work in the order of final cause. To question its validity is to demand action and at the same time, in the same breath, make action impossible.

A final, ultimate, supreme end, or goal, is necessarily solitary, unique. In simpler language, no man or woman can have two final goals at the same time, any more than a person can walk in two directions at the same time. Action is a majestic flight towards a landing field; and motion, swift or slow, crooked or straight, has only one final stopping place. The family likeness of all desirable things—goodness—is an unerring clue to their common origin and final resting place.

This ultimate, supreme goal is the giant power-house from which the current flows out to all other lesser goals. This is the head of the house of desirable things, from whom comes all the beauty and allure of the lesser members.

These lesser ends are intermediaries, steps, which have value because of their connection with the supreme end; separated from it, they are as pathetically useless as a bridge torn from the banks of a river it was meant to span.

In a very real, very objective sense, this supreme, ultimate good which draws forth all human activity is identical for all men. For on this one point are all men agreed; the purpose of their action is happiness. And it is precisely this supreme end which can fulfil that purpose. Actually, the ends of human activity are as multiple as the energies men put forth in search for happiness, as diverse as the mistakes men make in trying to determine just what that final, supreme good is. A man with a thick tongue and a headache is not a dependable judge of the tastiness of a breakfast; neither is a perverted will a dependable judge, of the object in which human happiness is to be found. Our next steps in the investigation of the essence of happiness will be the determination of the healthiness of the human appetite or will, the concrete discovery of just what particular object can confer happiness on man.

But first, and passingly, we might point out that the majestic force which has swept the universe on from its dim beginnings towards its final goal has made no exception in the case of man. He may be the very summit of nature, the lord of the world, but he is none the less a part of that natural order, subject to those same natural laws, and moving along with nature to the same supreme end. For it is quite true that the end of nature and the end of every man in nature is the same; as all motion must have had the one source, so it must have the one final resting place, the one goal. In this same sense, we might say that Admiral Byrd's plane, his dog, and himself all reached the same goal, the South Pole, but certainly not in the same way. So with the creatures of our universe: some by merely existing, some by living, others by living and feeling, reach a little image of that final good; while men and angels speed on to the very core of that final good on the wings of knowledge and love.

It is the peculiar genius of our race to be able to make mistakes. And that genius has been exhausted in the attempt to determine the object the possession of which will mean happiness for us. Men have placed their chips on every number that the universe offers in the gamble for happiness, and they have always been wrong. As a matter of fact only two classes of mistakes were possible: placing all chance for happiness in some external, particular good, or on some good within the nature of man himself, whether of body or of soul.

Of the external seducers, riches have played a leading role, but their beauty has been an illusion produced by make-up and a spotlight. For the ultimate goal of man cannot exist for anything else; because it is ultimate it is desired for itself, it is never a step but always that to which steps lead. And riches, whether natural (such as food and drink) or artificial (such as wealth) are always steps, always *for* something else: the first *for* the sustaining of life; the second, even more obviously, *for* the purchase of natural goods.

The other external goods—honour, reputation, power—are just as easily disposed of as being claimants to the place of honour in man's quest for happiness, no matter how many millions of men and women they have fooled. Natural and artificial riches, as instruments used by man for his ends, are servants, not the supremely desirable answer to his lifetime of longing. Honour and reputation are quite outside of the man himself and indeed often independent of his efforts; in any case they bring nothing intrinsically within the scope of a man's own being. Honour is rather a witness to excellence than the constituent of happiness. Reputation (fame or glory) is another witness, not in us at all but in those who are honouring or praising us. These are frail things, often grossly erroneous, as we well know, at the mercy of every circumstance, and presupposing, not establishing, some claim to happiness. No, these are not the reason for man's existence, the final goal of all his efforts.

If the supreme good to which every man dedicates his life could be conceived as capable of being utterly vicious, capable of being possessed and still leaving its possessor a fool, or even dragging a man down to the gutter, we might be forced to hesitate before the throne of power in determining the object which will give us happiness. Power is quite capable of all these things; but, by the same token, it is incapable of being the final answer to man's quest for happiness.

Since his happiness is not to be found in the universe in which he lives, man looks, quite logically, in the only other obvious place, within himself. But his body is no more helpful than was the whole scope of the universe. Its conservation, its health, its beauty, its sensitive acumen or vegetative prodigality, are no more the explanation of man's activity than the conservation of a ship is the real purpose, the last end of a captain. The captain's job is to make a port, to navigate his ship; everything else about that ship serves this master purpose. The body's job is to make possible that activity we call human and all of its various and complex workings serve that same master purpose; ministering the material to the intelligence and will which the body serves.

To pass immediately to a consideration of the soul of man would be to treat with contempt the mistake about happiness most common in our own day. And no human mistake deserves contempt, if only because there is behind it a human heart which, until its last beat, is capable of that incredible courage that snatches victory from despair. What of sensual pleasure? Can a man lose himself here and find the complete happiness whose absence has been the driving force of all his days? Because there is so much of the animal in us, this is a mistake easy to make and difficult to remedy.

But mistake it is. For if human activity is distinctive, the goal at which it aims is no less distinctive, not at all a place where we must lie down with the brutes. As a matter of fact, a child does not have pleasure because it is enjoying ice-cream, but because it has ice-cream to enjoy. In other words, pleasure, delight, does not cause itself, but is caused by possession of some good, some end. No pleasure can make up happiness; rather it must always follow humbly in the wake of happiness, like a train-bearer following a bride.

Our attempt to determine the object which will bring man his happiness has thus far been entirely a consideration of facts. It has been no more than a pattern of the final or the ultimate, demanded by every human act, laid on the actual choices made by men. We have not been theorizing, not preaching, but simply comparing facts and rejecting obvious misfits. This strict adherence to facts brings us to the last possibility—the soul of man. It is the end of a great experiment; the last step which many have not bothered to make because they think the answer could not be other than the right one, the one sought. But honest facing of the facts cannot allow cowardice to creep in at this last stage. Let us put that pattern of finality, of supremacy in the order of things desirable over the soul and its possibilities—and the answer again is no! They do not match.

Indeed, if they did match, there would be no necessity for the bustle of human life; man would be happy from the very beginning. The very urge of man's nature that he get out of himself, as well as the shrivelled, distorted result achieved by the introvert, are indications that man's happiness does not lie within himself. Man, by his knowledge, can in a sense take all things into himself. He can become all things, and so he can desire all good. But he *is* not all things, he is not God. Neither he nor any creature is all good; and only that which can satisfy man's desires can bring him happiness.

The object of his pursuit of happiness is not outside man and in the universe; it is not within man, body or soul. But this does not mean that the whole affair is a grim joke of cosmic proportions. It is still real, still decidedly objective, this beatifying object—but it is above man and the universe. It is the answer to the human capacity to desire all goods and be satisfied with none; it is the final good that can leave nothing to be desired; it is *the absolutely universal good, outside and above man, outside and above the world, outside and above any good that bears the brand of limitation, of particularity.*

A boy is not happy because an apple will bring him happiness; but because he has the apple in his possession. Neither is a man happy because the universal good will bring him happiness; but because he possesses that universal good. The attainment of the final goal, not its mere existence, marks the close of the pursuit of happiness. And that means no less than our having reached out and taken possession of the final good, bringing it into ourselves, making it our own. In this strictly formal sense, happiness, the final accomplishment of our human actions, is indeed within man.

Dr. Cabot of Harvard[1] insists that man's business in life is to grow. The dimly seen truth behind this statement is the same as that behind modern philosophers' insistence on progress, advance, constant change, evolution without end. For to the naked eye it is apparent that action and perfection have a strange affinity. When I have absorbed all that an educational system can offer me in the way of knowledge, quite patently I have more of perfection than I had in my grammar-school days. A potential opera

[1] *The Meaning of Right and Wrong* (New York: The Macmillan Co., 1936), p. 112 ff.

star has much less perfection of voice than the opera star who has realized her potentialities. It is quite true then that perfection is in exact proportion to actuality, as true of man as of plants, or indeed as of God.

Consequently, this ultimate perfection of man, which is his complete happiness, is to be found in his consummate, most perfect act. In modern terms, substance exists for the sake of function; the ultimate in perfection of any substance, then, will be its most perfect function. More simply, the goal of life will be the realization of the best that is in man.

This truth is so obvious that, stated in common-place language, it seems almost insulting to intelligence. Everyone knows that man's desires are satisfied only by his reaching out and getting what he lacks. Of course, since some object he now lacks will satisfy his desires, will bring him happiness, the thing for him to do is to reach out and get it—a feat that is accomplished by using the tools at our command, human actions.

Since we know what we are after—the universal good --we can immediately exclude all those operations that are not distinctively human, those sense operations common to all animals, whose goals are not universal but particular goals. This action must be a distinctively human action, i.e. an act of intellect or will. And again the process of exclusion is simple. I can desire a hat in a draughty room by a mere act of my will: I can enjoy the possession of that hat with my will. But if I ever expect to have that hat, I'll have to get up and get it. As a universal good is not something to be had by reaching out my hand, or by calling a servant, the only possibility of its possession is by an act of my intellect. Can I make it? Why not? That same intellect can know all things, even the universal; and it is the universal good that I am after.

But let it be well understood that no substitutes will do. My will can be satisfied only when I possess that universal good, only when it is present within me by my knowledge of it. The lofty considerations of truth offered by philosophy or science will not do; not even the absorbed contemplation of angelic beauty will be tolerated patiently. It must be all or nothing: either the universal, all-embracing good, or the failure of the pursuit of happiness. The intellectual perfection that will help me to take more steps towards a goal is not sufficient; rather that is necessary which will mean no more steps.

In plain words, I must see God. From the very beginning I have been driven by the desire to plumb the depths, to be unsatisfied with the superficial, to know the inner workings, the very essences of things. And having come upon the traces of God in nature, having learned of His existence, my nature will not be satisfied until I have seen the very essence of God.

So far Aristotle managed to trudge up the last hill in his pursuit of happiness. He saw man standing at the summit of the created universe; at the peak of man's nature was the intellect; and the zenith of that intellect's activity was the contemplation of truth. Here, he concluded, must lie the happiness of man: in the supreme act of his supreme faculty, in the perfect realization of his greatest potentiality.

Looking down from these heights, Aristotle was brought to earth with a crash. The men of that earth were real; the labours, interests, worries of their lives were decidedly real and left very little room for silent contemplation. Perhaps their offices were not as busy then as ours are to-day, but certainly their lives were. Moreover, how many of these men were capable of contemplation; and how long could the best of them keep it up? What an end to the quest of happiness! Such was the way Aristotle must have felt about the whole thing. His courage and devotion to facts were great enough to make him hold doggedly to the conclusions facts had forced upon him; but they were not great enough to make him take the last few steps that were possible to philosophy—to come out clearly with the last conclusions demanded by the facts. He chose to leave them vague.

Two obvious difficulties jumped at Aristotle—and at men ever since. For it seems evident that man cannot see God, and, even if he did, the act, like all his acts of contemplation, would endure for only a short time and could not give him happiness. To these objections St. Thomas had the infallible answers of divine faith. As a matter of fact, men do see God; and in their vision is their supreme happiness.[1] It is quite certain that the universal Good, the essence of God, cannot be crowded into a mental concept, nor be abstracted from sensible things; and yet that is the way our intellect works. Yes, the way it works naturally; the way it works at the present time, not because of its intelligence, but because of that crutch which intelligence must use and which we call reasoning. Man can be, and is, lifted above that lowest grade of intelligence; he is enabled to throw away the crutch and come to grips with divinity, not through an image or a concept, but in the way the divinity sees itself—through the immediate union of that supremely knowable essence to the intellect of man.

Supernatural? Of course it is supernatural. But that fact is no more of an affront to man's self-sufficiency, to the efficacy of nature, than is the fact that man is born without protection and clothes but is given hands and reason to make up for the deficiency. Here he is given a free will by which he can co-operate with the supernatural help infallibly offered him and reach the happiness which hangs over his head. That the contemplation of divinity is unsatisfying in this life, is beyond all question; and if reason could not have discovered that fact, faith would broadcast it to the four winds.[2] But that dissatis-

[1] Ex Constitutione Benedict XII, "Benedictus Deus", H. Denzinger, *Enchiridion Symbolorum* (Freiburg, Germany: Herder & Co., ed. 17, 1928), #530.

[2] Council of Vienna, condemned propositions of Beghards, 1, 4, 5. (Denzinger, #471, 474, 475).

faction is in this life, seeing that divinity through a glass darkly and while we are sadly pressed by all the necessities of physical existence. Aristotle was right as far as he went; but it had not entered into the mind of man that God would insist on such a perfect image of Himself in the unfolding of the goal of human activity.

Of this ultimate goal, then, it is strictly true that it is supernatural, not to be attained by natural powers. Yet, paradoxically, it is strictly personal attainment. No other creature, neither man nor woman, nor the highest angel in heaven, can get it for us; nor will God force it upon us. We approach it step by step, by our own human actions, working with the constant help of God; and the last and eternally enduring act by which we grasp God Himself is an act of our intellect, something that can no more be done for us than our thinking here and now can be done by someone else and still be ours. Once had, this supreme good which satisfies all our desires and puts an end to the quest of happiness cannot possibly slip from our fingers. On its part, the beatifying object cannot dry up and blow away, it cannot decrease or cease to be what it essentially is, the universal good; on our part, we cannot get tired of it, there is nothing else that can tempt us from it, that can seem to have something that is not contained in that ultimate goal. Otherwise it would not be the ultimate, the universal good. Just as now we must will everything under the guise and in the name of good, so then we must will everything in the name of the divine good—what attractiveness there is in other things, comes from this final end.

Summing this up: a universally good object and its attainment by us is required for our complete happiness. In that attainment of the final goal there is involved the intellectual vision of the beatifying object; not merely a passing glance, but a tenacious grasp, an enduring comprehension of that object, and, finally, the eternally enduring joy (or rest) of our will, our appetite, in the accomplishment of our goal, in the possession of the all-satisfying good.

All else that may be involved in our final happiness, however much it may contribute to the perfection of happiness, is secondary and relatively unimportant—a delicate touch perhaps, like a drop of perfume on the gown of a perfectly dressed woman, but adding nothing substantial.

In this way, the reunion of body and soul will add to the perfection of the happiness of man. After all, his body belongs to a man, the soul was made for union with that body, and without it, the soul is in a very real sense incomplete; but the addition of the body will not add to the essential joy and glory of the soul, rather the other way around. From the soul will come joy and glory to the body, much as at present a light heart gives buoyancy to our steps.

This overflow from the soul to the body will carry that body far beyond the limits of natural perfection. Often the body is in command of the situation at present, as the protest of our knees at an overlong prayer will testify; but then, the body will be completely subservient to the soul as it was meant to be. It would seem difficult then to find a place in the perfection of happiness for external goods. At present they are ordained to the needs of physical life; even the most sublime contemplative needs food and clothes. But the question of clothes in heaven would seem to be still very much open to debate.

Friends, of course, there must be, in the same way that we must have our bodies. They are our other selves; something of ourselves would be missing without them. And this is true, even though the principal end of friendship—the opportunity to help, to sacrifice, to give to others—will no longer exist; that subtler, infinitely precious joy in the beauty, the triumph, the happiness of friends will give a splendidly human air to the courts of heaven.

All of this may seem very far away, very unsatisfactory to men and women who are engaged in the actual pursuit of happiness—as always the tape at the end of a race seems infinitely distant from the starting line. We want happiness *now*. What can we do about it to-day? What, if any, is the possibility of some happiness in this life?

All of the answers to questions that might be put about present happiness are contained in what we have already said. Perhaps one of the most important is that no perfect happiness is to be had this side of death. It is an important thing to know. What happiness is possible can be had only by going in the general direction of that final goal, for because of that goal every other good is desirable, every other good has what power it possesses to satisfy the longings of our hearts. And what happiness can be had will be had slowly, trudgingly, little by little, with many an imperfection, distraction, interruption mixed in. The degree of present happiness is in exact proportion to our approach to the final goal of life, as the heat we feel from a fire is in exact proportion to our proximity to the fire. In utterly simple language: happiness, even the imperfect happiness this life can offer, is a matter of approaching God. The closer we get to Him, the greater our share of this imperfect happiness; the farther away we get, the less happiness we can expect to garner. The words of the child's catechism are an adequate summary of all we have said: man was made to know and to love God. The goal of life is the knowledge and love, the vision and enjoyment, of divinity; what happiness we get in this life will be through an imperfect knowledge or love of God, either in Himself, or in one of the mirrorings of divinity which we call creatures.

The rush of New York life is not necessarily an improvement on the sleepy quiet of a tiny Irish hamlet. Man gains his happiness by activity; but not by every activity, rather by activity that is going somewhere, going to the right place. There is such a thing as being so busy we have no time to live; having our heads so full of knowledge we have no chance to think; or our hearts so crowded that there is no place for love. Activity for activity's sake, bustling for its own sake, may help us to forget, may prevent our thinking, but it will not bring us happiness. Progress is indeed a measure of happiness—if it is progress towards God. But progress in time saving devices, or labour-saving devices, in wealth, health, strength, beauty, athletic ability, business efficiency—all of these can easily be synchronizing with flight away from the ultimate goal of human life. At best they are helps; at times they make that true progress easier. There can be no question that a young man of to-day has made less real progress as a result of fourteen or eighteen years of intensive educational efforts than did the Apostles by rubbing elbows with Christ for three years.

A man or woman who starts off in high expectations of grasping full happiness within the span of human life is headed straight for despair; for despair is the fruit of reaching for the impossible. The person to-day starting life with a denial of life's goal, of the ultimate universal good, has no choice, eventually, but to choke out life or to attempt to choke out reason. The first is despair. The second produces a weariness from trying to pretend that the petty particularities of the universe can be the absorbing explanation of human activity, the goal of human life, the reward for the pursuit of happiness. This is boredom.

CHAPTER II

(OUTLINE)

THE MEANS TO HAPPINESS

(Q. 6–10)

1. The means by which happiness is attained are utterly simple yet distinctive:
    - (*a*) Simple—at the finger-tips of every human being.
    - (*b*) Distinctive—proper to man alone.
    - (*c*) These means are human actions.

2. The distinctive core of human action is deliberate control:
    - (*a*) By this, man's life, his activity and his destiny are things apart in the universe.
    - (*b*) Fundamental character of modern errors on the nature of human action.
    - (*c*) Enemies of deliberate control:
        - (1) From within a man himself:
            - *a*. From the senses:
                - 1. In contact with evil.
                - 2. In contact with good.
            - *b*. From the intellect.
        - (2) From the outside.

3. The environs of human action in general:
    - (*a*) Their name and number: who, what, where, by whose help, when, why, how.
    - (*b*) Their importance:
        - (1) For the complete story of a human action; comparison of journalist's and theologian's quest for truth in human action.
        - (2) For judgment, public or private, of a man's act.
        - (3) For the individual's choice of action.
        - (4) For his very activity.

4. Particular conditions of every human action:
    - (*a*) Why:
        - (1) To attain the object of desire; always because of good principally because of the end or goal.

(2) Not exclusively but primarily because of the goal; every other object of desire is with reference to the goal.

(*b*) By whose help—the motive forces of human action

(1) Intellect's part.
(2) Part of the senses.
(3) Part of the will itself.
(4) External influences.
(5) God's part.

(*c*) How:

(1) Naturally.
(2) Necessarily:
a. With regard to a proper object.
b. Because of sense appetite.
c. Because of divine influence.
(3) Freely.

Conclusion :

1. The means to happiness are perfectly proportioned to the object whose possession gives happiness:

(*a*) They are universally possessed by men.
(*b*) Effective from the beginnings of reason.
(*c*) Rigidly personal.
(*d*) Completely sovereign.
(*e*) Utterly simple.

2. They are in complete harmony with the unity and effectiveness of nature and natural law.

3. They alone are worthy of the dignity and intelligence of man.

CHAPTER II

THE MEANS TO HAPPINESS

(Q. 6–10)

OUR task in this chapter is one in which philosophy needs no theological help. If we accept the quite accurate definition of philosophy given by a modern philosopher, "the attempt by reasoning to know what is ultimately real", we are quickly brought face to face with the absorbing problem that occupies us in this chapter.

Two very human pictures show how deeply this problem concerns the human heart. A mother, fondling her infant, wonders what the future holds in store for the baby. What will it become? Will it be happy? Behind this universal query lie the deeper questions: what is the meaning of this tiny life, what is it for, where is it going, how will it get to the goal where alone it will find happiness? "To know the ultimately real!" At the death-bed of his father, or of that same mother who had wondered about his life, the same questions meet the son. What becomes of these loved ones? What was the meaning of their lives? Was that long courageous trek through the years only for this? Or is there a further goal? And even where these questions have sure answers, there are the further questions that keep loved ones always close by keeping them always dependent: did they have the right tools for the carving out of their lives, did they know and use the means that would bring them success, did they take the steps that would bring them home? Bethlehem and Calvary, the two pictures—birth and death—which bring men and women face to face with the necessity of knowing the ultimately real of human life.

In the preceding chapter, in determining the object in the possession of which happiness alone could be found, we saw part of this ultimate reality. We saw the goal, the final end, the supreme answer to the quest for happiness. Here we are looking at a no less important angle of that ultimate reality, that ultimate meaning of human life, in examining the means by which we can reach that goal.

The answer is by no means merely a speculative one. If these means to happiness are open only to the very wealthy, or to the very poor, man's life takes on the proportions of a practical joke, played on a cosmic scale with a ruthlessly cruel lack of humour. These things cannot be the exclusive possession of the very wise or the very ignorant; of the very wealthy or the very sick; of the man of power or the timid weakling. They cannot be the private property of any class, any group, any nation, without making a farce of the very peak of natural perfection that is found in the story of human activity.

They must be utterly universal, and, despite their efficacy in bringing a man to his goal, must be of so uncomplicated a nature that a child can wield them with the sure touch which proclaims mastery. If human life has a meaning, if there is a final goal of human action, then that meaning, that goal, is proper to every human being. Not personality, not age, not talent, but the very fact of being human is the just claim to the possession of the means to happiness.

In our last chapter we said that happiness means the possession of the object which brings happiness, the grasp of the good which is back of all desire; and that this possession is the fruit of our own action. More concretely, we showed that human life has a goal—the supreme universal good; the individual man is happy when by his action he possesses that universal good, when he is brought into immediate contact with that final end through the vision of God. The steps to that final goal are simply human actions. These are the means by which man can attain to happiness, and these alone. And it is precisely these means that all men, women, and children, from the dawn of reason, have at their finger-tips.

It would be interesting to examine the false goals of human endeavour from this angle; to wonder, in a kind of stage whisper, how huge a wave of despair would sweep the world if it were true that health, food, pleasure, riches, fame or power was the final goal of us all.

But we have finished with the goal for the time being. Let us look more closely at the means to human happiness. A characteristic of these means, as striking as their universality, is their distinctiveness. While they belong to every single man born into the world as a natural birthright, not another creature in the world can possibly possess them. They are the family heritage which can be claimed only on the grounds of human blood; the pontifical robes of the lord of creation which no impostor can possibly wear. Only a human being can produce a human action.

A man can crash into a brick wall even more resoundingly than the blindest of insects, he can howl like a dog, be as vicious as a tiger, as stupid as a sheep. In fact, he can disguise or cast off the humanity of his actions to the extent of being more animal than the animal. But it does not work the other way around. For only a man is capable of that deliberate, that controlled action by which he can move himself to his goal. Everything beneath man is in the servant class, answering the beck and call of an outside power. Man alone is master of his life, of his action.

What is the secret of that distinctiveness? What is the human action's inner core whose presence makes such a startling difference between the wielding of a fork and the rooting of a snout? We could call it by several names.

Perhaps the simplest would be "control"; "deliberate will" would be another. Whatever its name, its presence or absence is the determining factor in the humanity of our actions. This control makes the difference between the fatal blow struck by the fury of blind rage and the paid assassin's silent knife-thrust.

At the roots of this deliberate control is man's unique ability to choose. Precisely because he can look beyond his action, he can control it; because he knows the connection between the job to be done and the tools at hand, he can pick his tools. Because in his heart he carries the image of the supreme good, he can see the defects in anything less than the supreme good, he can choose this because of its good points, reject that because of its defects, or sit back in contempt and refuse to be bothered with anything which does not bear the mark of complete perfection. Whatever the course of his action, he has exercised that solely human faculty of self-control. The trip from birth to death is not along a track utterly determining the course man will follow; because of the voluntary character of his actions, man is sitting behind the wheel in complete control.

Take away that control and you take away the human character of man's actions. By this control is man alone capable of triumph or failure. He is the only one in the universe with the paradoxical capacity for sin and sanctity, for mistakes and successes, for nobility and meanness, because he alone can answer for his actions.

It is not an easy thing to carry that responsibility. Perhaps unconsciously, men sometimes try to escape its difficulties, forgetting its privileges—and forgetting that there is no escape. One way of attempted escape is to take too much to drink; another way is to philosophize man out of existence. If man's actions are only the overflow of deep, unconscious surgings (Freud) or the swelling tide of an irresistible and blind life-force (Bergson), man hasn't any worries, nor has he any hopes. If his activities have no more significance than the arching of a cat's back at the sight of a dog, an animal response to external stimuli (Watson), he must make up his mind to lead a dog's life and like it. If his intelligence is merely the last phenomenon in a long and inexplicable process that cannot reach a goal without destroying itself, like the latest bubble on a glass of champagne (S. Alexander), it is silly to get excited about control, or goal, or happiness, or humanity. It may be comforting to make man an animal, or a machine, or a process; but it is not the comfort of truth, of facing the fact that man continues to be man. These modern errors are much more sweeping than has been realized by many people; and the devastation they bring is the result of their attack on the distinctive core of all human action—deliberate control.

This deliberate control is the result of self-movement with a knowledge of the relation of means to end. In other words, it requires over and above the intrinsic principle of movement common to all living things, a knowledge of the goal and the steps to that goal. Over and above the intrinsic principle of movement and the particularized, determined knowledge of sensible ends common to all animals, it demands a universal knowledge of the end and of the relations between that end and the means to it. In a word, it is self-movement, movement from within, which knows where it is going and why it is going this particular way.

We can picture this movement from within, this deliberate control, as a long journey from the inner recesses of man's soul. Looking at it in this light, we see again that it is not easy to be human, to hold tightly to our humanity. Within the kingdom of ourselves, the jealousy of the universe is concentrated, steadily directed at our unique privilege of acting humanly. We are masters of ourselves, but our subjects are always ripe for rebellion. As that journey from the inner recesses of our soul gets under way, it meets a formidable enemy in the animal life of the senses.

Whether that animal life is fleeing from impending evil or rushing headlong after an alluring good, it always carries with it serious dangers to the control of our actions. Indeed, as we shall see in more detail later on, it sometimes goes to the point of completely destroying that control, as in the terror-stricken mob that fights hysterically to escape from a burning theatre. When that happens, there is no longer any question of human action or human responsibility, of human progress towards a goal; the humanity of our actions is destroyed in the exact proportion to the interference with that control.

Where the attack is not so much on control as on the willingness of our actions, fear of evil and desire of good operate differently. A pilot, through fear of being forced down by ice on the wings of his plane, will lighten the plane by throwing overboard precious gasoline the loss of which will certainly shorten his journey and perhaps bring disaster to it. He does not want to lose the gasoline, yet in the circumstances there is positive eagerness to be rid of it. Fear makes him do something that in itself is displeasing, something that he does unwillingly; yet, in these conditions, the loss has his complete consent. The pilot is much like a man with a horror of bitter medicine, who is quite willing to take the medicine, not because he has changed his views on the matter, but because the bitter dose is necessary for his health. The allure of good, rather than cutting down our willingness, directly and immediately increases it. Our passion for the theatre may seriously threaten the control of our actions; but at no time do we trudge up to the box-office on unwilling feet, like a small boy returning to school after vacation, with an air of woeful martyrdom.

Even further back in the course of this movement from within ourselves, almost before the journey has started, a no less deadly enemy is met in the intellect itself, an enemy that goes by the name of ignorance. There is something particularly repellent about the word "ignorance" that makes us instantly resent its application to ourselves. To be called a rascal may mean that our morality is seriously being called into question; but if the epithet is "ignorant rascal," it is not only our morality, but our very humanity that is under attack. For the implication is that we are lacking in something we should have, something that directly affects that control of action which is distinctive of humanity. "Ignorant" is just a little worse than "half-wit" or "stupid", for these things cannot be helped; but ignorance implies that somewhere along the road we have failed to pick up what we should and could have had; something necessary for the manliness, the humanity of our actions.

This repulsiveness of ignorance is easily understood from its concrete results. When it precedes a particular action, it makes us do things that otherwise we would never think of doing: silly things like spreading shaving cream on a toothbrush, and eventually on our teeth; petty things like short-changing a newsboy in a strange city; tragic things like killing a man when we thought we were shooting a deer.

A more despicable type of ignorance is one which we are quite willing to tolerate, indeed even to protect, because it allows us to sidle out of things. It is a thoroughly hypocritical ignorance which gives an unhealthy odour to our bad deeds, as well as to the good, and which, though quite successful in destroying goodness, leaves evil intact. It is this sort of thing that keeps a man from looking at a calendar, lest he discover this is the day on which he must pay a bill, or that this is the day on which he cannot eat meat. It is the thing that closes our eyes and ears to the needs of others, lest the obligation of charity force us to open our purses.

A third type of ignorance affects our actions very little, for even if we were not ignorant, we would have done the same thing. The results would be the same; but the action by which those results are produced would be quite different. In other words, like all ignorance, this kind robs our activities of the human mark which alone gives us a title to pride or to remorse. So a gangster on a vacation, intending to shoot a bear, actually kills a rival whom he has been seeking vindictively for months. And not even a gangster can be proud of that sort of achievement.

Going back to our original figure of a long journey from the inner principle of movement, we can all appreciate the difficulty of being human when we get out of the territory within our control. There was difficulty from the senses and the intellect within our own kingdom; in the foreign territory of the external world, there is the enemy of violence. When we step into this foreign territory, the central core of distinctive human action, can and does, rely confidently on the magic cloak of its spirituality and wanders inviolate up and down the roads of the world.

Some of its messengers or its lesser lieutenants may be and often are captured, dragged into enemy ranks, shot down; but the commanding generals can never be taken. True enough, they are behind the front lines and far enough behind to be safe—as far, in fact, as the distance between the world of matter and the world of spirit. A strong man might succeed in forcing water down your throat, but he cannot make you want to drink; your finger might, by force, be pressed against a button that will electrocute a man, but you cannot be forced to want to kill. Violence may make you smell, or hear, or see, or feel; you may be forced to run, or to walk, or to dance. But nothing in the whole universe can make you will. That inner principle of distinctive human action is inviolable by any external power because there is no leverage for violence against spirit, such as the soul of man and its faculties are.

All this has had to do with the central core of our human acts. To be satisfied with this as the whole story of human acts, would be like conceding that a home consists only of four walls and a roof, all other appurtenances—light, heat, water, furniture, and so on—are totally unimportant. Or, more accurately, it is like feeling that we know all about a house from a photograph which completely isolates the house from its surroundings and gives a view of only one part of the exterior. As a matter of fact, the neighbourhood in which the house is situated is important: the house might be sunk in the midst of freight yards, enthroned in a private park, sogging in the squalor of a tenement district, or dwarfed by the brick walls of skyscrapers.

The same is true of a human act. We cannot really know it until we know its surroundings. The surroundings, the neighbourhood of a human act, are grouped together in the theological term, "circumstances". As a matter of fact, when we have run through these circumstances and discovered who did the thing, where it was done and why, when it was accomplished and how, and who helped, we have covered all there is to know about the event. We not only have a view of the neighbourhood, we have the whole family history and a fairly accurate prediction of the future.

A full grasp of the meaning of any act is impossible without a consideration of these angles. It may be a matter of no moment that a man trips over a dog and goes sprawling; certainly the identity of the dog hardly seems important. But if it happened to be the president of France who tripped over the favourite hound of Adolf Hitler, it would certainly make headlines, and perhaps, an international "situation".

This truth has been recognized since the world began.

In our modern times, a good example of it is the pursuit of news by a reporter. Newspapers recognize that news values may be hidden by the incompleteness of a story; hence the fundamental "w's" of every reporter (who, what, why, when, where) are no more than a demand for the complete story of any human activity. A theologian, indeed, is not looking for news value; but he is looking for the truth, and truth can be had only when all the returns are in.

In the example we have already given, of a man killing another while hunting deer, it changes the story completely when we know how and why the man was killed. To the confessor hearing a penitent confess that he broke open a door, it makes a great difference where that door was, whether on a tabernacle, a prison, or a burning theatre. Whether a penitent, taking a little drink, swallowed whisky or poison; whether it was Sunday or Monday that he got lazy and stayed in bed all day, these are not mere details, but elements necessary if we are to get to the truth of our own or any one else's actions.

There are times when a review of those circumstances might hold us back from action entirely, or certainly change our course of action. An honest man running for public office might well have his doubts about continuing the campaign when he discovers that the bulk of his support comes from politically entrenched gangsters. Or a parent might well halt the upraised hand, realizing that the reason for the spanking now being administered to a child is the parent's own indigestion. In fact, a person who cannot answer the question "why" relative to one of his actions, is a little bewildered and sneaks a look over his shoulder to see if anyone noticed him acting so foolishly. If the same thing happens often, he begins to doubt his sanity. If it is the usual thing, there can be no doubt of insanity and the individual is promptly locked up.

This or that particular action may lack one or other of these circumstances; after all, the furnishings of a mansion have no place in a four-room flat. But there are three general conditions that are to be found and investigated in every act which lays claim to humanity: why was it done; how was it done; by whose help?

What is the excuse for human activity; why is any human act placed? Why does a man work or love or suffer? The answer to that question was the whole burden of our last chapter. The answer is, briefly, to attain the object of desire, to satisfy desire; or, more simply, to obtain a good, for desire never seeks evil. Human action is a search for a good, and, ultimately, a goal; for every thing desired is sought either for itself or as a step to something else. Principally, then, man acts because of the end or goal of his life; he acts that he may attain happiness. Everything else that is desired, every other object of his activity, is such only because it has something of the goal, something of the end about it.

The helpers of a human act are those who contribute in some way to that movement from within which is the essence of living movement, to that deliberate or controlled movement from within which is of the essence of human life. In the first volume of this work we saw that will, the human appetite, was the principle, the starting point of all movement in man. Here, we are looking for the elements that might play some part in putting that motive principle to work, the spark that might start the engine of human activity roaring.

Within a man himself, the work of the intellect is primarily not to move but to know. By knowing it can contribute to the movement of the will; and it is precisely in that way, in recognizing good and presenting it to the will, that the intellect enters into the movement of the will. The intellect presents a target, stretches a tape across the track; the will must be at the root of the actual movement.

The intellect gives the will a look at the desirable object as it is in itself. The senses play a much more indirect, but very often a much more important and preponderant part. Waiters on Pullman cars very rarely make the mistake of tossing a cheery greeting in a man's face in the morning until they have served him coffee; not that the cheery greeting has changed in its desirability meantime, but the man has changed considerably. Watching a football game, an otherwise staid and responsible citizen considers it quite the proper thing to throw away his hat, shout himself hoarse, and pound a perfect stranger on the back; an hour later, in the privacy of his home, such actions are far from appealing. The dispositions of the senses can and do colour an object, hide or enhance its appeal, and so swerve the will away from or coax it into actions that would not be performed under other conditions. It is an indirect, a coaxing, movement that never has the efficacy of force but always has the subtlety of intrigue. Passion, prejudice, headache or plain grouch are by no means the prime movers in a man's life; but the part they play is not inconsiderable.

The influence of outside forces is of the same indirect type. Little Mary's smile may be most winning, but it cannot force the permission for just one more piece of cake. The heavenly bodies play their parts, as witness the power of moonlight, or zero weather, on the activities sponsored by our wills. But, in spite of the ludicrous faith that reads all future events in the stars while starving to death for lack of clients, no material thing, no external force, can reach into the sanctuary of a man's soul. That is another world; the world of spirit that is impervious to the clumsy pushings and shovings of the world of matter. The wise man dominates the stars, as he dominates all things else in the universe.

There is only one external influence of which the will is not independent; there is only one barrier between the will and complete independence. And this barrier is really a bulwark, for its absence would be utterly calamitous for the will, as it would be for any other creature; it would mean instant annihilation, for it would mean severance from the first independent source of all that the human will is or can hope to be.

Where you find complete independence, there you find God, the first mover, the source from which flows every perfection. On this first mover the will is utterly dependent. God can and does move the will of man. Indeed, the thing is self-evident, at least as regards the first movement of the will; for the particular will of any man started its activity some time and that is explicable only by going back to the first mover. Activity is not explained by inactivity, any more than apple pies are explained by apples.

It is not necessary to make a god out of the human will to safeguard that will's autonomy. The fact that there is only one first cause does not destroy but rather establishes the efficacy of nature's working; the fact that there is only one being who is life, does not destroy but rather explains the vital nature of every living thing; and the fact that there is only one first mover, does not weaken but rather establishes and fortifies the power of the human will to move itself.

And this brings us to the last general condition of every human act. How does the will move? It may be quite sufficient to know how to drive a car in order to make a transcontinental tour; but to know something of its inner workings, what makes it go, and, which is of more importance, what might have made it stop, is a decided comfort when something has to be done about a sudden breakdown miles from a repair shop. It might be enough for a man to know how to steer his actions to their goal in order to make a success of living human life; but to venture into the rough country of our materialistic age, to meet obstacles that challenge the power of those human actions constantly, it is more than a comfort, it is a necessary precaution to the successful completion of the journey to know just how the machinery of human action operates.

The man who seriously maintains that absolutely every movement of the human will is under the control of a man, is as absurdly optimistic as the man who would cure a broken leg by deep breathing or mental concentration. His account of things reads like the blurb on the jacket of a best-seller; trying to push man up into a class with the deity, he succeeds only in turning out an impossible freak which has no place in nature, in heaven or in hell. For the facts are plain; man is a part of the natural universe, not a discordant note in the harmony of the spheres. The laws that govern nature also govern man and move him to the end of all nature. It is nature that is the source of movement in other living things; and man must go back to the same source. It is not merely a question of parallelism, rather it is a matter of concrete facts. The foundation of all knowledge is a set of principles which we *naturally* know, not something that we figure out for ourselves. So the foundation of all movement in man, the source of all desire, is a movement that is *natural* to us, about which we can do nothing but submit; all other desires spring from a natural desire that makes its appearance as soon as we are capable of any desire. Towards these objects of natural desire, the will moves *naturally*, not freely; in the concrete, the will cannot but desire good, quite naturally it cannot act for evil. It naturally desires a last end, naturally desires all those things that belong to a man by his very nature, such as life, knowledge of truth, and so on.

As the will sits enthroned, watching the parade of particular desirable things marched before it by the intellect, it is indeed a monarch of all it surveys. No one of these things can snatch the will from its throne; the allure, the beauty of no one is so great that some flaws cannot be found. The intellect automatically and irresistibly must know truth that is clearly presented to it; the eye must naturally, necessarily see colour presented to it. For truth in all its forms is the object of the intellect, and colour is the object of the eye. But no good, short of the universal supremely perfect good, can rush the human will into necessary action, for only that supreme, final good is the adequate object of the faculty of human desire.

A man may have a seemingly irresistible personality; but there will always be someone who can find something displeasing about him, for, as a matter of fact, he is not irresistible. Nothing is irresistible but God. The appeals presented by our senses, by the passions, by the whole inferior nature of man, inflict necessity upon the will only in proportion as they interrupt the sway of reason's command over a man's life. The alcoholic is helpless in the presence of drink because he is not human in the presence of drink; but as long as our actions remain human, so long is lower nature our subject and not our master.

The miraculous works of Christ in Palestine consistently produced a double effect in the bystanders: an elemental fear, such as we feel in an earthquake, a fire out of control, or when standing close to a giant locomotive; and an admiration that was nothing less than astonishment, bewilderment. These are always the results of contact with the divine. Divinity touching the limits of the created world always puts a paradox before our minds, perhaps because our experience, however rich it may be, has mostly dealt with human, understandable things. It is no surprise to find the divine in contact with the human will offering us another of those divine paradoxes—the admirable, wholly astonishing, and utterly bewildering fact of the human will being moved by God and yet moving freely.

We can get some little foothold on this marvel but we can never take it apart, as we might an internal combustion engine. We have noticed the wind bending a small willow tree almost double, swaying the Empire State Building only a matter of inches, and picking up dust and carrying it across thousands of miles. Yet all this is without any change in the wind; the difference in the effect is rooted in the different natures of the things moved. In the same way, the divine movement of the universe to its end will move the tree, the cat and the man each according to its nature, each differently, none violently; always respecting, nay, perfecting, the intrinsic principles of each nature. And it is the nature of man, precisely because he can have universal knowledge, to be free in his choice of particular goods.

Let us not try to soften this truth any more than we would try to hide the artistic beauty of sculptured marble by draping it in clothes; rather let us bring the truth out in a strong light where every detail of its beauty can be appreciated. The influence of God on the human will not only respects human liberty, it causes it; without that divine movement, it would be impossible for humanity to enjoy the freedom, the control, that sets it apart from the rest of the universe. We went into this very exhaustively in the first volume. But it can be put thus briefly: the mode of the human action, its freedom, is as real as the action itself; and, like all reality, it must be traced back to the first cause of all reality. In other words, the causality of God, unlike our own, is not limited to the surface of things, to mere externals, but plumbs down to the intrinsic principles of nature itself. It extends, not merely to the act produced, but to the way in which this act comes forth into the world, whether that way be one of necessity or of freedom. The one can no more exist without divine movement than can the other.

"To know the ultimately real" of human life! an aim that tugs at the heart of everyone and makes every man a philosopher. This is a task that, if accomplished, presents us with a picture that explains much of the beauty we have half-grasped, expresses the thoughts that have haunted our minds, explains the power and significance we have vaguely glimpsed in human affairs. This present chapter presents the other half of the picture; and, showing something of the ultimate reality, it of course matches perfectly the fragment of the original masterpiece we have uncovered in the preceding chapter. That was the goal, these are the steps to it; that was the end, these the means; that was the destination, this is the course along which we run to it.

The goal, we have said, was open to all men without exception on the grounds of age, ability, power, wealth, health or any other consideration but that of humanity. It could be shared by all men and lose nothing of its splendour, its perfection, its satisfying beauty. It could satisfy the least and the greatest of all desires entertained by the human heart; and yet it was no mass happiness, but an individual affair, strictly personal, reigning supreme in the field of the desirable.

The means to the end seen in this chapter but bring out the further simple yet overpowering beauty of the original fragment of the picture. Human actions are the universal and exclusive title to eminence of every human being. They are at the finger-tips of every man, woman and child from the dawn of reason; and they are of a simplicity that makes their manipulation by a child accurate, masterful, effective. For how else could heaven be filled with those who were so heartily welcomed by Christ on earth?

Stirred into being by desire, these actions pursue the quarry relentlessly, tirelessly, as long as life lasts in man the hunter. No obstacle can hinder the pursuit, no violence lessen its effectiveness, no shortness or length of time be too little or too great for ultimate success. And each hunter of happiness goes about his business in his own way. Not only is each man an individual different from all others who have ever lived or ever will live; the means he uses (his actions) are his very own, mirroring his personality; yes, every single act will bear the stamp of the time, place and dispositions of the agent and be set apart as a thing distinct in the history of the universe.

Yet these means to happiness are a part and parcel of the universal progress of nature to the end which was also the beginning. Like every other living thing, the perfection of man is the full development of his nature, the perfection of his highest act, worked out from the principles inherent in that nature. Like every other created nature, the means to the individual goal are furnished to each member of the species from the very beginning. Man is not a freak dropped by mistake in a universe that is foreign to him; he is not the whole of it, not the ultimate end of it all, nor is he an accident, an unimportant, unforeseen phase of it all. He is at the peak of the material, at the lowest rung of the spiritual, moving, as is everything else, to God—but in man's own way of knowing and loving the God he seeks.

In a way Chesterton was right when he considered it an insult to suspect that a man was incapable of a bad action. For it is his unique privilege to be able to fail, as well as to be able to succeed. To a mind that can stretch out to universal truths, to a will that can thirst after the universal good, it is no less than an insult to suspect that the course of life will be marked out step by step with no choice, no variation possible. Man would rightly be as restless under a régime that laid out every step of his life in the instincts of his nature, as an intelligent adult is restless listening to someone read out the titles of a movie. He can look ahead of life, can stand to one side and be a spectator of the whole glamorous parade, even of himself; do not expect him to go through the motions like a robot incapable of thinking for himself. In fact, do not expect him to go through life in any way except as a man. Do not expect him to use means to win his way through, other than means that are worthy of his manhood, worthy of his intelligence. Insistence on anything more, on anything less, is not paying just tribute to God, to man, to nature, to positive facts. But rather it is plunging into the world of make-believe because the world of reality offers no escape from the humanity of man.

CHAPTER III

(OUTLINE)

TOOLS OF HAPPINESS

(Q. 11–17)

1. Necessity of familiarity with tools of successful living.
2. Necessity of familiarity with ingredients of these tools.
3. Two ways of considering human acts:
    - (*a*) Empirically (scientifically):
        - (1) Physiologically.
        - (2) Psychologically.
        - (3) Mathematically.
    - (*b*) Philosophically:
        - (1) In themselves.
        - (2) In their morality.
4. Story behind the controls of human action:
    - (*a*) General Principle—reason is the form of human activity.
    - (*b*) Story in detail:
        - (1) With reference to the goal or end—apprehension, volition, conation, enjoyment.
        - (2) With reference to the means:
            - *a.* On the part of the intellect—counsel, judgment, command.
            - *b.* On the part of the will—consent, election, execution.
            - *c.* Two characteristics—all are uniquely human; all are controlled.
5. Practical views:
    - (*a*) Birth and growth to maturity of human act.
    - (*b*) Decision and execution in every-day life.
    - (*c*) The government of the kingdom of man.

Conclusion:

1. Forging the tools of life, as well as wielding them, demands delicate balance:
    - (*a*) Blindness of sheer will.

(*b*) Practical sterility of sheer intellect.
(*c*) Despair of endless steps.

2. That balance makes the difference between bungling and skilful living.

3. Skill in living is essentially in the act of command:
   (*a*) What interferes with command interferes with our mastery of life.
   (*b*) By command man shares the labours of Providence.
   (*c*) Law and the reign of law are impossible without command which is the heart of control.

CHAPTER III

TOOLS OF HAPPINESS

(Q. 11–17)

IN the search for speculative truth, the farther one gets from the concrete, singular, matter-of-fact affairs, the closer one approaches to the truth sought. On the contrary, if the search be for practical truth, perfection lies in coming to grips with concrete details. A theoretical chemist can sit at his desk and, with no more help than that given by a sharp pencil, can pursue his labours happily and effectively; but the practical chemist must be mechanic enough to know how to assemble the apparatus for his experiments or even to create that apparatus, or he will get no results at all.

Our work in this volume is of a decidedly practical nature; so practical, in fact, that it is the business of every human being. Our task is the examination of the whole problem of human happiness. Every step we take is a step down into the every-day world of human affairs; in every chapter we come closer to the roar and confusion of human activity.

So far we have been looking at men and their deeds in a general way. We found what happiness consists in and how it is grasped by men; in other words, the meaning of human life and human activity. The problem of the last chapter was the humanity of human actions, the examination into their mysterious power to make a success of life, their ability to win happiness. And that secret was summed up in the words "control" or "deliberate will". We saw that it was by the actions under man's control that he wins happiness; that only such actions were admitted by men and women as human, and everything that could remotely affect that control was a subject worthy of investigation.

In this chapter we are coming down a step further, penetrating into the control-room of every human life, trying to discover what does the controlling and just what actions are controlled and how. Since it is by his activity that man makes a success or blunder of his life, these human actions are the tools by which his happiness must be worked out. To use tools effectively, one must be familiar with them. It is not mere superstition that leads the baseball-player or cricketer to insist on his own bat; the fact that I am using someone else's pen may not be the whole explanation of the execrable character of my penmanship, but it contributes a part; a stenographer trying out for a job on an unfamiliar machine is not necessarily offering an excuse when she says she could do better on her own typewriter.

For their effective use, tools must not merely be fitted for the particular job in hand. They must be practised with, weighed, measured, hafted. When it was said that one of the first requirements for a good surgeon is that he be a good mechanic, a great truth was expressed; for the surgeon, like anyone who must use tools, is great when he has made his tools a part of himself, an extension of his own hands, of his own brain.

We must be familiar with the tools we are going to use on the job of living. But a mechanic's knowledge is not enough; we cannot buy those tools, we must create, must forge them, we must know what goes into their make-up. A lawyer preparing his brief must view the case from every possible angle, and then very carefully include, and even more carefully exclude, material from that brief. A doctor who writes a prescription which stops dandruff but paralyses the patient has written a very bad prescription. In the same way, the man who looks at only one angle of the job of living, who considers only one phase of his tools, or who concentrates on one ingredient in their manufacture, will do a very bad job of living.

Actually we can exhaust the possible views of man's activity by looking at human actions from two angles: from the angle of science, looking for the answer to the question "how?"; and from the angle of philosophy, looking for the answer to the question "why?".

Science can, and as a matter of fact does, examine human actions. And this is quite proper. Man is a living organism, he is an animal, all of his actions create some little ripple on the pool of physical nature. Physiology can quite properly examine and correlate the results of its examination of the blood, the nerves, the muscles, the brain of man in his different activities. Experimental psychology can properly compare the common elements in human and animal activity; it can search out the physical basis of neuroses, the springs of hate and fear, anger, despair and all the rest. Scientists can measure and weigh, make up averages, statistics, ratios, quotas, and be entirely within their scope. All this is an invaluable contribution to human knowledge.

Tragedy enters the picture when it is supposed that all this, or any part of it, is the whole story of human actions; or, indeed, that it is the important part of the story. As far as human actions are concerned, science is always on the outside, looking in. It is just as unfair to expect the whole story from science, as it is to expect an account of a football game from the wistful boy standing outside the stadium listening to the cheers. The account becomes more accurate the closer we get to the inside; for the whole story, we must get inside the brain of the man who is running the team.

This mistake is not the mistake of scientists, but of modern philosophers. Each one of these sciences has been erected into a philosophy over the protest of the scientist. For example, in recent years an associate professor of psychology at a mid-western university, has expressly insisted on the fact that science is not seeking the ultimate causes, not seeking the answer to the question "why?", but only the proximate, immediate causes in answer to the question "how?". In other words, science, examining human actions, examines everything but their humanity. This last is the philosopher's task; and philosopher's task it will continue to be as long as it remains impossible to put the spiritual under a microscope or to dissect it with a scalpel.

The investigation of the empirical or scientific angle is something we can safely leave to someone else whom we consult from time to time as the occasion demands—or perhaps not at all. For the key to successful living lies precisely in the humanity of these actions of ours, in their subjection to our control. That angle we cannot leave to anyone but ourselves; that element must permeate every action in every instant of its existence, and is our business every moment of our lives. Whether we like it or not, we must be philosophers.

Do not let that frighten you. It does not necessarily mean long hair, fits of abstraction, or that vague far-away look which is such a deterrent to sprightly conversation. Many a farmer has raised successful crops, though he never saw an agricultural college; but he did go to school—to the very difficult school of experience. And that same school has, early in life, made a philosopher of every human being. It will be evident from the examples used farther on, that what is to be said in this chapter is not an abstruse, totally unfamiliar bit of doctrine. But rather, like all scholastic philosophy, is organized common sense.

From this all-important philosophical angle, which will give us the whole story of human action, we can look at the controlling and controlled actions of our everyday lives, cutting them off from every other consideration, and considering them solely in themselves, one by one, as they pour forth from the great centre of human movement.

That is the work of this chapter. In the next chapter our work will be to consider these actions in reference to good and evil, to their morality or immorality, to try to plumb the depths of a question which has turned the modern world upside down.

As we look into the control-room of human activity, we can see two great dynamos—the intellect and the will of man. The work of the first is to know; that of the second is to desire, to move, to enjoy. The will of itself is blind; like every other appetite in every other creature, it trails along, following and limited by knowledge. The intellect, of itself, is powerless to move itself or anything else. Yet from the combination of these two, we have that distinctive human product—movement with knowledge, controlled or deliberate movement, that is the means by which happiness is obtained. Not movement alone, not knowledge alone, but controlled movement makes a success of life.

Right here, in the very beginning of our inspection of the control-room, we seem to have met an insuperable obstacle. It is impossible to expect a movement from the will until some object of desire is known; yet there can be no movement to knowledge, or to anything else, without having recourse to the source of all movement in man, his will.

The answer is easy enough. But, to grasp all its implications, it is necessary to remember that reason is the form, as it were the soul, of human acts; as the soul of man gives life to his body, so the reason of man gives humanity to his acts. It is because he can know the universal that man can choose between particulars; because he knows the relation of the tools to the job in hand, because he knows why he is placing this particular action, man is in control of his activity—and only man. From the very beginning, then, reason must lead the way; until reason has placed its stamp upon the coin of human activity it is not coin of the realm.

The apparently vicious circle of the interaction of intellect and will is broken by tracing the beginnings of that interaction to nature and ultimately to the source of nature. Reason must lead the way; but the first movement of reason is inspired, not by the activity of the will, but by a push from nature.

Nor does this mean that man has been singled out from all the pupils in the school of the universe and made to stand in a corner alone and in disgrace. Rather, he is running along with "the gang," safe in the assurance that he is "one of the fellows." For no creature that has a beginning, telling later in life the story of its successful career, can make the boast proper to the so-called "self-made man." It must make the confession that it was given a start, it must trace back its earliest efforts to that solid power of natural principles. Or, going farther, everything that has a beginning, precisely because it began, must be traced to that which alone had no beginning, to the God of nature. This is true of everything—existence, life, sensibility, knowledge, activity of any kind; and so, of course, of human activity.

Keep in mind that when we speak of the beginning of human activity, we are talking of its end or goal. For it is because of the end or goal that human activity starts at all. A man does not adjust his false teeth in the morning for no reason; but for several good reasons. In fact he has a good reason for everything he does, or he must convince himself that he has; otherwise he will be forced to doubt the humanity of his own actions. And this is a very discomforting doubt. In other words, there is human activity because of desire for an object, because there is an end in sight. And the whole of that activity is moulded in view of the object of desire, or the end.

The beginnings of human action deal with the end of human action. Looking for the roots of that controlled action which alone is human, we must look first at the actions of intellect and will that deal with the goal or end. And of course the first act of the intellect deals with the work of knowing. The very first step is knowledge or apprehension of the end. The will, meeting this end proposed by the intellect, pays it the flattering tribute of wishfulness (volition). Further impressed by the desirability of this end, the will does more than merely wish; it wants this end or goal, and that means it is ready to take what steps are necessary to get it. Finally, when the attainment of that desirable object is over and done with, the will sits down to enjoy the possession of its goal.

A schoolboy taken on a tour of a hospital sees the surgeons actually at work. He thinks they are splendid and wishes he could be a surgeon. If he stops there, that will be the end of it. But if he goes further and *wants* to be a surgeon, if he thinks that is the greatest profession in the world and one that he is going to master, then there is some chance of his one day sharing the joy of surgeons.

This undoubtedly explains why so many of our "good resolutions" disintegrate so rapidly; they are not good resolutions at all. They are merely wishes, castles in the air; and of course when they come into conflict with something we really want, they come tumbling down without any noise, dust or confusion precisely because they are so very frail. I once knew a priest some six feet three inches tall and weighing close to two hundred and fifty pounds, who had always cherished a secret desire to be a jockey. All of us have some such sneaking desire: bankers seem to favour being railroad engineers in their dreams; politicians dream of heroic days as firemen; university professors prefer great detective deeds, and so on. It is a harmless sort of game, for we appreciate the fact that it is a game of dreams, of half wishes and not of real desires. We treat it as an absurd game and laugh at ourselves, unless we grow cowardly about life and try to exchange the world of reality for a world of dreams. Then we court disaster. But it comes as somewhat of a shock to realize that our unfulfilled resolutions belong in this same class of dreams.

No risk is taken with the beginning of all human activity. The goal that is naturally, necessarily known by the intellect is goodness; what the will necessarily wishes is the good, the desirable; moreover that is what it wants, what it will take steps to attain, and what alone will satisfy it. There is no question here of freedom, of control; but of rigorous, natural necessity. Never, at any time, under any circumstances whatever, will you find men or women willing, searching, pursuing anything but what is good, or what appears to them good. They cannot help it; they are built that way.

That solid foundation of human activity, the element of it that needs no control, does not detract from man's mastery of his life but rather makes it possible. If the front wheels of an automobile were not capable of being swung from side to side, we could not control an automobile's direction; but the same would be true if all the rest of the automobile had the same capacity for indirection. It is quite necessary that the seat remain stolidly beneath the chauffeur. A polo player can control his pony, but only because there are some very fundamental things about that pony that are beyond his control and independent of it, e.g. the dependability of the position of the horse's legs. A polo pony with legs as collapsible as those of a bridge table would not be of much help in a polo game. The variable ultimately rests on the invariable, as the dependent rests on the independent.

It is only when we come down to a consideration of the steps to the goal, the means to be used for the end, that there is question of controlled action. And here too, naturally, begins the question of human responsibility, human success and human failure.

The machinery of human activity is not unlike a gasoline

engine. We have an infallible automatic starter in nature; once started, the interaction of intellect and will is like the steady interaction of the different cylinders of the gas engine. The explosion in one prepares the way, gives the pressure necessary, for the succeeding explosion in the next; so each act of the intellect prepares the way for an act of the will, which in turn makes necessary an act of the intellect and this again is followed by an act of the will. When our human engine is running smoothly, it is difficult to separate the action of intellect from that of will, so quickly and intimately do they run into one another; but let one cylinder misfire, and we have a stuttering, coughing, creeping paralysis of the whole powerful engine.

These acts of intellect and will go in pairs, like policemen in an unsavoury district of a large city. It is, in fact, the only safe way to travel; for if we are to get anything done, we cannot do it blindly without disaster, nor yet can we accomplish it by mere thinking. Because human activity is controlled action, it demands both intelligence and power; for every ounce of power there must be an equal amount of direction of that power. The direction, the traffic officer of human activity, is intelligence; the source of power is the will.

If we follow the mental processes of a little girl investing the coin which has just been advanced from the family treasury, we shall have an accurate account of the process of controlled use of means to an end. This little girl knows that money exists to be spent, the end is clear, desirable and desired, indeed intended. The question is what means will best accomplish the perfection of investing it. So she takes counsel with herself and sees that both toys and chocolates are adequate and desirable means. She consents to the fact that both of these are good and desirable. But which one to choose? This demands a judgment between the two, which falls, let us say, on chocolates. That decided, she elects to buy the chocolates and is now ready to make her purchase. The passage from choice to actual purchase, the execution of that choice, is accomplished under the direction of the intellect's command, the end is in her possession, the chocolates in her hands.

Each of these acts flows into the following act and depends on the one preceding it. So the consent is reasonable because of the preceding counsel; the choice is not blind because of the preceding judgment; and the command is effective because of the preceding push of the election or choice. In spite of all the intricate dodging and ducking involved in running, the football-player invariably puts one foot down after the other: left, right, left, right, with never a break in the regularity of the succession. So in spite of the intricacy of the human activity under this or that set of conditions, invariably it will be the product of an act of the intellect, followed by one of the will, followed by one of the intellect, and so on—with never a break in the regularity of the succession.

All of these acts are under our control. We do not have to take counsel, we can rush into things, we can do the first thing that enters our minds. We do not have to consent to the material counsel has laid before us. We do not have to select one from the many good things to which we consent; nor is it beyond our power to refuse to make a choice at all, even when there is only one worth-while thing offered to us. We can take any or all of them; or we can leave them. And that very control gives these acts the stamp of humanity. We are in the driver's seat, doing the driving; everything else in the universe is driven by an irrevocable necessity.

Each one of these acts is different, in a class by itself. Counsel offers us an array of good things; judgment picks out one. Consent is but comfortable complacency in all the good things offered by counsel, without the labour of choosing any particular one. While command is like the pest at a week-end party who, full of energy, is constantly breaking into the moments of quiet loafing with the cheery exclamation: "Let's do something."

The whole purpose of human activity is, after all, to get something done, to reach up and to hold happiness. It is not at all surprising that the act of command should have very much the same part formerly held by commanding generals in the days when war was a gentleman's sport. Command dashes up and down the lines, dictating every move made. Whenever anything is done humanly, whether within a man himself or externally, it is because that act has been commanded; otherwise it escapes the mastery of the man himself and is no longer human, no longer controlled.

Command swings back and forth behind the lines of human activity, ordering every movement. Nothing that has to do with the means to an end is outside its authority. Counsel, consent, judgment, election—somewhere in all of them and behind them all you will find command. Not merely the movements of a man's hands and feet, but of his intellect and will are at his command, subject to the orders issued by his intellect.

Its very important position demands that we look at the act of command more closely. It is an act of the intellect, sandwiched in between the will's choice and the will's movement to execution or use, keeping intact that invariable succession of acts of intellect and will. But the very efficacy of command tells us that it is not merely an act of the intellect; it smacks of power, of effective movement, and that is the work of the will. In command, then, there is an element of intellect and an element of will; and at that, it is only right and just that such a responsible office-holder in the control-room of human activity should combine the two essential elements of all human activity, i.e. control and movement.

Perhaps the relative position of these two elements will be clear from the mere statement that command is effective orderly movement. It is not mere movement, but ordered, directed, aimed movement. The movement comes from the will; the direction and the communication of that direction to the executing potency—eyes, hands, feet, etc.—is the work of intellect. Before there is room for command, we must have arrived at definite choice; to step beyond this choice into the field of execution means that this movement to execution, like all movements of the will, needs direction, needs intelligent aiming. The movement which comes from the will flows along intelligent channels under the direction of the intellect. Command, then, briefly, is an act of the intellect, presupposing a movement of the will.

A tourist visiting the Cathedral at Cologne can become so enraptured of the detail work about the door that he never sees the inside and has no conception of the sweeping lines of the exterior. But if he goes back along the street which stretches straight out from the Cathedral and sees it as a whole, the very details which are so precious find their proper place in the plan of the whole and make a fitting preparation, as they were meant to, for the grandeur of the interior. The same is true of a study of human acts; we can so bury ourselves in details as to miss the beauty and significance of the whole.

With a better perspective we can see the ingenuous sweep of human activity, and it must strike us at once that the origins of human control can be accurately described in the homely terms of the human origins of every individual. The conception and birth of human activity is taken in hand by nature and runs its course to a happy conclusion necessarily, infallibly through the acts dealing with the end—apprehension, volition, intention or conation. The baby has arrived; the process of growth to maturity is ready to begin.

The beginnings of that growth will of course be under the protecting wings of home life—the period included by counsel, consent, judgment and election. The first effortless days of innocent, unworried childhood correspond to acts of counsel and consent. Rugged adolescence, with its mighty determinations and sweeping judgments, its trials, struggles, and high hopes, will represent the process of judgment and election. The final sortie out of the protection of home life into a cold world and to the ultimate triumph of founding a home is the phase taken in by command, execution and enjoyment.

A view of the imposing structure of human activity from yet another angle, enables us to see it as the double process of making up our minds and carrying out our intentions. As to the goal or end, there is no difficulty; our mind is made up for us by nature, leaving us no worries about apprehension of the end, its volition or intention. But making up our minds about the means to attain that end is another matter. We must shop about rounding up the means at hand by taking counsel. If there is only one way of doing the thing, of course we do not bother about counsel nor do we take counsel about unimportant trifles. There are no long mental processes involved in hitting a nail with a hammer.

Counsel is necessary and helpful. And it immediately involves our consent to the desirability of the means it has rounded up. But both counsel and consent become painful processes if they do not quickly lead further. An example of this is the mental agony of a woman with an extensive wardrobe who cannot get beyond consent to the beauty and desirability of all her gowns, even though her husband is shouting: "We will never make it."

If she is ever going to get to the party, she must make up her mind. She must judge which dress will be best for the occasion and then decide to wear it. This decision does not put the dress on for her, much less get her to the party in time. The decision must be carried through, must be commanded and executed or her intentions are never carried out. She cannot go to the party with only her mind made up.

I think it is fairly evident that all this is not mere theorizing, but a statement of homely facts with which everyone is familiar. From everyday life we have a whole host of exhibits of every one of these steps, caught as though they were suddenly frozen, or surprised and buried in just the exact posture by a flow of faithfully preserving lava. There is the eternally deliberate, over-cautious man who never has all the possible means rounded up, the budding novelist who is never quite ready to start his novel, the newly and secretly married couple who are still looking for better ways of breaking the news at home. There is the person who can never find anything good enough to win approval and consent, like the woman shopper who exhausts the clerk by "just looking." There is the child so enraptured of all the candy in the show case that it cannot make the bitter judgment which will exclude all others in favour of the one which its precious penny will buy; or the man faced by the problem of choosing between the peace and pleasure offered by an evening of poker with the boys or an evening at home. There is the procrastinator who never reaches a decision, who is always going to look into this or that, see about this or that; the man with a toothache who knows the tooth should be pulled but never quite decides to have it done; or the woman who knows her in-laws should be visited, but never decides just when that visit should be made.

When we come to the point of actually getting things done, the difference between choice and command jumps out at us from every day of our own lives. Hard as decision or election is, it cannot be compared with the encountering of actual details and obstacles involved in really doing the thing. How often we have chosen to clean up our desk on a certain day and how often we have scuttled out from under that choice. There is always much more embarrassment involved in coaxing a precocious child to speak its pieces before company than in merely electing to have the child show the company what an extraordinary child it is.

The whole process is indeed nothing more or less than the process of the government of the kingdom of man and his empire of the universe. It is the question of the intelligent control and direction of his life, his activities, his contacts with the universe to the one end of attaining happiness.

The ends or purposes of this government are taken care of by nature, the foundation is solidly laid by our naturally necessary acts relative to the end—apprehension, volition, conation. The deliberations and decisions of government, the weighing of the means and the choice of the particular one which will have governmental sanction, is the work done by counsel, consent, judgment and election. The legislative branch is entirely concentrated in the act of command; and the executive, carefully following the letter laid down by the law, extends to all that is subject to man's intellect and will.[1]

There will be the absolute subjects of intellect and will themselves, never giving an instant of worry about rebellion; the colonies, partly but not entirely subject, have some very definite powers of their own—the sensitive nature of man; finally the autonomous members of the commonwealth who can only be called subjects by a kind of courtesy—the vegetative side of man's nature. That is man's kingdom.

[1] These acts can be graphically presented in this manner:

ACTS OF INTELLECT	ACTS OF WILL
Dealing with the end.	
1. Simple apprehension	2. Simple volition
3. Judgment proposing the end	4. Intention
Fruition or enjoyment of end.	
Dealing with means.	
A. In Intentional Order.	
5. Counsel	6. Consent
7. Judgment	8. Election
B. In Order of Execution.	
9. Command or precept	10. Active use
Passive use in the executing faculties.	

His empire is the universe which he can and does use to his ends. His use of it is an expression of his power over it, of the ability he has to command.

The scholastics used to say that the superiority of man over the rest of the universe was plainly seen in the perfect balance of all the elements of the universe in man. He was a little universe in himself; yet a universe where no one angle protruded to mar the beauty of the whole. Certainly balance between intellect and will, starting out from the firm foundations of nature to the fitting climax of the vision of God, is the secret of the distinctiveness and effectiveness of human action. Let the will play an overbearing part and the result is a ruthless, blind release of power, a reign of unseeing terror whose only effect is incalculable damage to the individual and to everyone with whom he comes into contact. This is the tragic half-truth that the world would have us bow down before to-day when it tells us man is merely an animal. Subordinate the will entirely and there results a futile, cold, sterile creature incapable even of dreams; another of those tragic half-truths, a caricature sponsored by Descartes and his followers in their attempt to make man angelic instead of human. Deny to man the solid foundation of nature, the end from which activity starts and to which it unerringly goes, and man is placed on an endless treadmill with only the escape of despair and death. This is the third tragic half-truth, widespread to-day in the philosophers' insistence on man as a part of society, a part of a process of social development, and nothing else, coming from nowhere, going to no place, merely keeping the wheels of society turning.

Tragic as these half-truths are, they cannot compare with the catastrophe involved in the complete falsehood that would deny both intellect and will to man, that would deny both end and means, making him merely a machine. That is the uttermost depth beyond which one cannot go; its very depravity serves as a brilliant foil to bring out the sublimity, the brilliance, the vigour, and comfort of the complete truth about man and his activity—that he is the image of God, on his way back to God. We cannot take this or that part of man and neglect the rest without doing violence not only to truth but to man himself. We must take the complex whole, keeping a delicate balance between the control-room and the subjects of that control, and between the elements involved in the control-room itself. That balance makes the difference between man as he is and man as he is grotesquely caricatured to-day; maintenance of it makes the difference between bungling life and living skilfully. Let man bank too sharply to one side or the other, go up too steeply or down too steeply, let the engine falter, and the soaring flight of his activity comes tumbling down to crash in failure amid the things of mere earth.

That skill in living is epitomized in the act of command. What interferes with that command, interferes with our mastery of our own life. It makes no difference whether that interference comes from within or without us; when our ability to command weakens, we have begun to turn over the direction of our life to someone or something else. It may be the rebellion of passion, the inertia of boredom, the attraction of another personality, or a too great delicacy for the feelings of another, that is robbing us of command; whatever it is, it is making a direct attack on our ability to live successfully. Whatever contributes to that command, whether it be discipline, self-denial, or energetic use of our power to command, builds up our power for living. It may very well be that outside the kingdom of ourselves, our commands are entirely disregarded; but that does not make a great deal of difference. The important thing for successful living is that within our own kingdom, within ourselves, that command be supreme.

All other creatures in the universe participate passively in divine Providence by natural inclinations guiding them to their respective ends. They are mere subjects of that law. But over and above this, man takes an active hand in the affairs of Providence, he is not merely a subject but something of a legislator for himself, able not merely to be provided for but actively to provide for himself and others. And this active participation in divine Providence is immediately brought about by his act of command.

This is the law of his internal kingdom. By it the reign of law is set up and the anarchy, the brutality, the ruin of lawlessness stamped out. This is the deepest secret of the control which stamps an act with humanity; this is the heart of control.

CHAPTER IV

(OUTLINE)

HAPPINESS AND MORALITY

(Q. 18–21)

1. Comparison of physical and moral goodness and evil:
   - (*a*) Roots of morality.
   - (*b*) A definition of morality.
   - (*c*) Rules of morality:
     - (1) Proximate rule—reason.
     - (2) Ultimate rule—the eternal law.

2. Sources of modern attacks on morality:
   - (*a*) The identification of the real and the tangible.
   - (*b*) Rejection of a personal end of man.
   - (*c*) Attack on authority—graduated according to authority attacked:
     - (1) Divine authority.
     - (2) Ecclesiastical authority.
     - (3) Civil authority.
     - (4) Paternal or domestic authority.
   - (*d*) Conclusion to a morality that is irrational or, more logically though more rarely, to amorality.

3. Morality of human action in general:
   - (*a*) Sources of morality:
     - (1) Object of action.
     - (2) End of action.
     - (3) Circumstances of action.
   - (*b*) Acts good, evil or indifferent in themselves.

4. Morality of human actions in particular:
   - (*a*) Intrinsic acts—meaning of "good will":
     - (1) Dependence of this goodness:
       - *a.* On the object; part played by intention.
       - *b.* On the rules of morality.
     - (2) Sole norm of bad will.
     - (3) Conformity with the will of God.

(*b*) Extrinsic or commanded acts:
(1) A double standard of morality.
(2) Interrelation of these standards.
(3) Moral significance:
a. Of external acts.
b. Of the results of an action.

5. Consequences of goodness and evil in human activity:
(*a*) Sin and virtue.
(*b*) Praise and blame.
(*c*) Merit and demerit.

Conclusion:

1. Place of morality:
(*a*) In the order of nature.
(*b*) In the nature of man.
(*c*) With reference to religion.

2. Impossibility of escape from morality.

3. Morality and the pursuit of happiness.

CHAPTER IV

HAPPINESS AND MORALITY

(Q. 18–21)

IT is always disconcerting for human nature to discover reality where only the stuff of dreams was expected. A man who was dreaming that he was present at the Deluge, and wakes up expecting to stretch luxuriously in the enjoyment of a warm, comfortable bed, only to discover that the roof is leaking and he is being thoroughly drenched, is disconcerted. So is the man who dreamed about burglars, only to awake to a ransacked house. When we have nicely classified something among the intangible and unimportant material of dreams we like to have it stay that way. A little idiosyncrasy of ours, perhaps, but one that will make the subject-matter of this chapter decidedly disconcerting.

It has been quite a fashion these last years to contrast the physical and moral much as we would the real and the unreal: the physical is the strong, undeniable, dependable order of the natural; while the moral is in the class of the fluttering subjective or the intangible supernatural.

Let us look honestly at the two. Physical goodness is not hard to understand. A blind cat has not as much physical goodness as a cat with two good eyes, because it lacks something that a cat should have, that we can reasonably demand of a cat. So, in a very tense moment of a cat show, the decision of the judges must hinge on which of the contestants has all that a cat should have. The absence of wings will not affect that decision a bit; a cat just does not have wings, and the lack of them is no reflection on the cat. Our norm of physical goodness, then, is correspondence to the demands of a particular nature.

We can put this more profoundly by looking at what gives a cat, or anything else, what it should have, considering its nature. Hit fatally by an automobile, the cat in question ceases to have any of the perfections of a cat. So with a man, death robs him of the perfections due to human nature. He may make a wonderful corpse, astoundingly natural in appearance, but in appearance only. His soul, the principle bringing him his specific perfections, is gone. So the form or soul of a cat is the source of the physical goodness of the cat. When the cat has all the perfections its form can give, it is a perfect cat; it lacks goodness, or suffers evil, in so far as it lacks any of those perfections due to the form proper to cats. All this holds true of everything in the order of nature, indeed, in the order of reality. It is our knowledge of these natural forms, or essences, that enables us to judge between the physical good and evil.

If we apply all this to actions, we shall find an exact parallel. A horse's act of eating is good in so far as it has all we can expect of such an act, in so far as it measures up to that principle which gives it its perfection and makes it stand out as different from all other actions. Concretely, in so far as it does what eating is supposed to do, that is, nourish the animal, the act is good. The form of an act, the perfecting principle, which marks it as different from all others, is the object of that act; just as a motion is marked out as different from all other motions, by the goal or object of that motion. The goodness of an act, then, is judged in relation to its form. We are still in the physical, undeniably natural order; and, as is evident, the same principles that determine the physical goodness or evil of a thing as tangible as a cat or a mountain, determine the physical goodness or evil of an action in that same physical order.

To step into the moral order means no more than to step into the order of human actions. The query concerning their moral goodness or evil is no more than a query as to their goodness or evil precisely as human. Just as all other actions are judged good or bad in the light of their form, specifying principle or object, so also human actions are similarly judged in the light of their form, or object. The difference lies in this: the human action, precisely as human, is a controlled action, an action that is aimed, an action put forth under the guiding hand of reason. So the object of human action is an object responding to that principle of reasonable control.

In other words, a human action, like all other actions, indeed like all other things, is good or bad according as it has all it should have, or lacks something that belongs to it. To say that its goodness is moral is merely to insist that its goodness is human. To speak of human action, free action, or moral action, is to speak of exactly the same thing. Whenever a man places an unreasonable action, he places an immoral action. Driving along a mountain road and deliberately turning off over a precipice instead of following the road, a man has placed a morally evil action, because that action did not measure up to the object of human action, the object understood and aimed at by reason, even though the quick turn off may have been a clever bit of manipulation of an automobile.

There is no distinction between the real and the moral order; things moral are just as real as things physical, in fact more so. Their roots are buried in the same metaphysical beginnings of thought and being which make the truth and goodness of each a matter of exact proportion to their existence or being. Morality is not the ghostly door through which the sleepwalker passes unhindered, but the solid barrier that will wake him up with a crash if he bumps into it.

Morality, quite simply, is nothing more than the relation of a human action to its proper object, to its object as a human or moral object. One goat may butt into another, looking very much like one football player butting into another; but the acts are quite different, for one is human, the other is the act of a goat. One was placed in view of the end; the other was not. One has a moral object, the other has not.

The determination of the rule of morality is then ridiculously easy. The rule of goodness for a cat, a mountain, or a horse's dinner was the form of each of those things; the exemplar, the perfecting principle, which made them stand out from all others and to which they measured up. The same is true of the rule of human or moral actions: it will be their form, that which makes them stand out from all others as different. We have already seen that actions are human in so far as they are controlled; it is this which makes the difference between a man's hat being blown off and being thrown away at a football game. It is reason which aims human actions, which makes them human. The determining principle of goodness or evil then involves the principle of control; it is the end known and aimed at by reason. Reason is the immediate rule of morality.

The human reason is not a magician at the wave of whose magic wand morality comes into existence. It is a decidedly workman-like faculty whose job is to know and command. To cast it in the role of creator, as principle author of morality, is a silly contradiction of facts. Rather, the realization of just what reason is and does, indicates immediately that behind it is the first cause of morality, as behind the howl of the tornado is the first cause of all physical things. Behind human reason stands divine reason. To measure up to the rule of morality which is human reason, means to measure up to that supreme rule of morality—divine reason—which is mirrored in our own created reason.

Going back to that poor cat before it was hit by an automobile, no one of us makes the mistake of thinking the form, the soul, of that cat created the cat, even though here and now it was the measuring rod of the cat's physical goodness. Behind it was the eternally enduring essence or form existing in the mind of the creator, the eternally true exemplar by imitation of which the created form or essence was set up as the norm of feline perfection. So behind every created thing is the divine architect's model of that thing, the ultimate criterion of its truth, its goodness, its perfection. Behind every action, behind every human action, is that same array of plans in the mind of the divine architect; for action, and human action, belong in the real order and demand the same explanation as everything else in that real order.

Morality, then, is not something of caprice, not even of divine caprice; but part of the essential truth of things. It is just as impossible for anyone to make an essentially bad action good as it is to make the essence of a cat the essence of a donkey. Morality has the same solid roots, the same inviolable nature as the earth on which we walk.

All this is disconcerting, for it puts our modern world in the position of the little boy stoutly denying he ate the jam in spite of the generous layer of jam on his face. Our modern attack on morality is an attack on fundamental facts that simply will not be denied; and it is only by the exercise of mental gymnastics worthy of a mad-house that we can even imagine we are denying those facts.

Because the attack is against fundamentals, the roots of our modern scoffing at morality go back to fundamentals. One of the earliest roots, and one which is rapidly dying to-day through the advance of scientific discovery and consequently of scientific humility, was the identification of the real and the tangible or sensible. If the only real things were those which could be weighed, measured, cut up, used as subjects in a laboratory, then of course morality did not belong to the real order. For no one has as yet stumbled over morality in the dark or preserved it in alcohol. Unfortunately this also included loyalty, friendship, love, beauty, wetness and a host of other things that the world has always insisted were realities of no mean proportions.

Much more to the fore to-day is the rejection of a personal end of man. This rejection has taken various forms, subjecting the human individual variously to a mechanical, biological, or sociological process in which he is merely filling a gap. Whatever its form, it immediately does away with the necessity of morality by doing away with humanity. The precise mark of human action is control, the aiming of action; where there is nothing to aim at, it is silly to spend time correcting the sights of a rifle. Since human action and moral action are the same thing, the removal of humanity from an action is an effective squelching of morality in that action.

An older, but still strongly enduring source of this modern attack on morality is the attack on authority. It really should not be an attack on morality at all; in fact it can be such only by misunderstanding what and where morality is. From what we have seen, the essential morality does not depend on authority, even on the authority of God; but on the same foundations from which the physical order has its stability. But the notion somehow got around that human beings were moral because they were told to be so, because they were little children ordered about by a somewhat tyrannical parent; a lessening of the authority of that parent, then, was understood as a loosening of the reins of morality. So step by step we staggered down the ladder of authority. First, divine authority and that of the Church which claimed divine authority was rejected; then the authority of churches which admitted they had no divine authority. The next reigning authority was that of the State; from there only two more steps were possible—

to the paternal or group authority of the family and to the completely subjectivistic authority of the individual himself. At every one of these steps some men and women have stopped. You will find those who trace their morality to themselves, to social approval or tradition, to civil law, to dictates of ecclesiastical authority; and you will find others who have rejected all of these one by one until their theoretical morals consist in the arduous task of pleasing themselves.

This does not mean that the modern world has gone immoral. Not at all. Very often the proponents of these particular varieties of morality are themselves living up to a very high moral standard. What it does mean is that the modern world *should* have gone immoral. To propose a moral theory side by side with the contention that morality is not real, that man has no individual purpose or goal to his life, or that morality is merely somebody else's dictum, is absurd. It is unreasonable; it will not stand any searching criticism; it simply does not measure up to the facts. Building on such fundamentals, or lack of fundamentals, the really reasonable thing, the really rational conclusion, would be amorality—a denial of morality. Or, briefly, we are in the position of the boy with jam on his face; we are caught with morality in our very make-up no matter how loudly we may deny it. Our attack has been against a straw man; if we bend over closely enough to make sure the enemy is dead enough to justify a shout of victory, we cannot but discover he was stuffed with straw.

To discover the immediate sources of morality it is necessary merely to look closely at any human action. Take such a very ordinary thing as eating a meal. If we analyse that action, we obtain an accurate idea of what contributes to the human or moral goodness of dining. We will find that this action, and every human action, has three parts and from each part some morality can flow.

No matter who eats the dinner, what the diner's capacity, or who pays the bill, the natural object of a dinner is to repair the tissue burnt up by the expenditure of energy during the day. That is what dinners are for, that is the reasonable object, the end known and aimed at by reason. It is something quite independent of the individual diner; something universally true of all dinners that justly claim the name.

The second part of the human action lies in the purpose or intention of the agent. Perhaps a man is dining merely for sociability's sake—"he isn't a bit hungry"; perhaps because he wants just one more dinner before going to the electric chair so that the pangs of indigestion will make him forget everything else; perhaps he is so stuffed with food that one more bite will kill him and he has chosen this novel form of suicide. Whatever his purpose, it can go beyond that which naturally and essentially belongs to the dinner as such.

The third part of the human action is made up of the circumstances—the neighbourhood of a human act which must be known for the complete story of human goodness or evil. For instance, a man might carry his lunch to the opera and eat it between the acts; he might go at his dinner a little too ardently; he might eat it at midnight knowing it is going to keep him awake all night; and so on.

At any rate, considering these three elements of a human action, we have considered all possibilities; there is nothing else that enters into a human action. What morality, what human goodness or evil there is in an act, must come from these three sources. The first of these, the reasonable object of the act itself, gives the essential, necessary goodness or evil which will always and under all circumstances cling to the act. So theft's object is to take unjustly what belongs to another; that distinguishes it from all other human actions, good or bad, makes it essentially in all times and under all circumstances an act which is essentially bad, or bad in itself. The object is an intrinsic form giving the act its moral nature; to compare this form, giving the action moral life, to reason, giving the action humanity, is like comparing the form constituting a house distinct from all others, to the architect's conception according to which the house is built. As these objects, these internal forms constituting the moral essence of human actions, are good, bad or indifferent so also are the acts. In more concrete terms, according as the objects of these acts lead to the end or goal set by reason, they are good; as they lead away from or impede the attaining of that goal, they are bad; if they contribute nothing one way or another in themselves, they are indifferent. A kind act is always good in itself; an unjust act is always bad in itself; taking a walk is in itself indifferent.

Over and above this essential goodness or evil of the human action in itself, there is the morality added by the end or intention of the one acting. I can give a poor man five dollars in order to enlist him in the ranks of crime; I can murder a dictator in vindication of my democratic principles or I can take a walk in order to induce a heart attack. And in all these cases some added morality has come through my immediate purpose, regardless of the natural end of the individual acts in themselves.

Something like the effect a neighbourhood has on the desirability of a house, of the effect clothes have on the appearance of a man, is the effect of circumstances on the morality of an act. They are accidents, adornments or disfigurements; they may play as vastly different roles as a drop of perfume or a misstep plays in the magnificent entrance of a society leader. They may make an act better or worse, more serious or less so; but they leave the act essentially intact. When they do not, when they actually change the moral species of an act, they have given up the secondary role of circumstance and stepped into the stellar role of object. The fact that the man who receives a blow is a bishop may be only an added circumstance in one sense, making only an accidental difference; but over and above the essentially unjust nature of this act, is the added affront to religious reverence that gives the act an entirely new nature.

All this is very much like scattering the insides of an automobile over the floor of a garage and saying proudly to the owner: "Well that's what takes you from New York to Los Angeles." The owner might reasonably reply: "Yes, and that's what's going to take you from automobile repairing to piano tuning if you don't get it together again." We have taken the human action apart to examine its goodness and evil. But we must now put it together again to see how it drives toward good or wanders off after evil.

In the process of reassembling the inner parts of the human action we come upon friends from a former chapter. Among others there are those acts of the will which precede actual external action, that enter intimately into the making up of our minds and always precede the execution of our purposes—intention, consent, election or choice.

All of these flow immediately from the will and are produced without the help of clever fingers or stumbling feet. They are elicited by the will in contrast to the outside acts that are executed under the force of command coming radically from the will. Where do they fit in the scheme of morality?

They should play a very important part. After all, good and evil are the direct business of the will. It is the job of the feet to walk, of the ears to hear, of the intellect to understand; but it is the will's exclusive task to be engaged with good and evil. This division of good and evil is the proper division of the actions of the will. Put in another way, the end or goal of activity is the proper object of the will; and a thing is good or bad precisely because of its relation to that goal or end of activity.

One phrase of that last sentence is particularly important: the proper object of the will is the end or goal of activity. It is important because it greatly simplifies the question of the morality of these intrinsic or elicited acts of our rational appetite. To determine whether my almsgiving was good or bad, it was necessary to consider not only the natural purpose of almsgiving but also my intention in giving the alms. But in determining the essential value of these intrinsic acts of the will that is not necessary. In these intrinsic acts, the purpose of the one acting and the purpose of the act itself always coincide—the proper object of the will is precisely the end or goal intended. We give a person credit for his good intentions, and rightly so; not in the sense that such an intention justifies everything a man does, but it does at least justify the intention. The inner form, the specifying principle, that which marks this act of the will off from all others, is at the same time the object of this inner act and the end of the agent—they are one and the same thing.

This does not mean that we are setting up the will as a swashbuckling king who can do no wrong. It can do wrong; in fact it is the fountain source of evil as well as good. It is not an independent creator of morality, making good whatever attracts it, as Midas made whatever he touched into gold. Its goodness or evil is to be judged by the same rules that determine the morality of every other human action, i.e., first and immediately by the rule of reason.

The inner form which gives the intrinsic acts of the will their morality must be set alongside the outer form, the exemplar, to see how it measures up. That outer form, that architect's conception, is reason's knowledge and judgment of the human object of this or any other act. I intend to help my neighbour and that intention is morally specified by its object or end; but that end is good because it measures up to the rule of reason declaring that such an object leads a man to the goal of human life. On the contrary I intend to injure my neighbour; again the morality is determined by the inner form and it is bad because it does not measure up to the rule of reason, because reason declares such an act leads a man away from the goal of human life.

The sole standard by which men of good will can be distinguished from men of bad will is the rule of morality, which is reason. Reason proposing a good end to the will does not make that will good or bad; but the will is good if its acts are in agreement with that reason, they are bad in so far as they violate that rule. It is in acting against an end proposed by reason as good, or intending an end proposed by reason as evil, that the will is bad.

A good grasp of this notion takes all the trickery out of the difficult task of conforming our will to the will of God. A special revelation of God's intentions is not necessary; it is not necessary that we have a blueprint of all the detailed devices of divine Providence; we do not have to spend agonizing hours on our knees trying to discover if this is or is not the will of God. We have only to follow our reason. The human reason does not make up these moral values. The unchangeable moral essences are not the product of human but of divine understanding, they are naturally known, accurate mirrorings of the divine plans ready to hand for every man and woman without the laborious pacing of the corridors of eternity. In this or that particular thing God and ourselves may be at odds without our realizing it—we pray very earnestly, for example, for someone's health when as a matter of fact renewed health would be the means by which he would make a failure of the life he is now prepared to end so successfully. The difference, the disagreement with the will of God is merely material; formally, our ends are God's ends if our ends are the ends of reason.

All this will perhaps become more clear when we look

at the acts intrinsic to and commanded by the will, walking down the highways of life arm in arm. Of course they always do take their strolls in just that fashion when the commanded act appears at all. And with astounding results. Former friends may snub the commanded act unmercifully when they see his companion; or on another day, the commanded act may receive salutations from the influential who would not notice him alone, or would pay him only the almost unconscious tributes given to creatures on a lower stratum.

The commanded act, by reason of its own proper object and so of its own moral essence, is good or bad in itself. No matter what the intention with which it promenades, this goodness or badness remains intact. If the commanded act is itself indifferent, it will be good or bad according to the intention, the end aimed at.

Recently, walking up Lexington Avenue, I came to Fifty-Ninth Street and, inevitably, met the "sandwich men" stooping under their enthusiastic placards. Usually these people are quite indifferent to the world surging past them: eyes blank, or vague with dreaming of a hot cup of coffee, hopeful with the approach of the end of their long vigil. But this particular night one stood out, a young Italian girl, perhaps eighteen years old with that madonna-like beauty that is almost an Italian heritage. She stood absolutely motionless, facing down-town, her eyes tightly closed and with an agony of unutterable shame stamped on her face. Realizing that her tightly locked eyes alone prevented a flood of scalding tears, one could appreciate the sublime courage and desperate necessity that drove her through the long hours of her shame. And it was not hard to form an idea of how the virgin martyrs of early Christendom or the modern martyrs among the nuns of Spain must have looked enduring their martyrdom.

The object and moral essence of almsgiving is good. The act is good in itself. But if from a strain of sadistic cruelty a man approached that girl and offered her a coin, the almsgiving would have been horribly bad. Theft is bad; if, seeing this girl, a man thought how nicely she could use a thousand dollars and so went into the department store on the corner and somehow stole a thousand dollars with the best of intentions, the act would still be bad. Looking or not looking at a human being is a morally indifferent act; but to stop and stare at this girl to enjoy her misery would be bad; to tear one's eyes away in a rush of pity would be good.

As a matter of fact, all this can be morally complete without anything being done for the world to see. My intention to torment the girl, followed by my decision to give her a coin might stop right there; and morally the case is complete as I have just outlined it. Does the actual giving of the alms add anything to the sin already committed? Over and above the damage such external action might do (as in the case of theft) each external sin at least adds a note of intensity, fixing the will in its determination to go through with the act; the very doing of the act extends the whole activity of the will over a longer period; and sometimes it actually increases the number of these acts of the will. A timid burglar intends to humiliate his competitors by a huge theft and decides on a particular victim. Later he weakens and gives up the idea; but the next night his courage comes back and he enjoys a very successful evening. He has committed two sins of burglary, though getting only one bit of loot.

Looking back for a moment, we see the sources of morality as the object of the human act, the end of the man acting, the circumstances under which the act is placed and the external execution of the act; all play their part, and their success or failure is judged by the strict critic reason. But that is not quite the last act; we cannot ring down the curtain until the consequences of that external act have made their bow.

An aviator soaring over New York suddenly becomes bored with just riding around and decides to end the ride right there. If he jumps out depending on his parachute to land him safely, he has no right to indignation when a policeman arrests him for the murder of the people his crashing plane has killed. On the other hand, a joke told at a banquet with such success that a listener swallows his false teeth and dies does not mean that the wit has committed murder. Effects that naturally, necessarily or even usually follow from an action are intimately connected with it and cannot be disowned as so many illegitimate children. But effects that happen once in a lifetime, or that no one could foresee, have no claim on the heritage of good or evil left by the act itself.

Our modern repugnance to the word "sin" is nothing short of absurd when taken in connection with our modern insistence on right and wrong, our judicial paraphernalia, our uplift societies and official reformers. A human act is humanly wrong when it is unreasonable, when it does not conform to the rule of reason; it is right when it does. And that is exactly what is meant by sin and acts of virtue. This or that is a sin precisely because it conflicts with reason; it is good and virtuous because it conforms to the rule of reason. To demand the substance and scruple at the name is just a little childish.

Of course we are blamed for sin and praised for virtue; just as we are blamed for wrong and praised for right. These acts, because they are human, have proceeded under our full control; they are wrong because we steered them deliberately in that direction, right because we chose to act in that fashion. There is room for remorse and satisfaction because human nature is in control of its activity. There is room for merit and demerit because there is room for success and failure, because there is room for justice to ourselves, to the world, to the divine architect whose plans we are working out.

Perhaps one conclusion apparent by this time is that the question of morality is certainly a complex question. Of course it is; for human activity is a decidedly complex activity. But there are a few very simple, very fundamental conclusions which are evident from even this cursory glance at morality.

It should be clear first of all that morality is an integral part of the natural order. It is not something extrinsic, foreign, merely authoritative; but something that flows immediately and necessarily from the working out of natural laws. Like everything else in nature, man is governed by natural laws; and, like their operation in every other nature, those natural laws in man do not violate man's nature. Just as the fulfilment of those natural laws is different in a chemical and in a chimpanzee, so is it different in man, following the differences of his nature. With everything else, natural law uses the whip of physical necessity, driving to its ends without the possibility of mistake; but human activity cannot be subjected to physical necessity and remain human, for it cannot be necessarily produced and at the same time be under our control. The necessity induced by natural law in human activity is a moral necessity, one admitting of choice, of mistake and success, because man's nature is a moral nature enjoying the ability to choose its paths to the goal of nature.

Our human nature not only submits to morality, it cries out for it, it cannot exist without it. In every smallest human act, in exact proportion to its humanity, there is morality; for morality is nothing more than the fulfilling or violation of the law that governs human nature. According as a man's acts are directed to his goal, they are good; and so far as they turn away from that goal, they are bad. And every human action, as human, must be either for or against that goal; it is under control, going somewhere, either to the right place or to the wrong place. If we discover a man whose actions have no morality, either good or bad, we promptly lock him up; for by the same token his actions have no humanity, he is insane; they have no liberty and he is not responsible for what he does. Human, free, moral action are one and the same thing.

Evidently morality is not a mere adjunct of religion. It is not something reserved to pious people, to believers in religion, and forbidden to all others; rather it is something exclusively demanded of possessors of humanity. It is not religion which produces morality but rather morality that of itself will produce religion; for religion is but one of the commands of the natural law which governs man's actions—it is not the root or source of that law.

To escape from morality means to escape from humanity. The attempt to overthrow the moral order is an attempt to deny the authenticity of human nature, to fly from the order of liberty. Like a child in a halloween game, it puts a false face on human nature and expects the world to be frightened. The world is not frightened, it is amused; and if only the inanimate and brute creation were capable of amusement and laughter, the roar of amusement at the antics of these solemnly learned opponents of morality would fill all the vast spaces of the universe. It is impossible to run away from morality because it is impossible to run away from nature, because it is impossible to run away from humanity. In a word, there is no escape from the truth of things as they are.

Everything we have said in this chapter has an immediate bearing on happiness. Let us recall that we placed the essence of happiness in the possession of the goal of life; we said that what share we can have of happiness in this life comes in exact proportion to our approach to that goal of life; all our human activity is but the means to that goal, so many tools by which we carve out happiness. And morality? Morality is the exact measure of man's success in living. Man is happy in proportion as he approaches his end; man is morally good as he aims his acts at that end, morally bad as he aims his acts away from that end. Our morality here and now is a statement of our account in the bank of happiness. Virtue is its own reward in this sense; that every virtuous act is a definite step towards final happiness, every virtuous act is a pocketing of a share in that happiness towards which we are striding. We cannot speak of morality without holding forth on happiness.

V

(OUTLINE)

HAPPINESS AND PASSION I

(Q. 22–29)

1. Opinion and fact of passion:
    - (*a*) Passion outcast as unworthy of man.
    - (*b*) Passion enthroned as all of man.
    - (*c*) Passion welcomed as part of man.

2. Fact of passion is its own full explanation:
    - (*a*) Definition and characteristics of passion:
        - (1) Relation to knowledge.
        - (2) Subject.
        - (3) Goodness and evil.
    - (*b*) Distinction of passion:
        - (1) From reflexes.
        - (2) From feelings.
        - (3) From instincts.
        - (4) From habit.

3. Varieties of passion:
    - (*a*) Generic:—mild (concupiscible) and emergency (irascible).
    - (*b*) Specific:
        - (1) Love and hate.
        - (2) Desire and flight.
        - (3) Delight and sorrow.

            . . . . .

        - (1) Hope and desperation.
        - (2) Daring and fear.
        - (3) Anger.

4. Mutual relations of passions.

5. Theories of passions:
    - (*a*) Resultant—Lange, James.
    - (*b*) Concomitant—McDougall.
    - (*c*) Emergent—Cannon.
    - (*d*) Sexual—Freud.
    - (*e*) Scholastic.

6. The basic passions—love and hate:

   (*a*) Love:

      (1) Double method of treatment: experiment and contrast.
      (2) Varieties: natural, sensitive, rational.
      (3) Division: selfish and benevolent.
      (4) Causes: good, knowledge, similarity.
      (5) Effects: union, inherence, ecstasy, zeal.
      (6) Appreciation:

         a. Its value.
         b. Its effectiveness.

   (*b*) Hate:

      (1) Object and cause: evil and love.
      (2) Its comparative power.
      (3) Hatred of self and of truth.

Conclusion.

1. Balance of passions.

2. Passion and human nature.

3. Passion and human activity.

4. Passion and happiness.

CHAPTER V

HAPPINESS AND PASSION I

(Q22–29)

IT is a part of our American heritage, or perhaps more properly, our Anglo-Saxon heritage, to look upon passion much as a family arrived in society might look on a poor relation. It is something to be ashamed of, frowned on, denied in public, to regret. A severely reserved attitude seems much more worthy of us as men than does passion. So we go about looking very solemn in a silly way, like children desperately suppressing a giggle or a flood of tears, whistling to prove to ourselves and the world that we really are not afraid in spite of the knocking of our knees or the chattering of our teeth. Yet this puritanical attitude makes generous allowances for such passions as sorrow, anger or desperation; and its champions positively revel in the sticky mists of sentiment which enable their minds to become hopelessly confused in a mild, genteel way.

At the opposite extreme we have the fairly recent importation which identifies passion with all that is best in man. Thus all of man's troubles—nervous, domestic, social or even physical—have their roots in the fact that he has not given his passions full play. To be fully a man, one's passion must have had full sway from the days of infancy; otherwise a man is a neurotic or a weakling. It does not seem to be of any importance that following such a procedure man turns out to be a beast; perhaps because down in the hearts of the champions of this attitude, that is really what man is, merely another animal.

The clash of these extremes has tended to divide modern opinion into two camps, both of which are deadly enemies of the perfectly evident facts of human nature. No matter how many hours he spends practising facial immobility before a mirror, no man can tell himself that he does not feel love, desire, fear, hatred and the rest. No matter how loudly he may champion the virility of giving full play to his passions, every man knows that his actions are truly human only when they are under his control; and every man is thoroughly ashamed, or at least considerably embarrassed, at the note of insanity, of inhumanity, that rings out so discordantly from his uncontrolled acts. Children learn very early that the very best time to ask for extraordinary favours is shortly after their father has thoroughly lost his temper.

Somewhere between these two extreme opinions the facts of human life slip by, and placidly pursue their prosaic way, utterly indifferent to the ebb and flow of the battle which no one ever wins and where both sides are always vanquished.

Wherever there is a man, there will be found passion; and wherever there is human activity, there also is control, an actual aiming at a target by man himself. These two indisputable and obvious facts really tell the story of passion; an old, old story which has been told in countless ways, none more simple than by saying that man has a body and a soul. Because he *has* a living body, complete in its equipment for sensitive or animal life, passion is an integral part of his nature, as it is of the nature of all animals. But because he *is not* a living body but a rational being in control of his acts, passion can never be all there is to man. To deny passion is to deny the animal life of man in the face of such obvious facts as the necessity of breakfast; to make passion the full explanation of human activity is to deny intelligence—something that could not be done without intelligence, however unintelligent such a denial might be.

Perhaps even taxi-drivers enjoy a thrill of novelty in examining the latest models of automobiles: there is always some new gadget, some improvement, or alleged improvement, which puzzles the most experienced driver. The parts of the human machine are much more standardized; in fact no change has been made in the model, of which we have any historical record. Realizing that we have been driving this machine for years and years, it is no surprise to discover that we cannot be surprised. A statement of the nature of passion will bring nothing amazing; it has been a part of us from the very beginning and is as familiar as our own face, or our own hands. It is in fact a little surprising that men can quarrel so about it, particularly when it can be adequately described as nothing more than the movement of the sense or animal appetite in man.

It is as simple as that. Very often "emotion" is used to describe what we are calling passion, the word "passion" being reserved for emotion with its cap tilted toughly over one eye. There is no argument with such usage as long as the meaning intended is made clear. But it does leave us without a name for the movements of the rational appetite or will. It seems much better to reserve the name emotions for any movement of any appetite of man, passion exclusively for the movements of the sense appetite. It is in this sense that we will use the word passion throughout this and the succeeding chapters.

Taken in this strict sense, we can expect of passion what we know to be true of any appetite, i.e. that it follows knowledge. Knowing is not its work any more than hearing is the work of the eye; nor can it know any more than the eye can hear. It was not built for that. But unless something is known and presented to it, appetite can never operate. A man who has never heard of baseball does not waste his time writing for a ticket to a game. And that same thing is equally true of every animal; it is only very recently that dogs began to desire dog biscuits.

Like every movement of appetite, passion must come from a faculty whose job is precisely the job of desiring.

It belongs in the faculty of desire much as vision belongs in the organ of sight. Passion as a movement of sense appetite can be immediately located in the organ of sense desire. It belongs in the body of man; if at any time it wanders into the apartments of the soul it is only by accident, merely because the two are so closely connected that it is remarkably easy to pass from one to the other like an echo running upstairs, or an insoluble problem in mathematics bringing tears to a child's eyes in the midst of his homework. In this way the sorrow in the soul of Christ penetrated to His body, and the gloom of a rainy day penetrates to our soul.

Like all sense activity, passion involves some corporal changes. The word passion, in its widest sense, has the signification of receiving something, of suffering or submitting to action, receiving an action within ourselves. In this very wide sense, we might suffer an idea, receiving an idea through the activity of material objects upon us. However ideas, and everything received in the spiritual part of man, are acquired without suffering in the sense of corporal change. It is the thing which must be changed to enter into the spiritual area of our being rather than that our spiritual side be changed to accommodate the material thing. But this is not the case in the sensible part of man. I remember talking to a cook who assured me he never had to eat because he was constantly inhaling food. Perhaps he did not eat. But assuredly he did not adhere to even this delicate form of nourishment without corporal, physical changes. The whole question of passion is in the sensible order; and sensible contact involves sensible changes. A man will flush with anger, pale with fear, his heartbeats quicken with desire, his muscles tense with hate—whatever the passion and however profound the physical changes involved, physical changes there must be. An expressionless face and long training may hide many of these changes; but the lie-detector is just one source of evidence of the impossibility of ruling these corporal changes out of existence when passion comes into play.

From all this it is fairly evident that no amount of puritanical shrinking can confer the dignity of morality upon passion in itself; just as no amount of case records can sum up humanity in terms of passion. We have seen in the preceding chapter that a moral action and a human action are exactly the same thing; and the most unlettered man of the street demands the brand of control, of mastery, before he will accept any action as genuinely human. Morality is inextricably tied up with the control of action. And passion is merely subject to control; it can be controlled or it can get out of control, which is to say it can be either human passion or animal passion, or, saying the same thing in another way, it can be moral, immoral or amoral. Of itself, like everything in the sensible order, it is morally indifferent. Physically, passion is good, an integral element in the well-being of man; but morally it is what we make it.

On the purely material side, these are the things we find always and inevitably in matters of passion: some knowledge—"sensation, percept, imagery, idea";—movement of the appetite, i.e. "a tendency to merge with some external object or to adjustment bringing some change perceptible as agreeable or disagreeable"; and finally some organic, corporal changes which are nothing more than the recognition of stimulus—"discharge of nerve energy, physiological resonances". It is in the second of these, the movement of sense appetite, that passion essentially consists. The first, knowledge, is an indispensable condition for passion as colour is for seeing; the last, corporal change, an inevitable effect following passion like a fall follows loss of balance.

Modern investigations have served to confuse the nature of passions. There have been so many scientific bloodhounds back and forth over the trail of passion that a hound set on the trail now can hardly be blamed if he chases some other dog instead of keeping after the quarry. Science is of course strictly within its rights in investigating this whole problem of passion. After all, it is a question of the sensible order, an order for which the whole equipment of science was designed. And the findings of science have been overwhelming in their detail and of incalculable value. Their very number and value, instead of excusing them from the demands of order, rather demand more attention to order; as an overcrowded desk is a more convincing argument for orderly arrangement than is the desk of the lawyer newly admitted to the Bar.

Going through the terms intimately connected and often confused with the movements of the sensible appetite which is passion, the differences are startlingly clear once they are pointed out, like the defects in a masterpiece or a precious stone once attention has been called to them.

Compared to the reflex-arc which plays such a mighty part in behaviouristic psychology, passion is as different as the dog's grinding on a bone is different from the hum of a meat-grinding machine. A reflex is what happens, for example, in the winking of the eye when a doctor tries to pour drops into it. It is an immediate and mechanical reaction, totally unconscious, which makes no demands on previous knowledge. Passion is a conscious affair which cannot dispense with previous knowledge.

Feeling is the "affective tone of sensation, pleasant or unpleasant", like the overtone of a resonant singing voice, and is a radical pre-requisite of passion rather than passion itself. This affective tone can no more be separated from sensation than a smile can be cut off a face and put away in moth-balls. And sensation is at the roots of knowledge.

Instincts stand at the end of the scale opposite from feelings. Briefly, an instinct is "a function with a physiological and a psychological foundation, a complicated behaviour pattern purposive in character usually operating for the benefit of the individual or race". It includes cognitive, appetitive and motive functions. Like passion, it is decidedly conscious; it is not a mechanical chain of reflexes. In it passion plays its part; but to identify passion with instinct is like identifying yeast with bread.

Reflexes, feelings, passion, instincts are all part of our natural equipment. They do not have to be laboriously acquired. As an indication of the truth of that statement, we have only to look at the difference in the distribution of knowledge or money and the distribution of reflexes, passion and instincts. Habits, on the contrary, are distinctly the product of our activity; we have habits because we build them up. We can be proud of them or ashamed of them as a man is proud or ashamed of his work. But if we have pride or shame in our instincts, passions or reflexes we have little to do and we have not used our leisure for thought.

It is a fact, which by the way I will not attempt to explain, that the English language lends itself much more easily to arguments on politics than to philosophical exposition. Certainly it is not because of any scarcity of English words; we have so many we can throw them about with the utmost abandon. But looking through those thousands of English words for an exact expression of a philosophical notion is like thumbing through a box full of old keys in the vain hope of finding just the one which will open the door. It is not so surprising, then, that it is difficult to find words which will fit the generic classification of the passions. We can lift words over directly from the Latin and divide the passions into "concupiscible" and "irascible" passions—and probably frighten some readers into abandoning this book. Or we can use the term employed quite recently, and call them "mild" and "emergency" passions; and put ourselves in the position of maintaining, for example, that love or daring is a mild passion!

Whatever the name, the distinction is based on the fact that one set of these passions has to do simply with good or evil, no other consideration coming into play. These are the mild or concupiscible passions. The object of the other set of passions adds to the notion of good and evil that of difficulty; these are the emergency or irascible passions.

Translated into concrete terms, this means that all the activities of our sense appetite can be summed under two headings: its loss or gain of the good and its struggle with difficulties, two phases with which every one of us is familiar.

We shall treat every one of the passions in detail, starting in this chapter with love and hate. Instead, then, of stopping at each one for a miniature picture, let us try to get one sweeping view that will accurately locate each of these power houses of sensitive activity. Take, for example, the man to whom a long morning's sleep has been presented as an eminently agreeable, a good thing. He loves sleep whether he is actually enjoying it, looking forward to it, or merely remembering the one he had yesterday; with equal heartiness he hates insomnia whenever and however it is brought before his consciousness. He has been invited to his brother's place in the country for a quiet week-end and to-night as he rushes home on the subway he looks forward with eager desire to a long, refreshing sleep. Actually arriving at his brother's place, he learns that the neighbouring orphanage has burnt down and his brother is harbouring twenty-five orphans of tenderest age. He immediately takes the next train back to town in panicky flight from the inevitable insomnia that will rob him of his precious sleep; but the train is caught in a blizzard and he spends a miserable, back-breaking night in the smoking-car in profound sorrow at the loss of his sleep. The next night he makes up for all this and has the satisfying pleasure or delight in a long, long night's sleep.

Let us suppose there were no trains back to town that night. Here certainly is the place for emergency passions.

Sleep will represent some difficulties; but the women of the house assure him these children are well trained, they are accustomed to getting to sleep very early and if he will do his part by rocking, say, ten of them to sleep everything will be well. So with high hope of overcoming the difficulty he sets about the business of rocking the children to sleep. When he has reached number four, he realizes that it is not every night orphans have a fire—there is number one awake again for the third time. Despair creeps in; if this keeps up he will never get to sleep himself. Something must be done about it. With a daring extraordinary in so self-conscious a man, he puts all the children in bed and tries to sing them to sleep in mass formation. A few minutes of this makes him realize the hopelessness of the situation and he gives way to fear, the fear that there will be no sleep to-night. He finally gets angry about it, and the women of the house who rush in thinking another fire and panic have started, only increase his anger. He turns on the children viciously, shouting them down and announcing to all and sundry that the first one that so much as whimpers will have his ears bitten off. This immediately creates a homey atmosphere again, the children feel safe and sound once more and immediately drop off to sleep. The evil of insomnia has been routed.

A closer scrutiny of this example will show quite easily and quickly this interrelation of the passions. If this unfortunate individual did not love and desire sleep, looking forward to the pleasure of its possession, he would have known no hope, desperation, daring, fear or anger. The all-night taxi-driver does not mind excitement at any time of the night. It is always true that the mild or concupiscible passions are at the root of the emergency passions; in fact emergencies are radically due to the activities of the milder passions. An utterly bored individual has no use for emergency passions because nothing can interest him, nothing can arouse his mild or concupiscible passions.

Quite evidently, then, at the very root of the activity of the passions are love and its opposite, hate. If we wish to single out the most important of the remaining passions, we would not go wrong in picking hope, fear, joy and sadness. And the common bond tying these together, their common claim to importance, is the note of finality which rings out from each one, whether its peal be joyous or lugubrious. Hope stands last in the passions of pursuit (I love, I desire, I hope); fear holds the last place in the passions of escape (I hate, I fly, I fear); and at the very end of all passion's activities we have joyous possession or sorrowful loss. Anger, of all the passions, alone stands in proud isolation; it has no opposite, for its opposite—meek submission to an evil actually present—does not involve the activity of appetite but rather is a denial of this activity. At any rate the hero of our story is finally asleep.

The man has earned his sleep. Quiet has descended on the house, leaving us free to seek our excitement elsewhere. And there is no better place to find it than in the halls of science. Looking into this problem of passion, experimental psychology has arrived at various theories as to the nature of passion and where passion is to be located. One of the earlier opinions, that of James and Lange, identified passion with the bodily movements which are always found with passion. What we call passion is the result of organic and physiological changes; each distinctive passion is differentiated by the physiological changes in the subject of that passion. McDougall comes much closer to the truth when he ties emotion and instinct very closely together; but he tied the knot too tight. In his opinion each passion is always an indication and constant feature of some instinctive process; they always travel in pairs, one emotion to one instinct, with emotion the unchanging core of instinctive behaviour and instinct the great driving force of human activity. Cannon, who, with

Sherrington, experimentally criticized James' theory and proved that different emotions could not be differentiated on the basis of distinctive physiological characteristics, thought that the passions flow out (emerge) on the occasion of the animal organisms encountering certain stimuli or situations and mobilizing the resources of the body *for an unusually strong response.* Freud simplified the whole thing, lowering it to a plane where everyone could talk about it, by tracing all emotion to the master instinct of sex. The driving force of this master instinct, libido, is fundamentally a basic desire for the preservation of the race; and however innocent the particular passion may appear, it has a relation to the master, sex.

All these, with the possible exception of McDougall, make the mistake of interpreting the passions in terms of the purely physiological. The scholastics insisted that passion was a phenomenon of the whole animal unit, involving psychical as well as physiological activity. They explained it as we have in this chapter, an explanation that really meets all the facts in the case.

There is, for example, the matter of love. It *has* its explanations. We can set about explaining love in experimental fashion, that is in laboratory fashion, by subjecting all of its physical characteristics to experiment; or we can attack it more philosophically by contrasting the passion of love with the higher emotion of rational love, constantly setting one off against the other as a jeweller brings out the brilliance of a gem by the sombre majesty of the case in which it reposes.

The last method presupposes two kinds of love in every human being, a supposition that is by no means gratuitous when we remember that man has two appetites and love is the basic movement of appetite. In fact with one or the other missing, man would be no man but merely animal or utterly angelic. Fortunately man continues to be man.

As a matter of fact, by extending the term a little, we

can distinguish three kinds of love. In love's most essential meaning—the first response of appetite to an object known as agreeable, good, fitting to the particular nature involved—we can distinguish the response of plants to rain, of dogs to meat and of men to truth. The difference which irrevocably distinguishes the first from the other two, is that the knowledge followed is not the knowledge of the plant itself, but of its Maker. The plant loves rain in the sense that while the rain is good for the plant and the plant responds to this goodness, it does not know that rain is good; it merely follows a blind drive of nature. Both animals and men, however, have knowledge and it is their individual knowledge which leads on their particular appetites.

Of course all three are to be found in man: there is the response of his lungs to air, of his sense appetite to a cooling wind on a hot day, of his rational appetite or will to the generosity of Calvary. It is these last two in which we are principally interested at present.

To make the contrast between these two more striking, we have only to look back over a day or two of our lives. We have no difficulty in recognizing innumerable examples of selfish love. It must be understood that this word "selfish" is not used in a derogatory sense. It is merely descriptive of that type of love which seeks to assimilate the objects it desires, which seeks to swallow them up in itself, the love that puts in exactly the same class our love of a beefsteak, of a house, of a chair, of a book or even sometimes of friends. It is best expressed by the idea of ownership; this chair, this book, this house is mine, I own it, it is a part of me. This is the difference between *having* friends and *owning* friends. Selfish love has no regard for the substantial nature or personality of the thing or person loved except as it belongs to or is a part of the one loving. Absolutely all animal love, or the love of passion, is of this type.

In contrast to this is beneficent love which includes the true love of friendship and the love we have for God.

Instead of seeking to gobble up the thing loved, figuratively or literally, it has a profound regard for the individuality of the object of love. It does not aim at assimilation, at destruction, or possession of the object of love; but rather sees in the loved one another self. It is a multiplication of self rather than an aggrandizement of self; it promotes the intimate union demanded by love through union of will. This other self is the object of my efforts precisely because he is another self. What he desires is my desire, what offends him offends me, what thwarts his happiness thwarts mine, for we are one.

Rational love, the response of our will to good, can be either of the beneficent or of the selfish type. So it is possible to love a man because he is very wise in order to assimilate some of his wisdom; or because he is very virtuous in order to advance in holiness—neither of these can be the product of the passion of love, yet both are of the selfish or assimilative type.

Whether the love be rational love or the love of passion, the underlying causes are always the same and, very strangely, are remarkably simple and clear to the eye of the philosopher. The sweet mystery of love is not mysterious in its causes but in the infinite possibilities of the human heart for action in the name of that love. For there are just three causes of love, causes that are not mutually exclusive but rather one builds up to and is included by the other. They are goodness, knowledge, and similarity.

Knowledge is an indispensable condition for all love, as it is for all movement of appetite; the dream girl the bachelor seeks is not a creation but a composite of realities that have at one time or another entered into the bachelor's knowledge. It is not from love but from curiosity that a dog approaches his first dog biscuit. When people do not know quite as much about their partners as they thought they did, there is often more material for argument than for love. The element of goodness is no less fundamental, for goodness is the one and only object that attracts any movement of the appetite. No matter how scrawny or moronic a child may look, there is goodness there or there could be no love on the part of its mother. It is not nearly so true that love is blind as it is that love has a much more penetrating eye, plumbing the depths of a human individual and often finding pearls of great price overlooked by all others. Even the most utterly depraved of men who have sold their souls to vice, can be loyal to that vice only because they see it under the guise of good. This much at least must always be true: whatever or whoever wins our love must wear the robes of goodness or instantly suffer the loss of that love.

We have often noticed that very handsome men are an easy prey for very homely girls and vice versa; very vicious dogs seem to run with very timid pets; interminable talkers have excellent listeners for friends, and so on. We shrug it all off by saying "opposites attract". As a matter of fact in the field of love they do not, they repel. The attraction is similarity, a similarity that even a cursory examination quickly reveals.

We have said that beneficent love, or the love of friendship, sees the person loved as another self. Where this other self has our same qualities and excellencies in its actual possession, such an extension or re-birth of self is easy, natural. Remember now it is not a question of identity, but of similarity; the love springs from the precise points of agreement. We submit to this reasoning when we nod wisely and agree that "they were made for each other", "they are a perfect match". But we are apt to be irritated about the matches that are not so perfect, in the sense of not being so obvious; and in these cases we do not hesitate to contradict ourselves and nature by calling upon the moth-eaten doctrine of the attraction of opposites.

The real solution is that in the latter case we are dealing

with another type of similarity. Here it is no longer a question of both having the same qualities in their actual possession, but rather of one actually possessing some good and the other only potentially, or hopefully, in possession of it. It is from this type of similarity that the love of passion, and of friendship whose ends are utility or pleasure take their rise. The good listener has dreamed of being a great conversationalist and the very plain man has had visions of leaving whole clusters of girls stunned by his manly beauty.

Sometimes this works just the other way around, and instead of causing love it will cause envy and hatred, as, for example, when the excellence of another is conceived as standing in the way of our own perfection rather than contributing to it. So we have the refreshing variety offered by human life: we see strong men surrounded by weak ones who give undying loyalty; other strong men hindered, fought, even murdered by weaker men who resented this strength as an impediment to their own progress. We find wise men surrounded by fools; or wise men working hand in hand with other wise men towards greater wisdom; or wise men fighting wise men to the death, not because of their mutual wisdom, but because of what wisdom each was lacking.

It is a sobering thought, this realization that the objects of our love are so many mirrors giving us back accurate pictures of what we are or what in our hearts we would like to be. But it is still more sobering to step into the realms of love's effects.

We cannot possibly treat the effects of love adequately in this chapter; indeed, they will never be adequately known and appreciated this side of heaven. But at least we can touch upon these effects briefly. There is first and obviously the effect of union: the union of similarity in the very cause of love, the union of affection in our appetite's stretching out to the good loved or setting it up as another self, finally the resultant union that comes of love's coupling bond, either by assimilation or by the birth of another self. This latter is a union approaching as closely to identity as is possible without the destruction of either the lover or the loved and is best expressed in the reception of Holy Communion.

Just how close that union is can be made plain by a little insistence on the second effect of love—inherence. The very word indicates that the bond of love makes the parties concerned very nearly essential parts one of another. Taken literally it means that one inheres, exists in, the other. Perhaps that sounds exaggerated; but let us look at the facts. The person or thing loved is never out of our minds; our minds are like a home where the thing or person loved moves about with complete familiarity, leaving an impress on every thought, every image, every memory, and once the thing or person loved has passed out of our lives, our minds are left in a condition comparable only to a lonely, desolate, decaying house. This intimacy is not less but rather greater on the side of affection. If it is a question of the passion of love, there is either complete joy in the presence of the thing or person loved, or restless, haunting, driving desire for that presence. Rational love is calmer but no less intense, making the friend as close to our affections as we ourselves are, and stamping every good we wish that friend with the mark of its destination—to our other self.

That is only one side of the union—the presence of the object of love in the lover. Why can the lover never be content with a superficial knowledge of the object of his his love? What are the endless trifling things that lovers find to talk about? The answer to both these questions is found in the very necessity of the one loving to ponder, to inquire, to mull over and over every single thing pertaining to the object of his love. No, love is not blind, for always it must probe, must penetrate until it gets to the very heart of the one loved. Very simply, the mind of the lover inheres in, buries itself in, the thing loved.

And even more truly is the lover in the loved from the side of affection. So the passion of love will not be satisfied with mere possession, even with mere enjoyment of that possession; it goes further and seeks perfectly to assimilate the object to itself, to penetrate its inmost depths. That is why the ancient philosopher could so truly say a man is what he loves; whether that object be very far below and utterly unworthy of a man, or very high, even infinitely, above him—where his love is there is a statement of what this man is. For unlike the intellect which lifts up or drags down all things to its own level, the appetite must go out to the thing loved. If it be love of friendship, so deeply is the affection of the lover plunged into the one loved that good done to the friend is a personal good; evil done to our friends is evil done to us. We are, as far as is possible in this life, not two but one.

All the other effects of love really follow from these two. By "ecstasy" St. Thomas means here "being carried out of oneself", and surely if our minds and our hearts are buried in another, we are carried out of ourselves. Probably one of the reasons why the ordinary business house is willing to let an employee go off on a honeymoon is because long experience has shown that at that time he is not worth his salt in the office. After all, if a professor can be so immersed in a mathematical problem as to forget about dinner, what can we expect of a man who is immersed in the intense contemplation of love? This is the reason why women can live out their lives in miserable hovels in the name of love and be supremely happy; why men can dedicate their lives to a drudgery of uninteresting work; and why children can slave for parents until their own lives are nearly gone —and all be happy in the doing of these things for love. These people are working for their other selves; what contributes to the happiness of their loved ones is their happiness even though it mean the utmost of personal pain and suffering as it did, for example, to Christ in the Garden of Gethsemane.

Of course, what is evil for our friends is evil for us and is fiercely resented; or, in the passion of love, what interferes with our possession of the desired good meets with our immediate opposition. This is "zeal" in the sense St. Thomas uses it here. An intense movement to exclude everything repugnant to our love, its intensity is in exact proportion to the intensity of our love, a very valuable norm, by the way, for judging the place of anything or any person in our lives.

Does love do any harm? Is it dangerous? Well——! Anything as powerful as love *can* be dangerous; but it should not be. Its whole purpose is to supply us with perfection, to complete our nature. Certainly the love of friendship, beneficent, unselfish love, has no harm in it at all and can do nothing but constantly build up its possessor, working out the paradox that sacrifice is the most perfect way to the fullness, the perfection of our nature. But the selfish, assimilative type of love can be deadly, particularly when it fixes itself on an object unworthy of or dangerous to man. In fact any love is as deadly as the object loved; and this makes the eternally momentous difference between love of God and love of sin—always our appetite finds the level of the thing it loves. The material element in the passion of love, like the material element in any passion, can be dangerous in its excess. Men have been known to rupture a blood vessel or die of apoplexy in a fit of anger; and people have lost all desire for food and physically pined away in the name of love. Every passion involves some corporal, organic changes; and these changes can be carried to the point of organic destruction.

One more point. Put very simply by St. Thomas it is "love is the cause of all things the lover does". We can make this absolutely universal and say that love is the cause of all things that anyone does; and immediately we have furnished ourselves with material for infinite consideration. Think of that and then look at the terrifying complexity of human activity, the viciousness of diabolic activity, or the almighty activity of God himself! Or look at our own activities in the light of that statement and again we have an accurate indicator of that with which our heart is busiest.

There is little excuse for a man's ignorance of where his treasure really lies. Our zeal, the objects of our love, our activities, even our hatreds, are indicators of where our love is centred. For if there were no love there could be no hatred. A man without hates comes very close to being no man at all; for he is a man without loves and consequently a man without a goal, without an excuse for any activity whatsoever. An extremely broadminded man very nearly answers this description. We hate those things that are directly contrary to the things we love, as a woman who fancies cats will often hate the very sight of dogs. Very often a surprise awaits the man or woman who looks closely at the hatreds they cherish in search of the object of love which inspired that hatred. Of the two, love is the stronger, strong enough indeed, to cause hate; but of course we might very easily hate spinach more than we love parrots. Men and women have often twisted this truth of love's strength in the face of hate, but the mistake has its basis in the fact that hate is often more strongly felt than is love. There is no rest for hate, except in the climax of love; hate as long as it exists is a fiery, consuming passion, but love finds a quiet joy in the possession of the good desired—yet does not cease to be love.

Let us sum up this chapter briefly, much more briefly than the subject-matter deserves. It is not a sufficient excuse for gluttony or drunkenness to say that man has a natural desire for food and drink; nor is it a sufficient excuse for uncontrolled passion to say that the passion is natural. Of course it is natural, but whatever it is, it is only one of a host of natural passions. To allow one to run to excess is to snuff out some of the others, a decidedly unnatural proceeding. In the animals this balance of passion is kept instinctively and is thrown out of gear only by some extrinsic, necessary, physical cause. But in man that balance is kept by the command of reason and can be thrown out of gear at the pleasure of the individual. It is not natural for man to let any one passion take over the command of his life, for the essence of his human activity consists in its control by reason. Passion acting naturally in a man is passion acting under the control of reason.

To be lacking this or that passion is not subject-matter for a boast. No one boasts of being a freak; and the man or woman lacking any one of these passions is a freak. As a matter of fact, if such a statement were made, it would very properly be the subject of considerable doubt; as though a person were to smile gently and say in a pitiful voice: "You know, I have no brain." It would be at least unusual. Passion is an integral part of the nature of man.

More than that, it is an integral part of the source of motive power in man. All the drive behind human activity comes from the appetites of man, sensitive or rational; and passion is the natural movement of the sensitive appetite. It is not surprising that passion plays such a part in our activities—it should, for our two appetites are so closely connected they inevitably react one on the other. Under the control of reason, passion can be as much of a help to human activity, as out of control it can be of harm. Normally our natural equipment is not handed out in lopsided portions. There is usually a definite proportion between the power of the sensitive and the power of the rational appetite. To be the possessor of very strong passion is not a guarantee of a one-way ticket to hell; it is rather the statement of very great possibilities either for evil or for good, for loving greatly, wholeheartedly. The development of those possibilities is a question of the object on which we fix our love. The conversion and life-long loyalty of Mary Magdalen had their psychological as well as their supernatural explanations, as did the wise choice of Peter to be the successor of Christ as leader of the Apostles.

Happiness is the reward of human activity and the measure of man's steady steps towards his goal. Just as passion cannot constitute human activity, it cannot constitute human happiness. It is our common heritage with the brutes; what happiness it can give alone is brute pleasure that has always the taste of ashes in the mouth of a man. Passion can contribute mightily to happiness, as it can contribute mightily to the activity of man; passion can work mightily against happiness as it can operate mightily against the control that is the essence of human action. But whether passion, strong or weak, leads to happiness or away from it is in the hands of each man.

CHAPTER VI

(OUTLINE)

HAPPINESS AND PASSION II—CONCUPISCENCE

(Q. 30–39)

1. Pertinence of this subject-matter:
    - (*a*) To spoiled children of twentieth century.
    - (*b*) On the grounds of humanity itself:
        - (1) Place of activity and goal in human life.
        - (2) Place of mild passions in relation to activity and goal.

2. Passion of desire—concupiscence:
    - (*a*) Its essence and location.
    - (*b*) Natural and acquired desires.
    - (*c*) Aversion.

3. Pleasure and joy:
    - (*a*) Nature and distinction of the two.
    - (*b*) Their evaluation:
        - (1) In themselves.
        - (2) Relative to men.
        - (3) The scale of pleasure.
        - (4) Contrariety of pleasures.

4. Causes of pleasure and joy:
    - (*a*) Work.
    - (*b*) Movement.
    - (*c*) Love:
        - (1) Union.
        - (2) Action of others.
        - (3) Action for others.
        - (4) Similarity.
    - (*d*) Sorrow.
    - (*e*) Novelty.

5. Effects of pleasure and joy:
    - (*a*) Enlargement of soul.
    - (*b*) Desire and distaste.

(*c*) Keenness and dullness of apprehension.
(*d*) Perfection of operation.

6. Morality of pleasure and joy:

(*a*) Good and evil pleasures.
(*b*) Moral possibilities of pleasure.

7. Sorrow:

(*a*) Its nature; distinction of the passion from rational sorrow.
(*b*) Its contrariety:
(1) To contemplation.
(2) To pleasure.
(*c*) Scale of sorrows.

8. Causes of sorrow:

(*a*) Evil.
(*b*) Desire:
(1) For good.
(2) For unity and love.
(*c*) Power.

9. Effects of sorrow: impairment of nature.

(*a*) Blindness.
(*b*) Depression.
(*c*) Debility.
(*d*) Bodily injury.

10. Remedies for sorrow:

(*a*) Pleasure.
(*b*) Tears.
(*c*) Compassion of friends.
(*d*) Contemplation of truth.
(*e*) Sleep and a bath.

Conclusion:

1. Mild (concupiscible) passions are peculiarly modern passions:

(*a*) Economic theory and concupiscence.
(*b*) Advertising, scientific discoveries, amusement and pleasure.
(*c*) Vividly contrasting positions on sorrow and pain:
(1) Of horror.
(2) Of glorification.

2. Effects of this modern emphasis on mild passions:

(*a*) On make-up of man.
(*b*) On activity of man.
(*c*) On outlook of man.

3. Paradox of Man of Sorrows and His philosophy of joy.

CHAPTER VI

HAPPINESS AND PASSION II—CONCUPISCENCE

(Q. 30–39)

EVERY age in which man has lived has had its share of passion because men are men. Passion, as an integral part of human nature, makes its inevitable appearance wherever men are found. But history would make very dull reading indeed if in every age, or in every man, passionate activity were exactly the same. Fortunately the emphasis on different passions is as shifting as the interplay of light and shadow, rain and sunshine on a spring day, and with results just as interesting and individual. Our own era, in spite of the long centuries which have preceded it, is no more a mere replica of what has gone before than is the thirteenth child of a family merely a copy of the preceding twelve.

In this chapter we are talking of the mild or concupiscible passions—desire and aversion, pleasure and joy, pain and sorrow—a subject-matter which could expect attention in any age; but which *demands* attention and application in our own mild age. We are spoiled children. We have been treated far too well for our own good. Dr. Carrel has groaned in spirit and in print on the damage done to us by this constant coddling; whatever the damage, at least the facts are beyond question. It is not only true that our necessities were the luxuries of another age; we are dedicated to a programme of constant creation of new desires, new necessities. Every age has had its pleasures, our own has been overwhelmed with opportunities for amusement and self-indulgence and we are just starting. We are definitely committed to pleasure. We have developed a cult of joy which either shrinks in horror from sorrow and pain or goes to the opposite extreme of deifying suffering. At the very least our views of sorrow and pain are the sharp, vividly arresting views of extremists.

Merely as products of the twentieth century, mild passions have an absorbing interest for us. As men and women, moving in step with all the men and women of every age towards the goal of all men and women or away from it, these passions, like all passions, intrude on every day of our lives.

Human life is a swift movement to a definite end; it has meaning only because of the goal in sight; it is successful or unsuccessful, happy or unhappy as the goal is attained or lost. The dice the cast of which will determine that gain or loss are human actions, actions controlled, aimed at that ultimate target. These mild passions affect every action, they quicken every step or make it dragging, leaden, they colour every object which inspires that human activity. For they are nothing more than movements of the animal appetite in man, so closely joined to the intellectual appetite or will that the one is constantly affecting the other; and appetite is the principle of all movement in man, of every least activity and of activity's contribution to the goal of life.

All this sounds very serious indeed; and it should sound serious. The investigation of the passions is no mere satisfaction of a tourist's curious interest in strange sights, rather it is the strategist's close scrutiny of the field of battle. Familiarity with passion may inspire us with a bored confidence which is dangerous, like that of a man who strides confidently in the dark through a room in his own house, and, very effectively, falls over a chair that is just a few inches out of place either in his memory or in the room.

The obvious never seems very important, yet usually it is most important. Chesterton's remark that "it is not what a man proves that is important but what he forgets to prove" is a statement of a profound truth. It is the truths a man takes for granted that are the pillars of his intellectual life; just as it is the things he takes for granted which are the actual determinants of his actions. A novice at structural steel work very rarely falls; he takes nothing for granted. Our familiarity with passion, the fact that we come face to face with it in ourselves and in others in all our human contacts, is not a reason for dismissing it lightly, but for really uncovering all that we can about it.

It is, for example, important to know where such a very common passion as desire (concupiscence) belongs in our human nature. If we walk back into the store-room of sense appetite, we have only to reach up on the shelf between love and pleasure to put our hand on desire. It is always there and no amount of moving, of disarrangement, no external or internal turmoil will succeed in putting it anywhere else. It is our sense appetite's reaching out for a good that is loved but absent, a good the possession of which will give us pleasure. Scrutinizing desire we have infallible evidence of what we love, and what will in our estimation give us pleasure. Corresponding to this passion of desire in the sense appetite there is, of course, the emotion of desire in the intellectual appetite or will: the first centres on the attractions of the sensible world and always carries with it the organic changes that are the toll exacted by all passion; the other centres on the suprasensible delights which completely escape the animal world.

With all our effort to increase desire, there is one class of desires which the most ingenious advertising man cannot influence. The natural desires, whether in the sensible field of passion or in the spiritual field of will, operate in a closed shop and no length of apprenticeship can win a membership card in this union. Apprentices are not necessary, for members of this union do not die. The reason for this is the complete stability of the individual natures. Natural desires reach out for the goods nature must have;

and the nature of man, as long as he is man, always requires the same things for its existence and perfection. Limited in this sense, there is another sense in which these natural desires are insatiable. We may think we have enough sleep or food for the moment, but we are quite sure that it is for the moment only. Man is not one of the animals that take on enough food for the winter at one sitting; but even if he were, that desire for food would reappear with the chirp of the first robin. At the very moment when these natural sensible desires are satisfied, they completely disappear. This brings out sharply the dividing line between desire of an absent good and pleasure in a possessed good; never does food seem less desirable than immediately after we have finished a big meal.

The advertising man's genius has an opportunity to prove itself in the field of acquired desires. Here the limits of desire are as flexible as the limits of love, and love ranges the whole horizon opened up by knowledge. It is possible to teach a dog to drink coffee at night—and have him keep himself and everyone else awake. A bright dog can acquire many more desires than a stupid dog because he can learn of the goodness of more things. If the advertising business were strictly limited to dogs, the individual dog approached by a salesman would have every reason to be flattered. But it does not work the same with human beings. It is not a compliment to have a man edge up to us on a street corner and offer to sell a genuine diamond for fifty cents. Even the dullest man is capable of infinite acquired desires—not because he is so bright, but because he is a man and the human intellect, with the human will only a step behind, of its very nature reaches out for the infinite, is never satisfied with any particular good, or any number of particular goods. Every man was made for the universal good, the universal truth.

A man is quite capable of desiring riches without limit; but it is quite stupid of him to expect even limitless riches to satisfy his desires. Joyce Kilmer's poem, "Pennies", accurately describes the twist a man puts in his nature by centring his desires on particular goods. The poem pictures a little boy standing perplexed and sad with a few long-hoarded pennies in his hand, sad because the first delight of ownership has gone. Suddenly he drops the pennies on the ground and sees them scatter, and immediately his old zest returns and joy is born again in seeking the lost treasure. Desire is made to do the double duty proper to desire and pleasure; because we have learned so well that none of these things once had will satisfy, our pleasure is put into the hunt for them, not in the things themselves. It is as though we read a book, not for the story, but that we might turn the pages; or run a race in the fervent hope that it will never end. Of course there is no peace for such a desire, for peace is the end of desire and the end of such desires brings nothing but tears such as dimmed the eyes of Kilmer's "kilted Hedonist".

Arm in arm with the powerful passion of desire, like a weakling clinging to a strong man, or a fool to a wise man, is the pettiest of the passions. In the last chapter we called it "flight"; perhaps "aversion" would be a more concrete name for that turning away of the appetite from the disagreeable or evil. It is not to be confused with fear, for fear is by no means a petty thing. Aversion has for its object an absent evil, the kind of thing that furnishes so much material for worry; but the evil which inspires aversion is not a great, difficult, or even imminent evil—all those come under fear. It is not that we are afraid of this particular evil, that we are in any danger from it, we simply do not like it. The idea of caressing a pet snake, the surgeon's enthusiastically detailed account of an operation given at the dinner table, a graphic picture of a murder spread across a newspaper, all might very well arouse the passion of aversion, even with surprising organic changes.

A much more important passion, and certainly a much more joyous subject for consideration, is the passion of pleasure. Its consideration can be a thing of joy; but the passion itself can never bring joy. In that statement we have the very important distinction between the act of the sensible or animal appetite and the act of the intellectual appetite in the possession of good. Joy is the movement or rather rest of the intellectual appetite, corresponding to pleasure in the sensible appetite. Or at least it is in this sense that we shall use the terms. Both occupy the final position in the mild emotions, in fact of all emotions, for to them is ordained the activity of all others. This is the reason for desire, for hope, for daring—in order that the good loved might finally be possessed. They mark the end of emotion, as they do of life, for it is to this end that life and emotion began. Every pleasure, every joy, is a tolling of a great bell marking the passing of a struggle; perhaps that is why so often in the midst of pleasure or joy we pause to wonder if the prize were worth the effort and sacrifice that went into its winning. And often the tolling of the bell of pleasure seems to awaken us from a dream to the bitter realization of the shoddiness beneath the bright tinsel which deceived us.

It is sometimes surprising, though it should not be, how much of profound truth is expressed in our ordinary choice of words. We are quite willing to say that a warm sunny day gives us pleasure; but we would be reluctant to admit that our meals are a source of joy to us. We prefer to save that word joy for something less obviously sensual, or at least for something superlative. Taking joy as the intellectual emotion corresponding to the passion of pleasure, there is a great deal of truth in this practice of ours. For considered in themselves, in the abstract, spiritual joys are far greater than anything the senses have to offer. After all, they deal with much greater goods, and our union with these goods, from which springs our joy, is much more intimate, more perfect, more enduring. The contrast of the joy of friendship and the pleasure of a cigarette shows us there is no comparison between the two from the point of view of value. As for union, well, certainly the cigarette does not penetrate the barriers of our mind and will to take up an eternally enduring position which nothing can change or corrupt, as does the true friend, nor are we plunged mind and heart into the very essence of the cigarette.

From our point of view, however, the sensible pleasures may be, in fact usually are, greater. We are, on the whole, very much better acquainted with the smell of clean fresh air than with the odour of sanctity; scalding coffee is much more vivid to us than the imperfection of the words we use after drinking it, for the coffee—like all things sensible—extorts the toll of organic change, leaving us something by which to remember it. Perhaps an even stronger reason for the pre-eminence of sensible pleasures is that they are direct antidotes to sorrow, while spiritual joys have no corresponding sorrow, unless it be the sorrow of their loss. The sorrow of a child over its lost pennies can be combated effectively by the pleasure of ice-cream, where a sublime exposition of the beauty of poverty would leave the child unmoved. Spiritual joys help us to sustain sensible sorrows, but they will not drive them out of our lives.

Comparing the sensible pleasures one to another, the greatest in dignity, the supreme in reference to knowledge, is sight. This comes closest to the boundary lines of the spiritual and ministers more heavily to the intellect than do the other senses. Our pity for a blind man as against our annoyance at a deaf man has some basis in fact.

Very often, however, our pity is based on the helplessness of the blind man, from the view point of the utility of sight. Really from this angle sight ranks much further down the list than does the sense of touch and the pleasure it gives. A horse in a majestic pose looking towards the east at dawn is not lost in the beauty of the sunrise but alert to the prospect of oats. In all the animals touch is more intimately wrapped up with the conservation of nature and so is more useful than any of the other senses. All other pleasures are with reference to the pleasure of touch. The sight of a deer may give a lion as much pleasure as it does a man; but the lion's pleasure will certainly not be the pleasure of an aesthete.

It is not hard to see that sensible pleasures are often directly opposed. They are the result of movements reaching different goals; their opposition is the opposition of their goals. There is the vivid contrariety, for example, of sleeping and listening to a brass band, or walking in the rain. But this is not true of the joy of virtue; no virtue is opposed to another, for all regard the same landing place, the same terminal or goal—reason. If the act is virtuous at all, it will agree with all other virtuous acts in this one particular at least: that it is in harmony with reason, it is according to the rule of reason.

Although it will not be a joy of virtue, a man can act against reason and by his action win pleasure. In this sense, the pleasure of every sin is unnatural, unhuman, i.e. in violation of the rule of humanity in man, the rule of reason. The word unnatural, in ordinary usage, is reserved for things more monstrous than the violation of reason, though of course they include that. We apply the word only to violations of man's physical as well as his moral nature, things like cannibalism or bestiality. These totally unnatural things can bring man a pleasure, though of course it is thoroughly unnatural pleasure. This fact presents a real difficulty. Pleasure is a passion, and as such is an integral part of our nature, ordained by the author of nature to the full perfection of nature; yet here we find it in full vigour in an open violation of all that is natural to man.

The answer can only be that in these cases something is rotten in the individual nature. There is corruption there, a gangrenous decay which has eaten away some of the very bones of nature and left it lopsided. It might be a corruption of body, such as we get from sickness and fever; as a cold might make everything a man eats taste like so much leather, or a disease make sweet things taste sour, or make hot things feel cold. Some such physical corruption can make a man enjoy munching on a piece of coal or a lump of dirt. It may be a corruption of soul, a deterioration or obliteration or change of the natural inclinations of a man through bad habits, vicious education either by word or example, and from this latter corruption we have such practices as cannibalism.

The cause of these unnatural pleasures is significant. It means that where they have taken root, the nature of man has gone far along the way of corruption. This corruption has sometimes gone as far as actual putrescence, though accompanied at the same time by a kind of brilliance and unhealthy beauty, a brilliance that has been characterized quite rightly as the "phosphorescence of decay."

How can we win to that natural healthy pleasure and joy which is the natural goal of all our activity? Well, one way would be to stop pitying the postman's dreary trudging of the streets or the sailors' weary days and nights on stormy seas and watch them when they have a day free. The postman takes a walk and the sailor rows a boat about on some lagoon. There is a real pleasure in the exercise of any of our faculties; what we do well we enjoy doing, what we do not enjoy doing is usually connected with some impediment to the operation of our faculties.

It is pleasant to experience the movement from cold to warmth as we come home on a bitterly cold night; though the same thing is not so pleasant on a July day in the city. It is in this sense that St. Thomas takes movement as a cause of pleasure; the passage from one state to another, which of course would include such a thing as the movement from ignorance to knowledge. Not that St. Thomas would deny pleasure to an interpretative dancer through the exercise of her art; but he would insist that such pleasure proceeds from that very plebeian cause "work," the exercise of natural faculties.

There are many causes of pleasure and of joy flowing from love. There is the supreme pleasure of passion and the supreme joy of will in that essential climax of love which is union. We explained this quite thoroughly in the last chapter, but it is worthy of note here that it is precisely this union springing from and culminating in our love for God and God's love for us that makes up the central joy of heaven. The successful or triumphant actions of friends bring us joy, for we look on their success, their triumphs, as our own; the multiplication of self by beneficent love (which includes friendship) is also a multiplication of the sources of joy. We might receive considerable pleasure from the actions of mere acquaintances, when, for example, they tell us how wonderful we are; or when these actions are the means by which we obtain some good. Actions for others are a cause of joy springing from love, for they are really love in action, responding to that deep desire of love, not merely to wish good, but effectively to wish good to another, to get something done for another, to prove to ourselves and to the world that our love is not a matter of mere words. When one of the Fathers said "love is not lazy" he was giving a very laconic expression to this truth; it is the explanation of the Christian paradox of emptying oneself that one's joy may be full, of having nothing but possessing all things, the paradox that explains the Christmas spirit and draws our eyes to the spectacle of God giving Himself to man.

Because it is so intimately connected with love, similarity

is a great contributor to pleasure and joy. At the same time it may, quite accidentally, be a cause of hatred and sorrow, as in the case of the twins who are a great joy to each other until they both decide to marry the same man. The disappointed girl may then withdraw into a corner for a satisfying fit of melancholy; but do not sympathize with her too much, for there can be joy even in sorrow. That is what makes operations such an engrossing topic among erstwhile patients—the emphasis on such past sorrows if placed on the fact that they are past, or on evils that have been escaped, is a definite cause of pleasure. People who insist on knowing the worst, have joy as well as sorrow from the bad news; the joy which comes from knowing what should be known. Toyland or sightseeing is a perennial cause of pleasure and joy; the novelty of everything we see pleases us, not because of the ignorance of which it reminds us, but because of the knowledge it gives us, or at least the hope of knowledge.

Inevitably the effect of pleasure and joy is an enlargement of a man; the pleasure of passion is an almost literal enlargement, an aggrandizement which is the end of selfish love, an expansiveness easily seen in the pleasure afforded by a good meal. The same is true in the spiritual order, for there the possession of good is an addition of perfection to a man.

In the sensible order of passion, when our desires are satisfied, we enjoy pleasure, and we have enough. In fact if we have any more it will cause disgust and distaste; perhaps later on, when desire awakens again, but not now. For these sensible goods can exceed the demands, even the capacities, of nature; a man can literally drink himself to death. But the goods of the spiritual order, instead of exhausting nature's capacity, perfect that capacity. The desire for them is never satiated, too much of them cannot disgust us, for we cannot have too much of them; though now and then, quite accidentally, because of weak knees, a headache or an empty stomach, they can become a source of annoyance rather than of joy.

There is the same contrast between the passions of pleasure and joy in their effects on the mind of man. Joy increases the facility and effectiveness of reason, for the very workings of reason are themselves a spiritual joy, in no way hindering but rather increasing the joy of the soul. Sensible pleasure, on the contrary, impedes the reasoning of man in direct proportion to the magnitude or intensity of that pleasure. It is just as well that a man cannot talk with his mouth full of food; at least he will have more important things to say some other time. The vividness, familiarity and appeal of the sensible is too much of a match for the high aims of reason. It is this very power of sensible pleasure which makes physical relaxation and recreation such a boon to man. It really rests his soul, the way turning off a light rests a boy's eyes. And of course, as a final effect of pleasure and joy, our work improves. Not only is our soul rested by the pleasure, but what we like we work at more heartily, give it a more vehement attention and start the pleasantly vicious circle in which our work gives us more joy and our joy gives us greater capacity for work.

From what we have seen of natural and unnatural pleasures, it is evident that good and evil pleasures exist; the difference between the two is found in the object whose possession gives rise to the particular pleasure. For pleasure in itself, like any other passion, is neither good nor bad; it is the material from which we fashion good or bad deeds, the moral evil or moral goodness comes rather from our fashioning than from the material itself. What is true of pleasure is not necessarily true of joy, for the saint simply cannot make bad use of the joy of his virtue any more than a mathematician can square a circle.

The course run by appetite is the course run by human life. At the end of human life there is heaven and hell;

at the end of every human activity there is pleasure and joy, or sadness. These are the two great landing fields on one of which the soaring flight of every human action must come down. Perhaps many of us think we have a mechanic's job at the airport of sorrow; but that is usually an exaggeration. We are all inclined to be very gentle with ourselves and to extend a heartfelt sympathy to ourselves on the slightest provocation. One of the most ordinary foundations of this self-pity is the failure to make the same distinction in these emotions that we have made in all the others: one sorrow is passion, the sorrow of the sensible or animal appetite when evil actually enters the house; the other is the sorrow of the intellectual appetite or will under the enforced visit of the same unlovely guest. If we count up our sorrows we will be astounded to discover how few of them can make a serious claim to entry into the domain of the soul. Almost all will be flatly opposed to the passion of pleasure, to sensible pleasure; for that is the way of such pleasure, to be always dogged by its very opposite. No sensible pleasure escapes the existence of its horrible twin. But when we enter the domain of spiritual joy, there is real difficulty finding opposites of joy outside of the very patent sorrow over the evil of sin. Certainly there is no sorrow standing over against contemplation or knowledge, unless we have recourse to sensible nature again and point to fatigue of body, or such an impediment to contemplation as a headache.

Remembering that for sorrow there must not only be an evil present but we must know of its presence, it is not too difficult to see that interior sorrows are much greater than are the exterior ones. Martyrs were quite logically willing to undergo the pain of suffering and the loss of life rather than the loss of virtue. Exterior suffering, which affects us through our bodies, is undergone quite as a matter of course every time we visit a dentist; it is repugnant to the appetite because of its repugnance to the body, while the interior sorrow is directly opposed to the appetite itself. We can, and often do, undergo these exterior pains joyfully, even eagerly, in the name of a higher good desired by our will—like caring for a sick baby or having gallstones removed. Yet, counting over the sorrows that weigh us down, we find it is these lesser sorrows which make up the vast majority.

I remember, shortly after electric refrigerators and consequently ice cubes became a household word, seeing a very small child filch one of these cubes and crawl off to one side to enjoy himself sucking the ice. Suddenly he was screaming at the top of his lungs; his hand was so very cold it felt like it was burning, yet the ice cube was clutched in a death grip. Perhaps the child did not know the ice cube was causing his pain; or knowing it, wanted to hold the ice cube and escape the pain at the same time. At any rate he succeeded in giving a vivid portrayal of many of our relations to sorrow; very often we know what is wrong but we want to eat our cake and have it, and perhaps just as often the cause of the sorrow is by no means clear to us.

Yet in itself the cause of sorrow is ridiculously simple. It goes back, of course, to evil, but behind evil there is desire. Our constant effort to increase sensible desire is at the same time an increase of the causes of sorrow; a multiplication of pleasure inevitably multiplies its opposite.

An age of self-indulgence is invariably an age of discontent, disappointment and sorrow; it places its emphasis on the sensible side where every pleasure has its opposite pain. It is desire for good, for love, for the integrity and happiness of the things or persons we love that is at the root of sorrow, as love is at the root of hate. Our sorrows, like our loves and our hates, are invaluable indicators of what is closest to our hearts.

The mere existence of evil would not inflict sorrow on

us; there must be that union effected between ourselves and the evil, as the union of love joins good to us and gives us pleasure and joy. So that the really active cause of sorrow is power, a power which cannot be resisted and that therefore succeeds in thrusting this evil upon us. There is a great difference between running head on into a fog and running head on into a door; and that difference lies in the irresistible power of the one to inflict evil on our senses and the helplessness of the other. The weakening of our power of command is inevitably a multiplication of our sorrows; where our power of resistance wears down, we are really conferring power on enemy forces—and this is a corollary to self-indulgence which is constantly skimmed over though in itself it is a powerful argument for discipline and self-control.

Sorrow can be quite accurately conceived as a process of deflation. Pleasure and joy puff us up; sorrow puts a pin in the balloon and watches it collapse. That is exactly what sorrow does to us, it collapses us. A young wife whose husband has been killed in an accident will wander about in a daze, unable to think, with no interest in food or sleep, her step will drag, she will feel utterly fatigued, and that time of sorrow will be a serious drain on her strength. She is not necessarily a nervous type; these are not signs of hysteria. They are the normal effects of sorrow. It simply lets us down completely. In the extreme it can paralyse our reason, impede even our physical actions, actually do bodily harm. It does more than that; it turns the motion which is life in the wrong direction; instead of an eager pursuit of the goal of life, it becomes a rout, a constant attempt to escape, a flight from evil rather than a pursuit of good.

It is, in a word, something that must be remedied, and remedied as quickly as possible. This is not to be misunderstood: not every sorrow produces these effects fully, but every sorrow will produce these effects in some little degree. As a matter of fact, a moderate sorrow, while it cuts down our reasoning abilities, may actually contribute to the cause of learning; the old-fashioned use of the switch to make a boy learn his lessons, cut down the sweep of his mental wanderings but considerably increased his intellectual efforts on his studies because those intellectual efforts were the means by which he hoped to escape from his sorrow.

One way of eradicating sorrow is to remove the evil which is causing it. But that is not always practical. There are very many and very practical remedies for sorrow, of which perhaps the most obvious is pleasure. The radio has cut down the sorrows of sick men; and a good movie is a first-class remedy for a fit of the blues. Where the sorrow is a sensible one, we can easily and quickly attack it by ministering physical pleasure. In other words, we are puffing a little wind back into our collapsed human balloon, and things are looking up.

"A good cry" is not necessarily a sign of weakness; it may be the sensible thing to do as a remedy for sorrow. Actually it falls under the same heading as movies or radio, for it is a source of pleasure. It is always a pleasure for us to do what we are perfectly disposed to do at the moment; on a brisk day a man may feel like taking a walk, and it is quite true that "nothing would give him greater pleasure." The same thing is true of tears. When a person feels like crying, a flood of tears will be more than a relief, it will be a pleasure and will help very much in conquering sorrow. There is a deeper relief to tears than this. It is a dispersion of sorrow, a scattering of it to the four winds. Instead of pressing it down within us, we allow it to overflow outside of us, and immediately release the pressure of sorrow and rob it of much of its power.

Friends are a great help against sorrow, not only because it is a joy to know that we are loved, but also because their compassion shows us graphically that we are not carrying our sorrow alone. Going up the ladder of relief one step higher, mental concentration, contemplation of truth, is a very potent factor against sorrow, but only in proportion as we are lovers of truth. In itself it is the greatest of human joys and will one day make up the essential joy of heaven; but for a man whose love has been centred in the sensible world, whose pleasure has always been the pleasure of passion, there is little relief to be expected from contemplation. On the other hand, there is the story of St. Thomas whose ulcerated leg was cauterized very crudely by fire and the pain of it went unnoticed because of his preoccupation with a problem; while the martyrs, with their minds fixed on the eternal truth, could pass from life, as Thomas More did, with a laugh on their lips.

I am sure St. Thomas would be very impatient indeed with our preoccupation with sorrow if he could see our luxurious beds and abundant shower-baths. To his medieval mind, an immediate and practical remedy for sorrow is a sleep and a bath. When a Prime Minister told a former King to "sleep on it," he was giving sound Thomistic advice. We have said that sorrow deflates us, presses us down, actually drains us of energy and turns the whole motion that is life in the wrong direction, making it a flight; sleep and a bath renew our energy, restore the physical balance of our bodies so that we can and do take a saner view of our situations, and that saner view will of course include a condemnation of the attempt to run away from life. St. Thomas gives one more reason for the effectiveness of this last remedy: he says it is a relief by the subsequent pleasure it brings us and adds, in the laconic fashion of the schoolmen—"*quod patet*," "and this needs no proof."

If we look at Thomas's explanations of the mild passions and then glance at the tendencies of our time we must feel like a doctor who reads through a list of symptoms in a medical book and then listens to a patient recite that list as though it had been memorized. The applications to our time are so glaringly evident that we are almost forced to the conclusion that these mild passions are peculiarly ours, that in this twentieth century of ours they have reached one of the most flourishing states of their long history.

Let us look at the facts. Our economic theory calls for a constant increase of concupiscence or the passion of desire. To take care of the excess products of mass production and at the same time guarantee its profits new markets must not merely be found, they must be created. People must constantly be made to need more things, need new things, to have their desires always on the increase.

To this end we have one of the outstanding achievements of American genius in the field of advertising. Art, psychology, statistical science, modern printing miracles, untold wealth, all the genius of oratorical devices, of the theatre, and of the novel are poured into this great machine that out of it might come a flood of new desires.

Scientific genius is pressed to its utmost to satisfy these desires. Labour-saving and time-saving devices are necessities, the possession of which is not only a pleasure in itself but it releases us to sample freely the incredible opportunities for amusement and pleasure that are showered upon us from every side. We can see a very small but overpowering fraction of the possibilities our twentieth century offers the seeker after pleasure by spending a solid evening at the radio or attempting to read the titles of all the magazines which are dedicated to amusement.

Because of this dedication to pleasure, sorrow and pain take on the guise of utter catastrophes. We would very much rather hide sorrow and pain in institutions at any cost than face them or give them our personal ministrations. Physical sorrow, disease and poverty all put a check on pleasure, when they do not make it impossible; and to an age dedicated to pleasure, there can be no greater catastrophe.

Or, what is perhaps worse, pain itself is perverted, lifted up into the class of pleasures in the frankly militaristic states which are painting war under any form in such glorious colours. In Japan, for example, the highest joy in life is death on the field of battle; in the countries where the governing party has become a kind of deity, physical encounter and duelling are the great tests of manhood, suffering and death are supreme acts of worship.

All of this has made a deep impression on the modern man. Dr. Carrel does not go so far wrong in his pessimistic summing up of the damage done to us by the "benefits" of the twentieth century. From what we have seen in this chapter it is evident that such dedication to sensible desire and pleasure, such horror or glorification of physical sorrow and pain, have a deadening effect on the mind of man in direct proportion to the emphasis on pleasure. And if such a dedication deadens the intellect of man, it deadens his intellectual appetite or will. The multiplication of desire and pleasure is also a multiplication of sorrow with all the devastating effects of sorrow: blindness, depression, debility, sapping even our physical strength and turning life's motion completely around. And with this ever-growing physical sorrow there is an insensibility to the spiritual sadness that should be our greatest concern.

Consequently the activity of modern man is not likely to be aimed at a spiritual goal that will alone perfect his nature. In fact it is less and less likely to be aimed at all, for the increase in artificial sorrow means a constant weakening of our resistance, of our power to command or to aim our actions, and a constant approach to a more complete slavery to things unworthy of our high destinies. Preoccupation with the sensible tends to have us concentrate on the immediate, the concrete, the so-called "practical," to the detriment, even to the impossibility, of coping with the universal, the absolute, the enduring thing which is truth, the proper object of our intellects, the goal of our human lives.

It is not surprising that our age should be characterized by a philosophy that undermines intellect, by religious ideas that cannot ascend above man himself, by an acquiescence in the degrading conviction that man is no more than just another animal, or the despairing belief that man is only a part of something else, unimportant in himself: a part of a state, or of a party, or of a machine, or of a process.

If we could stand aside from the whole world struggle for just a moment, we would see a double paradox that staggers the mind: the paradox of an age dedicated to pleasure with a philosophy of despair; and the paradox of the Man of Sorrows who could leave His followers only a way of the Cross and a philosophy of joy. Part of the solution of this double riddle is hidden in what we have been saying in this chapter and in what we said in the preceding chapter. The passions are an integral part of man and so physically good; morally they are good or bad as they are aimed by us at the goal of life or away from it; completely out of control they rob us of all semblance of humanity in our actions by robbing us of control of those actions. They are then subordinate things, subordinate to the spiritual side of man; in comparison to the emotions of that spiritual side they shrink into insignificance, yet as part of the nature of man they are not to be scorned. The Man of Sorrows was never an instant without the joy of the beatific vision; the Man Who did not have time to so much as eat because He was healing all manner of sickness, Who did not shrink from the leper's touch, Who brought sight to the blind, hearing to the deaf and did all things well, had no scorn for the passion of sorrow. But because He came that our joy might be full, it was necessary that

He endure incredible physical sorrow in the name of an even more incredible spiritual joy. He did not pretend that man was an angel, nor did He tolerate his being merely an animal; but rather He insisted man was man, made in the image of God and destined to that supreme union of love which is the source of the supreme joy of humanity.

CHAPTER VII

(OUTLINE)

HAPPINESS AND PASSION III

(Q. 40–48)

1. Interrelation of mild and emergency passions:
   (*a*) Difference of goals.
   (*b*) Source of emergency passions.
   (*c*) Effects of emphasis on mild passions:
      (1) Decrease of power of command and lessening of emergencies.
      (2) Increase of sorrow and passions of defeat.

2. Hope and despair:
   (*a*) Their nature:
      (1) In men.
      (2) In animals.
   (*b*) Cause of hope—experience:
      (1) Paradox of hopeful youth.
      (2) Paradox of cynical old age.
   (*c*) Relation to love and work.

3. Fear:
   (*a*) Its nature and distinction.
   (*b*) Six kinds of fear—laziness, embarrassment, shame, stupefaction, admiration, anxiety.
   (*c*) Things to fear.
   (*d*) Causes and effects of fear:
      (1) Defects.
      (2) Power.

4. Daring:
   (*a*) Its nature and relation to hope.
   (*b*) Its origins.
   (*c*) Contrast of rational and passionate daring.

5. Anger:
   (*a*) Its composite nature and singularity.

(*b*) Its pre-eminence in man.
(*c*) Its causes and remedies:
(1) Excellence.
(2) Contempt.
(3) Satisfaction.
(*d*) Its effects:
(1) Pleasure.
(2) Bodily changes.
(3) On reason.
(4) On speech.

Conclusion:

1. Champions of concupiscence.

2. The twentieth century and the emergency passions:
(*a*) Passions of victory—hope, daring, anger:
(1) Effect of dedication to mild passions.
(2) Hope, daring, anger of modern times.
(*b*) Passions of defeat:
(1) The multiplication of fear.
(2) The surrender of despair.

Man the victim of the universe or its master.

CHAPTER VII

HAPPINESS AND PASSION III

(Q. 40–48)

THERE is a certain optimism intimately connected with the start of a New Year. The badly scribbled page of the last year is torn out and thrown away and a virgin page awaits our pleasure; we may write on it what we will and in just the way that pleases us most. It is a nice thing for the rest of the world, for it gives them, by a pleasant fiction, a taste of what the Catholic enjoys, by solid fact, from a few moments at the feet of Christ in the confessional. But for a man or woman to expect to go through a new year without meeting a difficulty or emergency would be even more absurd than for a Catholic to expect by a good confession a complete liberation from the occasion of or temptation to sin.

Of course there will be difficulties and emergencies in the business of carving out happiness, which after all is the business of human life. And because this happiness is an intimately personal thing and the tools we use to carve it out are our intimately personal human actions, the difficulties encountered will be intimately personal difficulties. It is just another evidence of the beautifully perfect attention to detail on the part of the divine Architect, that we are equipped with intimately personal means of coping with these difficulties and emergencies.

It would be a mistake to picture this emergency equipment as a vague precaution, like a fire-extinguisher gathering dust on the wall; in fact the frequency with which we must use our emergency equipment brings out the solemn truth that all of human life is an emergency permitting of no coasting, no loafing along. The whole gamut of emotions destined to play the part of inner principles of vigorous action in the face of difficulty gets little rest in the course of an ordinary human day. The emergency passions—hope and despair, daring and fear and anger in the sensitive appetite and the corresponding emotions in the intellectual appetite or will are like the crack troops of an army at war. Whether the army be advancing or retreating, they are in the thick of the fight as an advance or a rear-guard; even in the quiet moments of rest, they are the sentries guaranteeing the security of the army. For these emotions are indeed the champions, the defenders of the mild or concupiscible passions from which all activity springs.

In the last few chapters we have gone thoroughly into the mild or concupiscible passions of love and hate, desire and aversion, pleasure and sorrow. We have seen love as the basic passion, the foundation of all action, the source from which springs every other emotional activity. In the last chapter we saw something of the necessity of the other mild passions, their possibilities for good and evil and the real threat to our times in the over-emphasis of these mild passions, particularly through a constant deliberate increase of acquired or artificial sensible desires and pleasures.

There is an intimate link between the mild and the emergency passions. Because love is so basic, all hope or despair, daring or fear, all anger takes its rise from the fact of love and its consequent desire. Without the mild passions there would be no necessity for the emergency passions, for there would be nothing for these latter to defend. A man who is thoroughly bored has no use for anger, despair or hope; he has no use for anything because he has no excuse for activity and, as he sometimes discovers for himself, he has no excuse for living.

We might picture all emotion, except sorrow and pleasure, as a swift flight to or away from some goal. It is after all nothing more than the activity of our appetite seeking to attain good or to avoid evil. But if this picture is accurate, there is a striking difference between the mild and the emergency passions. The first, the mild passions, while travelling in pairs, really seek different goals; the goal which one seeks is good, that which the other avoids is evil. The emergency passions are grouped in pairs, but certainly they do not travel together; in fact each one of a pair rigidly excludes the other. They are flights that deal with the same landing field; one going to it, the other rushing from it. Hope and desperation look at the same difficult thing; the one rushing toward it, the other despondently surrendering before it. The saint, increasing his love for God, correspondingly increases his hatred of sin; but as his hope in the divine mercy increases, his despair and fear of the malice of the devil decrease even to the extent of enabling him to look upon the antics of the devil (as did the Curé of Ars) as a harmless and amusing break in the monotony of life, much as we might smile tolerantly on the growls of a toothless old dog.

There are only two possibilities in the face of a difficulty or an emergency: the one is to fight with victory in sight; the other, to admit defeat either by flight or surrender. The passions dealing with difficulties can be quite accurately classified, then, as passions of victory—hope, daring, anger—and passions of defeat—desperation and fear. Their mutual incompatibility is even more evident if we call them the passions of strength and of weakness; strength and weakness in this matter do not mix, as a strong stomach and a weak head might very well belong to the same man. What contributes to the weakening of man is a contribution to his fear and despair, an attack on his hope, his daring, even on his anger.

In a very general way, then, our last chapter gives us some insight into the intimate connection of these emergency passions with the mild or concupiscible passions. We noticed that our dedication to sensible pleasure and sensible desire undermined man's power to command his own actions, made him more and more a slave driven by appetite, rather than the master directing the course appetite should take. As this tendency increases, the very occasion for these emergency passions decreases; in the final analysis, the man thoroughly bored with life and the drug addict are in much the same position: the one has no reason for commanding or directing his activity, for he has no goal in sight; the other has no power to command his activity, indeed has no desire but that which will not obey his orders. The increase of sensible sorrow consequent on a dedication to the mild passions, is a direct attack on the passions of victory, an embracing of the passions of defeat. The very finality of sorrow is a death-stroke to hope and an invitation swinging wide the door to despair.

Hope and despair—at least here we are on familiar ground. Half our days and more than half our thoughts are charged with hope, surely no one can tell us much about that. Do we really know what hope is? A mother hopes her precocious son will become President some day, we hope some time to be able to sleep for about a week uninterruptedly, in our day-dreams we build up the towers of hope to heights that dazzle our friends and rivals. And none of this has anything to do with hope; it is desire, pure and simple. For while hope and desire both look to a future good and so are set off clearly from joy and pleasure in a present good, hope deals with a great and difficult good, precisely under the aspect of greatness and difficulty. One does not hope seriously that there will be tartar sauce with the fried oysters, that is much too petty for hope; and the one place where we experience absolutely no difficulty is in our day-dreaming.

The goodness of this future good of hope, sets hope off distinctly from fear slinking out of the shadow of evil; the possibility of the attainment of that future good marks the boundaries that separate hope from the withering deserts of despair. Like all the passions, hope and despair are motions, surgings of the sensitive appetites: the one speeding to a good that in spite of its difficulty and greatness is judged possible; the other fleeing from good because its very difficulty makes it appear impossible of attainment. Impossibility puts an ugly mask on the good which awakened love, a terrifying mask that makes us forget the good in an abject surrender which is as contrary to hope as flight is to pursuit.

Perhaps you have noticed how very calm a dog can be about a bone that is out of reach; much more philosophic than a man is about the last train to town just disappearing down the track. In fact animals are generally much more stoical facing the impossible, much less prone to despair than are men. They appear more philosophic only because they cannot be philosophic at all. That paradox is the answer to a puzzling difficulty. The very fact that hope deals with the future would seem to exclude it from the animal kingdom; the leaden feet of the material never outrun the twin guards of time and space. Material nature has been confined within the narrow limits of the concrete, the particular, the existing; only a spiritual nature, made very closely to the image of God, can, like God, escape from time and space, peer into the future and beyond it into the halls of eternity. Yet animals hope and hope looks only at the future.

St. Thomas insists there is a kind of hope in the animals, but a hope which is following in the steps of a knowledge that is not the animal's but God's. It is an instinct, placed in animal nature by God, which will send the lion racing after a deer that is not far off but which leaves the lion unmoved by prey much too distant to be possible of capture. Undoubtedly that is true. But actually the note of futurity disappears when we look more closely at the example, or indeed at the hope of any animal. That hope aims at a target within the limits of present, immediate possibilities;

it would never enter a lion's head to take a correspondence school course to build up the tremendous possibilities the advertisements guarantee. It would seem as though the instinctive judgment between the immediately possible and impossible is the outer boundary marking off the animal's view of the present, the immediate, the concrete.

It is not so with man. His hopes can scale the walls of heaven because his mind can know God; his despair can grovel on the lowest floors of hell precisely because his hope can aim so high. His despair can be a heart-breaking, shattering thing, tearing at the very roots of his being because man can look so very far into the future, because his hopes or the crash of his despair can be so long preparing. The animal appears calmly philosophic in the face of the impossible, because it lacks the key that would throw open the doors of philosophy and allow it to look down the long vistas of true hope—the ability to think, to know the universal truth, to see the invisible God.

There is a certain note of astonishment in our discovery of hope in an old man and that astonishment is unjust. The amused tolerance of the phrase "hope never dies" and the grim lugubriousness of the Latin proverb "While I live I hope" are really the fruits of a disappointed egoism. Age is not a destroyer of hope, it is the patient, solid builder of rational hopes. I do not suppose there are many men who have discovered latent acrobatic ability by falling downstairs without injury, but any number of parallel discoveries equally startling can be found without difficulty. The surprise of Matthew at turning out to be quite a good apostle left him practically speechless all during the life of Christ. Experience often shows us that things are possible to us which we had never suspected of ourselves. But it does much more than that; it puts new possibilities within us. After all, a man does not stand still at any stage of his career. Even though his job be so uncomplicated a thing as shining shoes, he grows through experience. By experience things become possible to us that were not possible in the bright days of youth. The death of a young doctor or lawyer is a loss to the community because of what that man *might have become;* the loss of an experienced professional man is a loss because of what the man *was.* A comparison of the earlier and the more mature works of St. Thomas brings this out clearly in the field of scholarship.

The one bad effect, if it can be called bad, which experience exercises on hope is to destroy false hopes. We expect hope to die out of a man in much the same way we expect his hair to fall out with increasing age, only because of the ridiculous over-estimation of our powers which has led us to so many disappointments. These disappointments have no basis in the transient qualities of the ideals we pursued; but rather in the acknowledgment forced on us by time that we are not quite the paragons we thought we were.

Yet, if we are in search of overflowing hope, it is not to old age we must go. The most hopeful people in the world, says St. Thomas, are young people and drunkards; defect of age or superabundance of wine is quite apt to paint the world in much rosier colours than the facts will allow. Nor is this unreasonable. After all, hope deals with the future and youths have plenty of future and very little past. Hope struggles hand to hand with the difficult and the great heart and abounding spirits of youth do not dodge but rather search out difficulties, champion hopeless causes and underdogs. Hope peers into the realm of the possible and youth has suffered too few repulses, faced too few obstacles to be anything but an easy believer in the possibility of things. A man in the expansive mood of too much good cheer is easily a match for the super-abundant spirits of youth; and there is probably no quicker way of making obstacles disappear and repulses slink into oblivion than to drown them in strong drink.

Perhaps another reason for the hopefulness of youth is that the loves of youth are deep, fast and strong; for love is, after all, the parent of hope. The grandchild of love might well be another love born of the family of hope; but the founder of the line must always be love. Urged on to what we love by a strong hope, we might very well learn to love a person who helps us in the attainment of what we hope. The benefits that God showers upon us are not merely proofs of His love for us, they are strokes of divine genius calling into life our love for Him from the clay of realized hopes.

Hope is an alert emotion that mirrors victory in its very face. It is dealing with the difficult and the difficult will suffer no slipshod attack to overwhelm it. It is difficult, for example, to walk on icy streets, so we give it our full attention. There is nothing lackadaisical about our stride, no peering at the sights or philosophizing on life in a great city. Our mind is fully concentrated on the business of keeping our feet; the one intention upon which our will is focused is that of pursuing our way in human fashion rather than on all fours. And, ordinarily, we make a good job of it. That is what hope does for all work undertaken through its inspiration; it makes it careful work, intent work and work well done which brings pleasure. It creates another of those pleasantly vicious circles by which our concentration on our work gives pleasure in the work and that pleasure increases our concentration.

The passion of fear presents quite a different appearance. It is a passion of defeat, somewhat less than sorrow because it deals with a future rather than a present evil; it is the immediate parent of desperation. It looks into the face of a future terrible thing that can hardly be resisted—and runs. No wonder it runs; for fear as long as it lives looks only on the face of evil. Perhaps that evil is one opposed to nature itself, corruptive of nature and contrary to the very desire to exist; or it may be opposed to a good we have learned to love and desire. But whether the fear be a natural or an acquired fear, it takes one look into the face of evil and flees.

The varieties of that flight of fear are illuminating, perhaps even amusing or embarrassing when we bring them down into our own lives. Fear is flight from a future evil which exceeds our power so that we cannot bear up under it. With that in mind it is easy to see that evil we fly from may be connected immediately with our own actions or with exterior things. The obvious evil connected with our actions is labour; and we fly from excessive labour by laziness. It is unflattering but true that a lazy man is a man in the grip of fear; the writer's difficulty in composing his first line gives him an appreciation of the solidity of the reduction of laziness to fear. The other evil affecting our actions is baseness or turpitude. The very red face and thoroughly embarrassed manner of a young nun going into the family entrance of a saloon to cast her vote is one of fear's ways of running away from this evil; the agonized shame of the woman taken in adultery and cast before the feet of Christ as her sin was bellowed to the four winds is another. One has to do with the baseness, immodesty or unbecomingness of an action to be done; the other with the discovery of a shameful act already committed—a distinction nicely stated in the Latin (*erubescentia et verecundia*) but impossible of statement in English.

As to the world about us, fear creeps into our hearts when we are confronted with magnitude, with the unforeseen, the unprecedented, the unpredictable. And our flight takes the form, respectively, of admiration (amazement), stupefaction, and anxiety. Let us look at these more closely. Admiration, in its strict root sense, is the emotion called forth by such things as a sunset seen from the height of an alp, a storm at sea, the vision of truth, or the death of God on the Cross. It is a form of fear which flies from present judgment, mistrusting its ability to judge so great and new a thing—but it inquires later on with the end of reaching an accurate judgment. It is rightly called the first principle of philosophizing. Stupefaction is a definite impediment to all philosophical inquiry, for it flies from both present judgment and future inquiry. It is a mental paralysis in the face of things that cannot happen but do; it is the way the Indians felt upon their first contact with firearms or the way the Apostles felt seeing Christ walking upon the stormy waters of the lake of Galilee. In fact, admiration and stupefaction are to the intellect what laziness is to the external members of the body; an inactivity, a refusal to operate in the face of difficulty, a kind of paralysis in its presence.

Perhaps the most common form of fear is what St. Thomas calls "*agonia*"—approximately translated by "anxiety". It deals with an evil that cannot be provided against because it is so unexpected, or so unpredictable. It is the kind of thing that spoils the start of a man's vacation by vague worries about what he forgot to pack, or makes a woman wring her hands. It finds eloquent and accurate expression in the agonized question "What shall I do?" and it is the emotion behind that activity that occupies so much of our lives—the business of worrying, a business that in spite of all our dissipation of energy by no means exhausts the infinite possibilities of the things that might happen.

What is it that induces these different types of fear? What is there for a man to fear? It is quite evident that a man in good health has not much fear of death—it is too far off; neither for that matter has a man facing the firing squad—it is an evil that holds out no possibility of escape, so he considers himself as good as dead already. Two conditions must be had in the future evil that frightens us; it must be imminent and it must admit some possibility of escape.

More particularly we fear what happens suddenly, what comes as a complete surprise. A safety island that pops up unexpectedly before a man's car always looks bigger than safety islands should decently look; it is imminent and our eyes must be as big as saucers to take in its enormity. As a matter of fact the imminent character of an evil robs us of the chance to prepare to repel it, by the very suddenness of the attack we are stripped of the remedies we might have found. The same is true of an evil that appears irremediable; precisely because there will be no way of remedying that evil, we fly from it most desperately. We are quite right in giving the palm of heroism to a doctor who faces imminent death to care for the victims of a plague; and even more reasonable is shrinking from the irremediable pains of hell.

But strangely enough, at first sight, there is no reason for fearing sin. After all, sin is wholly within our own powers; no one can push us into it, trick us into it, we cannot fall into it by mistake. The object of fear is something which exceeds our power to repel. We might quite reasonably be afraid of the occasion of sin, knowing our own weakness from experience, but not of the sin itself.

We can be, and often are, frightened by fear itself. In fact this chain of terror can be stretched out indefinitely; we can be afraid of the fear of fear. Fear as a passion is not completely under our control; the phantasms of terror it calls up are also in the sensible side of our nature and are not completely obedient to our intellect and will. In a very real sense, the passion of fear is an evil outside of our spiritual nature and one which may possibly overwhelm our resistance. But this is true of fear only in the same sense it is true of all the other passions; they can be controlled by reason, man can repel fear. And if at any time they overwhelm reason, the actions produced during the interregnum of passion are not the actions of a man but those of an animal.

Fear can indeed be a very terrible thing; yet it is love that gets us ready for fear. It is because of our love for a thing that its opposite takes on the form of evil; so that a catalogue of our loves is at the same time an indication of the roads by which fear can invade our souls. Sometimes, very indirectly, it works the other way around and fear disposes us for love; as when a man, through fear of punishment, begins to keep the commandments of God, then begins to hope and through hope is led to love.

A much more personal cause of fear is within our very selves—our own weakness. It is because of a lack of strength that we are unable to repel the invasion of evil; fear is not merely a passion of defeat, it is a confession of weakness. The effective, direct cause of fear is the power and strength that are able to inflict this evil upon us. Weakening our own powers almost guarantees the increase of fear with a double guarantee; a guarantee that assures our inability to resist evil and at the same time confers power and strength on our enemies. Yet the use of that power to inflict evil is something to be ashamed of rather than to glory in, for it is only by a serious defect in our sense of justice that we can wish to do injury to, inflict evil on, another. In the name of justice, such injury might be inflicted in retaliation; in the name of fear, it might be inflicted to avoid injury to ourselves as a nervous dog attacks a passing child; but to inflict such injury merely because we have the power is a perversion of the social nature of man.

Fear, particularly a great fear, is not to be lightly imposed on anyone. Man was made to reach out of himself to the world around him, to play host to the universe, bringing all things into his own mind, to scatter those gathered treasures in constant communication with his fellows and finally, to reach out and touch divinity itself. Fear reverses all this and drives a man into himself. As a citizen in a lawless town shrinks into the safety and quiet of his own home, or as the vitality of a dying man retires further and further into the depths of his being before quitting it altogether, so a man under the influence of fear shrivels up, contracts, withdraws into himself, even physically. We really shrink with fear; our feet get cold and our hands numb as we freeze with it. Our fingers tremble, our knees shake, we lose control over our exterior members through the process of shrinking into ourselves as a turtle draws itself wholly under the protection of its shell.

True enough, fear makes us much more willing to seek counsel and to listen to advice, but at the same time, like all passion, it makes our counsel much less excellent than if it were done free of the shadow of impending evil. If the lover sees all things through rose-coloured glasses, it is equally true that a man racked with fear sees all things through a fog of gloom; and the results of our thought are not worth very much if we are unable to see the truth before our eyes. Of course, a little fear may be a good thing, because it does move us to look about, to take counsel; as it grows it has the same effect on our mind, as it has on our hands and feet, seriously interfering with its operation when it does not totally impede the work of the intellect.

An imminent evil does not necessarily reduce us to this pitiable state of fear; it often awakens in us the contrary passion of daring by which instead of fleeing headlong to escape the danger, we hurl ourselves at it to conquer it. This aggressive approach to imminent danger flows as naturally from hope as desperation does from fear. The desperate man is essentially a coward, a beaten man, for fear is a victory over the man who is frightened; daring smacks of victory, as does hope, and is the passion most contrary to, most distant from, that of fear.

It follows, therefore, that whatever increases hope and dispels fear automatically contributes to daring. We may work on this double cause of daring, either directly, by working on the motion of appetite itself, or indirectly, by working on the organic changes which accompany this motion of the sensitive appetite. A man's knowledge of his own powers, the strength of his body, his experience in facing danger, the greatness of his wealth or any other like consideration which bolsters his estimation of the possibilities of successful action directly increases hope, for hope, like all passion, follows in the steps of knowledge. So the realization of the power of others who are on a man's side, his multitude of friends, his confidence in divine help, all flow into and swell the stream of hope into the charging torrent of daring. Fear is susceptible of exactly the same direct influence. The realization that a man has no enemies or, much more powerfully, the knowledge that he has injured no one, pushes whole masses of fear to one side; the man who has many enemies, especially the man who deserves to have many enemies by the injustices he has committed, has good reason to be haunted by many fears.

Indirectly, hope is increased and fear dispelled by what St. Thomas calls warming up the heart. We have said fear numbs, freezes a man, withdrawing his vitality into the depths of his being; while hope demands as its bodily accompaniment a great heart and abundant spirits. Anything, then, that contributes to the warming and swelling of the heart, the faster flow of the blood, the raising of the spirits, whatever acts against the shrivelling, numbing effects of fear, contributes to hope and daring. In the concrete, then, warm full-blooded people are naturally more daring; wine-drinking people have a ready source of daring at hand; while drunkards are daring not only because of the swelling of the heart and soaring of the spirits under the influence of drink but also because of the fog that clouds the brain and gives them illusions of grandeur as to their own powers. In this latter respect the inexperience of youth is a cause of daring by removing the cause of fear, i.e. keeping them in ignorance of their own weakness or of the presence of dangers. St. Thomas argues, on the authority of Aristotle and the scientific knowledge of his day, that a physically small-hearted creature should be more daring than one with a physically large heart—because the small heart is warmed much easier and more quickly than is the large one.

At any rate, a pertinent conclusion of all this is that martyrdom is really not so astounding in the saints; it is an almost inevitable outgrowth of their supreme hope and confidence in the almighty power of God. Even Aristotle noticed that those whose relations with divinity are amicable are always more daring; the devil, after all, really is a weakling.

To appreciate this more deeply, it will be a big help to contrast the passion of daring and the intellectual emotion of daring, daring in the will. The passion of daring is immediately dependent on sensitive knowledge; it is quite likely to be immediately aroused, to plunge into danger without realizing the difficulties to be met and consequently to be easily and quickly discouraged. The intellectual emotion of daring follows in the footsteps of intellectual knowledge, it depends on the judgment of reason. It stops to think and that often leads us to misjudge it. For example, during the days of war hysteria, anyone who had not rushed into a uniform at the first declaration of war was a coward; or, among the members of a juvenile gang, the boy who will not rush into any and every fight is necessarily "yellow". The real evaluation of the two emotions, sensitive and intellectual, must be made not at the beginning, but at the end of the emergency; there you will always find the deliberate, intellectual daring, the emotion which started slowly, looked at all the difficulties, and then plunged into the fight—that daring is always the strongest finisher. It is not surprised or discouraged at difficulties, it foresaw them; it is not downhearted at defeats, it expected them. It is, in fact, the emotion of a truly brave man, the emotion of a man who fully realizing the danger, cognizant of all its difficulties and defeats, still goes resolutely ahead to battle the impending evil. It is the daring of the ordinary Catholic in his battle against sin; the daring of the saints in their battles against themselves; the daring of the martyrs in their battles against the enemies of Christ. It is the kind of daring demanded by Christ of His apostles when He warned them again and again of what the world had stored up for them.

We come now to the last, and perhaps the strangest of the passions, the passion of anger. Its strangeness is the strangeness of the hybrid or the mongrel; it has a little of everything in it, but is a very individual thing. Like all the emergency passions, it has its roots in love, but unlike all the others, it arises only from the immediate conjunction of many passions: there must be, over and above love, at least sorrow for an injury done us and hope of revenge before anger is born. Unlike all the other passions, it has a double goal, a goal of evil and a goal of good: it seeks vindication as a good to be desired, hoped for and thoroughly enjoyed; it rushes aggressively at the injury done as at an evil to be remedied by demanding satisfaction for it.

Among all the passions, this one is very particularly our human passion; we have a special claim on it, we, far beyond all other creatures, have exploited it, and in a very real sense it is more natural to us as men than are any of the other passions. Considered from the part of the object, the passion of desire, at least the desire for food and sex, is more natural than anger. But from the part of the subject, while desire is more natural than anger to all the other animals, in man anger has deeper roots in the rational nature than has desire. Anger fits in very well with reason; in fact it demands a comparison, a weighing of the injury done and the satisfaction to be demanded, that can be had properly only by the medium of reason. There is no such intimate tie-up between the desire and reason as there is between anger and reason. What we call anger in the animals is very often sheer fright.

We can push this a step further and say that the naturalness of anger is greater than that of the other passions from the point of view of the physical constitution of the individual man. It is, for example, much more natural for a man with a choleric temperament to get angry than it is for a person physically inclined to coddle himself to be self-indulgent; the anger of the choleric individual will be aroused more quickly and thoroughly than the concupiscence of the effeminate individual. When we speak of being caught unawares by passion, of passion overwhelming reason before any defence could be mustered, our statements are more easily understandable of anger than of any of the other passions. Normally our other passions do not hit us over the head with the suddenness of a burglar's attack.

The very motive of anger is an indication of its profound basis in rational nature. We are never angry unless someone has done something against us—or we think he has. In other words, the real root cause of anger is another's contempt for us; and contempt is an injury that does not give us even the solace of being taken seriously. It is not too hard for us to be merciful, forgiving to a man who in an agony of pain heaps abuse upon us; he really does not mean it, it is the pain speaking; or to the dinner guest who holds the French up to ridicule not realizing that she is talking to a Frenchman. This contempt is the result of ignorance and is not personal. But one who despises us personally will have little trouble arousing our anger. The person who has such contempt for our hopes and efforts as calmly, indifferently, or even seriously but persistently to stand in the way of the things we are trying to get done will feel the full force of our anger. While one who offers us that climax of contempt which is deliberate insult presents us with the supreme cause of anger.

On our side, we are disposed to anger by the contradictory

qualities of excellence and defect. An orator might not resent a remark reflecting on his strength but he would resent a reflection on his oratorical ability; an opera singer might easily fly into a rage at the orchestra leader's pitying smile for her high notes. The more unjust such contempt for a real excellence, the more irritating it is. A wise man despised by fools or an aristocrat made the butt of a rustic's joke has more reason for anger because the contempt is so much more unjust. On the other hand, the very fact that anger arises from an injury done us makes those who are most easily injured most easily aroused to anger. So men who are sick are often querulous; a deaf man is sensitive about his deafness; a poor man about his poverty, and so on. From this same point of view, it very often happens that excellence is a protection against the injury of contempt; a man who is sure of his own pre-eminence, his own ability, who has no doubt whatever of himself, is not seriously bothered by whispering, jealousy or the activity of rivals. It is usually the small man, uneasy because of the slim hold he has on excellence, who resents competition or even the slightest whisper, for even so slight a breath of wind might easily dislodge him from his perch.

Anger has its compensations; one of its first effects is pleasure. There is joy in anger if it does not go beyond the bounds of reason and give us grounds for regret. Anger rises against an injury done and seeks, through vengeance, remedy for the sorrow caused by that injury. The pleasure of anger is in proportion to the anger and to the satisfaction obtained. If here and now we actually have our vengeance, if we succeed in killing the fly that has been irritating us so, the pleasure is perfect; if we are still looking forward to that vengeance, we enjoy it by making it present through hope or by rolling it over and over in our mind as a child rolls a piece of candy around in its mouth, savouring it. That pleasure will even penetrate into our dreams and give our vision of vengeance a decidedly enjoyable turn.

But on the other hand anger is a very disturbing passion. The motion of anger is one of pressing upon an enemy, surging against him; quite opposite to the motion of fear and desperation and with quite opposite physical effects. It brings a rush of blood, a tensing of muscles, an acceleration of the heart that is excellent for the purposes of vengeance but which does the use of reason no good at all. To use our reason we need certain sensitive powers and the actions of these sensitive powers are impeded by a physical disturbance of the body such as anger produces. If we see a man grow red with anger, see him bristle, his neck swell and his face turn crimson we might expect him to suffer a stroke, but do not expect him to produce the fruits of profound contemplation.

One effect of anger, which from different points of view may be good or bad and which is not an invariable effect unless the anger be very great, is to dam the flow of words. Whether with reason, or seriously impeding reason, anger in the bellowing stage is really a mild sort of anger; in a more advanced stage it robs us of the ability to talk. We are literally so angry we are speechless; the corporal disturbance set up by anger so hinders the use of the external members of the body that the tongue simply will not function, and so impedes the use of reason that we could not find words even if our tongue would function. In fact the organic changes induced by anger are most manifest in the powers which usually mirror the activities of the soul—the eyes, the face, and the tongue.

There are only two possible goals for all the activities of sense appetite, the goals of sorrow and of pleasure. To these all the others, and so, of course, the emergency passions, are ordained. Hope or fear, daring or desperation or anger are not stopping places for a man, they are means to the great final passions of the concupiscible appetite, sorrow and pleasure. They are the fighters or the quitters whose whole purpose is to rush to the aid of the mild passions or betray them by surrender. These emergency passions are the appetite's response to danger, to difficulty; an answer of victory or defeat.

What part do the emergency passions play in twentieth-century life? What is the height and depth, the fire and coldness of these passions to-day, together with their corresponding intellectual emotions? Our last chapter gives us the answer; let us compare it with the conclusions of this present chapter. We are definitely dedicated to the cultivation of the mild passions, to the constant creation of new desires, new necessities, to a coddling of our sensitive nature, to sensible pleasure. What does this do to the emergency passions of victory? Certainly our hope, daring, and anger will not be the high, bravely enduring, burning emotions proper to the spirit; for this insistence on the sensible attractions pushes the goods of the spirit farther and farther back into the dim recesses of our lives. There will be more of passion in our hope, daring and anger and less and less of intellectual emotion; which means that they will be scattered about on the million and one things that attract our animal natures. We will have many more hopes, many trivial hopes, hopes at the mercy of every passing circumstance; our daring will be of the rushing, passionate type which dies out as quickly as it flares up, which is easily disappointed, discouraged by difficulty, downcast by defeat; our anger will be more and more of the blind, brutal, unreasoning type with little regard for justice, but as our hopes spread wider and thinner, as they become more shallow and less enduring, we will have less and less to be thoroughly angry about.

And the passions of defeat? Here we really reap the fruit of a dedication to the mild or concupiscible passions rather than to their corresponding emotions in the will. We have said that our modern multiplication of pleasure automatically multiplies the possibilities of sorrow. It pushes farther out of reach the joy of the will which is the supreme antidote for sensible sorrow, the joy which is an integral part of the sacrifices of love and the death of martyrs. The spreading of hope in a shallow layer over the wide expanse of modern pleasures multiplies our objects of fear; there is so much more that can be taken away from us. And all down the line our power of command, of control over our own actions, is persistently weakened as, plunging further and further into the things of sense, we get further and further from that control-room of human actions which is our reason. Possibilities of sorrow multiplied, objects of fear constantly haunting us on every side, power of command and consequently of resistance steadily weakened—what is left for the creature that is man but the passions of defeat? Is it true that we are more and more haunted by fear? Look at the advertisements in the magazines and newspapers; study the tactics of almost any political power or political party; look at the methods of propaganda for almost any cause; look at the modern attitude towards the natural difficulties of life—towards marriage, childbirth, religion, work, thought, responsibility.

Is it true that we are more and more given to despair, that more and more we are willing to give up the fight in abject surrender? There are several signs of despair by which this question can be tested and answered; man can run away from the fight of human life in several different ways. He can plunge into a vortex of pleasure calculated to kill the operations of his mind; he can immerse himself in activities calculated to keep his mind from turning to the ultimate human problems; he can set himself seriously to forget these problems or can set out in the name of philosophy to attack their very existence; he can solve them all by deifying himself; or he can put a bullet in his brain and end the farce of being human without the courage to live humanly.

Actually man was equipped by nature for quite a different role. He was given an inner sanctuary inviolable to all attacks from all creatures; a source of joy, of hope, of love and all the rest, that could and should lord it over the sensible world, using it, as it was meant to be used, as a servant for his high ends. These champing steeds of human activity in the sensible order which we call passions, could and should be a mighty force under the intelligent control of well drawn reins. There is no comfortable middle way for man in this universe; he must be on top of it or at the very bottom. He is either master of the universe, of his passions, of himself; or he is the miserable cowering victim of all three. And it is only the individual himself who can effectively say whether he will be the victim or the master.

CHAPTER VIII

(OUTLINE)

HAPPINESS AND HABIT

(Q. 49–54)

1. Man of action and habit—an unjust contrast:
   (*a*) Animal "habits".
   (*b*) Absence of habit in God.

2. Basis of habit in human nature:
   (*a*) The limitations of human nature.
   (*b*) The limitless possibilities of human nature.

3. Essential notion of habit.

4. Location of habits in man:
   (*a*) Physical side of man:
      (1) Body.
      (2) Sensitive faculties.
   (*b*) Spiritual side of man:
      (1) Essence of the soul.
      (2) Intellect.
      (3) Will.

5. Cause of habit:
   (*a*) Nature and the seeds of habit:
      (1) Intellectual habits.
      (2) Appetitive habits.
   (*b*) Repeated acts:
      (1) Possibility of habit produced by one act.
      (2) Infused habits.
      (3) Some theories:
         a. Physical.
         b. Intellectual.

6. Increase of habit:
   (*a*) Physical and spiritual magnitude.
   (*b*) Means of increase—intensity of acts.

7. Decrease and corruption of habits:
   (*a*) Means of corruption—absence of acts.
   (*b*) Inviolable habits.

8. Distinction of habits:
   (*a*) Specifically—by *objects*, matter and principles.
   (*b*) Morally—by relation to nature.
   (*c*) The compatibility of habits.

Conclusion:

1. Habits and happiness:
   (*a*) Habit and action.
   (*b*) Significance of physical theories of habit.

2. Consequences of habit's relation to happiness:
   (*a*) Responsibility:
      (1) Of parents.
      (2) Of educators.
      (3) Of example.
   (*b*) Personal evaluation, forecast and improvement.
   (*c*) Relative importance of intellectual, moral and physical habits.

CHAPTER VIII

HAPPINESS AND HABIT

(Q. 49–54)

SO far throughout this volume we have done nothing but renew our acquaintance with the homely, familiar elements of our daily lives. The subject-matter of this chapter is no exception to this mode of procedure. Indeed we are going to rub elbows with what we usually consider the most humble, the most homely and disappointing of all the servants in our individual kingdom —our habits.

The very name "habit" calls to mind a whole series of homely, simple pictures, as the chance hearing of a consecrated phrase will bring up visions of a comfortable old chair, a sweet tired smile, or a bright curly head. "Habit" makes us think of umbrellas and rubbers forgotten because we so seldom used them, of people putting matches in their mouths and throwing cigarettes away, of absent-minded professors, worried mothers, and distracted sales girls.

Habit has the air of routine about it. It seems to belong most fittingly to those of us caught in a grey circle of sameness, drudgery, unromantic, unexciting, prosaic life. Quite the opposite is true of action, of danger, of the unusual, the extraordinary. We picture the man of genius as the man who steps out of this ceaseless round of the ordinary, who escapes from habit and startles the world by an unexpected, unprepared, singular action. Habit seems to cut us off from the class of genius and associate us with the plodding, cud-chewing cow, the puppy curling up in its accustomed corner at its accustomed time. The spark of divinity seems much brighter in genius than in the rest of us; we cannot even conceive God's being a victim of habit, perhaps principally because we cannot think of God mislaying His glasses.

This chapter is no exception to our policy of fraternizing with the apparently unimportant, familiar elements of our lives. And our notion of habit is no exception to the astonishing mistakes we make about the things that are closest to our own lives. We do make a truly astonishing mistake about the very nature of habit. It is strictly true that God cannot have habits, but it is no less true that an animal cannot have habits, while the man of genius is precisely the man with the most fully developed, most perfect habits.

Habit is something distinctively human. God does not have habits because His infinite perfection precludes them; the animal cannot have habits because its growth in perfection is completely arranged and wholly limited by the principles of its nature. But man cannot get along without habits and all his human powers are perfected only in proportion to the habits which he has developed. We can contrast human and animal nature as we would one of the Great Lakes and a small town reservoir; the possibilities of one as a source of drinking water depend on the pipe-lines that are run from it; the other has the pipe-lines already in and the slightest investigation will tell us immediately what its possibilities are. Or, looking at it from another angle, animal nature is a small cup full to the brim; human nature is an expanding vessel whose capacity grows with the amount poured into it; while God can have nothing more added to the infinite sweep of His divine nature. These additions, these modifications, these capabilities by which human nature alone grows are habits.

It is the imperfect, created character of human nature which makes habits necessary; it has not as yet all the perfection it can have; something can be added to it. And at the same time it is because of the indetermined, indefinite possibilities of human nature that habits are possible. Concretely, three conditions are necessary for the possession of a habit: first, that the subject of the habit have a potentiality still to be realized, and this makes habit impossible to God; second, that this potentiality be not to one determined object, as the nose is to smell; third, that this potentiality is capable of being realized, not in one definitely determined way but in different ways. The last two conditions make habit impossible in the animals.

An essential notion, then, of habit is determination. It is a limitation of a limitless faculty, a pipe-line from an immense lake. Our minds and our wills are capable of universal truth and universal goodness; that they get to work on particular truths, particular kinds of truth and goodness, it is necessary that they be pinned down, determined. Our acts are definitely determined, concrete, going towards definite objects; yet why should a mind or a will that is of its very nature indifferent to particular things and forced to action only by the universal, choose this action rather than another? The determination certainly did not come from our faculties, yet here it is in the act produced by these faculties, because of a further determination of those faculties by way of habit.

The work of habit is precisely to modify a man, to give a definite channel along which his limitless powers will flow. It is a determination, a qualification of a man disposing him well or badly either as to his nature itself or to the operations for which that nature exists. It is evident that here we must step out of that indifferent, amoral atmosphere which clings to the passions. Habit has quite frankly to do with the end of nature, and we insisted that human things were good or bad morally as they led man to his end or led him away from it. So habits are definitely moral. They are morally good or morally bad. They help a man to his end or they lead him away from it; they contribute to the perfection of his nature and of his operation or they detract from his nature or hinder his operation.

It would be an error to confuse habit with a mere passing disposition. It is of the very nature of habit to be permanent, or at least, looking at its causes, difficult to uproot. Habits are really capabilities that have been developed by hard, repeated effort, consciously, deliberately until these capabilities are as deeply embedded in nature as a grafted branch on a tree. They become second nature to us and, like the operations of nature itself, the habits at work give us that joy which comes with easy, dexterous, masterful action, there is joy in living, breathing, walking, and seeing; and there is much the same joy in every craftsman's skilful labour, in the artist's long concentrated efforts, in the singer's ringing notes, in the thinker's clean-cut incision through error to truth, in the saint's insanely daring love of God.

These habits are our very own, developed under our command. They never escape that command. It is unjust to associate habit with traits of forgetfulness, as though habit had betrayed us and run off with the command of our lives. It is not because habit is beyond our control that we pour soup on the table, not noticing that no soup-plate was laid out; that is because we did not give any attention to the operation of that habit. In the beginning of habit, our alert attention and forceful will are necessary; as the habit grows stronger, less and less of that intellectual effort is needed but always habit is the perfect servant of the true master of human life. Its task, like the task of every perfect servant, is to make the work of the house easier, more quickly, unobtrusively, joyfully accomplished.

If we keep clearly in mind the distinction between habits ordained directly to operation and habits ordained directly to nature itself and only indirectly to operation, the actual location of habits within ourselves is a fairly simple matter.

The type of habit that is immediately aimed at the

perfection of nature itself, such as beauty or health, the so-called "entitative habit," in distinction to "operative habit," is really more of an habitual disposition than a true habit. After all, beauty can be quickly lost, as can health; the causes from which beauty and health flow are themselves quickly and easily changed while a true habit has a hard, grasping durability. The entitative habits can be located in the body of man; that is, they can dispose the body of man more perfectly in accordance with his soul, his form. But the operative or working habits belong primarily to the soul, for the soul is the source of all human activity.

This is more clearly seen when we remember that the body, like all material things, runs along a one-way track that has been laid out to the last inch by nature itself. A habit in material things is no more necessary than a steering-wheel in a locomotive. No more determination is necessary; indeed, no more determination is possible. The part the body plays in the operations of the soul, a secondary, ministering, disposing part, is an accurate picture of the claim the body has to habits—a secondary, dispositive claim which would have no meaning whatever without the perfection of habit in the soul.

This will be true also of all our sense faculties, our hearing, sight, smell, memory and all the rest. Indeed it will hold true of the whole world of sense life. An official tea-taster, a piano-tuner, a pickpocket and a surgeon all have developed operating habits in their sense faculties. They can do what an untrained man cannot do. The same is true of the dog who has learned to fetch the evening paper at four o'clock. But actually these sense developments have a claim to habit only by reason of their relation to the command of man's reason. In other words, if men left them alone, the animals would never develop even such traces of habit; and if men did not steer their touch, hearing, or taste along these particular lines there would be no pickpockets, surgeons, piano-tuners or tea-tasters. Animals and sense faculties operate along lines strictly determined by the instincts of nature; of themselves they can go no farther, they need no greater determination. It is only the creative vision of man which sets up new ends and trains both animals and sense faculties to serve these ends.

It is, then, in the spiritual side of our nature that we must primarily look for habits in their full perfection. It is true that no natural entitative habit, i.e. no disposition whose end is nature, can be had in the soul, for the soul is the active principle of our nature, the source of all perfection, of activity; it disposes rather than itself being the object of disposition. A match is a great help in a dark room, but we do not hold it up to a burning electric bulb to increase the light. Yet because man reaches for things as high above himself as God, the soul can be disposed for this higher, supernatural life; and the disposition or entitative habit perfecting, disposing the soul for that supernatural life is called sanctifying grace and its perfect complement is the light of glory in heaven.

The operative habits of the soul belong, of course, in the faculties by which the soul operates, in the spiritual principles of action which are intellect and will. Here habits are not only possible, they are desperately necessary. The intellect does not run along a determined track, nor does it start out on the trip of life with a knapsack full of ideas. It is a blank page capable of receiving every truth; it can seek truth for truth's sake alone, or with the end of action in view; it can judge by first principles, or from immediate things of the world. Determination is essential if there is to be action; such determinations are habits and are called intellectual virtues.

The will is in much the same position. It is capable of all good, real or apparent; it can move towards its end or away from it; it can be good or bad; it is the great power-station of human life, but feeder lines must lead its power in determined directions. And on the direction of these lines depends the results of that immense power; as the electricity coming from a power-house can kill a man in an electric chair or save the life of a man on a surgeon's table, so the power coming from the will is quite capable of blasting man to hell or snatching him up to heaven. Habits in the will are the moral virtues and the vices.

It must be noted that habit occupies a strange intermediary position between what the Scholastics called potency and act. Relative to the faculty, the intellect or will, habit is an active, perfecting principle which brings that faculty one step nearer to its ultimate perfection of action; yet looked at in relation to the act of intellect and will, habit is itself perfected, completed, and in this sense is potential. So a person who had a collection of good habits and never used them would be like a man who had a collection of powerful automobiles but who never left his house Neither one would get very far. The habits would be as useless as the cars. The difference is that the very possession of habit is itself a good guarantee of the acts following from those habits.

Habits, then, are very necessary; we simply must develop them, and develop them we will. How do we go about it? Where do they come from? Perhaps these questions would be more exact if we put them in this form: "What can we do about habits?" and "What has nature done without our having any say about it?" The answers to these questions vitiate a great number of comforting excuses. We have heard of the "born musician", the "born worker", the person who is "naturally" patient, wise, humble, and so on. We say that because nature was not so kind to us —we appear lazy, or irritable, proud and all the rest. Nature at times is a solid comfort to our self-respect.

Nature does have a hand in habits, but to identify habits with the efforts of nature is to identify the full-grown plant with the seed from which it sprung. Habits have heir roots in nature, but only their roots. The rest of their growth demands some explanations that only we can give.

On the intellectual side we can really trace much to nature. One habit, common to all men, has substantial beginnings in nature, and that is the habit by which we understand first principles. Every man, once he knows what a part is and what a whole is, recognizes the whole as greater than the part. More indirectly, nature lays the foundations of intellectual habits in the perfection of the senses. Because we need the sense organs in the work of understanding, keen, alert sense organs are a decidedly good start towards intellectual habits.

On the side of the will the start given by nature is really the sowing of seeds. Our natural tendencies, natural inclinations, are the slight push which starts us off on the long voyage of life. From our physical constitution, too, we have just such a nudge in definite directions; so one man, from physical reasons, will be more inclined to meekness than to zeal, another more to chastity than to patience, and so on.

All of this natural equipment very often goes under the name of "temperament", a word used to cover a multitude of sins. The finished product, after the habits are built in, is usually called character. And really an artistic temperament, a bilious temperament or a choleric temperament is a very poor excuse for an utterly disagreeable character. Father Jarrett once said that a thoroughly nasty temperament was really a big help in the building of a very fine character, because it made us realize early the need of hard, earnest effort in the building of the right kind of habits.

Earnest effort is the solid cause of habit. No one but God can slip a habit into our souls as a handkerchief is slipped into a pocket. There is only one way to get a habit and that is by our own personal acts. A habit, after all, is a perfected disposition, a well-developed groove down which our activities slip easily, quickly, directly to their objects.

Our acts wear that groove deeper and deeper, smoother, surer. The golfer's tireless practice, the athlete's training, the singer's scales are all faint pictures of this from the physical side and bring out the fact that by our every act we are determining the course along which our powers will flow.

It has been pointed out significantly that a habit really starts with the first act, at least the surface is scratched and there is a faint beginning of a groove. Even more significantly, every habit is charged with the past and full of meaning for the future; it is an accurate history of past acts, an assurance of swift, easy, pleasant action in the present, and it offers good grounds for a prediction of the course of future acts, for habit is not to be snuffed out in an instant.

Nor is habit to be called into existence in an instant. Grim warnings are given that bad habits are often produced by one act. It simply cannot be done. True enough, on the intellectual side, a truth can be so clearly presented that the intellect at once grasps it and never relinquishes it; the result is an intellectual habit by just that one act. But outside of the intellectual order we need both time and effort to build up the solid structure of habit. So from the side of the appetite it is clear from daily experience that reason cannot dominate the will or the sense appetite as truth dominates the intellect. Our reason can show us that this one act is eminently desirable under these particular circumstances; but if we remember that our will and sense appetite can reach out to many desirable objects and in many different ways, it becomes clear that the domination of one grooved way of doing things is not to be brought about with one gesture. The entitative habits of the body might be produced by just one act, as health might be restored by one dose of powerful medicine, but these after all have not the enduring qualities of true habits but are rather habitual dispositions resting on easily hindered or helped causes.

All this is in the purely natural order. In the supernatural order we have a whole group of habits—grace and the infused virtues—which are caused instantly by God and not gradually by our acts. In fact, they could not be caused in any other way. They are dispositions or determinations to acts which are above all the powers of nature and they themselves are beyond the reach of any combination of natural forces. Because they lie completely outside the scope of the entire natural order they can come only from the one Being Who is not included within that circle of nature—God Himself.

Someone who looks on a man as smoothly sly can always hear insincerity in his voice. The same attitude makes supporters of a political candidate swell with pride at his remarks, while his opponents growl with disgust. This, of course, is the result of one-sided views; the other side also must be seen to discover truth. Modern philosophers have been occupied with a one-sided view of man ; so much so that they are now convinced that only that one side, the animal side, exists. In all of man's actions they note with delight the overtone of a snort, a growl, a grunt or a whinny. When such champions of the material look at habit, they see just what they are prepared to see—a purely physical, at most an animal, phenomenon. To some, habit is merely a chain of mechanical reflexes (Behaviourism); to others, stimulus and response do not quite sum up habit, there must also be a consideration of the history and present dispositions of the organism but merely the physical history and disposition (S.O.R. of Dynamic Psychology); still others insist it is merely a case of stamping in and stamping out physical associations (Thorndike). But to all of them it seems apparent that habit, like the rest of man, is not to be allowed to go above animal powers.

Perhaps some trace of this animal-worship has found its way into the writings of those who hold fast to man's spiritual soul; as though, because there are no muscles to kink, no co-ordination of parts involved in the operations of intellect and will, there is really no place for the kind of habit we have been describing, the habit which is really an accidental form determining and perfecting the faculty as the substantial form determines and perfects the body. They would prefer to have habits mere associations, but, of course, spiritual associations; or they quite frankly do away with habit altogether, at least in the will, reducing the whole differentiation of the will's acts to the power of the motive that is held before it. Unfortunately in this matter no compromise is possible; it is not merely that the facts will not allow it, the very indeterminate nature of the intellect and the will demands the determination offered by the accidental form of habit.

It is important to hold fast to the notion of habit as form, as simple active principle, if we are to understand its increase. As a simple form, a principle without parts, there can be no question of increasing it as we would increase a physical thing, by piling on quantity as though we were preparing a fat man for a circus side-show. Magnitude in spiritual things is not measured by poundage but by perfection; one angel is greater than another because it has more of being, more of excellence; one soul is greater than another supernaturally because it has approached closer to the source of all perfection, because it has more of charity; in the natural order, one soul is greater than another because it has more of the accidental perfection, the added forms of habit. Habit is made greater because somehow it is more perfect, either by extension to more things or by deeper penetration into the subject itself.

This sounds complicated but actually the extension of habit is as simple as the extension of health to more and more parts of the body, as the diffusion of love to more and more objects worthy of love, or as the discovery of more and more conclusions in a principle. Intensively a habit increases as it cuts its groove deeper and deeper, as, for example, the love of a married couple gets deeper, more solid, more a part of the married couple themselves with the intimacy and companionship of the passing years. Habit seeps into the marrow of our being as the heat of the morning sun seeps into the bones of the drowsy Italian sunning himself on one of the great rocks hanging over Amalfi.

Either way, true habits are increased by only one medium. That medium is our own acts; not by every act, but acts which are more intense, more earnest than the habit itself. Playing golf or tennis against excellent competition improves one's game, not only then but later; the thinker who limits his reading to detective novels or his conversation to mere gossip is on the down grade. One of the great virtues of good books is precisely that they keep us in the company of intellectual giants. A lazy, slouchy act, less intense than its habit, does the habit no good, in fact does it positive harm. After all, if the act is to be the cause of perfection to the habit, it must itself have something to give beyond the perfection of the habit. The act cannot just run along the groove, it must cut the groove deeper; it cannot itself be imperfect and hope to confer perfection on its habit.

This has the appearance of a contradiction—the act proceeds from the habit as from an immediate principle, yet must be greater than the habit to increase it. But think for a moment of what the habit has already done. It has made the act more natural, easier, more pleasant; so that with the same amount of effort our next act is immediately better. In other words, it has done away with much of the strain which was necessarily present in the first action, removed much of the resistance, cut a pathway through a forest, like the pioneer settlers of the early West. Of course the next settlers can travel the same trail much more easily and faster, and they improve the trail. Eventually the trail becomes a road, then a paved stretch along which cars can roll with practically no difficulty; eventually it becomes a four-lane highway which almost drives the car for us.

From the notion of habit as a simple form, a perfecting principle, it is fairly easy to see that a habit is corrupted by a contrary habit. Just as we cannot have a human body both living and dead at the same time, for life is the result of its form or soul and death is the expulsion of that form, so contrary habits cannot exist together. One destroys the other. The channel of a river cannot carry that river in opposite directions at the same time; our habits are the channels of our activity. And of course these contrary habits, like all habits, are built up by individual acts.

It is not even necessary to go to the length of opposite acts and habits for the destruction of already existing habits. Mere laziness or sluggishness will weaken a habit; complete disuse of a habit will itself destroy that habit. This is particularly true of the moral habits, or habits of the will. They deal with the regulation of external acts and the passions; and of course if these are not being regulated they are proceeding without regulation, for they do not stop. In more simple terms, a man who is not producing good acts is producing bad acts; when he is not using his good habits, he is building up bad habits as well as neglecting the good habits, for no human action is morally indifferent.

In the intellectual field, mere disuse very much weakens and sometimes totally corrupts a habit. So the man who continually moves in a circle far beneath him intellectually is rapidly retrogressing; the man who spends his time day-dreaming is decreasing his powers of thought and concentration; the man who spends his time reading trash is rendering himself less and less capable of reading anything but trash.

There are some few habits which no corrupting influence can ever reach. These are the intellectual habits which nature has had so nearly ready made from the very beginning, the habits of first principles, both speculative and practical. Upon this inviolable basis rests the perpetuity and validity of human thought and the absolute universality of moral principles. It would take a complete destruction of human nature itself to drive out of man the principle of contradiction, for example, and the distinction and obligatory force of right and wrong.

We have a great variety of habits. But it is relatively easy to distinguish them. They are, after all, principles of action; they are pointed to definite action, for they themselves are definite determinations. To avoid confusing them we have only to follow the direction in which they point. In other words, the objects of habits distinguish them as neatly as the different destinations announced for trains enable us to pick out the right train from the confusing number in the railroad station. So the habit of justice is easily distinguished from that of temperance; and both are different from the habit of prudence. In a general way, we can distinguish groups of habits according to their location, the habits of the intellect, of the will, and so on. But remembering that one faculty can have many habits, that its habits may be either good or bad, we can easily see that this is sufficient only to distinguish groups of habits, not the individual habits themselves. The same is true of the matter with which habits deal; it may serve very well to mark off groups of habits one from another, but we must go to the objects to which the habits are determined if we are to discover individual distinctions.

And habits are distinctly individual, as individual as the trains that look so much alike and pull out in the same direction from the same station. They are going to different places. It is as impossible to link habits together to make one long habit, as it is to couple trains with different destinations to make one long train. The case is different if parts are to be dropped at way stations; then the final destination gives unity to the train. Exactly the same thing is true of habits.

What has all this to do with happiness? Recall that in

the early stages of this volume we insisted that the tools by which we carve out our happiness are our own human actions. By nothing else do we make a success or a failure of our lives. And habit's whole task has to do with action, human action.

We have seen in this chapter that habit is a graft whose fruits are produced in a way so similar to that of nature that we rightly call habit "second nature". Like nature itself, habit makes our acts flow ever more easily, more quickly, more pleasantly. Look behind that statement. If that statement is true, which incontestably it is, then habit has actually increased our natural powers. It has removed much of the resistance to our action, made much less effort necessary, offered an inducement to action in the very ease and pleasure of the effort. It has been said truly that if the will always had to make the same effort to produce its acts, to direct the hands, feet, etc., man would never advance; if no trace of the exertion put forth yesterday were evident to-day, man would stumble through life like an infant that has never learned to walk. It is optimistic to say that man would stumble through life. He would collapse very early in life, he would give up the struggle altogether, through sheer exhaustion.

Habit is the condition of all progress, as it is a necessary condition for activity. Indeed it is progress itself. The man of genius is capable of his extraordinary contributions exactly because so much perfection has been added to his natural powers by way of habit, so much of his energy has been saved by his "second nature".

Habit is the condition for activity, the condition of all progress. From our habits flow our acts. What, then, if we limit the possibility of habit to the animal level? Why, of course our acts are limited to that level. And as our acts are the steps by which we approach our goal, our goal itself must be an animal goal. Then the high aspirations of will, the great visions of intellect crash down and there clang shut the prison gates of the material, sensible, measurable which confine us at the level of the brutes. And that is the finish for the creature formerly known as man! All this is not an exaggeration; it is the commonplace denial of the spiritual nature of man put forth by the proponents of the physical theories of habit.

It seems hardly necessary to point out the terrific responsibility of those who guide youth in the formation of their habits. What is this but to choose their destination, put them on the train and stamp their ticket? This is what it means to be a father or a mother—to have entirely at the mercy of your careless neglect and ignorance or of your zealous love and intelligent effort, the failure or success of your children's lives. It is a responsibility that cannot be shrugged off in the name of a bridge game or a set of nerves; nor is it work for a faint or cowardly heart.

This gives an insight into the tremendous contribution of the religious Sisters to the Church in America in the training of Catholic youth. Only God himself can compute the number of successful lives that must trace the powerful beginnings of their success to this source. It also gives us an insight into an entirely different picture, a picture whose background at least breathes of despair. I mean the picture of American education under the influence of physical theorists, the naturalistic psychologists of education. It is doubtful if ever before in history has so much damage been done to humanity itself as has been done these last few years by the dominance of such a school with its tremendous influence over the teaching body of American schools.

What we have seen in this chapter makes immediately clear the importance of example. What influences the actions of others influences their habits and so goes far in determining their future actions. And from the hero-worshipping boy to the no less hero-worshipping man, example has been proved by long centuries of experience to be a powerful influence on the actions of others. The man in authority, the man or woman constantly before the eyes of others, the Catholic whose very Catholicity makes him stand out from the crowd, all carry this terrific responsibility, whether they like it or not.

Habits furnish the element of unity in our actions. They are the record of the past, the force of the present, the prediction of the future. They bind the past to the present and future, tell us what we have done with the past, what we can expect of the future and what must be done if we do not particularly care for that prediction. In other words, for an evaluation of life up to the present moment, we must look to our habits; if we desire to improve, again we must look to our habits, but always with the realization that of all the habits, by far the most important for the success or failure of human life are those precisely which have to do with the goal of human life, with leading a man to or away from his end. Physical habits may improve the body; intellectual habits improve the mind; but it is only the moral habits that improve *the man.*

CHAPTER IX

(OUTLINE)

HAPPINESS AND VIRTUE

(Q. 55–58)

1. The opprobrium of virtue—some modern conceptions:
   - (*a*) Equipment for a reformer.
   - (*b*) For a hater of joy and humanity.
   - (*c*) Result of ignorance of workaday world.
   - (*d*) A neurotic inhibitionism.

2. Double basis of misconceptions:
   - (*a*) Ignorance of nature of virtue.
   - (*b*) Ignorance of nature of man.

3. The nature of virtue:
   - (*a*) An operative habit.
   - (*b*) A good habit.
   - (*c*) A definition of virtue.

4. The humanity of virtue:
   - (*a*) Its limitation to strictly human cognitive powers—perfect and imperfect virtue.
   - (*b*) Its limitation to strictly human appetitive powers.
   - (*c*) A sufficient division of virtue—intellectual and moral.

5. The intellectual virtues:
   - (*a*) Speculative—understanding, knowledge and wisdom.
   - (*b*) Practical—art and prudence:
     - (1) Their distinction.
     - (2) Necessity of prudence for good living.
     - (3) Adjuncts of prudence.

6. The moral virtues in general:
   - (*a*) Distinction from intellectual virtues.
   - (*b*) Interdependence of moral and intellectual virtues:
     - (1) Moral virtues without intellectual.
     - (2) Intellectual virtues without moral virtues.

Conclusion:

1. Virtue and successful action:
   - (*a*) In relation to particular ends.
   - (*b*) In relation to the goal of human life.

2. Moral virtues and fullness of human life.
   - (*a*) Their importance proportioned to importance of goal of life.
   - (*b*) Their rewards are those of successful living:
     - (1) Immediate—fullness of life.
     - (2) Ultimate—possession of goal of life, happiness.
   - (*c*) Their denial is a denial of humanity of man.
3. The moulding of men and morals.

CHAPTER IX

HAPPINESS AND VIRTUE

(Q. 55–58)

OUR subject-matter in this chapter is virtue. Probably there is no part of our human equipment that has been more thoroughly misunderstood and more viciously maligned. A close parallel to our modern treatment of virtue was given a few years ago by Russian peasants to modern tractors which they considered mysterious, incomprehensible, perhaps dangerous, certainly very extraordinary and suspicious contraptions. If we were to attempt to sum up briefly this modern notion of virtue, our summary would not have to go beyond the statement that virtue has a double connotation to the modern mind: repression and ignorance.

It was not mere coincidence that led cartoonists to picture the champions of the prohibition law as dressed in a funereal ministerial garb. Quite recently a newspaper carried a full-page feature in which two contrary opinions were given as to the manner in which New Year's Eve should be celebrated. One held out strongly for a riotous type of celebration, in fact made a consequent headache the measuring rod of the celebrant's humanity, good-fellowship and normalcy; the other was a very prim affair, advocating the gloomiest type of introspection as a fitting "celebration". The pictures of both authors were given as a graphic expression of this contrast of "virtue" with joyous humanity; the author of the first opinion was pictured as an attractive young woman, beautifully gowned, flaunting a charming smile; the other author glared out at the world from a battleship type of face, fittingly framed in the finery of the Victorian era.

This point of view is so common that it has an effect even on Catholics. How often do we picture virtue in terms of the very simple, naïve old pastor, the kind of person who is quite likely to mislay collar, vest or shoes; good as gold, with a heart as big as himself—but eccentric as the devil? Or we associate virtue with nuns, veils and cloisters as though it were a product of a super-human hothouse atmosphere. Virtue is looked upon as something to be taken cautiously, in small doses and in careful correlation to the individual temperament. The statement that all nuns are neurotic is not unusual, presumably on the grounds that nuns are virtuous and virtue is a neurotic repression vividly contrasting with the full, joyous, healthy expression of our human nature.

All this is, of course, sheer nonsense. But nonsense can be very deadly when it is taken seriously. It was nonsense that burnt witches and our present nonsense is much more deadly for the men and women, particularly for the boys and girls, of our time; for the agony it causes is not over in an hour or two, but drags its hopeless way through all of a lifetime and even all of an eternity.

Like all nonsense, this particular nonsense about virtue has its roots in dank ignorance, a double ignorance of virtue and of humanity. As long as virtue is looked on as something beyond the ordinary, like forced feeding or the over-training of an athlete, we are not likely to learn much about it. When it is considered as something unhealthy, like the sly smile of the demented, or as something hypocritical, like the guileless eyes of a vicious child, we are not likely to care to learn anything about it. And when we are told on all sides that it is something old-fashioned, immature, and unscientific, like red flannels, sulphur and molasses, or the dangers of night air, we become actually afraid of any familiarity with virtue, for we must keep up with the times.

We cannot even begin to understand virtue if we have

completely misunderstood man. To picture man as a machine or as a mere animal, rules out the very possibility of virtue as completely as it is ruled out of the clashing of gears or the whining of a puppy. We looked thoroughly into the nature of man in our first volume and saw that he was spirit as well as animal, possessed of a soul as well as a body. With that accurate conception of man before our eyes, let us look more closely at virtue.

Our very first glance at virtue brings out the astounding truth that virtue is not at all extraordinary, not at all mysterious, but rather a prosaic thing without which we simply cannot get through even an ordinary uneventful day. In plain language, virtue is simply another name for a certain kind of habit, namely for a good habit ordained to facilitating operation.

In the last chapter we noticed the striking difference between the equipment of man and of the other creatures of the universe. A chemical, such as sulphur, needs no education or training for its full perfection; it follows a rigid law of physical necessity which finds it fully equipped from its beginning for its one determined action which can be placed only in one determined way. Much the same is true of the perfection of the animals; even though they have knowledge, they follow the rigid law of instinct which plots out every step of their way, tying them down to one narrow path plainly marked and hemmed in by a barrier that admits of no trespassing. But man starts off with his intellect and will be tied down to nothing that is less than God; his powers are like the waters of a great flood that must be turned into definite channels to produce definite results. These channels are the habits of a man.

There is, then, a striking difference between the action of inanimate creation, of animal creation and of man. The actions of the first two are strictly determined by nature from the very beginning; that of man must be qualified, determined by the habits which a man develops. These grooves which he cuts so deeply that they become a second nature and give his actions a delight, facility and promptness comparable only to that of nature itself, are operative habits, perfections of his faculties which determine the path his activities will take, conserve his energy and make possible an always greater action, an always greater perfection.

If these habits direct his activity away from his goal they are bad habits or vices; if they direct his activities toward his goal they are good habits or virtues. Putting it in another way, we might say that a man is a very good thief, standing head and shoulders above his fellows in the quantity and quality of his plunder and the cleverness of his thievery; but of course we are speaking metaphorically. We could not say he was a virtuous thief. What we are saying is that he has habits that are excellent in their way, but that way is an evil, defective way; while virtue always implies perfection, the fulfilling of the possibilities of a man, the full realization of his potentialities. Virtues are good habits.

The identification of virtue with good habit immediately destroys the modern notion of virtue as a repression, an inhibition; habit is a principle of action, of activity. So that virtue is by its very nature a principle of activity; in fact it covers the whole field of good action. There are, of course, some very disagreeable people who operate in the name of virtue, people who, after the example of Martin Luther, are simply terrible when they are good. There is that whole class of the sanctimonious who shudder at contact with publicans and sinners. And there are those incorrigible gossips who are deeply irritated by one who refuses to speak unkindly. But none of this is virtue. In fact we could define virtue as a good habit by which a man lives rightly, without which he cannot live rightly, and which he cannot possibly put to bad use. If it is a human virtue, it is the result of our actions; if it is a supernatural or infused virtue, it is the result of the gracious kindness of God. But whatever kind it be, it cannot be the principle of those viciously unkind acts which are so often associated with the name of virtue.

You can hate virtue—as the gossip hates charity because it is a constant and well-merited rebuke. You can be stupidly proud of virtue and frown on everyone else who does not give first-hand evidence of possessing that same virtue. But to accuse virtue of being the cause of an evil act is like expecting one channel to carry water in different directions at the same time. Virtue is a power-line to one definite, determined destination; and that destination is in complete harmony with the nature of man, it is good.

Virtue is not, then, a grim enemy of jolly humanity. It is as distinctively human as a quiet chuckle, a sympathetic smile, or a roaring laugh. No creature but a possessor of human nature has any use for or any possibility of having virtue; it deals with the production of distinctively human action, it is the smooth path along which actions which alone are proper to man run a rapid, pleasant race to their goal. If we are in search of virtue, we have only to look at man, and within man himself, to look at the two great principles from which human action alone flows—the intellect and the will.

This double location of virtue, in intellect and will, brings up a distinction which answers a puzzling difficulty. It has often been noticed that a man can be an intellectual genius and a moral degenerate. A highly educated criminal is not only a possibility, but his very education makes his criminal activity more dangerous, more thorough, often more vicious. Socrates thought this could not be so, but the facts refuted him; our American educational system has made the same Socratic mistake and still cannot believe the facts can be right. After all, the whole purpose of virtue is to produce good actions; virtue in the intellect, then, certainly should make good men.

It does make good mathematicians, scientists, carpenters, and so on. But I can at least conceive of a carpenter being also a thief; and Bertrand Russell, who is an excellent mathematician, if he carries out one-half of his ethical principles is most certainly making a botch of his life. In other words, these intellectual virtues may make a man good in this or that line; they are incomplete or imperfect virtues. The explanation lies in this: some virtues give a man the ability to produce a good act but do not assure man of always using that faculty well; while others both give the man the faculty to act well and also guarantee the good use of that faculty. For example, grammatical habits give a man the faculty of speaking well; but even with those habits a man may speak very badly and certainly can violate the Ten Commandments. But a man with the habit of justice not only has the faculty of acting justly, but by that habit he does here and now act justly. He does an act of injustice only with difficulty and by deliberately pulling himself out of the groove of justice. In other words, these latter habits make a man simply good, not good in this or that line. They are the moral virtues.

This will be more clearly seen if we remember that the moral virtues reside in the appetite of man. As we have already seen so often, the appetite of man is the centre and source of all movement; its proper object is the end or goal of man and it is by reference to the goal of man that his actions are judged good or bad. We may say of the intellect that it is false or true; but only of the will do we say that it is good or bad. These complete or perfect virtues which make the whole man, not merely his faculties, good, belong to the will; and if they be found in any other faculty, it is only in so far as that faculty is moved by the will. Faith, for example, which is in the intellect, can perfect the whole man because the intellect assents to these supernatural truths only at the command of the will. Prudence, also an intellectual virtue, is a complete or perfect virtue precisely because of the order it implies to the will and the object of the will. But we shall see more of that later on.

For the present it is sufficient to stress this double classification of intellectual and moral virtues, as habits perfecting either the intellect or the appetite of man. The moral virtues, then, are good habits in the appetite of man, primarily in the will of man. We say primarily because there are the virtues of fortitude and temperance in the sensitive appetite of man, conforming his emergency and mild passions to the dictate of reason; but these virtues are virtues only in so far as the sensitive powers of man can participate in his spiritual powers. They are nothing more than the habitual conformity of the sense appetites to reason; in so far as they bend the activities and goal of the sense appetite to the activity and goal of the will they make a claim to be perfect or complete virtues.

The will itself has need of direct determination by habit. To move to its own proper good presented to it by the intellect, the will needs no help by way of habit at all. It was made for that, shaped for that type of action, determined along that line. But to reach out for a good that is outside its own field, the good of a neighbour, for example, or to a good that is outside the whole of the natural order—the divine good—it needs the habits which we call charity, justice, and the virtues connected with justice. More simply, for pursuit of a good pertaining only to ourselves our will needs no virtues; but for supernatural or altruistic goods we cannot get along without habits. And the exclusive pursuit of merely selfish ends does not develop or perfect man but destroys him, for it cuts him off from all social life, human and divine, and makes quite impossible the attainment of the goal of all human living in which the whole essence of happiness consists.

These, then, are the virtues of man: the virtues perfecting his intellect and those perfecting his appetite, the intellectual and moral virtues. This is a sufficient and complete classification of the human virtues, or of the good habits, in man, because there are no other principles from which human actions can flow. In other words, these are the two great dynamos to which the power-lines must be connected; there are no others. We shall treat of the moral virtues in greater detail in succeeding chapters; here it is enough to name them—justice, temperance, fortitude. Let us look more closely at the intellectual virtues with which our age professes to be so greatly in love.

I remember once seeing a seminarian, at home for a visit, greeted by a family of hard-working brothers. Everyone shook hands with him heartily and everyone immediately noted the contrast between his soft, callous-free hands and the rough hard hands of his brothers. The immediate verdict was: "Pretty easy; if you were home you would not have hands like that." I know the seminarian devoutly wished that the brain developed callouses that might be adduced as proof of work.

As a matter of fact that contrast has been going on from the beginnings of the human race. The man of action has been sneering at the man of thought as a dreamer, much as the French revolutionists hooted at the idleness and uselessness of contemplative religious Orders. And the philosopher, the brain-worker, has been looking with envy for generations at the day-labourer whose work was done when he laid down his pick and shovel. Whether thinking or acting is the harder job is unimportant here; but the contrast of these two is of immense importance, for it shows quite clearly the channels along which the activities of the intellect can flow and consequently shows the habits that may be developed in the intellect.

Intellectual activities that are not in view of something to be done or to be made are speculative activities and the habits or virtues perfecting the intellect for these activities are the speculative virtues: understanding, science and wisdom.

To-day we have picked out the middle virtue—science—and denied or neglected the other two, much as a woman might cling to youth and forget childhood, while vigorously denying old age, and just as impossibly. These are not three separable, unconnected habits but rather steps up in perfection; science supposes and absolutely demands understanding, while wisdom includes both science and understanding.

To grasp these virtues it is only necessary to look at the way our minds work. In the very beginning we gather first principles; from these we proceed to conclusions in this or that line; and finally we go back to the roots of things, to last causes, to ultimate explanations. The habit of first principles is understanding; as a habit of the first principles of thought it contains the seeds of all the sciences, as a habit of the first principles of action (synderesis), it contains the seeds of all morality and of all the moral virtues. Important? It is vitally important. Can we imagine a scientist proceeding to experiment without the principle of identity, of contradiction, of finality, or of sufficient reason; without knowing his right hand from his left, water from sulphuric acid, without seeking a reason for the unexplained? Yet modern philosophers solemnly assure us that this is the only valid way to gather knowledge. Moral life without that first principle, "good is to be done and evil is to be avoided", is just as impossible, for without it there is absolutely no basis for morality.

With the virtue of science we are quite familiar. Like all intellectual virtues it has to do with truth, with the firm certain hold on truth. The truth it seeks is that which can be deduced from the principles, or gathered from facts in the light of the principles furnished by the virtue of understanding. It always operates along particular lines: a science of mathematics, of chemistry, of physics, etc. We have let it stop there; but of course it includes much of philosophy and theology and is included in the ultimate reaches of philosophy and theology. Very simply, it is the virtue which deals with truth known through demonstration

Another name for the virtue of science would be knowledge. Stopping at this point and looking around the modern world we would feel very much at home. For the modern world has stopped at knowledge. And mere knowledge can be a disorderly, chaotic thing which can shatter a man's life just as a torrent of inharmonious sound can shatter a man's nerves or even his hearing. Knowledge of thousands of facts and conclusions from a dozen sciences may fit a man to be a robot in an industrial machine or to hold a chair in a professional school; but something more is needed to fit a man for living. A crowd of boys turned loose among the instruments of a symphony orchestra can undoubtedly produce as much noise, waste as much breath and work up as much perspiration as any symphony orchestra; but something more is needed for the production of music. That extra something is *order*.

And that is precisely the work of the virtue of wisdom. It is not satisfied with the immediate truth, as is knowledge; it wants the last truth, the last explanation. It is not satisfied to take a principle from some other science, it must go back to the very last and very first principle. Looking out from this vantage point, it sees the relation of one truth to another, one science to another, and, what is more important, the relation of all the truths, all the sciences, to the last truth, the final goal. Perhaps if we give this wisdom its ordinary names its work will be better understood: if it is divine wisdom we call it theology; if it is human wisdom it is called first philosophy or metaphysics. In either case it is the supreme speculative virtue necessary for any human life. It furnishes the answers to the fundamental questions of human life—why, whence and where—of the universe and even of God. It should be the prime object of education. The skeleton of it is given to the Catholic child in the catechism class; its possession can make the ignorant washerwoman very wise, its defect makes the learned professor very stupid. And it is one intellectual virtue which is a stranger to the American educational system.

So much for the virtues of the contemplative, the thinker,

the pursuer of truth for truth's sake. While they are imperfect or incomplete virtues, remember always that they can be meritorious of happiness under the command of the will and that actually they are the beginning, the foretaste, of the joys of heaven, for the essence of eternal happiness consists in the contemplation of truth, the beatific vision. How about the virtues of the man of action, the practical channels of intellectual activity?

Here again there is a clear-cut distinction between the maker and the doer, between the craftsman and the moulder of human actions. There is no one of us who escapes the work of moulding our own human actions, of steering them along the lines laid down by reason to the goal of human life. But a good many of us could eat a pile of lumber as easily as we could build a chicken coop; to some a hammer is an enemy with a personal grudge. The practical virtue dealing with the direction of human action is prudence; the other, the craftsman's virtue, is art.

It would seem as though our age had a positive genius for picking the unimportant and putting all stress on it. With only two practical virtues to choose from we pass by the one essential to human life, and exert our tremendous energies and undoubted ingenuity on the one that is not at all essential. St. Paul was, it is true, a clever craftsman; but I'm sure, hopefully sure, that heaven is full of saints who were clumsy with tools. Our great ability to make things, our inventive genius and technological perfection, our professional excellence and equipment has done some injustice even to art. While we have left the liberal or fine arts fairly intact, we have taken art out of the labouring man's life and in its place demanded only a monotonously precise speed to keep pace with the instruments of mass production.

Art is evidently an incomplete or imperfect virtue; it has no relation to the appetite of man. An atheist might make as good a violin as a saint. In fact an artist who deliberately violates the rules of his art, like the carpenter who wilfully hangs a door incorrectly, commits less of an artistic sin than the blundering artist who does not know any better. But quite the opposite is true of prudence; a man who deliberately steers his actions in the wrong direction is guilty of sin, while the man who steers his actions in the same direction not knowing it is wrong is guilty of no sin at all. The reason is that prudence is a complete or perfect virtue; it makes the whole man good. Nor is this a contradiction of what was said earlier about the intellectual virtues being incomplete virtues; for prudence is really an hybrid virtue, half intellectual, half moral. It is located in the intellect, but the material with which it deals is distinctly moral material, namely human acts; prudence works on the acts of seeing, hearing, thinking, willing, loving, and so on.

It has a most intimate relationship with the appetite of man. In the speculative order, as we have seen, the truth of a conclusion depends intimately on the truth of the principle from which that conclusion proceeds. In the practical order, the principles are really the ends of the actions; it is the end in view which determines the whole character of an action, that is indeed the reason for there being any action at all. Prudence, as the chauffeur of human life, steering human actions, presupposes right ends, right goals. In other words, prudence, before it can take a step in directing human actions to their goal, presupposes the rectitude of the appetite of man relative to that goal.

Remembering that good living is synonymous with good operation, that success in human life is measured by the goodness of human actions, or, in other words, by their approach to the goal of human life, it is easy to see how important prudence is in the living of human life and what a monstrous thing has been done to our age in cutting out these goals which are the foundations of prudence. For good operation it is not only a matter of what is done, but also of how it is done; it makes a big difference whether the action is the result of a rush of passion or of the deliberate, controlled direction of reason. And the work of prudence is precisely to furnish that controlled direction that makes human action coin of the realm for the purchase of happiness. In art, the goodness or defect is not a matter of the disposition of the artist, but of the quality of the work he has produced; but the goodness or defect of prudence is a matter of goodness or evil in the man himself. It is his very action that is the material upon which prudence must work.

In the next volume we will go into the virtue of prudence exhaustively. Here it will be sufficient to point out the obvious fact that prudence presupposes a certain perfection of counsel or searching for proper ways and means, and a perfection of judgment in picking out the best means at hand. Prudence, of course, as it deals with human action to an end, has to do only with means to that end.

Evidently these five intellectual virtues are not enough equipment for full, hearty, successful human life. The optimistic stand of Socrates in holding that they were—and our own American defence of the same position—is really based on the notion that the only explanation of sin is ignorance. The notion behind this idea is that since all human actions are acts controlled by reason, reason is the supreme power in the government of our lives, a power which has only to crack the whip to have its subjects jump to obey. There is something in this, but not enough. True enough, reason is supreme, the first principle of human actions precisely as human; but the command of reason is by no means absolute in its power. Over the spiritual, yes; but it has no command at all over the vegetative side of our nature and its power over the animal part of nature is by no means the despotic power of an absolute tyrant. It is rather a political power that may at any time be upset by a rebellion, is frequently resisted and only rarely get whole-hearted obedience. The appetite of man needs good habits, habits by which its activity flows along lines demanded by reason. The moral virtues are quite necessary, and as distinct from the intellectual virtues as intellect is from appetite.

They are distinct, but not at all unrelated. In fact, without some of the intellectual virtues it would be impossible to have any moral virtues at all. At least these two—understanding and prudence—are absolutely essential to moral virtue. The work of the moral virtues is to modify the activities of the appetite of man, to conform those activities to the demands of reason, to act as channels that will carry the flow of appetite's activities in the direction demanded by reason. They are elective habits, constantly making choices aimed at the goal of life; they demand by their very nature a striving towards the right end and the counsel, judgment and command necessary to select suitable means to the end in view. Counsel, judgment, and command are the work of prudence; the right leaning towards the true goal is the work of the moral virtues. More simply, it is impossible to produce right moral action without prudence; and prudence, as an intellectual virtue proceeding from first principles, is impossible without the virtue of understanding, i.e. without the habit of first principles.

It is a serious mistake to identify prudence with an extreme caution which goes about everything in the spirit that makes a man wear both suspenders and a belt. Prudence is not timidity or indecision or fear; it is intelligent moulding of human actions into tools by which happiness can be carved out. Prudence is not to be identified with education or learning; a very ignorant person can be very prudent in living human life, even though he can be easily deceived by an expert swindler in ordinary commercial affairs. Prudence is not something limited to one class or state of life, precisely because it is so absolutely necessary for all human life.

And this prudence is the only one of all the intellectual virtues that is impossible without the moral virtues. The interdependence of prudence and the moral virtues is complete: there is no moral virtue without prudence, and no prudence without moral virtues. Understanding, science, art, even wisdom can be had by a man who is thoroughly bad; but not prudence. Not every theologian is a saint, not even every great theologian.

The reason for this dependence of prudence on the moral virtues is that prudence really comes to grips with the concrete acts of human life. It cannot be satisfied with general principles, general conclusions, general rules; it must here and now have an intimate grip on the particular principles affecting this particular act. To put it more exactly, since the principles of prudence are the ends of action, prudence absolutely demands rightness of intention here and now, demands striving towards particular ends that are good here and now. And this right striving for good ends in the concrete is the work of the moral virtues, as, for example, a chaste man senses immediately, intuitively, the slightest trace of impurity in an action, a gesture, a word, or a glance, or a charitable person knows intuitively the thoughtful act, the word, the smile demanded by the tortured soul of a neighbour. With this to go on, prudence can steer its way to the goal; without it, prudence flounders in a world of general precepts like a correspondence-school detective who has forgotten his book.

Summing all this up briefly, it seems immediately apparent that the modern world has grossly misunderstood virtue in attaching to it connotations of ignorance and repression. Far from repressing human nature, virtue is an absolutely necessary principle of all good human actions, whether intellectual or moral. It is, very simply, a good operative habit. Every man to produce human actions must have habits; so habits he will build up, whether those habits are good or bad. Let him discard virtue, good habits, and he is dedicating himself to making a failure of his human life, he is twisting his own nature, stunting its growth, making it lopsided. For human nature was not designed for the pursuit of evil any more than a razor-blade was designed for sharpening pencils; to fill that nature with bad habits and then expect it to produce successful human life is like filling a razor-blade with nicks and expecting it to produce a good shave.

Virtues are the channels along which human actions flow to the goal of human life. They are the grooves, the trails cut by pioneer action, which make every other action that much easier, that much more perfect; they release a tremendous amount of energy for greater efforts, fuller perfections, fuller development.

While the intellectual virtues perfect a man in this or that way, develop this or that capacity, it is the moral virtues alone which perfect the whole man. If the attainment of the goal of life is man's one reason for living, if his partial happiness here and now is measured in terms of his approach to that goal, and his eternal happiness by his attainment of that goal, then there is nothing, humanly speaking, in this present life of ours outranking the moral virtues in importance. Their whole genius is the effective dealing with the goal of life and the approach to it.

Consequently virtue has not for its immediate result the sour face of the reformer, the fanatic egoism of the neurotic, or the stupidity of the superannuated. Its immediate result is a full perfection, a blossoming of the human powers of man, a release of power for the doing of extraordinary deeds, a more and more joyous tasting of that abundant life which Christ came to bring to the world. Ultimately the reward of virtue is that stamp of success on life, the attainment of the goal of life which constitutes the happiness of man. That happiness is carved out by the tools which we call human actions, human actions controlled, steered to that one goal; these moral virtues are precisely the immediate sources from which spring the only human actions capable of being used as such tools, good human actions.

A denial of virtue is a denial of good habits. And that means either the abandonment of man to bad habits, or the denial to man of any habits at all, in other words placing man on the level of a machine or of the animals. It is to take the very humanity out of human actions; or at least to take the successful note of humanity out of those actions. For the work of virtue is to mould men, to protect human nature against any influence that would drag it down, limit it, or make it less than it might be. Virtue breaks down the barriers to full, free, human living, sets the powers of man ever more free, free enough ultimately to soar up to God Himself. In a word, it makes men more human by making them more moral.

CHAPTER X

(OUTLINE)

STEPS TOWARDS HAPPINESS

(Q. 59–62)

1. The redintegration of human nature:
    - (*a*) Within itself.
    - (*b*) To God.

2. The redintegration of passion:
    - (*a*) Distinction of passion and virtue.
    - (*b*) Moral virtue as cause and enemy of passion.
    - (*c*) Passion as material of virtue.
    - (*d*) The joy and sorrow of virtue.

3. Factors of redintegration—good habits:
    - (*a*) Necessity of plurality of moral virtues.
    - (*b*) Personal and social virtues:
        - (1) The social virtues.
        - (2) The personal virtues.
        - (3) Aristotle's enumeration of the virtues: fortitude, temperance, generosity, magnificence, love of honour, magnanimity, meekness, affability, sincerity, recreation (eutrapelia), justice.

4. The leading factors: cardinal virtues:
    - (*a*) Their limitation to four: prudence, justice, fortitude, temperance.
    - (*b*) Their claim to leadership.
    - (*c*) Their mutual distinction.
    - (*d*) A scale of moral virtue:
        - (1) Virtues on the human plane.
        - (2) Ascending to the divine plane.
        - (3) Divine plane attained.
        - (4) The virtue of God.

5. Redintegration of human nature to God:
    - (*a*) Name and existence of theological virtues: faith, hope, charity,
    - (*b*) Distinction from intellectual and moral virtues.

(*c*) Their number and contrast with human faith and hope.
(*d*) Their scale of excellence.

Conclusion :

1. Virtues and the redintegration of human life.
   (*a*) Individual life.
   (*b*) Social life.
   (*c*) Divine life.
2. Virtue and complete human life.
3. Virtue and energetic human life.
4. Virtue and successful human life.

CHAPTER X

STEPS TOWARDS HAPPINESS

(Q. 59–62)

MODERN naturalistic education has much to say about the integration of personality. To these psychologists and philosophers of education, this integration is a goal to which all educational efforts must be directed. It is not so important to us here to notice how wrong these educationalists are in their notion of personality or of integration; what is important is that we notice how right they are in pointing out the delicate balance of the creature man.

It is puzzling for these modern educators to notice that man has something in common with stones, but is not a stone; he has life in common with plants, but is not a plant; and he has feeling in common with the beasts, yet of all the creatures he alone has need of having these elements properly balanced. The obvious explanation is that he needs balancing because he can unbalance himself; he alone has freedom. The task is really much more puzzling than these modern educators suspect: for over and above his extended substance, his life and his feeling, man has spirit in common with the angels and yet is no angel; he has an intellect and will that can reach to the uttermost boundaries of infinity, and which yet cannot say with absolute power what his feelings will be, how far they will go, or what preponderant part they will take in his actions.

Looking at man as we find him to-day, it is evident that his parts must be exactly proportioned and his energies be nicely balanced one against the other, if the whole man is to function smoothly as a man. In a word, it is much easier to upset that smooth functioning of man's personality than it is for the runner to pull a tendon in his leg; and the results are more disastrous.

We can go a step further and realize that over and above the nice co-ordination of the inferior parts of man to the one supreme director of human activity which is reason, there is a further co-ordination and subordination necessary for the full perfection of human development—a subordination, co-ordination, integration to the supreme director of all activity, God Himself. And then we feel a deep pity for the bewildered educationalist who is trying so futilely to assemble the parts of man in one harmonious unit, with no notion as to what the finished product should look like. No wonder he stands back and scratches his head in astonishment at all the parts he has left over, at the weirdly different results of his efforts like a little boy who has fixed the clock. He has none of the comfortable security of the expert assembling the bones of prehistoric monsters; the monstert will never come back to give the lie to the expert, but man is always present, haunting the naturalistic educationaliss with the bitter failure of his efforts.

Perhaps this need for integration is more vividly present to us who know so well that once man had that perfect subordination of sense life to reason and reason to God; and lost it. Because we know how it was once had, we know how to go about getting it again. If we lost our balance, at least we know it was lost and we know what is necessary for the maintaining of that balance. In very simple terms, we can pick ourselves up again because we know that delicate balance is obtained and maintained by the double medium of habit or virtue and grace.

It is unfortunate that our democratic traditions made the word "subordinate" and "subjection" so thoroughly objectionable. The notion of subordinating passion to reason seems to us to have something of the unpleasantness and unfairness of tyranny about it, like the frowning annihilation of an impertinent student by an impatient professor. And this notion has been given some substance by the uncompromising fashion in which some men proceeded to the integration of passion, of the movement of the sense appetites, in the human personality.

To one group it seemed quite evident that passion was unworthy of the human personality, something the virtuous man could not admit without shame; so the Stoics and the Puritans would integrate passion by blasting it out of existence, or at least by refusing to extend to it the social amenities reserved for the respectable citizens of the human kingdom. Still others were so impressed by the naturalness and force of passion, that they would integrate it to the human personality by blasting humanity out of that personality. This is the group that recently has been telling us such bogey stories about repression, inhibitions, and the necessity of self-expression.

Passion, however, is neither pariah nor king. It has its place; and the work of the moral virtues is precisely to keep it in its place. Of course moral virtues and passions are different things; but that does not make them inimical things. A loud senseless laugh may make many enemies, or at least many grouches, but certainly it will not find itself squared off in a battle to the death with the vocal cords from which it proceeded. It is true enough that passion is the movement of the sense appetite and moral virtue the immediate principle of that movement; but that links them arm in arm rather than putting them at each other's throat. Passion of itself is morally indifferent, while moral virtue is always morally good; but that merely indicates in a vague way the work before the moral virtues.

It is wrong to picture moral virtue, as the moderns do, as sitting on the lid of the passions as a man might sit on the lid of the safety valve of a steam-engine, an uncomfortable and dangerous position under the best of circumstances. This view allows our imagination to picture all sorts of things as happening within man himself because of the terrific pressure brought to bear by the virtues; we half expect the virtuous man literally to explode before our eyes. Or we can see passion as the browbeaten underdog and immediately our sympathies are heartily enlisted.

The moral virtues actually produce passion. Look at it this way. Passion starts from the sense appetite, and its goal, if it is to be human passion, is reason, measuring up to the rule laid down by reason, keeping to the road mapped out by reason; moral virtue starts from reason with all the charts and maps in its pocket. Its goal is the sense appetite which it is to steer along the road of reason. The only type of passion that virtue will operate against is the inhuman or beastly passion which disregards the rule of reason, which hurtles itself off the road of reason as a frightened horse might plunge over a precipice. And the moral virtues will operate just as earnestly against no passion at all as they will against this unreasonable, bullying, blindly crashing passion that is wrecking the whole delicate balance of human personality.

Passion, then, is not a browbeaten underdog, nor a simmering boiler of steam with no legitimate outlet. The other older notion, that passion is unworthy of the virtuous man, we have already treated of at some length. Let us stop for just a glance at one rather amusing angle of that opinion which our Anglo-Saxon civilization has taken to its heart. The ancient version of this angle was that the passion of sorrow had no place in the life of the virtuous man; it comes from evil actually present and the virtuous man allows no evil to happen to him. The modern version is that sorrow is unworthy of a man, by reason of his manhood; it is something for women and children—at least the expression of it.

There is a little something in each opinion. It is absurd to say that no evil can happen to the virtuous man. He is, after all, human; he can suffer misfortune in his external goods, pain in his body, sin in his soul. Even supposing that here and now he is in the best of health and good fortune, without a sin to his name, it is hardly likely that he never committed a sin for which he can entertain regret; even in this highly improbable case, he can always very laudably be sorry for the sins of others. But it is by no means absurd to say the sort of evil which makes a substantial difference in the success or failure of a human life—sin—cannot happen to a man. It does not happen; it is deliberately chosen.

It is quite silly to maintain that an expression of sorrow is a reflection on manhood, unless we insist that men are freaks with an essential part of their nature omitted while women and children are complete human specimens. But it is not absurd to say that such expression of sorrow, like all other passions, must be under a man's control, under the guidance of his reason; that unless it is, it is a serious reflection on the very humanity of the individual in question.

Important as it may be to see passion clearly as the material of moral virtues, it is equally important to understand that passion is not the sole material of the moral virtues, or rather that it is not the material of all the moral virtues. We may picture the moral virtues as governors sent out by the emperor reason to the colonies—the sensitive appetite. They arrive there, participating the power of the emperor, for the sole purpose of governing those colonies; and that means for the purpose of directing them to the common good of the empire. That common good will be the good of reason, according to the rules of reason, moving along towards the ends of reason. So that everything and anything that can be governed, ordained to that good of reason, is a proper subject of the moral virtues.

Concretely, it is not merely the passions themselves that must be conformed to reason if man is to have an integrated personality, his external actions must also measure up to this standard of humanity which is reason. Put in another way, we can say that reason not merely guides the sensitive appetite along its proper road, it also guides the intellectual appetite or will which is the root principle of all activity in man. Moral virtues are no less necessary in the intellectual appetite than they are in the sensitive appetite. In the latter they regulate the passions of man; in the former they regulate the actions of man.

The moral virtues of the will, in themselves, can operate without passion, as we can pay a doctor's bill without sorrow flooding our souls; passion, after all, is proper to the sense appetite, something we have in common with the beasts. But even here, because man is such a smoothly working unit, passion ordinarily makes its appearance. There is joy in the will at successful, smooth operation; and that joy reacts on the sensitive appetite to cause pleasure. As a rule the greater the proficiency and perfection in the will, the greater the joy and consequently, ordinarily speaking, the greater the passion responding to that joy like an echo responding to a shout in the mountains.

A man once told me of his operation. It seems that he was on time but, as sometimes happens, the doctor was late. So he was wheeled into a small side operating-room and of course the only way to pass the time was to look about the room. There for his interest and terror was a most splendid collection of bright shiny scalpels, scissors, pincers, a veritable armoury of instruments of torture. Somehow it seemed to him that operations would be much less terrifying if the doctor could do his job with just an ordinary knife; it would not be so bad if it were something like a boy-scout knife, full of gadgets for every purpose. But at least it should be simple, direct, to give less room to the imagination's frightful pictures. Perhaps much the same sensation comes upon a man the first time he stops to realize the complex assortment of virtues which a man must have to carve out a successful life. It would be much simpler if we were sent out to cope with life as the pioneers coped with the wilderness, with little more than our hands and our ingenuity; we would be hacking out our eternal homes as a pioneer hacked out his log-cabin with only an axe for an aid. But the finished product would not be much of a palace; and probably we would be scalped by Indians long before the house was finished.

No, the task of successful living is much too complicated a work. We need every one of the shining virtues which life offers us. One, no matter how complex, would only make a botch of the job. Looking at it from another angle, these moral virtues are governors of particular colonies participating in the power of the emperor reason; no one of them, however complex, could direct the whole moral life of a man, any more than a creature, however perfect and complex, can adequately mirror the beauty of God in which it participates.

Our shining set of tools for the job of living is easily divided into tools for inside and for outside work, or to call them by other names, virtues of passion and virtues of action, personal virtues and social virtues. Understand, of course, that every virtue has operations by way of effects, but here it is a question of the material upon which the virtues will work—some deal exclusively with the passions, others with the actions of man. In other words, the aim of these inside or personal virtues is the conformity of man's inner life to the rule of reason; the aim of the outside or social virtues is to regulate man's relations with others by the rule of reason.

The foundation of this distinction is important and like most important truths is familiarly within reach most of the time. Put it this way: drinking a single glass of whisky can be a difficult mortification undertaken in the spirit of Lent for the man who is used to drinking a pint a day; for another man the same act would be one of sottish intemperance. A book that would make one person blush merely produces prodigious yawns in another. But no matter how bored a man is as he goes about his murders, no matter how lightly they affect his sleep, or how good they are for his nerves, they are always wrong, wrong no matter who does them.

In plain language, there are some acts whose goodness or malice must be judged in reference to the individual performing them, according as they affect this or that individual differently, or even as they affect the same individual differently at different times. The virtues which deal with these, principally busy themselves with the emotions of the individual. There are other acts whose goodness or malice is completely independent of how we feel or think about them, for their goodness or malice is measured in terms of what is due to another. (The virtues of the first are the personal, of the second, the social virtues.)

It is immediately evident that the social virtues have one common note, a note that runs through them like a simple melody through all the complexities of a difficult piece of music. That note is one of debt, of what is due to another, of another's rights being respected. In other words, it is the note of justice. This is particularly important: important in its insistence on the fundamental truth that the bond of social life is mutual communication, the external relations of man to man, for only by such externals can man communicate with his fellowmen in this life; important to-day in its bald condemnation of any and all social theories that have lost sight of the rights of others in their scramble for vindication of one class, have lost sight of the necessity of fostering and regulating these relations rather than destroying them.

This does not mean, of course, that when we have placed justice, the equipment for successful social life is complete. Our debts to others are widely different: what is due to God, to parents, to civil authority, to neighbours, to subjects, to inferiors, what is due as result of a contract, of promise, in payment for a benefit received—each one offers a wealth of material for the labours of a virtue. We shall see each of these in some detail in the next volume.

The personal virtues, whose material is the passions of man, automatically split into the virtues of the concupiscible appetite (from which come the mild passions) and the irascible appetite (from which flow the emergency passions). But their classification is not so simple as all this. In fact it is not at all simple. We cannot simply stop with two virtues, any more than a surgeon can stop buying equipment because he has a jack-knife. Nor can we simply click off the names of the passions and tie a virtue to each one. Evidently a man's love of food, his desire for it and his pleasure in it are all regulated by one virtue, so intimately are the mild passions connected by their common object—the sensible good. Or again love and hate are the subject-matter of one virtue. Entering the field of the emergency passions, that intimate connection coming from a common object is missing; so we find hope and desperation dealing with a difficult good and regulated by magnanimity, daring and fear dealing with a great danger and regulated by fortitude, while anger is taken care of by meekness.

It all seems complicated, like the bewildering array of the surgeon's tools. I hope the reader will appreciate this complexity. One of the reasons why Aristotle's enumeration of the virtues is given in detail in the outline preceding this chapter is to win a hearty agreement on this complexity; such agreement, in fact, as will allow the unravelling of each particular virtue to be deferred until the next volume.

At any rate it should be a heartily comforting thought to everyone to realize all this complex assortment of virtues can be reduced to just four: prudence, justice, fortitude and temperance. These are the principal or cardinal virtues, the hinges upon which a man's life swings; they are the root virtues to which all the other perfect or complete virtues can be reduced. We classified the intellectual virtues as incomplete or imperfect because they perfected only a faculty of man without guaranteeing the good use of the faculty; or, in simpler terms, they made man good in this or that way, but they did not make him a good man. We are talking now of the integration of human personality, the assembling of the elements of humanity into a smooth-running engine which will carry man to his goal; we are speaking of the making of a successful, a good man. Looking for the leading factors in that integration, we have only to look for the principal virtues among the perfect or complete virtues which make the whole man good. Prudence is the only intellectual virtue included in this list of four; and it will be remembered from our last chapter that the material of prudence is moral material—human acts; while the principles of prudence are furnished by the moral virtues. In other words, the interdependence of prudence and the moral virtues is so complete that one cannot exist without the other.

These virtues have a much stronger claim to principality than mere convenience. If we remember that the goodness of man consists in conforming to the order of reason, then it is immediately evident that order can exist in reason itself (prudence); or it is imposed on actions (justice); or is imposed upon the passions, either in so far as they impel a man to something contrary to reason (temperance) or tend to withdraw him from something that is according to reason (fortitude). Even more simply, looking at the location of these virtues, we find prudence in the reason itself, justice in the will, temperance in the concupiscible appetite, fortitude in the irascible appetite. By these virtues we have the fundamental perfection of all possible sources of human acts.

As we have pictured it in this chapter, the world is a huge human workshop, an assembly plant for human personalities. We can make an approximate job of the assembly by comparing the parts one to another; but for the first-class assembly necessary for the long, rough road over which the human machine must travel we must have the model before our eyes all the time. And that supreme model, to which all men must conform for a successful living, is God Himself.

The creatures of the universe make up a great vague mirroring of divine beauty, as though God had looked into the still waters of the pool of the universe and sunk His image in their depths. Each creature, each part of every creature, is a facet of a great jewel, throwing back to divinity one reflected ray of the divine beauty. So all creatures make their way back to God as to the source from which they come; each reaches its perfect fulfilment as it approaches closer to the beauty, the perfection of God. And all this is true of man, of every part of man, and, of course, of the virtues of man.

It is ridiculous to speak of temperance, fortitude, justice and prudence in God in the same human way in which we speak of them in men. But vaguely they are moulded on the divine model. Trying to see that likeness, we see prudence as the very mind of God, temperance as the turning of the divine will to God Himself as in us it is the turning of appetite to reason; the fortitude of God is His unchangeable constancy, His justice the observance of the Eternal Law in all His works.

Perhaps it is easier to see the human personality's approach to that divine model by looking at the different stages of its assembly. In the first, purely human, stage man according to these virtues is more and more perfect in his handling of human affairs. Through the infused moral virtues, man comes a step closer to the divine model, for by them we find man rejecting all earthly things as trifles and directing all thought to divine things by prudence; by temperance, as far as nature allows, he edges away from the use of the body; by fortitude he strides boldly to the high things of God, unterrified by the thought of separation of soul from body; and by justice he wins the whole soul's hearty consent to this divine way of life.

Finally, when the human personality has come as close to measuring up to the divine model as the infinite generosity of God can allow, we see prudence penetrating exclusively into divine things, temperance undisturbed by temporal desires, fortitude indifferent to or ignorant of suffering, and justice perpetually associated with the divine mind through the amicable pact of imitation. These last are the virtues of the saints, whether in heaven or on earth. Sanctity is the ultimate of integration of the human personality.

It is to be noted that for that integration of personality we have frankly stepped into the supernatural. The infused moral virtues, which come not from any effort of man but only from the generosity of God as an infallible accompaniment of His grace, are only a part of that victorious sally into the supernatural which wins the essential happiness of man.

It is not to a happiness proportioned to his nature that man is destined, but to no less a happiness than the participation of the life of God. Yet he must win to that altogether supernatural happiness by the homely steps of his own human acts; even his part in the divine life must be the fruit of his clever use of the tools of life. Ordinary tools will not do; yet they must be the tools of man. God does not ask us to carve out a crystal palace with a sledge-hammer; He puts supernatural tools into our hands, rather He makes these human acts of ours supernatural, He gives them a divine edge, an eternal significance which enables a man to say to himself in heaven or hell that he was the workman who fashioned his destiny. This supernatural character is given to our acts by giving us supernatural principles of those acts, supernatural habits, supernatural virtues: one group supernaturally to regulate our human moral life—supernatural moral virtues; the other to lift us up, even in this life, to the point where we can come into contact with the divine life itself—the theological virtues.

These theological virtues, the virtues whose only object is God Himself, are utterly supernatural and utterly necessary, supernatural because they can come only from God, be known only through God's revelation, and go only to God, necessary because the goal of man is completely beyond his natural principles of actions, his natural virtues.

These are not intellectual virtues, nor are they moral virtues; their object is not the intellect of man, nor the appetite of man, but God. They are theological virtues. And yet they lift our whole moral and intellectual life to a supernatural plane. Put in another way, we can say that God equipped us no less adequately for the supernatural life, through grace, than He did for the natural life through nature itself. The knowledge of first principles upon which our whole intellectual life is based is natural to us; the will of man naturally tends to its natural object, naturally grasps that object when it is present. Faith makes the knowledge of supernatural principles connatural; hope makes the striving for the supernatural goal connatural; charity makes union with the supernatural goal, God, connatural. In other words, by these virtues we move about the broad fields of the supernatural with the easy familiarity of natives; we breathe the rarefied air of heaven as if our lungs were made for no other; our intellects and wills join in the family life of God as though this were our home. And indeed it is; for by these virtues the supernatural is made second nature to us.

We might possibly make a modern mistake by underestimating faith and hope. If we draw an exact parallel between these virtues and human faith and hope, our pride will make them seem unpalatable. For faith and hope, in the human sphere, have something defective about them, a note of uncertainty, of lack of insight, of helplessness. Surely they had none of the strong, sure stride of virtue about them. That is strictly true; for human faith and human hope are not virtues. But that uncertainty, helplessness, that staggering stride is not present in supernatural faith and hope which are backed up by the infallible authority and omnipotent strength of God Himself.

As the fulfilment of man's age-long dream of becoming "like God", these virtues are infinitely precious, a treasure to be fondled again and again, to be dreamt over, to be guarded at any cost. We know whence they come. In running these jewels through our fingers again and again, the desire constantly comes to know more about them, to know all about them. We shall fulfil that desire as far as possible in our next volume. For the moment it will be enough to insist that since they are infused with grace all three appear instantaneously in the soul; there is no first, second and third. But, as we understand them, the order of their generation is: first, faith—for we must know before we can love; then hope, for our goal must be possible to us; finally charity. But in the order of their excellence, charity leads all virtues, the other theological virtues included, for the object of charity—union with God—is the goal of all the virtues, all the actions, all the aspirations of man. It is the final goal of all human life, the essence of human happiness.

We can sum this all up briefly by going back to our starting-point, the redintegration of personality. A stone exists but has no personality; a plant lives but is not a person; an animal has feeling but no one attempts to develop a dog's personality. Personality is more than mere existence, life or feeling: it is the peculiar characteristic of a living, feeling, intellectually knowing substance that is responsible for its acts. In other words, a person is one who has freedom, whose acts are under his commands, whose life answers to his steering.

The perfection of that personality, then, will be the perfection of that mastery of life, that command of action; or, in the terms we have been using throughout this book, the redintegration of personality consists in bringing the whole of man under the sway of reason, of extending those controlled acts that alone are human to every department of man's activities. The human personality is redintegrated, perfected, in so far as the will and the sensible appetites and their passions come more fully under the control and direction of reason. Even more simply: personality is redintegrated in proportion as the individual grows in virtue, for the whole purpose of virtue is precisely the extension of the sway of reason, the conforming of appetite to the rule of reason, the creation of grooves along which human action flows to the end of reason or the goal of human life. For the smooth unity, the easy, faultless functioning of this creature man, virtue is indispensable; without it man is hardly a unit, but rather a chaotic example of constant civil war. His individual life is nothing but the wreckage left by the warring armies that have passed again and again over every inch of its territory.

As virtue binds the energies of man into one mighty unit, it also binds men together into the unit we call society. It is the cement holding the bricks of society together, harmonizing, regulating, controlling all the external means by which alone men can communicate. There is no other means of holding men together except that of force; and where the mailed fist is the symbol and explanation of social unity, there is not a society of men but of slaves. It is justice alone that makes society possible; every attack on justice is an attack on society, every society based upon injustice has the seeds of its own dissolution within itself. It must cease to exist or its subjects must cease to be men. For without justice there is no human society, there is no conformity to the rules of reason, no travelling along the road of reason to the goal of reason, the goal of humanity.

Virtue is the great integrator. Only by it can man live with himself; only by it can he find life with his fellows; and only by it can he live with God. It is the great peace-maker, putting man at peace with himself, at peace with his fellows, at peace with God. In its supernatural form it is a magic instrument lifting man from the natural universe to the supernatural life of God, stamping each of his smallest actions with the mark which gives it supernatural value, giving every moment of his life an eternal significance that makes his lightest step echo for ever in heaven or in hell. And only when that last destiny has been for ever determined will man be fully integrated, or spend an eternity completing his disintegration.

From all this it is evident that virtue is not an integrating force in the sense of dwarfing half of man's nature, of blasting out his passion in favour of his reason or his reason in favour of his passions. By virtue alone can *all* the energies of man have their complete development; only by virtue can man live a complete, a full human life. He is not mere animal; nor is he pure spirit. That delicate balance between animal and spirit which will extinguish neither one but fully develop both can be had only by the inculcation of virtue.

Only the virtuous man is able to use his human energies to the full. All the sweeping force of passion and the sublime soarings of will are harnessed to the goals of reason and rush along the road of life in giant strides by virtue; without it man is like a mad dog, rushing now in this direction, now in that, retracing his steps only to come rushing back again, but always effectively barring himself from advancing towards his goal. Will and passion can accomplish great things when they are working together; but they work together only when they work under the order of reason. Working against reason they produce nothing but shattered hopes, fruitless quests, despairing hearts. Success in human living can be summed up in terms of good action, action in conformity to the dictates of reason; and the principles of good actions are good habits, or virtues. This is the end of education, this is the redintegration of the human personality that means complete, energetic, successful human living—sanctity.

CHAPTER XI

(OUTLINE)

HABITS OF HAPPINESS

(Q. 63–67)

1. Two ways of considering a finished product:
   - (*a*) That of the busy genius, equipped with secretaries and assistants.
   - (*b*) That of the leisurely craftsman:
     - (1) Gathering up the shavings, putting things in order.
     - (2) Remembering, pondering the labour, the aims, and results of work.

2. The finished product of virtue is second nature at its best.

3. The labour of producing second nature:
   - (*a*) Nature's part.
   - (*b*) Man's part.
   - (*c*) God's part.

4. The aims of second nature:
   - (*a*) The ultimate aim.
   - (*b*) The immediate aim—mediocrity and the mean of virtue:
     - (1) The mean of the moral virtues.
     - (2) Of the intellectual virtues.
     - (3) Lack of a mean in the theological virtues.

5. The results of second nature:
   - (*a*) The co-ordination of parts:
     - (1) Connection of the moral virtues.
     - (2) Connection of the moral and theological virtues.
     - (3) Connection of the theological virtues.
   - (*b*) Balance of the whole structure of virtue:
     - (1) Equality.
     - (2) Inequality.
     - (3) Comparative excellence.

6. Durability of the finished product:

   (*a*) In time.
   (*b*) In eternity.

Conclusion:

1. Virtue and pride of accomplishment.
2. Virtue and humility of the craftsman.
3. Virtue and gratitude.
4. The finished product—second nature at its best.

CHAPTER XI

HABITS OF HAPPINESS

(Q. 63–67)

WE men and women of to-day have lost something very precious. As so often happens, the tragedy of that loss is increased by the illusion that the loss is itself a gain. It is bad enough to lose a friend, but to rejoice in the loss of a friend is tragedy! This modern tragedy is vividly exemplified in the story of a famous novelist who made it a practice to rise very early every morning, and write madly for three or four hours, sweeping the numbered sheets off his desk on to the floor. Then, while he took his morning stroll, his secretary gathered up the manuscript, arranged the numbered pages and packed the finished product off to the publishers.

Somehow that appeals to our love of the efficient, of speed, of accomplishment. Creative genius cleaning up after the work is done, sweeping up the shavings, arranging the loose ends, putting things in order is genius wasting its time and gifts; it is as incongruous a picture as that of a prima donna washing her own clothes or the mayor of New York dusting the furniture every morning before going to the city hall.

I wonder if our familiarity with machines has not begun to warp our vision, to make us see all things, even men, in terms of a machine. Surely we are inclined to forget to-day that man, like God, stamps his image on his works. Something of our personality, something that no other force in the universe can contribute, goes into our labours and makes them really a part of ourselves. This is the foundation of the pride, the affection, even the tenderness of the true craftsman for the finished product of his labours. The wrecked safe bears the mark of the particular expert who ransacked it, as the perfectly rounded, clear note of the singer, the products of the carpenter, the bricklayer, the lawyer or the surgeon, all tell an intimate story of their authors as the universe tells an intimate story of God.

What we have lost is that exquisite joy of the old craftsman puttering about his shop, putting things in order in an easy, leisurely fashion that gives him time to stop a moment and run a hand over the smooth perfection of his work. What a time he had getting this particular part of the work done, how he planned, dreamed, worried; how eagerly he went back to the job as his dreams began to take shape; what secret pride there is in this child of his genius, even though none of his works seem quite to catch the elusive beauty and breath-taking grace of his dreams! He has not forgotten that when God finished His work of creation He surveyed His creatures and saw that "they were good". This is the way Adam would have worked naturally if sin had not distorted the very nature of work.

And that is the way we are going to work in this chapter. We have spent several chapters painting the picture of second nature at its best, laboriously painting in every detail of the structure of good habits in man. Now the work is done and of course things are scattered about. Let us stop and put things in order, pick up the odds and ends, pausing every now and then to steal a glance at the beauty of that painting, to remember smilingly the effort which went into it and the pride there is in it even though there is always a pang of disappointment that the reality never measures up to the dream.

It is well to remember that it was necessary to build in a second nature for man because of the paradoxical combination of imperfection and perfection. Because only the infinite can measure up to human powers, to tie those powers down to the finite and particular would be like holding down a spirited thoroughbred to a sedate pace. Or, to put it in another way, the tremendous energies of man's appetites, the tremendous horizons of his mind, had to be applied to particulars. Man's intellect and will are great power-houses from which the power flows along the power-lines of habit. They are like a great reservoir from which channels must lead in different directions, according to the ends for which the water is to be used. These modifications of man's powers, these feed-wires, these channels, are the habits of man; and when they are good habits, they are virtues.

We have said it was important that these channels or grooves be built into man. He could not get far without them. Yet they had to be *built* in; they were not furnished by nature like a set of teeth, strong lungs or a pleasant smile. The best we could hope from nature was a nudge, a push in the direction of second nature. Or perhaps it would be better to say a shove; nature is never over-delicate and has definite notions about what man must construct within himself to make the most of his powers.

Nature is not over-delicate; to some she must appear niggardly. The natural inclination to know first principles instantly, the natural inclination to desire good, seem, from one point of view, slim foundations for our whole intellectual and moral life. Even granting that each individual has positive leanings, by his very physical constitution, towards this or that good habit, towards justice, or temperance, or fortitude, those leanings are inevitably balanced by others that make the acquiring of other virtues extraordinarily difficult. All in all, nature did not monopolize the task of producing man's second nature.

A child puzzling over her homework probably feels hurt that the family will not tell her the answers and she feels she is neglected because she must work out the problems herself. The family is niggardly with its knowledge. But when she has solved the problems, not only the answers but the principles from which she proceeded will be *hers*. The case is the same with the niggardliness of nature. It is because man's acts are to be his, not nature's, that the immediate principles of those acts, the habits, must also be his. We are not mere animals with tough hides, long sharp teeth, and no hope; our goal is our own, our acts are our own, and we fashion those acts through the medium of the virtues or the vices.

This, then, is our part in the building of second nature. We are trying to make our powers respond to a command like a squad responding to a drill sergeant's whistle. The whole purpose of virtue is to conform action to a rule; and human nature has the double rule of its own reason and the reason of God. What falls under the rule of human reason, falls under the rule of divine reason. The one is in perfect accord with the other as the teaching of a bishop is in accord with the teaching of a pope. But it does not work conversely, for God is not limited to the capacities of human reason any more than the powers of a pope are limited to one diocese. We cannot bend our energies to all the mysterious goals of the divine reason; that is God's work. But we can, and must, cut grooves within ourselves along which our actions will flow to the goal of human reason.

We start from the push given by nature, much as the pioneer started from the push given him by the crowding of later immigrants. And like the pioneer we blaze the trail along which all other acts will follow, follow more quickly, more easily, more perfectly. The demand that our actions produce the habits from which they will proceed ever more easily may seem like asking the kitten to produce its mother before it can be born. But that is because we are underestimating that impulse of nature. The act produces something more perfect than itself—its very principle—only because it is supported by the powerful forces of nature itself, much as a physically timid king can rule whole races because of the backing of his army and navy. For just as the principles of intellectual knowledge are higher, wider, deeper than the conclusions which follow from them, so the broad inclinations of nature are more powerful than the habits which proceed from them through the agency of acts. Each act cuts the groove just that much deeper and makes the next act go just that much more surely to its appointed goal.

All this every man can do, must do. But only God can steer man to a goal above all nature; so only from God can come the habits which will give our actions that supernatural significance which enables us to penetrate the walls of heaven. The theological virtues, coming immediately from God, give us a start towards the supernatural goal of all men, much as nature starts us off towards a natural goal; to enable us to cope with the detailed means to that supernatural end, God infuses in us a complete set of moral virtues—supernatural prudence, justice, fortitude and temperance.

However, a coin tossed down in the name of supernatural justice makes exactly the same clink as a coin which is given from natural justice. The temperate acts of a pagan give no clue by which they can be distinguished from those of a Christian. But they are distinctly different, as different as time and eternity. Even though it is impossible to detect the difference in the actions themselves, it is very easy to see that the infused virtues directing man's acts to the eternal vision of God, are very different from the acquired virtues ordering human acts to a conformity with reason. There is a difference even in regard to the immediate object of the different virtues, even though that difference is not immediately seen in the acts. So, from the acquired virtue of temperance, a man might curtail his too ardent desire for food for the sake of the health of his body or for the better operation of his mind; while, from the infused virtue of temperance, his aim would be to reduce that body to further and further subjection to the soul.

In other words, these infused virtues are not called supernatural merely because they come from God. They are above all nature, they cannot be acquired by any activity of ours, and their goal is no less above nature than their origin. Even their immediate object and the mode (of charity) in which they proceed place them in a class infinitely above the acquired or natural virtues. This is God's part in the production of this second nature of man—to give us with grace the infused theological and moral virtues; and an enormous part it is.

We have all heard thousands of times that virtue consists in a happy medium between excess and defect. Somehow, we have difficulty in being proud of that fact. It seems strange that we should demand such intimate and powerful activity on the part of God to make a man respond prudently by saying "harumph" instead of "yes" or "no". Actually that is not prudence at all; it is diplomacy or timidity. A happy medium is not a statement of a policy of straddling, of perching our soul on the topmost bar of the fence and taking good care we do not allow it to drop on one side or the other. It is not walking backwards down the middle of the road in order to confuse everyone, including ourselves, as to where we stand. It is not a dedication to an anæmic life of grey mediocrity where nothing must be allowed to happen which is out of the ordinary.

We make these mistakes by forgetting that "happy medium" is a technical term with a technical meaning. Virtue, as we have seen, is the one possible source of the extraordinary. By its nature it guarantees a steadily better, easier, more perfect result. In its supernatural form it is the secret of the mad romance with divinity itself, the hidden spring from which bubble up those impossible accomplishments, incredible hopes, and that constant reaching for the stars that give heroic proportions to the dullest of human lives. There is a huge difference between mediocrity and the medium of virtue, as great a difference as between the blustering cowardice of Pilate and the wide-flung courage of Paul.

This difference is vividly clear when we say quite simply that the medium of virtue is that demand which a man must meet to be worthy of his manhood; the medium of supernatural virtue is what a man must meet to be worthy of the friendship of Christ. Excess and defect, too much or too little, always have reference to some rule, to some norm which is the standard. A manufacturer has produced small whisky glasses which are graduated: the lowest mark has over it the caption "ladies", the second, "men"; the third, near the top of the glass, has no word at all, merely the picture of a very fat pig. Those lines are norms laid down to guide or shame the drinker into taking just enough. The rule of virtue is the rule of reason; excess is going beyond the bounds of reason; defect is offering less than reason demands. In matters of temperance, for example, excess is the glutton's gorging; defect is the miser's starvation. In either case there has been a defect of conformity to the rule of reason; the individual in either case has been somewhat less than a man.

In fortitude and temperance particularly this excess and defect, as far as quantity itself is concerned, is a matter to be judged with reference to the individual himself; to what is excess or defect for this particular man. But of course the other circumstances of the act, the "when", "why", "where" and so on, must also be considered. In matters of justice, on the contrary, this happy medium of virtue is definitely objective. Justice does not deal with the passions, which vary in every man, but with external actions and words, with the means of communication among men. The material of justice always has reference to another, it is the altruistic, the social virtue, its medium is not proper to this or that man, but to all men. Even though I have not acted unjustly because of my ignorance, the thing I have done is still unjust, for it falls short of the objective rule of reason determining what is due to another.

As a matter of fact a "happy medium", in this technical sense, goes far beyond the field of the moral virtues. It is indeed universally true of anything that can be gauged or measured, that its good, its perfection, consists in a happy medium which does not go beyond the rule by which it is measured but which nevertheless meets the requirements of that rule. So an architect's plan is the rule according to which a house is built; it would be an odd house, indeed, which would astonish its own architect by its bizarre arrangement of rooms.

In this sense, then, the immediate aim even of the intellectual virtues is to establish a happy medium, to conform to the rule by which the intellect is measured, to avoid going beyond it and at the same time not to fall short of it. That rule of intellect is the world of things as they are. The intellect is measured by the reality of things: when it attributes reality to fiction it fails by excess; when it denies reality to fact it fails by defect. Here we have again that beautiful gradation of thought, being and action which anchors all three to the world of reality and, ultimately, metaphysically, to the supreme reality. Here there is no possibility of endless vicious circles, of being lost in a subjective fog of value that is valueless; every step of the way our feet are on solid rock. The rule or measure of human actions is the reason of man; the rule or measure of the reason of man is the world of things as they are; and the rule or measure of the world of reality, the world of things as they are, is the mind of the God of things as they are. Or, coming down the steps instead of climbing up, the mind of God is the architect's model to which the reality of things must correspond; the real world is the model by which the mind of man is measured; and the reason of man is the model to which the actions of man must conform.

This is important for any slightest insight into that extravagance peculiar to human relations with the divine—the faith that walks gaily through impenetrable darkness, the hope that no defeat can beat down, the love that is for ever doing impossible things. By this grasp of how things, and actions, and men are measured, we can see that the theological virtues are beyond measure. There is no excess or defect in faith, hope and charity; they have no rule, they have no measure. Rather they go straight to the rule and measure of everything, to God Himself. Any degree of these virtues exceeds all created rules; their perfection is limited only by the unlimited possibilities of the human mind and heart. A man who thinks he will reach heaven without sorrow for his sins is guilty of presumption, not because he has too much hope in God but because he overestimates himself, as the victim of despair underestimates himself. There is absolutely no limit to the flight of the human soul to God.

The modern contempt for some of the virtues was brought home to me in a conversation with an aviator whose sympathy for religious under their strict vows and for the sad plight of an unmarried clergy was touching. Eventually he confessed that he had never before talked to a priest; and for a very good reason. He lumped priests and ministers of all kinds in one delicate pink class whose chief avocation was gossiping with idle women and drinking tea. His attitude had been very much that of the precocious columnist who remarked that he would like to be present when the meek inherited the earth—to see the not-so-meek take the earth away from them.

Both of these men would be astounded to know that a man cannot have the virtue of meekness and not be strong, that sanctity and effeminacy are mutually exclusive terms, that in fact a man cannot have any virtue without having them all. Yet that is precisely the case.

We can put this briefly by saying that prudence, in the natural order, and charity, in the supernatural order, tie the virtues together very much as the soul binds together the powers of a man. Destroy the soul of a man and every one of his lesser powers ceases to exist; destroy those lesser powers of man, corrupt his body, and the soul departs. Prudence is the form of the natural virtues giving them life and movement to reason's end, just as charity is the form or soul of the supernatural virtues, giving them supernatural efficacy and movement to the end of charity, to God Himself.

The inter-connection of the virtues is as intimate and necessary as the union of soul and body. Let us consider the cardinal virtues (as do many of the Fathers) merely as general conditions of virtue: then discretion belongs to prudence, rectitude to justice, moderation to temperance and strength or constancy to fortitude. To attempt to picture any one of these virtues without the others and still call the resultant acts the strong, smooth, goal-gaining acts of virtue is ridiculous. The Jews, for example, with extraordinary righteousness flung the woman taken in adultery at the feet of Christ—but without discretion, without moderation, even without strength, for it was a cowardly thing to do.

Or let us take these cardinal virtues strictly as virtues, each busy with its own proper object. Then we have prudence as the chauffeur of the moral life, steering every action to the goal of reason; an act of fortitude, justice or temperance without prudence means that such acts are without order to the goal of reason, they blindly slam into the world of men and women regardless of results. And prudence is no less dependent on justice, fortitude and temperance. Whether it is a question of making things or of moulding human actions, in the field of the practical the starting-point is always the goal, not every goal, not a vague universal goal, but the immediate particular goal, as definite as the architect's goal of a house. These particular, immediate goals of human action are furnished to prudence by the moral virtues. In other words, the very principles from which prudence proceeds come from the moral virtues; while the whole direction of the moral virtues comes from prudence.

It is quite true that a famous criminal operated soup kitchens for the poor. Some champions of temperance have been notoriously imprudent, some of them quite unjust. A woman of the streets might be, indeed usually is, generous to the poor, the neglected, the weaklings. All these are facts. But they are not facts that militate against the strict connection of the virtues. At the very most these things can be called "imperfect virtues"; usually they are not virtues at all, but rather inclinations flowing from the physical make-up of the individual or from pity generated by personal experience. The criminal, the imprudent reformer and the woman of the streets produce these imitations of virtue to please themselves, because they like to do those things; not because reason dictates these acts, not because they are striding swiftly to the goal of reason. For, as a matter of fact, their contempt for other virtues is itself a contempt for reason and the goals of reason.

These are imitations wearing a false face of virtue, uninvited guests at the party of human respectability. They might escape detection in the crush at the height of the party; but if we watch them on their way home, if we notice the direction they take, what their goal is, it is immediately evident that they are impostors.

We can, indeed we must, carry this connection of the virtues much further, even up to the heights of charity. Prudence is the form that breathes life into the moral virtues in the natural order; and in the natural order that living moral organism is quite independent of charity.

It is at least possible that a pagan without charity should have a very high degree of the four cardinal virtues. But evidently the supernatural moral virtues are something else again. They come with grace and charity, exist only for the goal of charity and are lost completely with the loss of charity. Charity in the supernatural order occupies the same place as is occupied by prudence in the natural order: its task is to steer every activity of man, every other virtue, to the supreme supernatural end of man. Without that helmsman there is no possibility of any member of the crew reaching port. We can put this even more strongly by saying that life goes out of these supernatural virtues with the passing of their soul, which is charity; they are dead, and, with regard to the infused moral virtues, that means that they are non-existent.

With the other theological virtues, it means that they are dead in the sense that without charity they cannot move a step towards the goal of life which is the goal of charity. The directive power is missing. But they are not non-existent as are the infused moral virtues. A man tears down his whole spiritual structure by mortal sin; but the foundations of faith and hope are still there for the work of rebuilding. It is only by presumption, despair and infidelity that man can totally destroy the work of God in the building up of his second nature. Faith and hope remain but imperfect, crippled, ineffective virtues which bring man no nearer to the goal which is the reason for all virtue.

Of course all this is true the other way around. To postulate charity without the moral virtues is like expecting a painter of miniatures to produce perfect specimens of his art with a whitewash brush. It is an insult to God, making the inference that He works much more clumsily in the order of grace than in the order of nature, for in nature He furnishes not only the drive to the goal but the means by which that goal can be realized. The same is true of the relation of charity to faith and hope. Charity is love. That a man has charity means that he is in love with God, that he has a love that is in a very real sense divine. Could that love exist without faith in the Lover, without hope in His strength and fidelity?

This is the high standard of perfect virtue. This is the closely-woven fabric of man's second nature; not a thread can be pulled out without the whole unravelling. But this does not make the second nature of man a standardized unit like the product of a mass-production factory. Saints do not come tumbling out of the workshop of virtue as alike as two cigarettes tumbling out of the same machine; nor do the virtues themselves follow one another about looking as much alike as identical quintuplets. Of course one is greater than another, charity, for example, and temperance; that is perhaps why they fit so beautifully together. And of course one man can be more virtuous than another, or more perfectly virtuous at one stage of his life than at another. There is a certain latitude in virtue, as there is in all things human, a scope which stretches from minimum requirements to full perfection, the distance between the humble Catholic barely squeezing between the closing doors of purgatory and the saint rushing directly into the arms of God. But there is too a certain equality, an inevitable equality, in the growth of the virtues in any one man, an equality of proportion like that of the growth of the fingers on a man's hand in spite of the difference in size between those fingers. A man may have more inclination to one virtue than to another, whether that inclination has its roots in his physical nature, in long hard practice, or in grace. But the actual increase in virtue is not a race that leaves some of the virtues trailing far in the rear, gasping for enough breath to keep them alive.

Within the great clan of the virtues there are varying degrees of beauty, excellence, perfection. One branch of the family has a clear claim to nobility: the intellectual virtues perfect the highest faculty of man. In a sense they have a right to be a little superior; but they are a sterile branch, limiting their activities to the perfection of that one faculty—producing good mathematicians or good carpenters, but not good men.

Still, remembering the high place of reason and the pre-eminence of reason in the direction of human life to its goal and even in the actual possession of that goal, it is as easy to graduate the moral virtues as it is to trace a family likeness. Justice stands at the top—it comes closest to reason, it resides in the rational appetite, and like reason it is not content to stay within man himself but extends to all his relations to others, even to God. Next comes fortitude, again because it has more of reason, it brings greater realms under the sway of reason and bows down to reason the very appetite that has to do with life and death. At the bottom of the scale is temperance, regulating the appetite for the things that contribute to the life of the individual and the life of the species.

Within the intellectual branch of the family of virtue, wisdom stands at the very top because it aims at the highest perfection of the highest faculty, it includes within and reserves to its own judgment the far-flung fields of all the intellectual virtues. In the same way charity stands at the summit of the theological virtues, as aiming at the highest goal of all goals, directly at God. We can extend this perfection of charity further and say quite accurately that it is the absolutely supreme virtue, for its object is the goal which is the very reason for the existence of all the other virtues; the others are steps on the way to the final resting-place which has belonged to charity from the beginning.

It is a beautifully balanced product, this second nature of man. One part blends into another with all the delicacy and unobtrusiveness of twilight fading into darkness. But it has all the sturdiness of hard, solid stone. True enough we can blast away the whole supernatural structure by mortal sin; and we can undermine the edifice of natural virtue by neglect or by serious cultivation of the vices. But short of all that, virtue carries on indefatigably up to the very gates of Paradise. What then? How much of all this laboriously wrought second nature will endure into and through eternity?

Of course the saints in heaven do not have to repress inordinate desires for food or drink, they do not have to steel themselves to endure suffering and death, or to resist temptations to theft. The material of the moral virtues is missing in heaven, except justice's constant rendering to God the things that are God's; but the perfect order those virtues strove to impress upon our lives is there in all its perfection. Much the same is true of the intellectual virtues. Their formal element, the ideas we so laboriously acquired during life, will certainly remain, for they are part of the intellect's equipment; but just as certainly, until the general resurrection, all the elements of our act of understanding which have a measure of dependence on physical nature—the phantasms, the process of abstraction from the phantasms, the recurrence to phantasms—cannot remain.

There is certainly no room for faith, hope or charity in hell; and in heaven what need is there of faith when we are seeing God face to face, or of hope of attaining His blessed presence when we are eternally united to Him? Charity alone, of all the virtues, remains in its full and perfect operation; for in this life its work is to unite us to God, and that is a work which it will continue to enjoy through all the long stretches of eternity.

Let us go back to the workshop from which we started this chapter. It is all cleaned up now, the odds and ends have been gathered up, things put in order, the shavings swept off the floor. There is the finished product of man's second nature before our eyes. Humanity has every reason for a great pride in that product. It represents the slow, careful, minutely detailed labour of many years. It has been built up, stone upon stone, by patient hands, by hearts that refused to be discouraged, by hands and hearts such as flung the medieval cathedrals against the sky even though the daring gesture took hundreds of years. It is like a path through a wilderness that only thousands of steps by feet that were too often weary could ever beat into such smooth hardness. Its progress was like the conquering of a wide empire which allows no slackening of command, of discipline, of vigilance or of alert devotion to the emperor, reason. It is what a man can become, must become, if he is to be worthy of his manhood, if he is to make the most of those tremendous energies, high hopes and keen vision that are his peculiar gift.

Yet we must stand amazed before it like the craftsman before the beauty of his work, wondering if after all we could have produced it. If we are completely frank with ourselves as we look at that completed product of man's second nature, we realize that actually we are looking upon the inner workings of sanctity—for sanctity is the goal of virtue as it is the goal of life. In the face of sanctity the most thoroughgoing egoist is reduced to humble wonder. Is it not an incredible thing that man should be lifted up to the heights of God and live the life of God? Yet what else does sanctity mean? And we understand better why God takes such a personal interest in this work, why He throws all the force of His divine ingenuity into the making of that supernatural second nature by which man can come to God now that God has come to him.

It is an incredible thing, this personal interest of God. Even more incredible is the set of tools He has delivered into man's hands, the almost miraculous instruments that turn the passing gesture of a man into eternal music, the yearnings of human love into a divine fruition, the vague gropings of a stumbling mind into the vision of the face of God. But all this is incredible only because we try to measure the generosity of God in terms of the generosity of man. Only because we are so very small is it difficult for us to believe that there can be One so very big.

There it is. The finished product of the united efforts of God and man, second nature at its best, an array of habits of happiness that marches stoutly to the goal of man, the vision of God.

CHAPTER XII

(OUTLINE)

THE BREATH OF HAPPINESS

(Q. 68–70)

1. Historical visits of the Holy Ghost:
    (*a*) Annunciation.
    (*b*) Baptism of Christ.
    (*c*) Pentecost and the Apostles.

2. Christ's promise of the Holy Ghost and His work.

3. The Holy Ghost and Christ's followers to-day:
    (*a*) The Church.
    (*b*) Individual Catholics: gifts, fruits and beatitudes.

4. Immediate preparation for divine-human action—the gifts:
    (*a*) Their purpose.
    (*b*) Their nature.
    (*c*) Their necessity for salvation.
    (*d*) Their number.
    (*e*) Their relation to the virtues.

5. Divine-human action—the fruits and beatitudes:
    (*a*) That action in general—the fruits of the Holy Ghost:
        (1) Their significance and distinction from beatitudes.
        (2) The field of this action: man in himself, among his equals, towards his inferiors.
    (*b*) In particular—in its perfection: the beatitudes:
        (1) Distinction from virtues and gifts.
        (2) Their double content—disposition and beginning of heavenly life (merit and reward).
        (3) The work of the beatitudes in voluptuous, active and contemplative life.
        (4) The rewards of the beatitudes and of human life, voluptuous, active and contemplative.
        (5) An accumulation of happiness.

Conclusion :

1. A justification of astonishment:
   (*a*) The usual effect of divine action.
   (*b*) Of complete change.

2. Paradoxes of Christian life:
   (*a*) Having nothing but possessing all things.
   (*b*) Losing life and finding it.

3. The ordinary Catholic and the breath of divine life.

CHAPTER XII

THE BREATH OF HAPPINESS

(Q. 68–70)

IN this chapter we are stepping into the region of unspeakable things, of things that are properly seen only by the eye of God, into a region that has been one of impenetrable darkness to the mind of man from the beginning. It is a region of mysterious and paradoxical things, like lights too bright to be seen or sounds too loud to be heard; like sights and sounds that leave a man blind and deaf by their very superabundance. Yet to us it is a friendly, familiar darkness, like the darkness in a home we have known from infancy, or of a house that has been so perfectly described to us that we find our way about easily, without fear, without stumbling, without hesitation, even very often without wonder.

In this chapter we are to examine nothing less than the movement of divinity, the activity of the Holy Ghost. It was a field particularly dear to St. Thomas as a Dominican, for a Dominican is himself a paradox whose only explanation is a burning love of truth; and of course one in love with truth is enthusiastically interested in every detail of the doings of the Spirit of Truth, the Holy Ghost.

There is a certain characteristic in these activities of the Spirit of Truth, we might say almost a divine trademark stamping them as belonging to the Third Person of the Blessed Trinity. It is somehow fitting that we should depict the Holy Ghost under the symbol of a dove; for the outstanding characteristic that marks His works is one of flowing grace, swift power silently speeding down only to soar up to greater heights. When the angel Gabriel told Mary of the coming work of the Holy Ghost he insisted that "the Holy Ghost shall come upon thee, and the power of the most High shall overshadow thee"; at the baptism of Christ, the dove was seen to come down, hovering over His head; on Pentecost Sunday there was the sound of a mighty wind filling the house, and tongues of fire sat upon each one of them. In each case that powerful sweep from above. And in each case a soaring to heights, possible to men only by a very great change. From the low hills of Galilee the pure maid of the royal house was snatched up to the heights of divine maternity; the simple Carpenter of Nazareth, by a change not real but symbolic for our instruction, became the crusading Messiah whose victorious throne was a cross; twelve weak, badly frightened men became the fearless apostles whose footsteps made the square stones of every Roman road echo a march of victory wider than a Cæsar's dream. And men, looking on, saw only darkness: a quiet woman from an obscure Jewish village, a criminal hanging on the cross, twelve madmen whose end could only be death.

All this was not the end but only the beginning of an activity by the Holy Ghost which would become so frequent as to be commonplace to us, though it always remained impenetrable darkness to a mere spectator. Christ at the last supper encouraged the despondent apostles by His assurance that He would not leave them alone, that He would not leave them orphans, but would send them the Holy Ghost, the Comforter, who would teach them "all things and bring all things to your mind, whatsoever I shall have said to you". A significant promise! It is an assurance of the constant presence and activity of the Comforter and the supreme Teacher, of the Spirit of Love and the Spirit of Truth; an assurance that men, for all the coming centuries, will be soaring to ever new heights of truth and love, while other men peer into darkness.

Men, understand; not merely an institution. Twenty centuries of infallible pronouncement and defence of truth, twenty centuries of dogged loyalty to the Master on the part of the Church do not exhaust that promise. It is a promise made also to individuals. A very rich meal, masterfully cooked, is rarely appreciated by those to whom it is served; it is more or less taken for granted by jaded appetites. But let a hungry man express his appreciation, not by words but by actions; or give the gourmand the time and opportunity to savour each morsel! Very often we Catholics are neither starved for spiritual things nor have we the keen, critical, insatiable appetite that alone does credit to the spiritual banquets served to us. And so the fact that this activity of the Holy Ghost is a personal matter to everyone of us, that every individual Catholic by the gifts, fruits and beatitudes of the Holy Ghost is the subject of this breath-taking activity of the Spirit of Truth, is practically taken for granted. Yet in us, as in those others, the divine trade-mark is always the same.

The activity of the Spirit of Truth within us is summed up prosaically in the three terms: the gifts, fruits and beatitudes of the Holy Ghost. But even such a cursory glance as we are able to give these three reveals something of the glory of Pentecost in our daily lives, something of the divine trade-mark of the Holy Ghost.

Perhaps we can understand this best if we keep in mind that notion of breathing upon, of inspiration, of swift, easy movement. Looking upon man as the subject of movement, as one moved, we can see immediately that the movers of man, the effective movers, are just two: reason within man himself, and God. Now the whole purpose of the gifts is to get man ready for the movement of God, to dispose him for easy speeding along the path towards the altogether supernatural goal of the vision of God. That some special preparation is necessary seems evident. Quite recently in this country we turned to high-speed railroad travel. On some roads the desired speed was obtained by simply perfecting the locomotives, on others not only the locomotives but every car on the train was specially built with that high speed in mind. The difference between a ride on a very old coach behind one of these high-speed locomotives and a trip on one of the streamlined trains makes concrete the difference between a perfect disposition in the thing moved and a disposition not nearly so perfect. Or, to take an example much nearer home, in the explanation of a particularly difficult doctrine the preliminary notions, the foundations which prepare the mind for that doctrine, are absolutely essential; and the more difficult the doctrine, the more perfect must be that preparation.

That is precisely the work of these gifts. They are gifts, not merely because they come from God, but because they prepare us, in a way totally above our own powers, for prompt, easy movement under the inspiration of God. For the movement of reason, man is prepared by the virtues; for the movement of God, by the gifts of the Holy Ghost. We have summed up the absolute need of that preparation by the virtues by saying that if the same effort were required for every one of his acts as is necessary for the first, all man's progress, indeed all his action, would soon cease from sheer exhaustion. If, for example, every man had to put the same effort into walking as does the infant just learning to walk, how many twenty-mile hikes would ever have been taken? But after habits have been acquired, after man is more perfectly disposed for the movement by reason, the actions flow ever more easily, more perfectly. The preparation for the movement by God is no less necessary.

In fact so necessary is this preparation for divine action, that every man must have these gifts of the Holy Ghost if he is to save his soul. A young externe, starting his career as a surgeon, does quite a good job with an experienced surgeon looking over his shoulder; but he needs that older head for a while because the art of surgery is not yet perfectly his. The moon on a summer night does a fair job of shining; but because the light it gives is not its own, it badly needs the sun if it is to continue to give that silvery light. With us, in what is our own, what belongs to our very nature, we need no particular help. But the fact is the whole supernatural life, supernatural action and supernatural goal are not our own, they are not a part of our very nature; the supernatural virtues do a good job of making that supernatural life possible, but we need something more to follow the swift divine instinct which makes supernatural action an actuality.

That extra help we get through the gifts of the Holy Ghost. Just what are they? Let us turn back for a moment to our chapters on the virtues. There we said that the whole work of the moral virtues was to make the appetites of man, rational and sensitive, readily obedient to man; the gifts of the Holy Ghost can be accurately compared to these moral virtues. As the appetites of man are made obedient, easily subordinate, to reason by the moral virtues, so the whole man is made obedient, easily subordinate, readily moved by the Holy Ghost through the gifts. Like the moral virtues, then, these gifts are habits. Thoroughly mysterious, extraordinary in their effects, yes. But utterly prosaic in their character of habits. They are a part of the supernatural furnishings of the house of our souls; we can bump into them, stumble over them, profit by them, forget about them as we do with an old familiar chair. That is often exactly what we do. It would seem as though it were a part of our human pride to be unimpressed until we are overwhelmed and to forget as quickly as possible that we have been overwhelmed.

The gifts have all the characteristics of other habits; but they are in no sense prosaic. True enough, like all habits, they are immediate principles of action. If we are looking for them we have only to look where all the other habits of man are crowded together like a mass of intricate cables, in the two great power-houses of human activity: the reason and the appetites of man. In reason we will find the gifts of understanding, knowledge, wisdom and counsel; in the appetite there are the gifts of piety, fortitude and fear. Like all other habits they have a solid permanency about them that makes us look on them as a part of us, like friendly slippers or a comfortable chair. But unlike all other habits, they produce their acts in a fashion not human but angelic or divine.

This last point is important for an understanding of the gifts. That divine-human action which proceeds from the gifts is our action but produced in a way far superior to our mode of acting. Take, for example, the gifts perfecting the intellect by completing the virtue of faith. By the gift of understanding we penetrate revealed truths, not by pondering over them, deducing conclusions from them or thinking up arguments to bolster them; but swiftly, instantaneously, intuitively, with an action like the flashing dart of an angelic intellect or the probing glance of God. By the gifts of knowledge and wisdom we judge created things and divine things in this same way; not by laboriously comparing concepts as a child might painfully trace the resemblance of two pictures, but rather in a flash that gives us the conclusion without the slow hobbling steps of reason down the hill to that conclusion. By the gift of counsel we apply these truths to individual works, but again in that swift, infallible, angelic way. The gift of piety perfecting the proper action of justice, i.e. the actions which have reference to others, fortitude perfecting the appetite against fear of dangers, fear perfecting the appetite against inordinate pleasure, all have this same divine mode of action. The Holy Ghost is breathing upon us.

But these actions are ours. It is a mistake many authors make to-day to suppose that we are passive instruments under the action of the Holy Ghost; that He is doing the moving and we are passively moved. An adult makes an error against tact when he offers to carry a child who has just learned to walk, or to work out a puzzle for a child who is quite sure it can solve the problem alone. The child is insulted, resentful at this reflection on its own powers. God is never tactless. What we can do He allows us, indeed encourages us to do, He demands that we use our powers to their utmost; what we cannot do He generously makes possible to us by His help. God is very careful not to do our thinking, our knowing, our desiring for us; in fact not even God could know or desire for us. That we must do for ourselves. The astonishing beauty of this whole action of the Holy Ghost in us is not the marvel of divine action—we have long known the infinite possibilities of God; it is the fact that these actions are ours. The mode of acting is God's, the very possibility of the action comes from God, but it is our reason that intuitively penetrates, judges, counsels; it is our appetite that plunges instantly to the heart and perfection of good. That vital assimilation of truth and goodness can come from no other but ourselves.

With all their glory, there is a note of humility about the gifts which brings them close to our human hearts. Utter perfection, unless it be the warm, sharing perfection of God, frightens us by its cold beauty. So in human affairs, high walls shutting off one heart from another often come tumbling down at some little sign of weakness—a tear, a stumble, a defeat. It is not with real regret but with a feeling of friendliness that we see the gifts taking second place among the virtues. Their work is very much like the work of the moral virtues: the one perfects the faculties of man in relation to the movement of reason, the other, the whole man in relation to the movement of the Holy Ghost. Just as the moral virtues are inferior to and dependent on the intellectual virtues perfecting reason itself, so the gifts are inferior to and dependent on the theological virtues which have God Himself for their object. Again, just as the moral virtues are connected in and dependent on prudence, so the gifts are connected one with another in charity and dependent on charity. They come together with grace and charity, and with charity they go; there is no such thing as the possession of one gift without the others, though indeed the operation of one may predominate in one individual.

The gifts prepare us. With these divine habits in our soul we are like an aeroplane drawn up to a starting line as its motors get the last warming up; it is straining to go, almost lifting itself off the ground, in need only of the petty touch of the pilot's hands to go soaring off. But in our case, we are not merely driven as is the 'plane; the flight is ours as well as the Holy Spirit's. We are ready for the divine-human action which is called the fruit of the Holy Ghost. That is the very simple difference between the virtues, the gifts and the fruits; the virtues and gifts are habits, the fruits are the result of habits—they are acts.

The term "fruit" is itself significant. It practically demands a bit of dreaming, as the scent of a flower in midwinter will snatch us out of ourselves into a forgotten summer day's caress of sun and wind. We are almost doing the word an injustice if we do not have a picture of long rows of old trees, gnarled like an old woman's hands which have seen too much hard work. And there is in the word "fruit" something like the pride of accomplishment, that makes the woman forget her hands, looking back over the years and see what those hands have made possible for a son or a daughter. Just so a tired old tree could look back through the long days from the first budding leaves, through the beauty of blossom and the anxious days of young fruit, to this final day when the ripe, luscious fruit is offered as the supreme accomplishment and the tree prepares to die for another winter.

In this case man is the tree. The fruit of man is his action. There is the same note of finality about the actions of man, a finality to be explained only by looking back along the rough road that made this action a reality;

and there is the same fullness, the same lusciousness about them, for in them is packed all that man has to offer. It is the final offering, the supreme accomplishment of virtues, natural and supernatural, and of the gifts. Sometimes the fruit is rotten, and its rottenness finds its explanation deep in the man who produced it. This was the foundation of Paul's startling contrast: "Now the works (i.e. fruits) of the flesh are manifest, which are fornication, uncleanness, immodesty, luxury, idolatry, witchcrafts, enmities, contentions, emulations, wraths, quarrels, dissensions, sects, envies, murders, drunkenness, revellings and such like. . . ." ". . . But the fruit of the Spirit is charity, joy, peace, patience, benignity, goodness, longanimity, mildness, faith, modesty, continency, chastity. Against such there is no law" (Gal. v. 19).

There is a humourless trick which consists in the endless enumeration of details when the details are infinite and simply cannot be enumerated. It is the trick which has made so unpleasant huge tomes bent crooked with their load of footnotes, university dissertations with their staggering bibliographies and philosophers with endless authorities for things that need apology rather than confirmation. Fortunately St. Paul had a sense of humour. What a weary book he would have written if he had tried to name all the fruits of man and the Holy Ghost! One can find plenty of reasons for Paul's stopping at twelve.

Even with these twelve St. Paul, in the estimation of St. Thomas, covered roughly the field of human action. After all, the joint work of ourselves and the Holy Ghost is limited by our very nature; when we have spoken of man's actions in relation to himself, to his equals and to his inferiors, we have fairly covered the human field, for of course in perfecting himself he is acting in relation to his superiors. It is under these three headings that St. Thomas divides the fruits of the Holy Ghost as given by St. Paul.

The disposition of a man in himself is either to good or evil. In other words, we start from the rock-bottom of all human activity and see man disposed to good through love and we have the first of the fruits, "charity"—an act, not the theological virtue. Then comes the immediate consequence of love which is "joy", followed by the perfection of joy which is "peace"—not the stagnant peace of inactivity, but the progressive, vigorous peace of a heart undisturbed by outside attractions and free from the horrors of civil war, a streamlined peace of ordered energies concentrating on the one goal.

In relation to evil, man is protected from the confusion and turmoil of imminent évil by "patience"; and from the over-long delay of looked-for good by "longanimity".

Relative to our neighbour, we will to do him good and the fruit is "goodness"; we can put that will to work and we have "benignity"; receiving evil from our neighbour, we tolerate it with equanimity and we have "meekness"; we refrain from injuring that neighbour by deceit or cheating and we have "faith". Relative to inferiors, we have "modesty" in external actions, and "continency" and "chastity" in our internal actions. The whole is in vigorous contrast to the subversive, disintegrating, befouling fruits of the flesh enumerated by St. Paul.

In this matter of detailed enumeration, his Master showed a greater sense of humour than did Paul; surely He showed a profound knowledge of and consideration for us who were to try so clumsily to follow the long strides He took on His way to the Father. Out of all these fruits of man and the Holy Ghost, Christ carefully picked the outstanding, the most perfect, we might say the heroic fruits; then He gave His special blessing to those who should produce these fruits, leaving us the eight beatitudes as the cream of the crop, the most proper effects of the divine-human action coming from the gifts of the Holy Ghost. There is no mistaking Christ's special emphasis on these eight acts;

but with an eye to our facility for making mistakes where mistakes are apparently impossible, He outlined these eight targets of our highest efforts in a way that made them conspicuous to the blindest of human beings. To each of these acts He attached an explicit reward. Not only an eternal reward which might be far distant, but a reward that should begin here on this earth, a reward that we can reach out for now and put in our pockets.

In each of these beatitudes, then, a double element is to be seen: an element of merit (the act itself) and an element of reward. It was as though Christ, knowing we would always remain children, realized that we would most certainly forget many things while running that short errand from birth to death; but with rewards promised immediately for these eight fruits, surely we would not forget them. Looking at this double element of the beatitudes from the vantage point of happiness, we see the element of merit as a disposition for happiness, the reward itself as the beginning, or—in heaven—the consummation of happiness.

The beatitudes, as their name implies, fall immediately into the classifications of happiness possible to men. Whether we are looking over the shoulder of Christ two thousand years ago, peering at medieval castles through the eyes of Aquinas seven hundred years ago, or glancing about the streets of a twentieth-century city, we see the same possibilities of happiness seized on by men. Then, as now, men sought happiness in voluptuousness (the affluence of riches, honour or passion), in activity or in contemplation. The first is an impediment to the true happiness of man, the second can well be a disposition to the true happiness of man, while the third in its imperfect state is the beginning of that happiness, in its perfect state, the very essence of that happiness which is the goal of mankind.

Since there is no human act worthy of the name which is not pointed to or away from true happiness, these highest acts of man—the merit of the beatitudes—are most intimately wrapped up with that happiness; they of all others go directly to the goal.

The falseness and irrationality of voluptuousness, the fact that it is a positive impediment to happiness, make it the object of attack for every good habit within man; the attack of the gifts is devastating. While the virtues move a man to moderate the use of riches and honours, the gifts make man totally despise them, make men "poor in spirit". Again the virtues moderate the fears, hopes and angers of the irascible appetite, while the gifts set man tranquilly free from them, make men "meek"; the virtues counselling moderate use of the concupiscible appetite's delights and sorrows cannot compare with the bold strokes of the gifts completely rejecting these things when necessary, or voluntarily assuming them in the face of necessity—so there are those "who mourn".

In the active life the work of the gifts is not to attack, but, with a shouting enthusiasm, to transcend the dreams of men. The happiness of the active life can come only from our double action towards our neighbour: the action of justice or of liberality, of giving what is due or spontaneously giving of our substance to those who are joined to us by some bond. The justice of the gifts is an eager justice, like the grasp of a man dying of thirst for a bottle of water; it is a hungering and thirsting after justice for which eagerness is a languid word. Their liberality is not limited by bonds of union, but by any and every necessity that allows that liberality to come into play; a liberality that is a rampantly charging mercy.

The contemplative life of men on earth is not so much a merit of happiness in itself, but rather a beginning of happiness. It has about it the quiet security and aloofness of a frail child marked for an early entry into heaven. The merit assigned for the beatitudes having to do with the contemplative life is really a merit of the active life, an effect of the gifts and virtues perfecting man in himself, making him clean of heart (unstained by passion or ignorance) or perfecting him in relation to his neighbour by giving him peace.

These are the heights to which men soar on the wings of the Spirit of Love and of Truth: poverty of spirit, meekness of heart, recognition of and regret for mistakes, a hungering justice, an unquestioning mercy, cleanness of heart and peace. In this way shall man escape the fruits of the flesh, to these ends shall man devote the tremendous energies of a nature that mirrors divinity, by these acts shall man taste on earth something of the happiness of heaven.

For the rewards are concrete and immediate; yet they are only a beginning, a foretaste of what is to come, like the snack given to a child impatiently waiting for the serving of Christmas dinner. Yet these very rewards are as paradoxical as a virgin who is yet a mother, a Man who is God, or ignorant fishermen who are teachers of all the world. Probably no single truth gives us a clearer insight into the profound meaning of St. Paul's magnificent paradox than does this truth of the rewards of the beatitudes: " . . . as dying and behold we live; as chastised and not killed; as sorrowful, yet always rejoicing; as needy, yet enriching many; as having nothing, and possessing all things".[1]

For the excellence and abundance men seek in honours and riches, the poor in spirit, despising honours and riches, receive the excellence and abundance of the good things of God, the source of all good things—the Kingdom of Heaven. The security and quiet possession that fighting men seek by quarrels and wars, the meek have given them; a solidity of possession of eternal goods that no word of ours will express except that firm, unyielding term "earth", "land". For the consolation against life's labours and sorrows which

[1] 2 Cor. vi. 9 and 10.

is sought in the pleasures of the world, those who mourn have the consolation of the Comforter Himself.

It is the same story in the active life of men—the old story, the paradoxical story that is characteristic of the meeting of divinity and humanity, "he that loseth his life shall find it". While unjust men roam the long highways of the world plundering, taking what belongs to others that they might have their fill of temporal goods, those who thirst for justice shall be filled, filled with the joy and consolation of the Holy Ghost, filled with the good things of God. While men and women carefully push the misery of others from sight and mind in an attempt to escape the inescapable, they merely put themselves outside the bounds of a mercy that belongs to the merciful who have sought out misery to receive mercy. And as the final rewards, rewards which the heart of man cannot conceive, come the vision of God to the clean of heart and the sonship of God to the peacemakers who have so closely imitated their Father Who is in Heaven.

All through this discussion of the beatitudes mention has been made of only seven. The eighth has not really been lost or overlooked. Although with seven gifts, twelve fruits and eight beatitudes to be treated in one chapter, it might seem not unlikely that at least one should be forgotten. The real reason for not mentioning the eighth beatitude has been that it does not need to be mentioned; understanding the other seven, we have a good grasp of the eighth, for the eighth is a summary both of the merit and the reward, of the work and the happiness of the other seven. Martyrdom lifts man to the heights of divine-human action and gives him instantly the fullness of reward; "those who suffer persecution for justice sake" quite fittingly are given the kingdom of heaven. In that work are all works, as in that reward are all rewards.

In fact each of these beatitudes is a summary of what has gone before; they are not disconnected, unrelated acts but progressive steps to always greater happiness. To possess something is much greater than simply to have it for the moment, for much that we have we do not firmly and peacefully possess. Even what is ours is often possessed with difficulty and sorrow to which consolation adds a note of perfection; and being filled with consolation, filled with the Comforter Himself, is much more than a passing smile of pity or a momentary handclasp of sympathy. Going swiftly up these steps—we receive the mercy which, makes consolation unnecessary, we see the face of God which is the supreme mercy and finally we are sons of God. Beyond this even the ingenious generosity of God could lift only one creature making her His mother.

All this is not only a matter of eternity; it has its beginnings here and now. Now as in the beginning men are astonished. The crowds of Jerusalem were astonished listening to the Apostles and hearing every man his own tongue; and that astonishment never died down while the Apostles lived. Men and nations have never recovered from the astonishment of seeing God nailed to a cross, of seeing a Jewish maiden holding God, her Son, in her arms. Of course they were astonished. Men have always been astonished at sight of divine activity in the world of men. Christ walked up and down Palestine working miracles and leaving behind him a trail of very great fear. For what is astonishment but a form of fear, a fear that either drives us to our knees or sends us raging blindly to destroy what has awakened that fear; to kneel before the Cross with Mary and arise to follow the footprints of the apostles, or to tear Christ from the Cross, Mary from her throne and draw the curtain of oblivion across the dramatic picture of apostolic courage.

Now, as then, men are astonished, are afraid. They see a complete change, a startling change, yet peering they can find no explanation but only impenetrable darkness. The human eye cannot see into these realms, for they are divine. The careful preparation of the soul of man by the virtues and gifts is a secret of God's and the soul, a secret that might never disturb the equanimity of men. But the divine-human action of the fruits and the beatitudes is something that no human being can ignore; it comes from God, and God, whether we like the fact or not, is the beginning and the end of every human heart. No human being can stand in the crowd along the road and see God passing by without crying out—in prayer or in hatred. The part of the Holy Ghost in this sublime action is itself enough to bring the strong legions of men to a clashing halt.

But when the incredible truth is met face to face, the truth that this soaring to heights undreamt of by men is still the action of men, there is reason for astonishment, for fear, for angry disbelief! To see utterly drab men and women snatching the prizes of happiness by turning their backs on all that the heroes of the world have treasured, is to see again the victory of the Cross and the death in the arena of the conquerors of death. It is to see the gifts of the Holy Ghost at work. It is to come face to face again with the eternal paradox that takes its rise from the blending of the energies of God and man, to meet again the "things that cannot be and that are", to see men and women having nothing but possessing all things, losing their lives that they might find them. And that is very often too much for the pride of men.

Yet as long as there lives one follower of Christ, this divine breath of happiness will lift men beyond the stars. In the soul of every Catholic in the state of grace there is that full equipment of virtues and gifts. For our very salvation these gifts are necessary—and their acts are the fruits and the beatitudes.

CHAPTER XIII

(OUTLINE)

HABITS OF UNHAPPINESS

(Q. 71–74)

1. The familiar but strange face of sin:
   - (*a*) Denied to be embraced.
   - (*b*) Denied to be shunned.
   - (*c*) Recognized to be fought.

2. Sin and human nature:
   - (*a*) Denial of possibility of sin an insult to humanity.
   - (*b*) Recognition of possibility of sin a tribute to humanity.
   - (*c*) Commission of sin a betrayal of humanity.

3. A contrast of friend and enemy: virtue and vice;
   - (*a*) Their incompatibility.
   - (*b*) A definition of sin (Augustine).

4. Distinguishing marks of sin:
   - (*a*) Its accidental character.
   - (*b*) Its motive or object: God, self, neighbour.
   - (*c*) Some non-specific distinctions of sin:
     - (1) Mortal and venial.
     - (2) Commission and omission.
     - (3) Thought, word, deed.
   - (*d*) Place of circumstances.

5. The disorder of sin:
   - (*a*) A step towards chaos.
   - (*b*) Inequality of sins:
     - (1) Essential gravity.
     - (2) Carnal and spiritual sins compared.
     - (3) Factors in gravity of sins:
       - *a*. Will and sense appetites.
       - *b*. Circumstances.
       - *c*. Damage done.
       - *d*. Condition of person sinned against.
       - *e*. Condition of sinner.

6. The home of sin.

Conclusion:

1. Sin and the modern world:
   - (*a*) Hatred of sin by Christ and by the modern world.
   - (*b*) Foundations of modern stand:
     - (1) Misconception of sin.
     - (2) "Not strong enough to fail."

2. Sin and successful living:
   - (*a*) Individual life.
   - (*b*) Social life.
   - (*c*) Divine life.

3. Sin and happiness.

CHAPTER XIII

HABITS OF UNHAPPINESS

(Q. 71–74)

TO continue with this volume we must literally come down to earth. In our last chapter we scaled the heights of human possibilities in the line of virtue, in the climb towards happiness. Beginning in this chapter we must start to dig down, to look into the depths of human possibilities in quite another direction, in the direction of unhappiness, of sin. For it is true that in every one of us there are unsuspected possibilities of sanctity and of vice, of success and failure.

I think we are indeed down to earth again when we start this chapter by observing the technique of a great insurance company; at least we have come down a long way when we have passed from the activities of the Holy Ghost to the activities of an insurance company. The insurance company of which I am speaking has adopted a method of procedure well known to St. Thomas and spread it all over America in full-page advertisements in practically all magazines. The business of that insurance company is to keep people alive as long as possible; no one regrets a funeral more than an insurance company. In order to do that, the company has seen that it is not enough to tell people where good health lies, what it looks like and what its benefits are; it is also necessary, indeed more necessary, to see to it that people understand what ill health is, what it looks like, its symptoms, dangers, remedies and preventions.

The business of St. Thomas was to lead men to happiness. To do that he recognized seven hundred years ago, as did Christ two thousand years ago, that it was not enough to talk about virtue, to explain what it was, how it worked, its full benefit of happiness; it was also necessary to say a great deal about sin—what it is, what it looks like, its symptoms, dangers, remedies and preventions. The insurance company is not an enemy of human health because it warns so emphatically against sickness; nor are theologians enemies of human happiness because they warn us so constantly against human misery in its acute form of sin.

The insurance company stands solidly against the enemy of man's body; the theologian, against the enemy of man's soul. One is the sworn opponent of the enemy of human health; the other of human happiness. Both are fighting in the name of humanity. Yet the one has all the world for an ally; the other fights alone. Our nation and our time is always on the alert for the enemy of health, positively eager to talk about symptoms, operations, infallible remedies. But of the enemy of happiness?

Our time certainly does not want to hear about sin. To many, such an enemy as sin cannot be admitted as existing; because sin makes such a charming companion for a while, thinking of it as an enemy would spoil it all. We have an attitude like that of a small boy who stoutly denies the existence of measles and disregards all warnings because he sees great possibilities in a good case of measles. There is no sin, there cannot be, it is silly to be careful about sin—because after all sin holds out some tremendous possibilities.

Still others wander through the streets of life carefully side-stepping sin, crossing the street to avoid the remotest contact with it. And all the time they proclaim to the world that their peculiar actions have no special meaning, they are a little eccentric, perhaps a little insane; but there really is no such thing as sin. There is no such enemy to run from; please do not pay any attention to the spiritual gas-masks, rifles, bayonets and hand-grenades—these are just little eccentricities adding a touch of gaiety to life like the trappings of a masquerade ball.

There is finally that alertly courageous group that refuses to surrender and refuses to run; the men and women who may be beaten to earth again and again but are still "strong enough to fail" and to fight again. This group looks on sin as the rest of the world looks on sickness, recognizing sin as just as much, indeed very much more, of an enemy. It is an enemy, therefore something to be fought. It is not to be hidden in the bosom of our families, not to be ignored while it does its deadly work, not to be wished out of existence, but to be recognized as the peculiar problem of humanity.

While sickness is something we have in common with all living things, sin is an enemy about which only men have to worry. Sin is the story of man's failure; and only man can fail because only man can succeed. Only man has control of his actions. Sulphuric acid never makes the mistake of freezing a man instead of burning him, nor does a dog make mistakes though he does meet with accidents. To say there is no sin is to insult the humanity of man; it is to put man in the class of inanimate or brute creation every moment of which is fixed, every step accounted for along the narrow path laid out by necessary physical laws from the very beginning. To deny the possibility of sin is to deny the humanity of man or to make him a freak in nature.

The recognition of the possibilities of sin on the contrary is the rendering of due tribute both to man and to nature. It is an insistence on the humanity of man, on his control and mastery of his own actions; and it is an equally emphatic insistence on his integral place in nature. He is not a freak, alone of all creatures excused from that general law which moves all things to the ends of nature, each according to its proper gifts; rather he is one with nature, moved by the laws of nature to the ends of nature—but moved as a *man*, morally not physically. There is an even greater tribute to man in this recognition of the possibilities of failure, a tribute not of word but of deed. It is the tribute a man gives to his own humanity when he has the courage to face the terrifying truth of that humanity and its responsibilities; it is the courageous tribute given by the most abject of sinners who knows and admits he has sinned, a scathing denunciation of the cowardice of the man afraid to face his humanity.

But while paying that tribute to what nature is and should be, the sinner is actually betraying his humanity by his sin. He is twisting, perverting, turning that nature away from all it was intended to be and to do. That nature is a rational nature; in it reason should be king, all its energies should move smoothly along under the direction of reason to the goal of reason in which alone there is happiness for man. The sinner, whatever his sin, dethrones reason and puts some usurper on the throne of his soul; his energies are aimed, not by reason, but by the usurper, not to the ends of reason but against all that reason reaches out for. Every sin is unnatural, against nature, a betrayal of nature because every sin is against reason.

The more profoundly we become acquainted with ourselves, the easier it is to understand why we call God "Father" and why we are always children in His eyes. We never really grow up. An instance to the point is our delight in the childish device of vivid contrast—beauty and ugliness, colour and drabness, laughter and tears. It was part of the gentle humour of God smiling on children that made of contrast the simple key to beauty, to love, even to wisdom for men. It was another evidence of God's stooping to men when He made contrast the gay path along which alone man walks to knowledge: of all the creatures beneath him, only man is capable of contrasting; and of all those above him, man alone stands in need of constant contrast.

It is not astonishing, then, that our best insight to sin is obtained by placing it in vivid contrast to its opposite, by putting the enemy of human happiness side by side with the indispensable friend of human happiness. Sin and virtue, darkness and light, ugliness and beauty, decay and health, all are in that one contrast of good and bad habits.

We have said that virtue was a good habit; its opposite, a bad habit, is strictly called a vice. The fruit of the spirit and the fruit of the flesh, these two are an adequate statement of the opposite acts of good and bad habits, of virtuous acts and sins. The first proceeds from the spiritual faculty of reason in command, the second from the rebel forces which have overthrown reason. Sin, then, is the act which proceeds from a bad habit and goes into the formation of a bad habit. Goodness and evil are the opposite dispositions left in a man as a result of these habits and acts.

These two, sin and virtue, are sworn enemies. No house is big enough for them, no reasoning, pleading, excusing is powerful or pitiful enough to keep them from each other's throats. It is sometimes a question as to whether vice or virtue will come hurtling out the window; but always we can be certain of a fight. If the actual guests at the same inn happen to be mortal sin and the infused virtues, there can be no question but what one of them must take the road again seeking other lodgings. Mortal sin is not so hard on the acquired or natural virtues; a natural virtue, after all, is not destroyed by one act. Venial sin does much to destroy the genial air of hospitality, but can get along in a strained, weakening atmosphere with either the acquired or the infused virtues.

By contrasting vice and sin with virtue and acts of virtue we have an accurate idea of the nature of sin and vice. This accurate notion was stated briefly by Augustine when he said that sin was "a thought, word or deed against the Eternal Law". Thoughts, words and deeds are the material, the brick and mortar, from which sins are constructed; the formal element in sin, what sets it apart from virtue, is its opposition to the Eternal Law.

The catechism defines sin as "a thought, word, deed or omission against the law of God". But the word "omission" is a little unfortunate. It has the air of the accidental about it, like forgetting to take medicine or absent-mindedly going out without an umbrella. Actually sin is impossible without some positive act back along the road from which that sin has come. Sins do not just happen, they are willed; they are not accidents that stain our souls as ink might stain a table-cloth, we must deliberately throw the stain at our souls. For sins are human acts, acts for which a man is responsible, which proceed under his control and to an end which he has freely chosen. Otherwise acts, no matter how evil they may be in themselves, are not sins. So somewhere behind an omission, either by way of cause, or occasion, or impediment, we must be responsible for the omission; which means that somewhere we must have willed it, whether directly or indirectly.

Yet in another sense, sins are indeed accidents. The commission of sin puts us in the position of the little boy who wants to eat green apples but does not want the inevitable stomach-ache that goes with eating them. Nevertheless he eats the apples. The stomach-ache is an accident as far as his will is concerned, certainly his mouth does not water in anticipation of a stomach-ache; yet in another sense he is quite willing to accept the stomach-ache as the price to be paid for eating green apples. No man wants to be a sinner, wants to turn his back upon God, wants to give up all chance for happiness and condemn himself to eternal misery. But if all that is inevitably connected with what is desired here and now, the sinner is willing to pay that price for his sin. We never quite grow up; and there is no more convincing evidence of our constant immaturity than the childish reversal of values involved in sin.

Stepping into the world of sin is like stepping into a dank

tropical forest nurtured to unbelievable growth by a sun of desire which kills healthy plants. The variety of sin rivals the variety of tropical growth, in fact surpasses it; for the variety of sin is limited only by the possibilities of a will whose limit is the infinite. It is of no use to look to that will for a distinction of the various kinds of sin; an examination of the motives of sin, meaning by motives the causes which produce sin, can tell us only that this act was or was not human, that it was or was not sin. From a terrible fear of humiliation or from a wildly passionate love can come the same sin of lying or murder; from the one motive of anger can come sins as widely different as blasphemy, theft and murder.

The reason for this is that sin, like every other human act, is a motion to a goal. In the world below man we can easily determine the nature of a motion by looking either at the goal or at the active power that produced the motion; for the powers beneath man run along a determined track that leads always to the same goal. But the powers of man have no set channel along which they must necessarily flow. So for the determination of any human act, virtuous or vicious, we must look to the goal towards which it is going, to the object of the act, to the thing desired that first set in motion that activity of a human being. In other words, the specific character of any sin, as the specific character of any virtue, its very essence, is to be judged by the object to which it is directed.

These objects of sin fall easily into a very general classification since the field of sin is the same as the field of virtue, indeed the same as that of every human action. A human act has to do with God, our neighbour or ourselves. There is a profound thought behind this classification of sins into sins against God, ourselves or our neighbours, a thought we have met before and will meet time and time again, and yet one which continually slips into the back of our minds. That thought is the solemn truth that every creature beneath us is merely a tool or a servant; the universe is ours to use for God, ourselves and our neighbour—but neither God, ourselves or our neighbour is to be used for anything in the universe no matter how powerful or attractive it may be.

Another way of stating this foundation for the essential distinction of sins is to say that man is governed by a triple rule: the rule of the reason of God, the rule of human reason directing the individual activities of man, and the rule of human reason directing the social activities of man. This is the triple law of human action: divine reason, personal human reason and political human reason. The first contains the second and third, for the reason of man has its validity precisely in so far as it is acting in the power of the divine reason. The dedication of men or society to any end less than the ends of man is a perversion, a twisting of nature, a rebellion against divine reason whose outcome is not freedom, not divine supremacy for man, but slavery—a chaining of man to the world that should be his servant and his tool.

Every sin, then, has its essential character from its goal, as every motion has its specific character from the place to which it is going; surely the contrast between a baseball thrown for a perfect strike and one thrown at a spectator's head presents us with a picture of essentially different motions. We applaud the one and resent the other, particularly if we are among the assaulted spectators. Any consideration other than this one essential point of the goal of sin, may tell us something about sin but it will not distinguish one sin from another.

For example, we distinguish between mortal and venial sins; but this distinction does not set aside different sins. The same kind of sin, for example theft, might be either mortal or venial; so a Catholic confessing "his many mortal sins" is no help at all to the confessor. The reason is easily seen. We cannot distinguish a man from a monkey by saying the human animal is bald; that is an accident and we are looking for an essential, specific difference. We can distinguish one man from another by saying that one is a barber and the other a priest, because there is no essential distinction, no specific gap between men. The mortal or venial character of sin tells us graphically what the sinner can expect from his sin or what he has done by his sin, i.e. either he has irreparably destroyed the very principle of his order to the goal or he has wandered from that order without destruction of its principle. But, as far as the sinner is concerned, both of these are accidents as deplorable as the little boy's stomach-ache from his feast of green apples. Like everything else, sins are not distinguished by accidentals.

The same will hold true of sins of commission or omission. "Omission" or "commission" tells us how a sin was committed, whether the sin violated a positive or a negative precept; but it does not tell us what sin was committed. I remember a very small boy who came to confession and, after much embarrassment and many hacking coughs by way of getting a start, solemnly assured me he had, in the past week, "had five thoughts". It was quite a remarkable feat in this day and age. It seemed to me the matter called much more for congratulation than for absolution. As a matter of fact he had merely stated the first grade of all human action. In the order of sin that first grade is fulfilled and rises to its consummation by the steps of word and deed; as, for example, an angry man first has thoughts that will not bear printing, then words that will not bear repeating, and finally the full perfection of his anger blossoms out in mayhem or murder.

Perhaps we keep the rest of the parish shifting from one foot to another while we tell the whole family history of our sin, its neighbouring surroundings, and all the circumstances that could possibly or impossibly have entered into it. All these may be important, they may vary the gravity or responsibility of the sin; but they do not let the confessor or anyone else into the secret of what that time-consuming sin was. For it is only the goal, the object of that sin, that gives it its essential character; and unless a circumstance steps out of its minor role of decorating that sin into the stellar role of object, it does not specify the sin.

It is important that we understand this specifying element in sin, important for several reasons. First of all, it gives us an insight into the terrifying variety of sin; and with that insight we can appreciate something of the dank disorder in the fetid life of the tropical forest of sin. We described virtue as the path along which human acts run to the goal of reason, as the channel leading the energies of man to reason's goal; and we said this was true of every virtue. All have the same goal; the man of virtue is a man of streamlined energies moving with smooth, easy grace and harmony to one end. The essence of sin is the disregard of the rule of reason, indeed of any rule but that of immediate desire for this particular object. The sinner is a victim of civil war. By the very nature of sin all order is disrupted: a thousand and one goals, even contradictory goals, are strained for at the same time; his soul is a chaos in which nothing can be accomplished, where even life itself is intolerable so that a man must get outside himself or go insane. That is the secret of the difference between the quiet peace of Christ coming from the unveiled face of God and the riotous peace of the world that dare not stop its wild pace an instant lest chaos overtake it, but must charge ahead carrying chaos with it, plunging with every step into greater and greater chaos. The virtues are intimately connected; but every sin is not only an enemy of God, an enemy of man, an enemy of society, every sin is a bitter enemy of every other sin, each striving for a mastery that will be its own destruction.

For sin, like every evil, would destroy itself if it could only be carried to perfect fulfilment. Like a disease which must have some healthy tissue to feed on destroys itself by its very growth, so sin by its growth eats away the thing which makes it possible—the freedom of man. If it were possible for sin to go its full length, its end could only be the destruction of itself in the destruction of the reason of man.

Sin can go as far as the destruction of man's freedom by making him a slave to his senses; but, thank God, it cannot go the lengths of destroying reason, for reason is a spiritual faculty against which no created force has any leverage. But the comparison with sickness gives us a clue to the different gravity of different sins. Just as one sickness is more grave than another, so is one sin more grave than another; the one as it more seriously attacks the principle of physical life, the other as it more seriously attacks the principle of reasonable life or of the life of grace. To put it another way, on the basis of our classification of the objects of sin we have an easy classification of the gravity of sin. All exterior things are ordained to man, and man is ordained to God; so sins directed against the external possessions of a man (such as theft) are less serious than those which are against the very substance of a man (like murder), and these in turn are less serious than those whose target is God Himself.

In so far as the objects of sin are opposed to the ends of reason, the sin has gravity; in so far as the virtues are tied up more intimately with the ends of reason, they have greater dignity. It is on the whole a fair arrangement. There is no unfair matching of a heavyweight sin with a lightweight virtue, cabin-boys do not fight admirals, raw recruits are not pitted against seasoned veterans. The graver the sin, the nobler and more dignified the virtue it attacks. In fact the arrangement is even more fair than this would indicate. All side-issues are thrown out, all petty annoyances brushed aside, when a greater virtue and a greater sin enter into their mortal combat; if there is a struggle at all it will be to the death. For of course the very nobility of a great virtue will easily sweep aside all but the correspondingly great sins, as a defending army will mow down the advance-guard of the invaders.

We could make a neat division of greater and lesser sins on the simple grounds of spirit and flesh; but in such a division it must be remembered that the comparison is general and supposes a parity in every other line. Otherwise we shall put ourselves in the silly position of a sports writer comparing two pugilists by putting the strength of one against the curly hair of the other. On this strict basis of gravity, then, the spiritual sins belong among the great, the carnal sins among the less great sins. There is of course much more shame and infamy attached to the carnal sins, as the course of the ages and the uplifted noses of the terribly righteous will testify. They do bring man down to the level of the beasts and no one realizes this more keenly than the carnal sinner himself. But from the point of view of the formal element of sin, the actual aversion from God and reason, there is much more of conversion to the creature than of aversion from God in the carnal sins, while the opposite is true of the spiritual sins. Again the spiritual sins are flatly directed against God and neighbour, both of whom we are bound to love more than our own body which is the object of the attack of the carnal sins. There is much more of deliberation and malice in the spiritual sins, much more of impulsiveness and the drive of passion in the carnal sins and in the matter of sin, the more a man is pushed the less is his guilt, because sin is always a matter of deliberate choice. Briefly, the spiritual sins to which we pay so little attention have more of the formal element of sin (aversion from God), more deliberation and malice, and are directed against a greater object. The sheep and the goats are not to be separated on the grounds of the carnal sins.

An absent-minded attendant at a shooting-gallery who shoots the clients in his fits of abstraction would be a great nuisance but hardly a great sinner. The rabid baseball fan who actually kills umpires in the excitement of a disputed decision is not to be compared to a cold-blooded gangster shooting his enemies in the back. For in establishing the gravity of a sin that deliberate will, which makes the spiritual sins so outstanding, holds absolutely first place. As a general rule, we might say that anything which adds to the deliberate will increases the gravity of sin; anything that detracts from either the deliberation or the willingness lessens that gravity. Indeed in this latter case the gravity and even the sin itself might disappear altogether—when, for example, the rush of passion or the fog of complete abstraction destroys the humanity of the action.

Deliberate will increases the gravity of sin by giving it concentrated power, boring in more deeply much as a hot iron can give a bad, even a fatal, burn though it is applied to only one spot. An equally fatal burn can be given by applying the iron to a wider surface, even though it does not burn so deeply. In the same way sin's gravity can be increased by spreading it over a larger surface, making it extensively greater even though intensively it does not bore so deeply. This is ordinarily the role played by the circumstances of a sin. Over and above the essential evil given by the object of the sin, they add the accidental malice of time, place, manner, and so on. Of course it is possible for a circumstance to change the whole character of sin, as, for example, in the beating given to a wife and the beating given to a nun; but then we are no longer dealing with a circumstance but with a distinctly different object of sin.

Among the other factors contributing to the gravity of sin, a place of dishonour must be given to the objective damage done by our sin. Perhaps we intended the damage; or perhaps we foresaw it and did not particularly care;

perhaps we did not foresee it through sheer negligence; or maybe the damage was not foreseen, not intended, but nevertheless was directly connected with our action—in all of these cases there is sin because in all of them there is an element of will, of effect flowing from our controlled action. Where that element is lacking—for example, when the damage done is embarrassment to a lady by falling into her lap from a ten-storey building—then the damage is not to be put on the bill of sin. It is just an accident.

It makes considerable difference who is committing the sin and against whom the sin is committed. We have said that in a general way the objects of sin are the objects of virtue: God, ourselves and our neighbours. Thus sacrilege against persons or things consecrated to God, even sins against persons who are very closely joined to God by virtue, will in themselves be more grave in proportion to the intimacy of that union with God. Sins against a mother or a father, against our children, against husband, wife, relatives, in fact against anyone who is joined to us either by a bond of blood, of natural necessity, or of gratitude, will all be more grave in proportion to the closeness of their union with us. In a way they are one with us, in sinning against them we are sinning against ourselves. The sins against a neighbour are more grave as they affect more of our neighbours: so an attack on the President is more grave than an attack on a private person because it really injures the whole community; or an injury done to a famous person will be more serious than the same injury done to someone who is entirely unknown, because of the scandal and turmoil it causes among the people.

On the other hand, the sins of the saintly man are much more serious by reason of the high state of virtue he had reached. There is so little to excuse them. He cannot plead weakness with the same honesty as the poor sinner whose life is a long series of falls; his sin is a much more unforgivable evidence of ingratitude for the graces and friendship he has received; he was far, far better prepared to withstand the assaults of sin. So of course his fall causes much greater scandal than would the sin of anyone else. "To whom much is given, much is expected." Indeed the saintly sinner can expect much himself by way of punishment.

It has been a persistent modern mistake to look for sin in the nerves, muscles, health or illness of a man, in his home life or in his surroundings. Of course the object of that search has persistently eluded the searchers. This or that has been improved and we lean back to watch the death of sin; but sin does not die. Really we have not touched the stronghold of sin; nor can we remotely approach that stronghold until we have recognized the humanity of man and man's control of his actions. For it is precisely in that control-room, back in the spiritual citadel where only guests ever penetrate, that sin is to be found. Sin is a human action, proceeding from a human habit; and the habits of man are to be found in the one place where habits are necessary—in the principles of human action.

As we have seen, the prime mover of man is the will of man. Here is the last stronghold of sin, of evil as it is of good; for it is the work of the will, not merely to move, but to move towards or away from a goal, towards or away from good. In the will first, and in the other faculties in so far as they are moved by the will, we find sin—in the intellect, in the sense appetite for good, in the sense appetite to and away from difficulty, but always in so far as these things are subject to the movement of the deliberate will of man. Sin is essentially a rebellion; and a rebellion is possible only where government is possible. The supreme victory of sin is had when it has successfully rebelled against the government of reason not only in the colonies of the senses, but in the high seats of reason and will themselves.

This, then, is our preliminary survey of the field of sin. It leaves us with some rather astonishing results.

Not the least of these is the contrary nature of the hatred of Christ and the hatred of the modern world for sin. Christ hated sin from the very depths of His divine being: sin is against all that God stands for, since it is an offence against the very mind of God; just as positively it is against all the God-man stands for, since it is the one enemy of human happiness. The Son of God who became incarnate that men might be free from sin, Who dedicated His life to the work of teaching men the truth that would make them free, of giving them an ever more abundant life, of leading them step by step to the goal of human life which is happiness—of course He would hate the enemy of human happiness which is sin. And of course He would demand a like hatred as the badge of distinction from His followers: "If you love me, keep my commandments."

The hatred of the world for sin is hardly less thorough, but it is directed against the name, the idea, of sin rather than against sin itself. This hatred finds its most natural expression in a vituperative attack on those who insist on calling a sin a sin, who defend the exclusive privilege man has of making a mistake. Actually what the modern world hates seems rather to be the ostracism which sin is made to suffer; it would like to do away with this caste system of good and evil in the society of human actions. Looking at this hatred of the modern world objectively, we are forced to the conclusion that it is directed much more against men and women than it is against sin; for faced with the dilemma of admitting the possibility of sin and all its terrible consequences or of denying the humanity of man, the modern world turns all its guns on the humanity of man, determined to reduce it to the level of the chemical and animal world above which it towers.

To us who are so familiar with our own times, this modern attitude, unreasonable as it is, has its explanations. The modern world is fighting sin because it does not know sin; and it cannot know sin as long as it remains ignorant of man. It is impossible to understand the indignities of which man is capable until we have some understanding of his dignity; and in a world where the spirit is laughed out of existence, there is no possibility of grasping even vaguely something of the dignity of man, of the necessity of habit and of the possibility of that bad habit which is sin. Even where the pressure of the years pushes men and women to an uneasy suspicion of their humanity, of their high destiny and eternal possibilities, the recognition of sin comes hard; for sin is human failure with human responsibilities for that failure. Always there will be those who are "not strong enough to fail".

This is one of the great reasons why our times are making such a botch of living. If we let this enemy of successful living have the run of the house, we can be sure there will be little of success individually, socially or supernaturally. The secret of successful living, as we have seen, is in the unification of the energies of man under one command, in their harmonious concentration on the one goal worthy of man. Sin is a disruption of that command, a dispersion of that concentrated power with a resultant state of civil war in the individual, of a scattering of his powers on goals totally unworthy of his manhood; it is a wasting of human energy, a complete failure of accomplishment, a smashing of the mirror in which was imaged the beauty and power of God. Every appetite is for itself here and now; the riot, confusion, total absence of peace in the soul of the sinner is a picture and a prophecy of the horror of hell.

In society it is every man for himself; and, as in the individual, it ends up by every man being against himself. As in the individual, we find men used as tools, ordained to the ends of things beneath them, the masters shining the shoes of the servants—men bowing and scraping before military prestige, financial power, class domination, and so on. For here, as in the individual, the unifying goal of reason is swept to one side; the one possible means of cohesion for human beings—a mutual respect for rights—is made a thing of words with much the same results as in the individual: slavery or destruction, in the one case destruction of life, in the other, destruction of human society.

Our world is in a bad way; men and women of that world are in a terrible way, for their very humanity is under fire. But even more terrible, their aspirations to the life of God have been definitely surrendered. Man is asked to find his peace, his hope, his courage, his complete happiness in this individual world of civil war, in the social world of slavery, with never a glance above the dreary scene that men have painted to inspire other men. For sin is, above all, rebellion against God; it is a deliberate descent from the plane of divine life, with the knowledge that no power but that of God can ever lift us up to that plane again. And even God will not lift us up against our will. Sin is a surrender of all that gives meaning to that swift motion which is human life, for it is a surrender of the goal of that motion.

Sin and happiness? The confirmed sinner has a solid grasp on the bitter knowledge of the unhappiness of sin. He has found out for himself that neither in this life nor in eternity can sin bring happiness to man. Perhaps only the saint realizes as keenly that the happiness of man consists in the approach to and possession of the goal of man and that sin is a despairing flight away from the goal to its complete loss.

CHAPTER XIV

(OUTLINE)

THE CAUSES OF UNHAPPINESS

(Q. 75–78)

1. Double root of modern discontent:
   (*a*) Ignorance of cause of happiness.
   (*b*) Ignorance of cause of unhappiness.

2. An analysis of unhappiness—sin.

3. Possible causes of sin:
   A. Internal:
      (*a*) Proximate and immediate: intellect and will.
      (*b*) Remote: imagination and sense appetite.
      (*c*) Sole sufficient cause: will.
   B. External:
      (*a*) Movers of senses.
      (*b*) Movers of reason.
      (*c*) Other sins:
         (1) As efficient cause.
         (2) As material cause.
         (3) As formal and final cause.

4. Intellect as a cause of and excuse for sin:
   (*a*) Ignorance as a cause of sin.
   (*b*) Ignorance as a sin.
   (*c*) Ignorance as an excuse for sin:
      (1) As a total excuse.
      (2) As a partial excuse, diminishing gravity.

5. Senses as a cause of and excuse for sin:
   (*a*) As a cause:
      (1) Sense appetite as mover of the will; directly and indirectly.
      (2) Sense appetite as conqueror of reason:
         a. Indirectly, by impeding action of reason.
         b. The sinner's syllogism.

(3) The first principle of sin: inordinate love of self:
   a. Conversion to creature.
   b. Concupiscence of the eyes, of the flesh, and the pride of life.

(b) As an excuse for sin:
   (1) Partial excuse: antecedent and consequent passion.
   (2) Total excuse.
   (3) Possibility of mortal sin of passion.

6. The will as a cause of sin, never an excuse:
   (a) Sins of malice, ignorance, weakness:
      (1) Sins from habit.
      (2) Sins from will.
   (b) Comparison with sins of passion.

Conclusion :

1. Root cause of unhappiness—bad will:
   (a) Modern remedies for unhappiness.
   (b) Norm of good will.
   (c) Means to good will.

2. Good will and peace.

3. Good will and happiness.

CHAPTER XIV

THE CAUSES OF UNHAPPINESS

(Q. 75–78)

NEARLY every good-natured unmarried brother has found himself, at some time or another, in the uncomfortable position of being left to mind an infant nephew or niece. It is a difficult position, for babies are mysterious creatures, particularly to unmarried brothers; if they could only speak up and ask for what they want instead of just sitting there howling! So the family comes home to find both the baby and its guardian exhausted. In front of the baby are piled up all the odds and ends a distracted mind could locate, like peace-offerings before the idol of an angry god; the guardian has sung songs, done tricks, made faces, poured out all his charm to no other end than the desperation of both the baby and himself. But two minutes after the family has returned, peace settles down on the house again.

Doctors are to be pitied on much the same grounds, though their difficulty does not come so much from the attempt to discover what the patient wants as from trying to uncover the things that he does not want. It must take a tremendous effort on the doctor's part to look confident and undisturbed when he has not the remotest notion of what is wrong with the patient and yet evidently there is something very seriously wrong. Unless the doctor can find out what is wrong he is in as uncomfortable a position as the unmarried brother who could not find out what was right for the baby. And of course the patient is even more uncomfortable than the baby.

Watson, the founder of Behaviourism, once said: "Give me the baby", meaning that he could then make the adult to order. Well he certainly got the baby. In fact all of modern philosophy has been left with the baby in its lap and the howls of discontent and unhappiness grow louder, more despairing, day by day. All the odds and ends that a distracted philosophic mind could think of have been piled in front of the baby, like peace-offerings before an angry god: philosophy has sung songs, dreamt dreams, done tricks, laughed and frowned, suggested and threatened, but still the baby is unhappy. We saw some of these philosophic antics earlier in this book: playing that men were machines, or that men were animals, that they were processes, or periods, or even commas; men have been offered riches, liberty, sensuality, oblivion, slavery, glory, power and despair. But still they are unhappy, still the howls of discontent make the walls of the world shudder. Modern philosophy cannot make men happy; it does not know where that happiness lies.

But the situation is much more desperate than this; it is not merely a question of humouring the baby. A patient is groaning in agony and the doctor has no notion of what is wrong with him; modern man is desperately unhappy, and his doctors do not know where to look for that unhappiness. All kinds of remedies have been tried. It was thought that inhibitions were at the root of the trouble, that religion was to blame, that men were not educated enough, amused enough, comfortable enough or healthy enough; one thing after another was amputated—the intellect, the will, then the sense appetites, but still the patient groans. And he will continue to groan. For just as modern philosophy is ignorant of the cause of man's happiness, it is also tragically ignorant of the causes of his unhappiness.

Our frowns at the clumsiness of modern philosophers are very much like the dagger-glances the mother throws at the worn-out guardian of her child. The answers seem so very simple to us. In the first chapter we saw what makes men happy, where alone happiness is to be found. In this chapter, beginning the investigation of the causes of man's unhappiness, we will find the answers just as plain, as concrete, as solidly true as they were in that first chapter. Peace descends on the house again; or it would descend upon the house if these inexperienced guardians did not insist on pushing the knowing mother into a corner and continuing their attempts to placate the baby, utterly undiscouraged by the disastrous results so far achieved.

The modern world never will discover where human happiness or unhappiness lies until it gives up the attempt to prove that men and women are not human. The unhappiness of human beings is not to be explained on the same grounds as is the wilting of a flower, or the misery of a shivering, half-starved puppy. There is vegetable life in man, there is animal life in man, and both of these can suffer adversity; but the whole point of human happiness is that there is human life in men and that human life can also suffer adversity. Of course that adversity is centred on the principles from which human life flows: it has to do with the intellect, the will, the soul of man. Quite simply, its name is *sin.*

This is the root of human unhappiness. Other things may make life unpleasant, uncomfortable, extraordinarily difficult, but not necessarily unhappy. We can find happiness amidst the most abject poverty, in squalor, in sickness, in ignorance, in terrible physical fatigue, in back-breaking labour. But happiness is not to be found in the heart of a sinner. He may wear the mask of pleasure and carry an air of bravado about with him as a protection from the pity of others. But no one knows better than the priest that no great sinner needs to be urged to shame and remorse; that sinner has drunk deep of the cup of misery and knows well its bitterness.

What brings this miserable unhappiness into being? What is the cause of sin? To answer this question is our work in this chapter, a work that will be completed in the following chapter. The answer is easy if we approach the problem in orderly fashion. In our first volume we learned something of God by looking closely at the world; we know that in our daily life we can get a good knowledge of a man by looking closely at his work. In the same way we can get a good idea of the cause of sin by looking closely at sin.

The very first glance gives us an obvious clue. Sin is proper to man, and that means it is a distinctively human action. Here we are on familiar ground, for we have looked thoroughly into human action, particularly into human action's principles of intellect and will and its all-important characteristic of control. Sin, like any other human action, is an act proceeding under a man's controlled direction to a goal of his choosing. In this, sin is like every other human act: it belongs to the man producing it, it is his responsibility, his tool. But unlike every other human action, there is something the matter with sin, something wanting, some serious defect which places it below the level of other human acts. It is precisely this missing element, this defect, that is the formal constituent of sin; this is the real root of human unhappiness.

We might explain this defect of the act of sin by saying that sin is a human act going to the wrong goal; or by pointing out that it is an act which has strayed off the road mapped out by reason, it is a builder's blunder as a result of disregarding the architect's blue-print. What is lacking, then, is the direction to the right goal, the conformity to the rule, to the plans of reason.

A room might be nearly pitch dark at high noon simply because of unusually dirty windows. It would not be a complex matter to flood the room with sunlight by washing the windows, though it might not be an easy job. The room's darkness is a defect, but not the same kind of defect as is found in sin. A room has no intrinsic claim to light, darkness is not a privation of something that belongs to a room by its very nature. It is a mere negation of light, a negation that can be corrected by simply removing the impediment of dirt from the windows. The defect of sin is more than a negation; the thing missing in sin actually should be there, it is a part of human action, without it sin stumbles along like a man deprived of his sight. We are not seeking here the cause of a negation, but the cause of a privation; no mere accident or impediment explains sin. There is something much more solid behind it.

Let us suppose a woman is in the flurry of last-minute preparation for a dinner. The guests are nearly due, so she takes ice cubes from the refrigerator and, in the confusion of giving three or four orders at once, she puts the ice cubes where they will not fall and can be easily found —on top of a hot oven. A few minutes later she turns to the ice cubes to discover in dismay that an essential element of ice cubes is missing; an ice cube should not be fluid. There is a real privation—not only for the ice cubes, but for the guests. What caused it? The fire of course. Still there have been fires burning for centuries before a single ice cube lost its solidity; certainly destruction of ice cubes is not the reason for the existence of fire. As far as the fire is concerned the result is entirely accidental. Fire has its own proper effect, but the accidental effect on the ice cubes is necessarily bound up with the natural action of fire, granted there are any ice cubes near the fire.

The same is universally true of the cause of privation as distinct from negation. Because a privation means the defect of what should be present, there must be some positive cause at the root of the privation; not that privation is directly produced by this cause, but rather this cause, producing its own effect, accidentally brings about the defect which is a privation of a due perfection. This is the case with sin. The defect of sin is not a mere negation; it is a privation of something that should be in a human act. It must be traced back to a positive cause, to the cause which in producing its own effect, brings about the inordinacy of sin. In other words, it must be traced back to the cause or causes producing the positive part of sin, the human action from which this ordination is missing; it must be traced back to the causes or principles of human action.

The causes of sin, then, are the causes of human action, causes with which we are thoroughly familiar whether they be the immediate and proximate principles from which these actions flow (intellect and will) or the more remote principles (senses, imagination and sense appetite). Putting it in another way will perhaps make clearer the part of each. In sin we have an *apparent* good inclining the appetite of man to action. The brick and mortar of this sin—the apparent good which is the motive of the whole action—is furnished by the senses and the imagination; the first inclination to this apparent good, by the sense appetite; the absence of regulation is due to the intellect where prudence should be alertly directing every action of man rightly. But so far we have nothing at all: an apparent good, an inclination that as yet has no morality, and no regulation or direction, for there is nothing to be directed. It is only when the will, the first principle of movement in man, gets in its work of motion to the positive act involved in sin that we have the sin present. As we have just said, the cause of the privation is the same as the cause of the positive side of the act of sin.

Right here enters the very human procedure of shifting responsibility to shoulders other than our own. If something goes wrong in a corporation, the investigators discharge the lowest clerk; if a battleship runs aground, the sailor with no one beneath him is cashiered. Adam started it by blaming Eve for his fall and she promptly laid the blame on the serpent. That is what our age has been trying to do with sin. We have passed the blame from intellect to sense appetite, to imagination, to the senses themselves; finally sin finds itself tossed into the lap of heredity, environment, or even the weather.

But it simply does not do in the case of sin. It did not do for Adam and Eve and it does not do for us. Actually we make ourselves a little ridiculous when we try to trace sin's cause to the outside world. A glass of whisky does not ordinarily club a man into drinking it; it is only after he has taken it that it does any clubbing. In fact nothing necessarily moves the sense appetite unless that appetite is already disposed in that particular direction; a great deal of money and labour go into the making of a drunkard. Even if the senses were captivated immediately and necessarily, they are, after all, only the servants of reason and will, not giving the orders but taking them; and if they go to the impertinent heights of giving orders themselves, the humanity disappears from the action—neither the senses nor anything else is doing the steering, giving the orders, for there is no order, no direction, in the act.

Much the same is true of the intellect. Unquestionably a man cannot tell himself the lawn does not need cutting when the evidence plainly says that it does, for the intellect cannot resist truth. But how often will such evidence result in the actual mowing of the lawn? No outside mover can force the intellect to the actual accomplishment of things. Of course the will, since it must be free to sin at all, free here and now, cannot be forced by anything external to itself to the action involved in sin. These are the principles from which sin flows: intellect, sense appetite and will. Any action brought to bear on them may be some inducement to sin, but only an inducement; the real cause of sin must be found within a man himself.

Such a conclusion immediately opens up the possibility of the cause of sin being sin itself. Certainly experience offers evidence enough that one sin leads to another, that once we start downhill the pace is rapidly accelerated;

and sin is within man himself. What part does one sin play in causing another? It seems quite clear that by one sin we can and do remove the things that hold us back from other sins; the first murder is always the hardest, not because the next one is any easier but because the sinner himself is hardened through the diminishing of shame and the loss of grace. It is also true that sin, like any other human act, cuts a groove along which other sins of the same type run more easily, smoothly, pleasantly. One sin may act as the labourer bringing up the material necessary for other sins, as the miser prepares the material for sins of injustice. The swindler tells many a lie in order to accomplish his clever theft. But in none of these cases is a sin produced by a preceding sin; it is only made easier, more appealing. We are still left facing the unpleasant truth that sin must be traced back to the principles from which flow the acts that are wholly our own. Our task, then, is simple: which of these principles of a human act is the sole sufficient cause of the inordinacy which is sin—reason, sense appetite or will?

The contribution of intellect to the perfection of human action is one of knowledge and intelligent direction based on that knowledge. Its part in sin, then, will be a part played by the contrary of knowledge, i.e. ignorance. Understand, of course, that not every lack of knowledge is ignorance; very few passengers on a transatlantic liner could navigate the ship, but they are not all ignorant, for ignorance is a lack of knowledge that should be had.

Not every kind of ignorance will do for sin; it must be that very particular kind of ignorance, an ignorance of that which, known in time, would prohibit the act of sin. A man might commit patricide either because he lacked the universal knowledge that patricide was wrong, or through lack of the particular knowledge that this man was his father; but in either case, unless the ignorance entered into the act, the patricide would come about ignorantly but not from ignorance. Even when all the conditions are perfect for ignorance to get in its contribution to sin—where there is a defect of knowledge that should have been had, and this defect enters into the act itself—ignorance is still only an accidental cause of sin, a cause in the sense of removing the impediments to sin much as washing the dirt off the windows would be a cause of sunlight flooding a room. As a sufficient cause of sin, ignorance breaks down badly; we shall have to look to the senses and the will for the answer to the fundamental question with which we are dealing.

As long as we have granted ignorance this audition we might as well listen to its songs and see what it can do, even though we are already sure it cannot play the leading part. It cannot be the cause of sin, but perhaps it could be a sin; and here is a possibility that is positively intriguing. Submitting a sin to the powers of absolution, the Catholic has the sin completely destroyed; how convenient it would be if the ignorant Catholic could confess ignorance and by absolution have the ignorance destroyed, have knowledge poured into his head like water into a kettle! Nevertheless ignorance is a sin, but the absolution does not remove the ignorance but rather is directed against the negligence or malice which made this particular ignorance culpable. For patently not every ignorance is culpable; surely not that which cannot be overcome (invincible), nor even every ignorance that can be overcome, but only that which deprives us of a knowledge that we could and should have, like the lawyer's ignorance of the law, or the doctor's ignorance of medicine, or a professor's ignorance of the subject he is teaching.

As an excuse for sin, the capacities of ignorance are also limited. We could put this role of ignorance briefly by saying that ignorance excuses from sin in exact proportion as it destroys the voluntariness of the act of sin. So the man who shot his father thinking he was shooting a deer is certainly not guilty of patricide. If he did not know it was his father he was shooting but did know it was a man, he would be guilty of murder though not guilty of patricide. In both these cases the act of patricide was altogether involuntary. But if the hunter were a gangster who mistakenly shot a long-sought enemy thinking he was shooting a deer, then the ignorance would have nothing to do with the case at all; even if he knew better it would have made no difference in his action.

There are two rather distasteful conditions under which even the type of ignorance which renders an act involuntary does not excuse from sin. One is the case of affected or hypocritical ignorance, the kind of ignorance which makes us dodge knowledge for fear we will discover that this thing we are so in love with is sinful; the other is a lazy negligent ignorance by which a man does not know the very things he should, indeed must, know here and now. These are distasteful because they smack strongly of a cowardice that is totally unworthy of man, the cowardice that makes a man cringe from life, from the responsibilities of being human. It is a futile attempt to escape from reality into the world of make-believe and pretence. And that is exactly why it does not excuse from sin; it does not really make this act involuntary, it just pretends to do so. Far back down the road up which this particular act travelled we will find the voluntariness trailing along, keeping far behind so as not to be identified with the act that here and now is begging pardon for itself on the grounds of ignorance. As a matter of fact the ignorance itself was *willed.*

A grasp of the validity of ignorance as an excuse for sin makes it easy to see the part ignorance plays in diminishing the gravity of sin. Evidently, the ignorance that totally excuses from sin, that totally destroys the voluntariness of the act of sin, also destroys the whole gravity of sin. Ignorance that is not the cause of the involuntary character of the act neither diminishes nor increases the gravity of sin. The ignorance that was willed directly in the voluntariness of the negligence which caused the ignorance does to some extent diminish the gravity of sin because it diminishes (though it does not destroy) the voluntariness and the contempt ordinarily involved in sin. But that hypocritical ignorance which is directly willed in order that we might sin more freely instead of diminishing the gravity of sin actually increases that gravity.

There is a point here worth noticing relative to the diminution of the gravity of sin through negligence. When we speak of the gravity of sin we are speaking of the evil of sin judged from the double viewpoint of the object of the sin and the malice of the sinner. Of course neither negligence nor anything else can change the objective, essential gravity which comes to a sin from its proper object; but the malice of the sinner can be affected, even though this lessening of malice results in an increased number of sins. So a motorist who has killed a person through negligence may not have committed as grave a sin as the assassin, but he may also have committed more sins in that one act than did the assassin.

Coming back to our original question of the cause of sin, we find there are only two candidates still claiming the dubious honour of principal cause of the unhappiness of man: the senses and the will. Of the two, the senses will lead in most popular balloting probably because of their vociferous demands for attention. Comparing the two, the senses seem to be in much the position of the unimportant cog in a political machine who struts about grandly informing his simple-minded constituents that he is dictating the policies of the governor. Really the comparison is quite exact; from the very nature of sin as a human action, an action proceeding from deliberate free will, it is self-evident that the senses cannot be the whole cause, in fact cannot be a cause at all except in so far as they influence the principles from which that deliberately free act flows. Like the petty politician's influence on the governor, the influence of the senses on the intellect or will is decidedly indirect.

Certainly the senses cannot stroll up to the will and tell it what it must do; in fact nothing can do this. What they can do, all they can do, is indirectly to induce the will to follow their suggestion. It is a fact that when a man is intent on a problem good cooking is wasted on him; or when his energies are concentrated in one direction, his other powers are bound and gagged. As examples of this there are the injuries that go unnoticed in a football game; on a more heroic scale, the unperceived agonies of the martyr who is caught up in an ecstasy of love. It works as well the other way around: not only does a concentration of our mental powers dull the perception of the senses, but a concentration of the sense appetite, a vehement rush of passion, saps the strength of the will. More simply, our powers are rooted in the essence of the soul; when any one of them is vehemently pursuing its object the others have to wait their turn or take a minor part in whatever operations are going on at the time.

This is one way the senses can influence the will. The other is by blocking the intellect thus leaving the will without intelligent protection, as putting a bandage over the eyes of a blind man's dog leaves the blind man helpless, dependent on the leadership of anyone who comes along. In other words, the senses can sometimes impede the work of reason, and so influence the will. This impediment to reason may come about through the concentration of the powers of the soul in one direction, as we have explained about the distraction of the will; it may be a case of the soul being pulled in contrary directions by passion and reason; or it may be by a positive physical impediment to reason comparable to the impediment of sickness, sleep or drunkenness. It is almost literally true that a man in a violent fit of anger "sees red", or at least that he is incapable of seeing anything else, perhaps of seeing anything at all.

We can put this more concretely by saying that a man might know murder is wrong and even that his particular act is murder; but the rush of the sense appetite impedes him from using the knowledge he possesses. Commonly this impediment of the sense appetite hinders a man from applying this universal knowledge to a particular case. The sinner, like every other man proceeding to a human action, arrives at his decision to act in this particular way by a syllogism, or a train of reasoning following the rational form. But instead of arguing rationally from "revenge is wrong", through "this act is revenge", to the conclusion, "this act is wrong and to be avoided", the sinner starts from a double principle. Side by side with the principle "revenge is wrong" he has the principle "revenge is agreeable, a source of pleasure". The rush of passion completely blocks the first; and the sinner goes on from the other to argue, "this act is revenge", "therefore this act is agreeable and a source of pleasure, a thing to be done". For it is always true that man must make all his acts wear the appearance of rationality, not only by way of protecting his own self-respect, but by way of protecting his own sanity.

This is the explanation of the pitiful cry of the sinner who says "I know I should not do this" but who nevertheless does it. He does know in an abstract, speculative way; but that knowledge is not allowed to proceed to the strict command or prohibition that would directly guide the action. In other words, the sense appetite swerving reason from its path is a sickness, a weakness that holds a man back from producing results worthy of his manhood, as an infection in the eye would keep a man from seeing with his usual clarity.

What is behind this rush of passion and its desperate attempt to cripple reason and sway the will, to rob the actions of a man of their humanity? The same thing that is behind every sin, the enthronement of ourselves. Here and now we want this desirable thing, we want it so badly that nothing else matters; that our desires be satisfied is more important than anything else, than any other consideration. In other words, we have placed self-satisfaction at the top of our scale of values; we have loved ourselves above all else. Yet in effect we have thoroughly hated ourselves. For this is not the healthy self-love which leads a man to God and to happiness; but a self-love that involves contempt for God and by that very fact a contempt for ourselves, for it dedicates us to things beneath us, to trifling things that leave our hearts emptier than before.

That is the root of sin, the ultimate to which all sins can be reduced. More immediate roots or sources of the sins flowing from the passions are given in St. John's phrase "the concupiscence of the eyes, concupiscence of the flesh and the pride of life": "of the flesh" indicates sins of what we might call natural passion—gluttony, drunkenness, lust; "of the eyes"—those sins of passion following in the wake of sense knowledge, imagination, sins turning about money, clothes, glory; "pride of life"—sins flowing from the irascible or emergency passions, sins that have to do with fear, presumption, anger and the rest.

But whatever their immediate source, it is not hard to see what gravity the sins of passion have, to see how much of an excuse passion offers for sin. Evidently if I know some particular line of thought is going to make me very angry and I deliberately sit down and occupy myself with this train of thought, the flare of anger which follows does not offer an excuse for sin; it was itself deliberately willed, it is a sign of my complete willingness, and as a matter of fact by its intensity it sweeps aside all hindrances to that willingness. If I stamp on my own corn to arouse anger I have no excuse for what follows; but if someone else stamps on that corn very much against my will, I may have a very good excuse indeed. In fact there may be no sin at all if the rush of passion destroys my use of reason altogether, so that I am really blind with anger. But if it does not go so far as that, the sin is less grave in exact proportion as reason is deprived of its rightful command. As long as reason still has some command, it is possible to stem the flood of passion, diverting it, insisting on its obedience, refusing to give it the formal recognition of consent without which it cannot take its place within the august assembly of human acts. Is it possible for a sin flowing from passion to be a mortal sin? Of course: of its very nature passion is not the enemy of reason and will but their servant; a servant that can also be sent on serious errands of sin.

Not reason, nor the senses are the sufficient cause of sin—there is only one possible answer remaining to the fundamental question we set ourselves to answer in this chapter; for there is only one other principle of human action to consider—the will of man. If we turn back to an earlier example we will find that the answer to that question was really contained in the question itself. The sufficient cause of the darkness in the room was the dirt of the windows —that was sufficient to account for a negation; but the fire was the sufficient, if accidental, cause of the melting of the ice cubes. This last was not a mere negation but a privation a defect of a perfection that should have been there. That is exactly the case in sin. It is not sufficient to point to ignorance or passion which might suffice to explain a mere negation; for the privation involved in sin we must go to a positive cause, a cause producing something directly, a cause whose effect accidentally causes this privation in sin. In other words, we must go to the cause of the positive element in sin, to the cause of the physical act of sin, to find the cause of the privation of sin. That cause is the will of man. If we are looking for the cause of the privation involved in theft, we must go to the cause responsible for the physical act of taking a wallet.

The will is the sufficient cause of sin, for it is the only direct positive cause involved in that human act of sinning. The malice of a sin, then, is directly traceable to the part played by the will in that sin; the sin is more malicious as the will plays the greater role. Where the intellect plays the greater part we have a sin of ignorance, for that is the intellect's contribution to sin; where passion has most of the lines, we have a sin of weakness, for that is passion's contribution to sin; but where the leading man is will we have a sin of malice—malice is the will's contribution to sin. It is true enough that in most sins there is some ignorance, some weakness; always there is malice or there can be no sin. It is a question of which plays the leading part; to say that one or the other enters into the sin is no more than repeating the evident though shocking truth that sin is itself a corruption, its brightness, like the flush of fever, proceeding from corruption and leading to an even more serious corruption. For the very fact of sin presupposes corruption in the intellect, in the sense appetite, and always in the will.

Where the will chooses sin without the rush of passion or the fog of ignorance entering largely into the choice we have what is called a sin of malice; the same type of sinning is variously described as "sinning from industry", "knowingly choosing evil". Not that there is not choice in every sin, but rather that not every sin proceeds principally from the choice of the will. It may seem difficult to understand how the will, made to search out good and pursue it to the heights of divine good, can deliberately turn aside to evil; the answer is not so difficult though there must always be something obscure about sin—it always remains "the mystery of iniquity". There are just two ways in which this mystery can be accomplished: by a corruption that makes the evil particularly appealing, even similar to the desires of the will, much as an eye infection will make light unpleasant and darkness agreeable; or by the removal of the things that keep us from sinning, the impediments to evil choice—hope of eternal reward, fear of hell, shame, etc.

Doing away with the impediments is like taking the sign "explosive" from a box of dynamite, for those impediments make evil stand out in all its hideousness. The corruption involved in a sin of malice is a more subtle and therefore more dangerous thing. It may be a physical corruption, like sickness or positive physical inclination, that makes this evil thing appeal to us so much; or, as is more usual, it may be the corruption of habit. The work of habit is to make our actions easier, more pleasant, second nature to us; and if those habits be bad habits, they make evil actions easier, more pleasant, more a part of our nature, with something like the appeal that nature itself has; something like the spontaneous response of will to nature is found in will's response to habit.

All other things being equal, a sin of malice is much more grave than a sin of passion precisely because there is more of the will in it, and the formal gravity of sin is a matter of the deliberate will to sin. This is the fundamental explanation of the easy and deep remorse of the passionate sinner as contrasted with the stiff-necked stubbornness of the sinner from malice. The victim of passion has really sinned half-heartedly, his whole will was not in it and he comes stumbling breathless back to God as soon as passion has subsided. We might say the passionate sinner has really been interrupted in his pursuit of God and hurries to take up that pursuit after the unfortunate interruption. But the malicious sinner is a whole-hearted sinner, he does not find it easy to come back, he has not been interrupted in the pursuit of God but rather he has deliberately taken after another quarry. If that sin of malice be from the corruption of habit, it has a permanency about it that only the grace of God and a heroic human heart can prevent enduring through the eternity of hell.

This, then, is the sole sufficient cause of sin, the bad

will of man. This is the root of human unhappiness, as distinct from the adversity of the plant or the brute, the malicious will of man knowingly choosing a temporal good that brings with it spiritual ruin. This is what is the matter with the baby left in the lap of modern philosophy, this is the trouble with the patient groaning while helpless doctors look on and speculate. Remove this and you will find human happiness wherever you find human hearts: in the poor, in the ignorant, in the sick, in the wealthy, in the learned, in men, women and children. For human happiness is no surface decoration to be snatched away by any passing wind of illness, misfortune, poverty or wealth; it is a treasure buried deep, as deep as the soul of man. It is locked up in the human heart, a treasure-room inviolable against any attack of any agency, a strongroom where only the master of the house or those to whom he has given the key may enter. It can be plundered only by its owner, squandered only by the man to whom it belongs.

How far wide of the mark we have gone in our times searching for remedies for the unhappiness of man! We have piled up gifts before man like peace-offerings before the idol of an angry god, remotely hoping that some one or the other would please him. On the positive side we have talked of better housing, better food, more education, more culture, more leisure, more health—all of them good; but was it not evident from the first that thousands of men and women who had all of these things were desperately unhappy? So we went to the negative side, saying it was not something that men lacked, but something they already had which was making them unhappy. We took away the notion of sin, of God, of a soul, of a free will, even of an intellect; we took away all restraint from the passions, all responsibility from actions, all meaning from life. And was man more happy? God alone will ever know how much damage was done to humanity; only the men and women who were the victims can say what a bitter, despairing drink we made of unhappiness. We failed, utterly, miserably. And we will continue to fail until we are willing to face the awful but inspiring truth that the will of man is the sole sufficient cause of the unhappiness of man: awful because it puts the responsibility directly into our hands; inspiring because it puts the destruction of unhappiness within our power.

The remedy for unhappiness is good will—not in the pietistic sense of a revival meeting; but in the solidly human sense of a will that is pursuing its proper goal, striding along the road of reason to the goal of reason and tasting at every step something of the invigorating happiness of the goal, as a man approaching the sea will smell and feel the tang of it while still miles away. This good will is not something mysterious, esoteric; it is not something about which we wonder whether or not we have it; it is not something that claps us on the head like a falling brick. Any man by a few moments' thought can immediately determine whether or not he has good will; it takes only an examination of conscience, a perusal of the Ten Commandments and an application of them to our actions. For if our will be good, our actions will be good; and our actions are good or bad as they measure up or fail to measure up to the Ten Commandments. Or, in more philosophical language, our actions flow from our will and they are good or bad according as they move to our goal or away from it. The Ten Commandments express the minimum of goodness demanded for "good will".

How is this priceless boon of good will, this foundation of human happiness, acquired? Again there is no hocus-pocus. It is simply a case of living up to the demands of reason, to the demands of our humanity, living the life of virtue. It is brought about by just those means the Catholic uses to insure the observance of the Ten Commandments: by doing what he can in building up the good habits or virtues, attacking, rooting out, avoiding the bad habits or vices; and for what he cannot do, calling upon the One Who can give him what he lacks—by prayer, the sacraments and all the supernatural equipment God has so graciously put at our disposal.

It was most fitting that the message of the angels, "peace to men of good will", should have been delivered to ignorant shepherds. It should have shocked us into the realization that good will is independent of the circumstances of life; that good will is the ultimate foundation for peace even in this life of ours. For where can there be peace where there is no happiness; and where can there be happiness without the cause of happiness? Of course God would not put us at the mercy of circumstances which for the most part are out of our control; if human happiness was important enough to the divinity to warrant Calvary's sacrifice, it was something intended for every man, put within the grasp of every man, independent of the world he lived in, independent of the activities of other men, of devils, even of angels. It was to flow from the good will of the individual man.

CHAPTER XV

(OUTLINE)

UNHAPPINESS FROM THE OUTSIDE

(Q. 79–81)

1. The inviolable sanctuary of the human soul:
    - (*a*) External forces and sin.
    - (*b*) External agents and sin.
2. The fact of sin and human dignity:
    - (*a*) Enemies of humanity:
        - (1) Betrayers of freedom.
        - (2) Destroyers of freedom.
        - (3) Betrayers of truth.
    - (*b*) Defenders of humanity:
        - (1) Of human intellect.
        - (2) Of human freedom.
3. God and the inviolable human soul:
    - (*a*) God's positive part in sin:
        - (1) The act of sin.
        - (2) Temptations from creatures.
        - (3) Punishment.
    - (*b*) God's negative part in sin: blindness and hardness of heart:
        - (1) Turning from good and embracing evil.
        - (2) Withdrawal of grace.
4. Helplessness of the devil.
5. Power of the devil:
    - (*a*) Limited field of his operations.
    - (*b*) His activity material for virtue as well as vice.
    - (*c*) Limited character of his actual activity.
6. Hereditary sin and the inviolable human soul:
    - (*a*) Fact of Original Sin and its transmission a certain truth:
        - (1) Nature's indications.
        - (2) Authority's proof: Job xiv. 4. Council of Mileve, Canon 2 (Denzinger, ♯ 102), II Council of Orange,

Canons 1 and 2 (Denzinger, # 174, 175), Council of Trent, Session V, chapter 2 (Denzinger, # 788–791).

(*b*) The mystery and its difficulties:
  (1) Voluntariness.
  (2) Justice.

(*c*) Theological explanations:
  (1) By the transmission of the human soul.
  (2) By transmission of corporal defects.
  (3) By transmission of human nature (St. Thomas).

7 Heredity and personal sins:

(*a*) Strict limitation of transmission to Original Sin.
(*b*) Universality of transmission to all men.
(*c*) Fundamental condition of transmission: "active principle of generation".

Conclusion:

1. Basis of modern revolt against God:

(*a*) Original sin.
(*b*) Personal sin.
(*c*) Physical evil and punishment.

2. Sin as evidence of the perfection of divinity:

(*a*) Nobility and generosity.
(*b*) Respect for inviolable sanctuary of human soul.
(*c*) Beneficent ingenuity and merciful justice.

3. Sin as evidence of dignity of man.

CHAPTER XV

UNHAPPINESS FROM THE OUTSIDE

(Q. 79–81)

PERHAPS one of the most distasteful tasks in the world is that of the man or woman engaged to demonstrate a product in a shop window. No human being enjoys being an exhibit. We put privacy near the top of the list of the individual's sacred things, privacy of thought, of desire, of the home. We can easily understand the unpleasantness attached to fame when an avid public gorges itself with details of wardrobe, breakfast and dinner, literary tastes, family history, and anything else that dogged reporters can ferret out. Curiosity, critical or admiring, easily reaches the point of persecution and is justly resented. We should have something of our own, some rooms which only our guests may enter, some doors that only love throws open, some inner sanctuary where the curious and unfriendly cannot wander about to gape and snicker.

Human dignity suffers only one greater affront: the affront offered to a henpecked husband or to the citizen of a state ruled by a tyrant. It is an insult calculated to drag men down with a crash by snatching from them the fundamental control that makes their actions human. We resent being pushed about and we exalt the contrary idea of independence. And rightly so, for the very heart of the humanity of our actions is precisely their independence; they are human because they are ours and no one else's, because they are proceeding under our control to goals of our choice.

This resentment is not the unreasonable indignation of the man whose flattering day-dreams are brought tumbling down about his ears by stern fact; it is the righteous anger of the man who has been robbed. We have not deluded ourselves into thinking we have this inviolable independence, it is not the product of recent theories or pet day-dreams; we have known through the ages that we have an inviolable sanctuary because we have always known that we are human. We are not making a revolutionary claim to independence of action, because we have known right along that these actions are human, they are ours, they are dependent on no one else.

In our last chapter we were forced to the disagreeable conclusion that the one sufficient cause of that distinctively human unhappiness which is sin is the will of the individual man or woman. Disagreeable, yes, but in itself it is a confirmation of and tribute to the inviolable character of our human dignity. We are not pushed about in our human acts, even in such unworthy human acts as sin. Ignorance and passion may try to coax us or trick us into committing sin; but we commit sin only because we have so decided. Heredity, environment, the state of our nerves, our digestion, or any other factor external to our own will can offer no more than an inducement to sin. We have our own sanctuary, inviolable by any force; we are masters of our own deeds and not slaves plodding helplessly under the sting of the lash. For we are men.

In this chapter we come to a consideration of the influence, not of things, but of persons, upon our human actions, specifically on the human action of sin. From our own experience, from our dealings with other men, we have an accurate idea of our independence and of the limitation of these external agents. We can make a child drink its glass of milk; but we cannot make the child want to drink the milk. Consider the full implications of that: the child is physically insignificant, intellectually just beginning life, totally devoid of experience, of the wiles of diplomacy, without powerful allies or the massive threats of great armies and navies; yet not all the military power of all times, not all the devils in hell, not all the wisdom of the ages can force that child to want a glass of milk! And sin is possible only under condition of being wanted, of being voluntary.

It comes as a great shock to men or women not afraid of their humanity but courageously proud of it, to find others positively eager to escape from that humanity. There is, for example, the great throng who would like to slip from under the heavy weight of human action and put the whole responsibility upon God, particularly the responsibility for that human action that is sin (Pelagius, Calvin, Zwingli). They would like to believe that we are helpless, driven mercilessly, necessarily into each particular sin by a totally contradictory deity. Others, on theological grounds, would believe that every action of every man is necessarily sinful; he cannot help himself and no one else can help him. All that God Himself can do is to blink at the sins and pretend they are not there (Luther).

Much the same destruction of human freedom has been attempted on scientific or philosophic grounds in our own day; though, by way of a sop, we are told to cheer up, even if we have nothing to say about our actions, there is no need to worry, because there is no sin. As if that in any way lightened the sweeping insult of denying humanity to men and women! It is no wonder that we resent this sort of thing, this insistence that we be content to be moved like pawns on a chess-board. It is not only an insulting denial of our freedom, of our mastery of our own acts; it is a shameless betrayal of truth, a demand that we embrace the absurdities of an evil divinity, of a godless universe, of a man who is not man, of a freak in nature absolved from natural law. The smile of friendship does not conceal the real enmity towards humanity there; if friendship there is, it is extended only to the streak of cowardice that is rare enough in a human heart and is always the guest of a shamefaced host.

Friendship is made of sterner stuff than the sentiment that gives a child pastry and chocolates by way of dinner. The surgeon's knife is often mercifully kind; a brutal truth usually springs from a much deeper affection than does a pleasing lie. The real friends of humanity have kept their eyes fixed on human happiness, on human dignity, on human freedom, on the truths of man, rather than on the lies that would please him for the moment. So, as we saw in our first volume, Christ and His Church through the years have been the defenders of human intellect,[1] of human freedom,[2] of a really divine God[3] and of a universe with an intelligent purpose behind it.[4] The booming thunder of authority was heard again and again when men, to deny their humanity, turned away from the persistent whisperings of reason. The real friends of humanity have insisted on the inviolable character of the human soul; our sins are our own because we are human, because we possess a citadel that no siege can reduce.

There are parents who rigidly forbid anyone to touch their children for any reason whatsoever, the type that rushes to the superior of a school demanding instant punishment of the teacher who has dared to frown at, rebuke or slap their child. Yet that child is being for ever knocked about by his own parents. That is exactly the position we would be putting God in if we held that, after He had built an impregnable wall of freedom to protect the humanity of our actions from every created force, He Himself should step in to violate that humanity, to cause our sins. It would be no more comfort to us to be free from the molestation of the world than it is for the child to be free from the beatings of everyone but his parents; for we would know that at home, within our own souls, we could expect our humanity to take a constant beating.

[1] Vatican Council, Sess. III, chap. 2, canon 1 (Denzinger, # 1806).
[2] Council of Trent, Sess. VI, canons 4 and 5 (Denzinger, # 814, 815).
[3] IV Council of Lateran, chap. 1, "De fide catholica" (Denzinger, # 428). Vatican Council, Sess. III, chap. 1 (Denzinger, # 1782, 1784).
[4] ibid.

But God is not like that. He demands respect for the humanity of our actions from every creature He has produced; and He gives that humanity the same respect. There is no such thing as God pushing a man into sin as we might push a child into a swimming-pool; we have to jump in ourselves, for we alone are the direct cause of our sins.

Nevertheless, indirectly, God has something to do with our sins; He must have because there is something very positive, very real about our sins and every reality must be traced back to the first cause of all reality. Remember we defined sin in the last chapter as a human act that has turned off the road of reason; an action with something essential missing, an act deprived of the regulation of reason. The positive side of it, then, is human action; the negative side, the privation of something that every human action should have. This positive side can be explained only by having recourse to God; God does cause this positive element of sin, as He causes our other actions—not destroying our own casuality in the matter.

As a matter of fact God could not be responsible for the privation of sin. Concretely this privation means turning away from our goal or last end; and that last end is God Himself. To suppose that God is the cause of the formal negative element in sin is to suppose God puts Himself in the ridiculous position of turning away from Himself, of making the absurd mistake of supposing something outside Himself is more desirable than His own infinite goodness. It would be as though a woman, looking into an old, cracked, distorted mirror were to think the face mirrored there much more perfect than her own.

In the negative side of sin we need no help from God. We cannot lay the blame for this defect of sin anywhere but on our own will. The staggering gait of a locomotive with flat wheels tearing over crooked rails is not to be traced to the power of the steam driving the locomotive.

The flat wheels and crooked rails are sufficient explanation. A steel worker who disobeys the safety rules of the plant by using a cracked hammer puttering around the top of a crane is himself responsible for the cracked head of the man beneath him who is felled by the flying hammer; or the field manager of a large concern who disobeys the orders of the home office is himself responsible for the results that follow from that disobedience. The negative side of sin is precisely the result of going outside the field of the first cause, of disobeying the orders of our superior; for that we ourselves are alone to blame.

Ah yes, but God permits it! Could He not prevent all men from ever sinning? Well then, why doesn't He? It is the old cry of those afraid of life who would throw out merit, love, triumph, virtue and heaven because they are afraid of demerit, hate, failure, vice and hell. To ask why does God not do away with the possibility of sin is to ask why does God allow men to be men? Why does He not make them machines, or chemicals, or plants, or animals? Why do we have to face these terrible possibilities of failure? Why? Because we can face these other tremendous possibilities of success.

God can prevent all sin, but should He? Is there an obligation of justice on His part to stop sin? Unless there is, we certainly have no claim to think injustice has been done to us. God does permit sins, permits even the negative side of sins according to the ends of His sublime wisdom and justice. The guilt of Roman tyrants fashioned the glory of the martyrs; many a proud soul in imminent danger of hell has been brought weeping to the feet of Christ through the humiliation of a degrading sin of the flesh, for always it is true that the evil God permits is ordained to some good. It is not always for the good of the individual sinner; sometimes it is for the good of others, sometimes for the good of the whole universe. But even the sinner himself is again and again the object of the divine mercy and the watchful providence of God; often we are allowed to fall into sin that, knowing the bitter taste of that joyful-looking cup, we might come to ourselves, know the reality of sin and, humiliated, come back to God. And where mercy has worked again and again in vain, the sinner's act will not escape the divine power for good; if it cannot serve the health of the sinner and the mercy of God, at least it will serve the divine justice which flows from that mercy.

Remember now it is not a case of God's doing evil that good might come; we do the evil and the divine workshops are kept running at full capacity to turn that evil to some good. That is strictly true of the evil of sin. Of the evil of punishment, it is indeed done that good might come; that is its precise reason. Many an optimistic parent has placed great hopes in a spanking which was decidedly evil for the child; in fact it is only love and justice that can administer punishment and if we insist on running away from love we are actually insisting on embracing the punishment of justice.

There is a point here well worth mention by way of putting still more of our feeble human excuses for sin definitely out of the running. One of the older ecclesiastical writers was quite sure that women were created to torment men. There was something unfair about the beauty, grace and attractiveness of women; and he greatly suspected that women had learned their feminine wiles from the devil himself. No doubt there are the elements of a sincere compliment in this opinion. Unfortunately we cannot lean back comfortably and laugh at antiquity from our superior age; for even to-day there are people who are sure drink is a curse originated for the degradation of man. Probably a little research would uncover many other instances of this mental kink that insists creatures were created to tempt men. Of course this is absurd. All that God made was good and ordained not to the downfall of man but rather to the attainment of his end; the universe was planned as his tool. Doctors have slashed their wrists with scalpels; but the scalpel was not designed as an instrument of suicide or murder. Creatures were not made to coax man into sin; it is rather the stupidity of men that perverts creatures to uses foreign to their original design, much as a contractor might conceivably turn out a machine-gun nest from material the architect had planned for a pent-house.

There is another angle of God's part in sin that meets with much unjustified complaint from men. Among the effects of sin frequently mentioned in Scripture is "blindness and hardness of heart"; a perversion of reason and will, of intellect and affections, that leaves the sinner buried in his sin as though he were put bodily into setting concrete which grew more rigid with every passing day. The blindness is a conversion to evil, a turning away from divine light comparable to the impatient movement of weakened eyes away from light in search of darkness; the hardness of heart is a reversal of the normal course of the affections of man so that instead of seeking the things that would turn man from evil he despises these aids to good. This blindness and hardness of a sinner are what make a death-bed conversion a marvel of God's grace; and which all too frequently result in death-bed tragedies that tear the heart out of the most experienced priest as he watches the sinner go defiantly down the road of death.

What part has God in all this? It is again the story of sin and its punishment; man furnishes the sin, God the punishment. In this perversion that appears in the habitual sinner, there is a double element: the adherence to evil and the revulsion from good; and the subtraction of God's grace which illumines the intellect and softens the heart of man. In their proper order we have first the placing of an obstacle to grace—the sin of man; then the refusal of grace by way of punishment; finally the result of this punishment is blindness and hardness of heart. In other words, the cause of it all is the sin of man, for by sin alone is punishment merited. Why does not God overlook the sin? Ah, but He does time and time again, though each time this punishment was well merited. God does not turn away from us, it is we who turn away from Him; and even then the "Hound of Heaven" keeps relentlessly on our track until divine mercy itself surrenders before the obstinate will of the creature made to the image and likeness of God.

The devil may go about the world as a roaring lion seeking whom he may devour; but as far as directly causing sin is concerned, he is a toothless old lion. The devil is as helpless as any other extrinsic force or agent in his attempt to force his way into the privacy of our souls; in spite of the marvellous perfection of his angelic nature, he is as helpless as the toddling infant. This sanctuary of ours is absolutely inviolable. We have no more reason to fear that the devil will make us commit sin than we have to run in terror from the gurgles of an infant on the same grounds; the Curé of Ars plunged to the heart of the truth when he chuckled at the antics of this droll companion of men. The thunders, knockings, mysterious whispers and broken furniture were all part of a satanic masquerade calculated to have the same effect on men as a Halloween false face might have had on children thirty years ago.

However, the devil has enough to keep himself busy. He can cover the whole field of material and human operation in influencing our human acts; that means he can go from the senses up to the phantoms of the imagination—and not a step farther. In other words, he can offer us inducements to sin as a merchant might offer us inducements to buy his wares; but he cannot make us want to buy. More concretely, the devil can produce in our senses all the results produced by external stimuli; all the physical and organic changes which ordinarily accompany the passions; he can induce phantasms in the imagination. And what is all this but saying a spirit can work on a material thing?

He can do all this—if he is not restrained by God. The general lack of experience with diabolic activity is more than sufficient evidence of the extensive restraint imposed on the devil and his angels by the infinite mercy of God.

The devil started his downward career with a mistake and has been making them ever since. Imagine a football coach, because of his dislike for a certain athlete, putting him through twice as rigorous a training as the others; and as a result turning out a far superior specimen of physical ability. That is the sort of thing the devil is doing all the time. For all these inducements are the brick and mortar from which a splendid house of virtue can be erected; they are opportunities for the exercise of good habits, for cutting the groove of virtue deeper and deeper into our souls.

Ordinarily we do not cheat the devil of any credit he deserves for our sins and our temptations. In fact we give him much more credit than he has any claim to, not because we are inherently generous but rather because we are so eager to think well of ourselves and so reluctant to disturb the foundation of those very kind thoughts of ourselves. The self-made man who traces all his success to the excellence and persistence of his own efforts, and the town drunkard who lays all his misfortune at the feet of bad luck are extremes of the same human vanity which never tosses a morsel to a guardian angel but heaps the refuse on the head of the devil. Even if there were no devil at all, there would still be ignorance and passion to offer a line of sin attractive even to the connoisseur. However, in one sense we can blame the devil for our troubles; after all, he started them all by tempting Eve.

And speaking of Eve, and of course of her husband, we come to the one effective cause of our sins from the outside; a cause which yet, in a mysterious way, is not outside at all. Original sin with which we are born apparently violates that inviolable sanctuary of man's soul; apparently one sin has slipped into our private quarters without an invitation. But only apparently.

It is necessary, before going into this question, to insist that original sin is definitely not a matter of myths, ignorant superstitions or inferiority complexes induced by a scheming ecclesiastical organization for its own ends. Original sin is a fact. Even nature itself gives us an indication that there is something wrong with man; in fact the modern world is quite ready to admit there is a good deal wrong, even to insist that almost everything is wrong so that the individual must be cared for like a helpless infant by his betters or his Government. But the modern world is not at all prepared to admit that this human defect is a matter of sin. But then the modern world does not know much of anything about the cause of human unhappiness, as we saw in our last chapter. It seems evident, though, that man alone, of all the creatures of the universe, is poorly equipped for the human things he is expected to do. A chemical, a plant or an animal is marvellously well equipped for every function nature demands; but man stumbles into the universe as poorly equipped as a Roman captive staggering into the arena. Considering the usual wisdom and efficiency of nature, this is very strange; considering the benignity and mercy of God and His providence it is inexplicable except on one ground: something has been taken away from man, he has been punished; and the one cause of such spiritual punishment is sin.

These are only indications of a fundamental truth. Its absolute certitude is based on the solemn declarations of infallible authority. Our human minds might overlook or misread indications of a mysterious truth, indeed they might be blind to the valid proofs of an evident truth; but there is no room for human error. The fact of sin and of its actual transmission comes from a source that cannot deceive or be deceived. A few of the references are given in the outline of this chapter; let me repeat the solemn words of the Council of Trent: "If anyone says that the sin of Adam injured only Adam himself and not his descendants; that losing the sanctity and justice he had received from God he lost them only to himself and not to us; or that through the sin of disobedience only death and the corporal penalties were handed down to the whole human race, but not sin—let him be anathema."[1]

For Catholics there can be no doubt: the fact and transmission of original sin are solid truths infallibly established. Precisely because we must believe, we are free to take this truth, turn it inside out, let our intellect run with the exhilaration of a man on skis down to the depths and up to the heights. Strange how men ever came to look on our dogmas as a limitation of truth. A scientist who has only an absolutely empty test-tube with which to engage his scientific energies might as well be paralyzed. Energetic investigation is possible only when he has something to work on. Our dogmas are distinctively positive things; they give us something and thus open up unsuspected fields for further inquiry. A denial of them just slams another door on the human intellect.

We might consider just what original sin is, what its effects are, just what man has lost; and we will consider all these things in our next chapter. Here we are interested in just one phase of original sin—how does it get into our souls? How is such a mysteriously spiritual thing passed on from parents to children; how can it possibly measure up to the essential demand of all human acts, that of control and voluntariness; and what is the justice of our coming into the world with such a stain as this on our souls, even granted that it is a sin?

With the easy familiarity of Catholics accustomed to rubbing elbows with patriarchs, apostles, martyrs and virgins, of linking arms with the Mother of God and ushering the Son of God into the unpretentious cosiness of their own souls,

[1] Sess. V, chap. 2 (Denzinger, # 789).

the theologians of the Church from the very beginning made no excuses for their bold attempts to answer these questions. Augustine thought perhaps the sin was transmitted from parent to child by the transmission of the soul itself; an opinion of which he was dubious himself before his death, and rightly so. For the parents do not transmit the soul, all they can do is prepare the material into which God infuses a soul He has newly created; a spiritual soul is not the product of material agents, even of exalted spiritual agents such as men and women, it is not to be made out of something, but to be carved from nothing by an almighty stroke of an infinite sculptor's chisel. So other theologians decided that perhaps the transmission of original sin was to be explained by the transmission of corporal defects which certainly fell within the power of the parents; then the soul being infused into this infected body would itself become infected with original sin. Unfortunately for this opinion, the harbouring of the guilt of the wrong human act within the confines of a material body is simply inconceivable; that guilt is a stain on the soul, a spiritual stain; and we can no more make a material body the subject of something spiritual than we can wrap an angel in cellophane; look at the terrible time our modern philosophers have had trying to place intelligence in animals and to keep free will out of the human soul.

No, these two opinions will not do. Even if it were possible to transmit the sin by transmission of body or of soul, there would still be the enormous difficulty of keeping that sin a voluntary act; and voluntary it must be if it is to be a sin. To St. Thomas these opinions seemed to involve more than great difficulties; they involved impossibilities and that itself was enough to justify their discard, for we are not asked to believe impossible things. St. Thomas pointed out that there was a third possibility: original sin was not transmitted by the transmission of the soul, nor by the transmission of the body, but by the transmission of *human nature*.

Let us look at it this way. In the individual there are properties that are common to all human nature and there are family traits like long noses or red hair; both types of traits are passed on to the next generation according to definite laws. There are still other strictly individual traits which belong to the individual and die with him. In other words, in the individual nature there are some things that belong to nature; and there are some that belong to the individual, things that are acquired over and above the natural or specific perfections. The same was true of nature in the beginning: it had some traits that belonged to it as nature and other perfections that came to it by grace, perfections that we will see in detail in the next chapter.

If we imagine an individual given the chance by one trial to have the privilege of passing his strictly personal traits on to his children or to lose them both for himself and for his children, we have a fairly accurate picture of the position of Adam in the beginning of the human race. He had the chance by one trial to win for his children, or to lose for both himself and his children, the privilege of passing on not only human nature's own traits but the perfections that came to it in the beginning by grace. And he lost.

In other words, Adam was the head of the race, not only biologically, but also spiritually. Through his elevation to the supernatural order he was constituted by God the spokesman and agent of humanity, just as by his creation he was constituted physical head of the race.

This original sin, then, is my sin, not in so far as I am a person but precisely as I have received human nature. It is not a personal sin but a sin of nature, a sin committed for all human nature by the head of human nature, and coming down to every individual human being who receives human nature from that first head of the human race. So in the human seed original sin is present, not actually, but virtually in so far as that seed virtually contains human nature.

Actually this is my sin; I have sinned in Adam, not in the mere physical sense of being contained in Adam as in an ancestor, but in the sense of Adam having acted for the whole human race. Perhaps it will be more clear if we visualize all human beings as members of one body of which Adam was the head, the director; then somewhat the way that sin is in the assassin's knife-stroke because his hand is moved by participating in the action of his will, so sin is in the descendant of Adam: the sin of Adam is participated by his descendants even though thousands of years have intervened.

Immediately an objection comes into our minds: why did we have nothing to say about the choice of this head of humanity? The answer is fairly obvious. If we waited for an election until every human being had a chance to cast a vote, the whole thing would have been ridiculous, for the great majority of the human race would have been long since dead and beyond any personal interest in the outcome of Adam's test. It was something to be settled immediately if the descendants of Adam were to reap any benefit by it; and there were no electors handy. Moreover, if we had been present and had a chance to pass on Adam's qualifications as head of the human race, we would have seen the most perfect man God ever produced (except Christ Himself Who was God) physically, intellectually and morally. Would we have been willing to make the gamble? Would we have been willing to accept the rewards if Adam had made a better fight of it?

Ah yes, but after all sin has to be voluntary to be sin at all; yet original sin invades even the womb of the mother to infect the soul of the still unborn child. Surely the child at that age is not exercising his free will, not producing voluntary acts. Of course not. Original sin is certainly not voluntary by an act of my personal will; but it is voluntary and mine as proceeding voluntarily from the head of the human race, the champion of the human race, the champion who failed.

It is evident from this that the personal sins of Adam, the personal sins of any of our ancestors, are not part of our heritage. It is only this sin of nature that comes down to us, for only in this limited field did anyone have the power to act for us. We lost the acquired perfections of nature; but the other perfections come to us intact. On the other hand, no descendant of Adam escapes the contagion of this sin; it comes with the nature received from the head of the human race. The solitary exception is our Blessed Lady who was never contaminated by original sin through a special privilege of God in anticipation of the merits of Christ; and that is what we call the Immaculate Conception. Christ Himself, of course, did not have original sin; but He was not an exception to this universal rule for He did not descend from Adam by carnal generation. Carnal generation is the absolutely necessary condition for the transmission of this sin; just as the hands or feet can participate the sin of intellect and will in so far as they are subject to the movement of intellect and will, so all men participate the sin of Adam in so far as they are moved by Adam through the motion of carnal generation, i.e. in so far as they receive human nature from Adam.

St. Thomas expresses this again and again by saying that the sin is transmitted by the active principle of generation, the father. That statement has been persistently misunderstood. The argument proceeds from Adam's headship of the human race, from the immediate father's headship of the family. The sin comes down through the male line precisely because Adam was constituted head of the race, the father constituted head of the family. To throw out St. Thomas's opinion on the grounds of modern medicine, *if* modern medicine has grounds for rejecting the scientific stand of the thirteenth century on the active principle of generation, this is to misunderstand St. Thomas. Carnal generation is the instrument of transmission of human nature and thus of original sin. The basis of our participation in original sin is the headship and consequent orderly subordination necessary for the good of the race and the good of the family. But it does follow from this that if God miraculously generates a man (as He did Christ) or if the scientist were to produce a man in a laboratory, in either case there would be no original sin, for the necessary condition of its transmission is missing, i.e. reception of human nature from Adam.

The modern bitterness against God has more than one explanation. There is, for example, the jealous preference of men for the idols materialism has set up; and this is no more than the logical climax of the gradual development of philosophy these past few centuries. A more recent source of this bitterness, recent only in its extension and in the sweeping devastation of its denials, might be dated from the despair of the World War. It is engaged primarily with the problem of evil and bitterly rejects God because of the evil it finds. Actually it is a strange mixture of insults to God, insults to men and absurd flatteries of humanity; like the incoherent ravings of a man gone mad.

There is first of all a violent rejection of a God Who would usher into the world men loaded down with the weight of sin and yet demand that they measure up to heights of virtue. This, they say, is a cruel, bitter, mocking divinity without the elemental justice of a crooked politician; a monster who made the world for the torture of men. Then, coming down a step further and taking the picture of God drawn by the destroyers and betrayers of human freedom as an authentic photograph, they vent their mad wrath on a straw god who never existed; on a god who creates men for hell, who pushes them into sin and awaits gleefully with a whip in his hand to punish the evil he himself has caused; on a god who should have prevented all this evil and did not. After having insulted God and insulted men by denying them the fundamental control of their actions, they leap to absurd heights in supposing the puny intellect of the creature they have so insulted is capable of taking in by one glance the sweeping plans of infinite wisdom. They meet hunger and thirst, pain, accident, death and injustice and demand to know why they cannot understand these things happening in a universe ruled by a good God. Why should not the creature who cannot master one human science grasp all the intricate workings of infinite wisdom ruling a universe from His eternal throne?

Perhaps they are a little mad. At least they are a distinct disappointment to the race that bore them; for surely we, with our great gift of intellect, should be able to appreciate the patent evidence of divine perfection which sin parades before the world. The very possibility of triumph and defeat, of virtue and vice, of success and failure, of heaven and hell, is both a tribute to man and a generous sharing of divinity's power with humanity. Only a master sure of his power, supreme in his greatness, would dare to give so much independent power to his subjects; only a being infinite in his goodness would invite such a hopelessly inferior subject as man to share his own divine life; only a mind infinitely wise and a heart infinitely generous could have put into the hands of man the tools which would make that brilliant participation of divinity's life the product of man's own efforts. He could have made man merely an animal, a plant, a chemical. He could have put man on a spiritual dole and freed him of responsibility and self-respect; He could have tossed him the scraps from the tables of heaven as to a beggar who had no claim. But the astonishing thing He did was to treat man as man.

It is not well, in talking of sin, to forget Bethlehem and Nazareth, and the long, weary, discouraging years that led up to the climax of Calvary. It is not good to forget the bread of angels, the picture of the slave nourished on the body and blood of his Master, the strong flow of grace, the wide horizons opened by faith and hope. In a word, we are blinding ourselves if we refuse to see the manifest evidences of divine love as well as of divine justice, if we refuse to see that God has treated us not merely as men, but as friends.

But even as men, the very nature of sin itself shows us the thoughtfulness of God. He gave us the privacy our nature demands; an inner sanctuary that no force, no devil, no man can violate. And He himself refuses to challenge the inviolability of that sanctuary. That soul is our own; its actions can be forced by no one else. They are ours; they must be ours if we are to be held accountable for them, for only by proceeding under our control to our goals are they human actions. The same is true of our sins, for they too are human actions.

Even the abuse of our mastery of our actions furnishes overwhelming evidence of the beneficent ingenuity and merciful justice of God. Time and again our sins are turned to good; time and again we are snatched from the hardness of pride through the humiliation of other sins, brought to our knees by the awful face of sin and the kind face of God. Again and again suffering and misfortune serve as steps to bring us closer to the divine heights. Even the raging activity of Satan himself is made the material by which the sanctity of the friends of God is fashioned. And when, after years of patient search for sheep that insisted on losing themselves, after silent years of unbearable insult, divine mercy sees the quest for love is hopeless, the very damnation of the sinner is made to serve the double purpose of warning, helping others and fulfilling divine justice.

Why should we have to face these awful possibilities? Why must we play the game of life and run the risk of defeat? These are the questions of the man or woman afraid to live, afraid to be human, the questions of the coward. These are the questions of those who would sacrifice freedom for fear of making a mistake, give up intellect for fear of ignorance, give up action for fear of failure, give up heaven for fear of hell, give up life for fear of living. We cannot have anyone of these without the possibility of the other; and our dignity as men is precisely that we can have, if we will, the most perfect of all, the triumph of life, a share in the life of God.

CHAPTER XVI

(OUTLINE)

EVOLUTION OF UNHAPPINESS

(Q. 82–85)

1. Beginning of sin in the individual:
   (*a*) Original sin—a disposition of nature.
   (*b*) Original sin—not a principle of action.
   (*c*) Original sin—singular in each individual.

2. The essence of sin's beginning:
   (*a*) Original sin formally—the privation of original justice.
   (*b*) Original sin materially—concupiscence.

3. The equality of sin's beginning:
   (*a*) Original sin equal in all men.
   (*b*) Inequality of inclination to sin not from original sin.

4. Place of sin's beginning:
   (*a*) Place of adherence—the soul.
   (*b*) Its place in the essence of the soul and the faculties of the soul:
      (1) First in the essence of the soul.
      (2) By way of action in the faculties, first in the will.
   (*c*) A defence of humanity:
      (1) Bad will and corrupt nature.
      (2) Infection in lower faculties.

5. Damage done by sin to human nature—"de fide" doctrine:
   (*a*) To principles of nature.
   (*b*) To original justice.
   (*c*) To natural inclination to virtue:
      (1) Never totally destroyed, even in damned.
      (2) Infinitely impeded by actual sin.

6. The "wounds of nature": Ignorance, malice, weakness, concupiscence:
   (*a*) With regard to pure nature.
   (*b*) With regard to nature in state of original justice.

7. Death and corporal defects as results of sin:
    (*a*) Of original sin.
    (*b*) Of actual sin.
    (*c*) As natural to man.

8. Root and beginning of personal (actual) sin.

9. Sin's decoys—capital sins:
    (*a*) Meaning of capital sin.
    (*b*) Distinction from mortal sin.
    (*c*) Division and objects of capital sins.

Conclusion :

1. Original sin and the individual:
    (*a*) Integrity of his nature.
    (*b*) His inclination to virtue.
    (*c*) His sovereign independence.

2. Personal (actual) sin and the individual:
    (*a*) Its attack on nature's integrity.
    (*b*) Its attack on the inclination to virtue.
    (*c*) Its attack on independence.

3. Plan of sin revealed.

4. The individual, sin and happiness.

CHAPTER XVI

EVOLUTION OF UNHAPPINESS

(Q. 82-85)

IT has become the fashion in our day for great minds to escape their tremendous labours for a few hours by reading utterly fantastic stories, preferably detective stories. These are calculated to fire the imagination and to set the mind completely at rest; in fact they forbid the use of intellect under pain of ruining the story. The large number of great minds revealed by a check of the circulation of these stories is a little incredible. At any rate in one of these stories a doctor succeeded in accomplishing the impossible—exchanging the souls of two men: the one was a middle-aged man, a chronic invalid who was forever taking medicine, suffering attacks of pain in the region of the heart, dragging himself along carefully, miserably, without hope; the other was a young man, vigorous, who had never known a day of sickness and who had all youth's hope for the future. Five years after the operation, the splendid young body which the chronic invalid had purchased was unrecognizable, floods of medicine were again necessary, the heart pain was present once more and the future looked as dark as ever, while the decrepit old body taken on by the youth was operating perfectly, charging vigorously ahead into the alluring future.

Utterly fantastic, of course, but it brings out a point that is not at all fantastic, the point that our present activity is moulded by our future; and our estimation of the future is largely based on what we have received from the past. Many a rich man's son has ruined his life because the future was too securely fixed by the labours of his father in the past; and many a son inheriting a disgraced name dragged that name still further down because the future was so hopelessly black.

Much the same is true in the moral order. Some men have been terribly cruel to their fellow men because their own salvation (they thought) was perfectly arranged for them no matter what they did; others have been incredibly vicious because they were sure they had no chance for eternal happiness. Some men have given up the struggle before they had fairly started, sure that no man could win in this fight with the corrupt nature he had inherited; while others have taken disastrous risks serenely sure of the perfection of human nature.

We saw in the last chapter that man did inherit sin, that he was born with original sin on his soul by the very fact of receiving human nature from the first head of the human race. It is important that we know just what that inheritance is. We must know what the past has given us, because the present will be formed by our outlook on the future and our estimate of the future is largely based on our inheritance from the past. Many a game has been won or lost before the teams took the field; over-confidence or defeatism, the conviction of a superiority that makes effort unnecessary or of an inferiority that makes effort worthless—one is as dangerous as the other in facing the game of life.

Even an atheistic doctor would be reasonably astonished if the new-born baby he was handing to the nurse were to speak up and flatly declare itself an atheist. We do not expect that sort of thing at that age. The baby can and does become mightily irritated at the way it is handled and gives voice in no uncertain terms to anger, fear, sorrow and pleasure; but it does not begin life by sowing wild oats. Whatever sin is on the soul of that infant is certainly not a personal sin but a sin of nature. It is something habitual, not a passing action; yet not a habit built up, for example, like chewing tobacco or dropping ashes on the rug.

In fact it is not a habit in the sense we have explained habits; it is more of an habitual disposition of nature itself. To visualize original sin in terms of habit leads us to make the mistake of considering original sin as a principle of evil acts from which all sorts of sins pop out at the first opportunity as mathematical solutions leap from the mathematician's habits of thought, or as thoughtfulness slips silently from the Christian's habit of charity. A much more accurate picture would be that of a symphony orchestra in which each man decided to be his own leader and express his personal moods in his music. Original sin is precisely that: a dissolution of the harmony of original justice. Picture it in terms of a complicated chemical substance where all the elements were beautifully balanced and then suddenly that balance was destroyed, as, for example, in the explosion of T.N.T. or dynamite; or, more humanly, as the attack of an illness which destroys the harmony and smooth co-ordination of our physical organism. That is original sin—a languor, a sickness of nature, a destruction of the smooth harmony of humanity.

It is possible to look upon original sin as multiple in as much as it is the beginning of sin in the individual, as the other sins of the individual are virtually contained in it; or considering that first sin of Adam with its elements of pride, disobedience and gluttony we can call original sin multiple. But strictly speaking, original sin does not multiply in the individual as lies do in the confirmed liar —until they have formed a maze from which even the ingenuity of a liar cannot escape. There is just one original sin to each man entering the world. Adam, after all, had authority to act for us in only his one particular: the gaining or losing of the gifts nature had acquired by grace. What he did with the rest of his life, what sins he committed or what temptations he resisted has nothing whatever to do with the inheritance which comes down to us. This is evident from the nature of original sin: it is a dissolution of harmony, the discordance of the elements of human nature. One such discordance is all one man can accommodate in the small house of his soul. The absolute authority of the head of the house has been destroyed and every member proceeds on the assumption that there is no one in command. It is very much the same as when the principle of harmonious operation in the human body, the soul, departs and each ingredient of the human body goes about its own proper function independently, separately, to the ultimate dissolution of that body; so with the destruction of original justice, the principle of harmonious operation in the soul of man, the faculties of man go their own discordant ways.

Suppose a sword were made out of the only material available—tin. The workmanship might be perfect, but the result would be a poor fighting instrument; at the first stroke it would bend out of shape. If the material had been glass, then in spite of supreme craftsmanship, that sword would be brittle and would shatter the first time it was used. God, in creating man, set about to make a creature that would link the material and the spiritual world. Man was to be a small universe in himself, a difficult combination of the powers of the plant, the animal and the spiritual world. The precise difficulty came in linking the animal and the spiritual powers; to co-ordinate and yet not impair one or the other meant that in the one creature there would be two sources of activity, each with its own proper motion, stimuli and goal—the animal and the rational appetite or will. By the very nature of the material with which He worked, God could produce only a delicately balanced, nicely harmonized but decidedly unstable creature; always the animal appetite would have its own field of activity, its own motion which would inevitably clash at times with that other independent motion of the human will. With the one seeking the supreme, universal good, and the other by its very nature concentrating on the immediate, the sensible, the particular good, civil war was inevitable.

From the very material that must go into human nature, then, there goes inevitably a defect just as in the tin or the glass sword. Naturally speaking, man must be defective in comparison with the rest of nature. God, in the beginning, overcame this natural defect by preternatural and supernatural gifts; and this state of defective nature preserved from its defects we call the state of original justice.

Original justice consisted precisely in the perfect subordination of the will or rational appetite of man to God and, as a consequence, the perfect subordination of the animal, indeed to some extent of the plant life of man, to his rational appetite or will. Briefly, it was an absolutely perfect harmony, the perfect balance, of the volatile ingredients of human nature. Original sin strictly and formally consists in the disruption of that harmony, in the insubordination of the will of man to God. From this fundamental insubordination all the rebellion of the lower side of human nature to the higher followed, much as the crash of the top of a huge smokestack follows on the blasting of its foundation.

When St. Augustine and the other Fathers speak of original sin as concupiscence they are describing the material or consequent side of original sin, the toppling of the upper structure of the smokestack. They are distinctly not speaking in terms of the gorgings of the glutton or the lust of the libertine; they are speaking of that general scattering of the animal appetites of man, each to its proper object, regardless of the welfare of the whole man.

There is an important point here, a point we have touched on before but which in this day well merits a repetition. The control of animal appetite by the will, the repression of anger or sorrow or lust, is not an act of violence against nature from which we can expect the awful punishment that nature inflicts on those who transgress her laws. Rather the refusal to repress those appetites, the grant of full play to passion in the name of nature, is a mockery that nature promptly and ruthlessly resents. For human passions, the animal appetites in human nature, were designed to be guided by reason. We are, as a matter of fact, acting humanly only in so far as we have those passions under control.

There is no ebb and flow in death as there is in life. So we are rather indifferent to the training of a guardian of a morgue; but not at all indifferent to the training of a hospital staff. If the morgue guardian were to make the rounds of his clients in an effort to see which was the deadest, it would only be because he had tired of playing solitaire. Death, as the absence of life, is absolute and equal in all men; original sin, as the absence of original justice, is just as absolute, just as equal in all men. The fact that one man has more inclination to murder than another is not because he has a bigger original sin than his neighbour, as one victim of an accident might have a bigger lump on his head than his fellow victim. The difference is due to differences in physical complexion, plus, of course, the difference built into each man by the personal habits he has acquired by repeated acts.

If I have a heavy dictionary and a newspaper side by side on a small table, I can efficiently and expeditiously put them both on the floor by simply pulling the table out from under them. The difference in the crash they make on landing and in the speed with which they fall is not accounted for by saying the table was pulled out from under each of them in a different fashion, or that one lost more of the support of the table than the other; rather the difference is bound up with the physical characteristics of a newspaper and a dictionary. Original sin has pulled out from under us the support of original justice; it has destroyed the leadership of our human orchestra; the difference between the racket made by the first violin and the bass drum is the difference between violins and bass drums.

We cannot, then, walk along the street detecting original sin in the shifty glance of one man and the bullying threats of another. We are often sure that just by looking at a person's face we can read his character, and sometimes that is true, but sometimes it is false. We must look deeper than the face for original sin.

Like all sin—all virtue too—this sin resides in the soul of man, for only by reason of his spiritual soul can man either sin or be virtuous. But even that leaves a great deal of latitude, for in the soul we can distinguish the essence of the soul, the intellect and the will. Then, too, there are those subject faculties, the irascible or emergency and the concupiscible or mild appetites. Where does original sin fit in? A clue to the answer is had in the commonplace contrast of the man who drinks himself into a stupor to drown his worries and his companion who goes blithely along the road to stupor with him because he likes it. Both have committed the sin of drunkenness; but in one that sin is in the irascible or emergency appetite running away from a difficulty, in the other it is in the concupiscible or mild appetite seeking pleasure, even the pleasure of stupid oblivion. The difference is in the goal first reached by the motive cause of the sin. The motive cause of original sin is the transmission of human nature and its first complete goal is the soul precisely as the form of the body, precisely as the vivifying, specifying principle of human nature. Original sin finds its secure home in the very essence of the soul.

From this depth of the human soul, the sickness of nature which is original sin spreads out to affect the actions of man, gradually becoming less and less virulent in its effects as it gets farther and farther from the focus of infection. It is like a strong light which becomes fainter and fainter as the length and width of its beam grow greater and greater.

In relation to actions, original sin in its indirect fashion affects first the proximate principles of human action—the will and the intellect—and then the more remote principles of the animal side of man's nature. But first and principally it affects the will. After all, it should, for its opposite, original justice, fell principally on the will, completely subordinating it to God; then, too, the will is the first principle of action and motion in human nature. If original sin is to affect human actions it must get at the root principles of those actions.

This obvious truth is of tremendous significance in daily human life. It means that the infection which really must be worried about is the infection in the will, the insubordination to God; and that brings us squarely back to our analysis of the sole cause of human unhappiness in which we traced that source of unhappiness to bad will. In other words, if that first principle of human action is not pointed at the goal of reason we have an enemy in the heart of our own camp; while if the will is subordinate to God, if it is a good will, the infection in the lower appetites is relatively unimportant. It is not only possible to look upon the rebellion of the sense appetite as morally irrelevant; that is the only true way to consider this rebellion and, as a corollary of practical moral guidance, a smile of contempt is a much more deadly weapon against such a rebellion than hours of worry.

Perhaps a good deal of the over-emphasis we give to the infection of the sense appetite is due to a misunderstanding of the Fathers. Very often they speak of the sense appetites of man as being most infected by original sin and they especially single out the generative faculties, the sense of touch and the concupiscible or mild appetite in general. But always they are speaking of this infection in relation not to personal but to original sin. In other words, these things are said to be more infected because by them the infection is spread, for by them human nature is passed on to succeeding generations; they are not said to be more infected because there is a greater moral deficiency in them.

In fact in relation to our personal or actual sins, these appetites are much less infected. They are on the outskirts of the metropolis where the plague has struck and they receive only a slight attack. The intensity of their rebellion against reason and will is no indication of the infection they have suffered; that is merely the nature of the senses. Of course the senses move more intensely to their objects; their union with their objects is more immediate, the object is a concrete, immediate good producing vividly real physical changes in the organism itself. But this is not due to original sin. From a moral point of view this intensity has no significance whatsoever beyond that given to it by deliberate will; in other words, this intensity is significant only in so far as it is the creature of our deliberate control.

Let us look at this concretely. Just what damage has been done to human nature by sin? Or better, just what damage can original sin, or any sin, do to our nature? Are we down in a gutter, foolishly thinking we can reach the stars when as a matter of fact we cannot drag ourselves up the few inches to the top of the kerb?

As we have already seen, the infallible authority of the Church solemnly declares that the will of man remains free despite original sin;[1] that the intellectual operations of man have genuine validity, can actually work to a sure knowledge of God;[2] and the hopelessly pessimistic claim of the reformers that every act of man is necessarily sinful has been solemnly condemned by that same infallible authority.[3]

[1] Council of Trent, Sess. VI, canon 5 (Denziger, # 815).
[2] Vatican Council, Sess. III, chap. 2 (Denziger, # 1785).
[3] Condemnation of the errors of Michael Baius in the Bull "Ex omnibus afflictionibus", Pius V, prop. 25, 35, 40, 67, 68, 74 (Denziger, # 1025, 1035, 1040, 1067, 1068, 1074). Condemnation of errors of the Jansenists, decree of the Holy Office, Dec. 7, 1690, Alexander VIII, prop. 2 and 8 (Denziger, # 1292, 1298). Confer appendix to chap. XX *infra*, p. 434 ff.

Examining the matter in more detail it is self-evident that original sin, or any sin, is incapable of destroying the constitutive principles of nature. A man caught in the grip of sweeping anger may do things that are not at all human, but he is no less a man after the anger than he was before. Body and soul, and the faculties of body and soul which are of the very nature of man, remain intact; the nature of man cannot be changed without destroying man and no sin destroys the humanity of man.

It is also self-evident that the original justice of man was destroyed by original sin. At least it is self-evident that such perfect harmony of subordination of the will to God, and of the lower faculties to the will, no longer exists, and our Faith tells us that the cause of this was original sin. Certainly we have not the preternatural gifts of immortality, freedom from suffering and pain that our first parents enjoyed.

This much we know: nature remains intact and the gifts acquired by nature through grace are lost. What worries us is the inclination to sin, the damage done to man's natural inclination to virtue, the upset caused by original sin to man's inclination to act according to reason, to follow the paths of reason to the goal of reason where human happiness is found.

The statement of the question gives the lead to its answer. This inclination to follow reason is natural to man, it belongs to his very nature, and as such it is indestructible. In other words, it is an integral part of his rationality and that rationality cannot be taken away from man. This is so absolutely true that even in the souls of the damned in hell that inclination to virtue, to follow reason, must still persist; and it is precisely the existence of that natural inclination which accounts for the terrible remorse of hell.

Perhaps this will be clearer if we look at this inclination to virtue from different angles. There is first of all its starting point in the soul, then its goal in virtuous or reasonable action, and finally the sensible faculties which it must often use to accomplish that action. From the first angle, the starting-point of the inclination in the soul, the inclination to virtue is absolutely indestructible. From the second angle, the goal of virtuous or reasonable action, this inclination to virtue can be infinitely impeded by our personal sins; by our actual sins we can pile up the chairs, tables, beds, mattresses, pianos against the door lest that inclination to virtue break through from our soul into action. But that is blocking it from the outside, not trying to blast it out of existence. From the third angle, the sensible faculties used in the virtuous action, of course we can root out the physical grooves cut by former virtuous actions; we can tear up the natural physical propensities to this or that kind of action by building up the physical propensities to contrary action, or even by such things as diet, disease, surgery and so on we can so change our physical make-up as to reverse the physical tendencies to this or that type of action.

I remember meeting a totally astonished and considerably crestfallen young doctor who, because of inexperience, had made the serious error of curing a chronic invalid. His patient was a middle-aged woman who during her long years of illness, had seemed an almost perfect character; always cheerful, smiling, patiently enduring her sufferings, creating an atmosphere that drew a constant crowd of visitors, not so much to give their sympathy as to be inspired. Then along came this bright young doctor and practically overnight he effected a cure. There could be no doubt about the cure. It was so complete that the patient herself could not even feel sick, could not possibly stay in bed and retain any shred of self-respect. And overnight the perfect character turned into a shrewish, ill-humoured, discontented person who could be borne with only from a sense of duty. Of course the full brunt of her discontent fell on the head of the young doctor. He was as astounded as the good

Samaritan would have been had the victim of robbers curtly ordered him to get out of sight until the photographers had arrived. The doctor could not understand that now this woman had no way to express the nobility of her character except by washing dishes and she did not care for the change; there could be no more lofty patience, no floods of sympathy from friends, no complete release from worries that might upset her. The doctor, in fact, had wrecked her "career".

A detailed explanation of this doctrine of original sin usually calls forth the immediate protest: "How about the wounds of nature?" It is a protest made in an aggrieved tone as though human nature has been done an injustice by being stripped of so many perfect excuses. Well, how about the wounds of nature? Theologians teach, quite accurately, that human nature has suffered four wounds: ignorance in the intellect, malice in the will, weakness in the irascible appetite and concupiscence in the concupiscible appetite. The positive side of that teaching is that the prudence, justice, fortitude and temperance of human nature have been damaged, that all the principles of activity in man are considerably less efficient than they were in the beginning of man's career.

That is all true. But what human nature is under discussion? The purely hypothetical human nature that has all that naturally belongs to it and no more? Of course not. The human nature in question is that with which man started his career in the universe, the human nature that existed in the state of original justice, the human nature that had not only what naturally belonged to it but in addition had the supernatural and preternatural gifts by which God corrected the defects inherent in the very material from which human nature was made. In other words the theologians are engaged in a *de facto* discussion. From this point of view human nature has certainly been wounded.

Suppose we were to take two infants, both normal and healthy, and rear one of them in a nudist colony, the other in a socially prominent family in New York. After twenty years we bring the two together and put them on absolutely equal terms by stripping the clothes from the New Yorker. The product of nudist training does not consider his nakedness an injury; but the New Yorker is furious in his indignation at the injury done him. After original sin, we are in the state of the indignant New Yorker. Nothing that belonged to nature has been removed, only those acquired perfections that came to nature through grace have been stripped from us, and we very rightly feel that we have been injured. We have. But our nature has not been degraded; it is not a beaten, half-living thing that must drag itself bitterly to the performance of impossible tasks.

Take the obvious defects of death, sickness, injury, hunger, thirst, and so on. They are all unquestionable defects resulting from original sin. But they are also defects that flow from the very nature of man. If there had been no original sin and no original justice with its exceptional gifts, man would still face death, sickness, and all the rest. His nature contains the seeds of its own dissolution in its material composition. Original sin caused these defects only in so far as it removed the wholly supernatural and preternatural impediments to them by destroying original justice.

We can summarize this doctrine by noticing the action of our own actual or personal sins. These personal sins of ours can also produce just such effects as death, sickness, injury, and so on. The point is that it is not precisely as sins that they cause this damage; it is as physical acts. It is the substance of the act, not its deordination or guilt that produces these physical effects. In other words, the object of the attack of any sin, as sin, is grace, but the grace attacked by original sin had dependent upon it a shining array of gifts to nature that were cast aside when that grace was rejected by Adam.

This is our inheritance of sin. With this heritage we start to carve out our own lives; slowly, step by step, day by day, action by action, we build up to splendid success or down to abysmal failure. We have already seen the elements that go into successful living; what starts us on the road to failure? What is the very beginning of the purely personal failures that ruin our lives?

Like all beginnings, the beginnings of personal sin are very simple, very clear. Sin, like all human action, is aimed at a goal; the beginning of our sins, then, can be traced to that first wrong goal which we placed before ourselves as the target of all our actions. More simple, it is an inordinate appetite for our own excellence that goes by the name of pride. We want this or that partial good for ourselves so badly that we turn away from the universal good and to ourselves. The formal element of sin, the aversion from God, belongs to the very nature of pride, whereas it is only a consequent of other sins, something accidental that is ordinarily quite beyond the intentions of the sinner.

This is the beginning, the end or goal in the mind from which all sin comes. As far as execution or the acts leading to that end goes, the first place is given to avarice, to the inordinate love of money. Not that every sin must come from avarice, but avarice is to other sins as the root is to the tree; it gives them nourishment, giving to man the faculty of both desiring and committing every other sin. There is no sin which the avaricious man will not commit to satisfy his avarice and every kind of sin can and ordinarily does arise from this inordinate love of money.

These are the two great starting points of sin—pride and avarice; these are the two great first principles of human failure. Ranked just beneath them we have the sins that have come to be called the capital sins. There has always been much misunderstanding about these capital sins, a misunderstanding that has arisen from the notion that they are singled out as capital because they are so terribly evil in themselves. They are not. As a matter of fact some of them are essentially venial sins. Their precise danger lies in their ability to call so many other sins into being. They are the sirens of sin, the decoys that allure men to their doom. They are capital sins because they aim at partial goods which are outstanding in their attractiveness; they aim at particular goods that have a general appeal, goods that can be attained in different ways and so they almost automatically call into being a whole host of other sins as partners in attaining their ends.

A few chapters back we touched on the various ways in which one sin can cause another. We noticed how one sin starts a groove or habit that makes the next sin of the same type that much easier and more attractive, as, for example, in the sin of drunkenness; again, one sin can be the labourer bringing the material for many other sins, as, for example, gluttony for the sins of luxury; finally one sin brings on another in acting as an end or final cause, as the avarice of the swindler generates fluent falsehoods. It is in this last way that the capital sins do their deadly work; it is only in this last way, by way of final causality, that one sin formally causes another. We may have two vessels designed to hold water but they will be decidedly different in form because we design them for decidedly different ends—for bathing and for drinking purposes. The end determines the form of an action; so these capital sins, acting as ends or goal, formally call into being the other sins that help to attain their ends.

This will be a little clearer if we glance at the partial goods which are outstanding in their attractiveness. Descending the scale of attractiveness we come first to the goods of the soul and see our own excellence with its corresponding capital sin of pride or vainglory; then the goods of the body, either individual or specific, with the corresponding capital sins of gluttony and lust; for external goods, there is the capital sin of avarice. All these have direct and immediate appeal. A hardly less powerful impetus is that to escape evil joined to good, with its corresponding capital sin of spiritual sloth striving to escape the labour involved in attaining the goods of the soul; the evil joined to the good of another is evaded either without violence by means of envy, or with violent resistance through anger. This is the field of the capital sins and it is the fundamental nature of this field, not the essential malice of these sins, that makes the capital sins so dangerous.

Although the capital sins themselves are very dangerous, a knowledge of their nature and significance is of incalculable advantage both to the confessor and to the layman in the regulation and improvement of everyday life. It is, as a matter of fact, not extraordinary to have a penitent confess to boasting, vanity, quarrelling, disobedience, with no mention of pride; or to confess malicious gossiping and detraction with no mention of envy. The sins actually confessed are really symptoms; if they are recognized as such, it is possible to attack the moral disease at the point of infection and to produce some remarkable results in a short time. The attempt to battle each of these so called "daughters" of the capital sins results in little more than complete discouragement; failure is almost inevitable, for the real cause of the whole disorder is left unchecked, indeed unnoticed. In other words, the list of capital sins is not the fruit of a theological passion for systematic arrangement nor a memory-test for the child learning the catechism; it is a list of the fundamental diseases which produce human unhappiness. We make a serious and discouraging blunder by occupying ourselves solely with symptoms, mistaking the symptoms for the disease which calls them forth.

Summing this up briefly, we find that we have wasted a good deal of sympathy on our poor human nature. The injuries done to human nature by original sin do not give us grounds for excusing ourselves from the business of living. True enough we have lost much by original sin; but nothing to which our nature gave us title. In the beginning of man's life on earth God corrected the defects which necessarily followed upon the very material of human nature by supernatural and preternatural gifts dependent on the grace first given to Adam. The loss of that grace through original sin stripped us of all the extras God had heaped upon our nature; but no damage was done to nature itself. There is nothing wrong with our nature; but it could have been much better off. As it is, the constitutive principles of that nature remain intact with all that nature intended man should have; but within that nature are the seeds of civil war and ultimate dissolution. For within that nature is a delicate balance of contrary elements that make for discord in action and ultimate dissolution, the discord of animal and rational appetite, the dissolution inseparable from material things.

Our inclination to virtue, rooted in the very rationality of nature because it means no more than the inclination to act according to reason, cannot be blasted out of existence. It must endure even through an eternity of hell and there furnish the basis of the terrible remorse of the damned. The sovereignty of the free will of man is still guaranteed; no amount of rebellion, no amount of external force or internal collapse can make the human action of a man other than an action proceeding under his deliberate control to goals of his choice. In a word, coming into the world even with original sin on our souls we are still masters of our actions, masters of our lives, and with the assured help of the grace of God we are still capable of carving out an eternal niche in heaven by our seemingly insignificant actions. We still have human lives to live and we still have the means to live them successfully. Even now failure is our own because our actions are our own.

Our actual or personal sins may, when built into habits, be immediate principles from which flow other evil acts. But this is never true of original sin which causes other sins only because it has pulled out from under us the support of original justice by which those sins might have been impeded. But even these actual, personal sins cannot take away from the integrity of our human nature; man's nature cannot be changed without being destroyed and no man is destroyed by sin. These personal sins can pile up infinite obstacles to the operation of the natural inclination to virtue, they can block up the doors by which that inclination might have proceeded from our souls to action; but they cannot remove that inclination to virtue from the soul of man. Granted that they can break down or remove the physical propensities to this or that act of virtue, the propensities that follow from our physical constitution, they must leave us rational creatures possessed of the inclination to follow the paths of reason to the goals of reason. They may attack the liberty of our wills, but again the attack is from the outside, doomed to failure before it starts. The rush of passion may set up a great clamour, the slow building up of habits may present serious difficulties, but always it remains true that the human action of a man is an action that has proceeded under his deliberate control, an action which is man's very own and for which he alone must answer because he alone was master of that action.

We cannot escape the task of living human lives by pointing to our inheritance of sin, or even by pointing to long lives of personal sins. As long as breath remains in the human body, man's life is his own. He is still capable of success or failure. It is no small help, in the living of that life, to know so surely just what methods of attack will be used to wreck human life. We do know. The plan of sin is briefly summed up in the capital sins, for their objects are the partial goods of outstanding appeal to human nature. It is certainly along these lines that sin will attempt to enter our lives; and it is these capital sins that will call others into being to attain their outstanding ends. The other sins are much more symptoms of these radical diseases, symptoms that patently indicate to us the root of our unhappiness and the means that must be taken to cure the diseases they reveal.

The individual man facing the risks of failure and the chances of success in human living faces one enemy—sin. He faces that enemy from the moment human nature is had. But always he faces it in the secure knowledge that it is not the kind of enemy that can overwhelm him by surprise or coerce him by force; rather it is an enemy that can enter the inviolable corridors of his soul only by invitation. It is not even a subtle enemy. All its plans of attack have been known through the centuries and its every appearance promptly indicates which of the limited number of roads it is using to approach the soul. Every man still faces the tremendous possibilities of human life, must face those possibilities. Their realization is through virtue moving to the goal of happiness; the failure to realize them is through sin moving to eternal misery. It is the individual man who must make the choice.

CHAPTER XVII

(OUTLINE)

THE RESULTS OF UNHAPPINESS

(Q. 86–89)

1. The cult of beauty—a modern paradox.

2. Beauty of soul—the splendour of natural and divine light.

3. Immediate and fundamental result of sin—ugliness of soul:
   - (*a*) Sin as cause of the staining of the soul.
   - (*b*) Essence of this stain: darkness.
   - (*c*) Duration of this stain.

4. Consequent result of sin—punishment:
   - (*a*) Debt of punishment as result of sin:
     - (1) Natural punishment.
     - (2) Sin as penalty of sin.
     - (3) Supernatural eternal punishment:
       - *a*. Fact of eternal punishment.
       - *b*. Its reasonableness.
       - *c*. Its immediate causes.
   - (*b*) Quantity and duration of punishment.
   - (*c*) Duration of debt of punishment.
   - (*d*) Sole cause of punishment:
     - (1) Guilt of sin, actual or original.
     - (2) Vicarious punishment.

5. Comparison of personal causes of punishment: mortal and venial sin:
   - (*a*) Their points of agreement and difference.
   - (*b*) Venial sin a disposition to mortal sin.
   - (*c*) Possibilities of venial sin becoming mortal and vice versa.

6. A reversal of scale of values:
   - (*a*) Modern attitude towards mortal and venial sin.
   - (*b*) Carelessness towards venial sin:
     - (1) Its foundation.
     - (2) Its gravity—results of venial sin.
     - (3) Venial sin a fault proper to fallen man.

Conclusion :

1. Some definitions of beauty.

2. Beauty and modern world:

   (*a*) A surface worship.
   (*b*) A worship that destroys its object.
   (*c*) A worship whose end is despair.

3. The home of beauty.

4. Beauty and happiness.

5. Beauty and God.

CHAPTER XVII

THE RESULTS OF UNHAPPINESS

(Q. 86–89)

PERHAPS one of the saving graces of our age is the fact that we have begun to bring beauty back into the everyday life of man. Kitchens, bathrooms, peeling knives and face cloths are recognized as capable of attractiveness as well as of utility. That note of splendid order has crept into our designs of motor-cars, locomotives and railroad coaches. And perhaps we are beginning to imagine that we belong to an age that is in love with beauty; in proof of which we might adduce the constant interest in beauty contests, the elevation of actresses and actors to the rank of fabulously salaried individuals, our horror of ugliness, pain and suffering.

But against all this we would have to balance the ugliness of our industrial centres, the disorder of our economic life, the terrific toll we have taken from industrial workers, our lack of interest in the human things of human life—the spiritual values of man. In other words, only a superficial observer could make the mistake of thinking we were in love with beauty. Only a superficial observer could fail to see that we have been robbing man of his capacity for appreciating the beautiful, blinding man to the sources of beauty, depriving man of his greatest beauty. There is a significance in the design of our streamlined locomotives, a significance that is made startlingly clear as one sees them slide beneath the huge buildings that now serve as railroad stations, as an insect scuttles beneath a rock to escape the healthy light and air of a summer day. For all our love of beauty presents the constant paradox of love which destroys, the paradox of a creature made for the spiritual world vainly attempting to satisfy himself by burrowing into the sensible only to destroy both himself and the sensible world with which he has fallen in love.

There is a spark of that forgotten spiritual beauty in every man, or at least the possibility of that spark of beauty; a spark, tiny in comparison with the infinite fire of supreme beauty, but still bearing all the vital brightness that clings to the child of such a divine fire. It is very difficult to translate the Latin word used to describe the beauty which belongs to the soul of man (*nitor*). It expresses the sheen of new garments, the pure brightness of gold, the gleaming beauty of silver. Perhaps the best translation would be "lustrous splendour"; whatever the translation, it must call forth the image of pure streaming light, of bright beauty breaking forth from the soul to adorn the actions of man with splendour, like a burst of sunlight escaping from the splendour of the sun to breathe the breath of beauty into the lifeless, stained-glass windows of a cathedral.

We can gain a deeper insight into the beauty of the soul by looking for a moment at one of the briefest definitions of beauty. Beauty has been called the "splendour of order"; order, in other words, so clearly breaking through the material in which it is found as to command our attention and admiration. It is a profound, a compact definition, one that could well stand long and serious examination. But even a cursory glance at it gives us the clue to the essential beauty of the soul, for the soul has a double principle of order; the reason of man and the reason and wisdom of God. Both of these carry with them the notion of light, of clarity, of splendid illumination: the one the light in the hands of a wayfarer, guiding each of his steps, sweeping about the dark world around him in a constant revelation of truth, of goodness, of beauty; the other the powerful creative beacon that calls into being the path followed by the pilgrim man, that creates the beauty he sees, that calls him home to the source of all beauty.

It is in this double light that the soul of man was meant to bask. It should never for an instant be out of the field of this double light. All of its actions should shine forth with this brilliance which penetrates the very essence of the soul. This is the beauty of soul which is so hard to describe in stiff language: the splendour of the light of human reason, of divine reason and wisdom, breaking forth from the soul to give life and beauty to the actions of man.

The beauty of a stained-glass window could be destroyed by hurling a brick through that window; or that beauty could be rendered ineffective by hiding the window in a dark cellar where streaming sunlight could never filter through it. There is no brick that will shatter the soul; once called into existence it must go on and on through all eternity. But it can be hidden from the streaming light of human and divine reason; it can escape the paths mapped out by reason and slink into the dark by-ways of sin. In those by-ways it comes face to face with ugliness; in those foul alleys a man sees sights that take the light out of his eyes, the spring out of his step, the hope out of his face, that leave his soul stained and befouled.

For there is more to the ruin of the beauty of the soul than mere darkness. In our earlier treatment of sin we spoke of its double element: a turning away from reason and God and a turning to the partial goods the world has to offer, an aversion from the last end and a conversion to creatures. The first robs the soul of the splendour of the light of human and divine reason; but it is the second that befouls the soul. Every sin is unnatural, is irrational, every serious sin is a revulsion from the true goal of reason and of human life. But every sin is more than that. Every sin is a dragging of the human soul through the mud of earthly aims that destroys the sheen of humanity's splendid garments.

The pure, rich beauty of gold is destroyed when gold is mixed with some baser metal to form an alloy. Silver is tarnished by exposure, its beauty lost when it is bound to rougher, coarser metals to do the work of man. In much the same way does man stain his soul, mar its beauty with ugliness. We must stoop to something beneath us, tie ourselves in intimate union with the world that was made to serve us, if ugliness is to enter our souls.

St. Thomas could have accurate, scientific knowledge of all the base things of which men are capable and yet be the "Angel of the schools", for he was not stooping to the level of these things, but rather bringing them up to his level; what a man knows he brings into himself, stripping the object known of all the material elements incompatible with existence within the mind of man. On the contrary, we are dragged down to the level of the things we love, for love goes out to the object loved and embraces it. Let a man's love soar above himself into the regions of divinity and man is lifted out of himself; but let that love plunge into the world of the beasts and man becomes a beast. In other words, we are brought back to our old conclusion that human unhappiness—sin—is in the will of man; it is by the act of that will, love, that the soul of man can be dragged through mire or can be mixed intimately with baser things and so robbed of the lustrous splendour that belongs to it on its own level or on the heights of divinity.

This accurate notion of the immediate and fundamental result of sin brings out some discomfiting truths. It lends a deeper meaning to the title "Prince of darkness", for it reveals that prince as the prince of sin. With sin and darkness so closely linked, we can understand why it is that only in the state of sin do the slinking inhabitants of the dark corners of the soul dare to make a bold appearance, like so many bats or owls which would flee from the blinding light of the sun. It is easier to understand that there is no beauty in night precisely as night; its beauty lies in what little light still exists, a light which because of the overwhelming darkness takes on greater value. The beauty of this pale light is a beauty of dreams, of fiction, covering up ugliness and allowing us to pretend that ugliness is not present. In the clear, bright sunlight we see things for what they are. Perhaps the truth is harsh, much less seductively soothing and flattering than the dreamlight of the stars. But we can make no such grotesque mistakes in broad daylight as we can under cover of darkness. The saints were not by any means "queer people", thoroughly eccentric, if not a little insane; they were rather persons of eminent sanity because they were walking in the light of day and seeing things for what they really are.

Unlike the course of physical darkness, the darkness of sin is not something that automatically comes to an end. It is caused by a turning away from the light of reason, not by reason turning away from our acts. It endures just as long as we remain turned away from the double light of human and divine reason, just as long as we give our love to things beneath us rather than to the goal of all humanity. It is a darkness that may last only for an instant, for a day, or a month or a year; or it may last through all the reaches of eternity. But certainly until a man turns back to the light of reason and God he is asking the impossible when he demands that darkness cease while at the same time he forbids all light.

It is not enough to claim that a man had stopped committing murder years ago. Sin, like every human action, is a motion to a goal but to a goal that is off the track of reason. Mere stopping at the goal does not effect a return to the path of reason; the sinner must turn around and come back, he must retrace his steps to the point where the road of reason was abandoned for the alleys of sin. He must turn from the creature in which he has placed his end and go to God.

This is the first and fundamental result of sin, though oddly enough we are much more perturbed at the consequences of this ugliness of soul than at the ruin of the soul's beauty. It is odd. After all, we do not rail at the natural law that makes the rain pour through a broken window, nor at the wind that is carrying the rain through the broken window. If we have any growling to do, it will be at the little boy who has broken the window. What is more important, we shall do something about the broken window. That is the natural thing to do. But we are not at all natural in our attitude toward sin, perhaps because it always hits so close to home.

Instead of looking at the cause of the punishment of sin—at our own deliberately controlled action that brought the whole thing upon our heads—we prefer to grumble about the type of punishment, the duration of it, the unkindness of God in demanding our punishment. As a matter of fact, we are demanding our own punishment. This act of sin is ours and we cannot deny the parentage of our own child; we have stained our souls and it is that stain that demands punishment; we have turned away from the light of human and divine reason, and so long as we stay turned away, we are crying out for punishment.

In ruining the beauty of our souls we are rebels against order; we have attacked and reduced to ruin the splendour of order within ourselves. It would, as a matter of fact, be disastrous if this were a one-battle rebellion, if the order we have overthrown did not rise up in anger against us. For that would mean that we would be left undisturbed in the confusion and horror of disorder, in the darkness of ugliness; it is the ultimate of punishment in this life for the sinner to be delivered over to his own desires. That rising of the injured order in its own defence is the essence of the punishment of sin.

I am not at all sure that a worm does turn; at least it does not seem that it could do much damage even if it did turn upon its tormentor. But if it does not turn, at least it offers the defence of flight; and here it is one with all nature, for every order in nature rises in immediate defence against the attacks of an enemy, because every order has within itself the principle of self-conservation. The sinner has rebelled against a triple order; and all three of those orders rise up against him, defending themselves by punishing the rebel that threatens their integrity.

More concretely, the sinner has risen up against the order of his own reason, against the civil order—political, economic or ecclesiastical—if his sin be external, finally against the divine order. By each of these orders is he punished. And he is wholeheartedly punished, for in a very real sense this rebel has attacked everything contained in those orders. Order implies a bond of unity, such as the bond of charity that makes all Christians one, tying them together so intimately that an injury to their order is an injury to every Christian.

Still more concretely, we might say that the punishment inflicted by God for the attack on the divine order is the slowest, the most merciful, the easiest to escape. That undoubtedly sounds ridiculous to the modern mind; but look at the facts. Let a man knock down the mayor of a city, start a rebellion against the Federal Government, blow up a few department stores, or run off with the gold reserve of the Federal treasury and how much explaining could he do? How much absolution would he get? How many times would he be forgiven and told not to do it again? Who makes any effort to determine the quality of the contrition of a spy or a traitor during a war?

The punishments of nature are more severe, more relentless. Nature takes its toll regardless of the disposition of the sinner. A practical example of this to-day is found in the young couple who start off married life intending to violate nature's order, but only for a few years, until they are financially secure, until they have a better social status, or for more individual social activity. It reads, to-day, like a sensible programme. But only too frequently long before the allotted time is up, the wife hates the husband or the husband hates the wife; nature is exacting its toll for the abuse of love and no amount of sorrow, of absolution, or resolutions will soften that punishment. There are, of course, the more obvious punishments of nature: remorse of conscience, loss of self-respect, building up of inclinations to sin and tearing down of inclinations to virtue, physical toll exacted by sin, and the increasing slavery of the senses with the consequent lessening of capacity for love, for joy, for any activity that does not furnish fuel for that devastating fire of introversion.

St. Gregory's description of the physical effects of envy brings out vividly another angle of this automatic punishment of nature: " . . . paleness seizes the complexion, the eyes are weighed down, the spirit is inflamed, while the limbs are chilled, there is frenzy in the heart, there is gnashing with the teeth." Even the sin itself can be its own punishment. Even more patently a sin is its own punishment sometimes from the very external difficulties which must be overcome to commit the sin; after all, the burglar does not enjoy climbing up ladders to rob second-storey apartments or unwittingly commandeering a radio car for his escape. Indeed the very essence of sin is itself a punishment, for, as we have seen, the sinner does not want to turn away from God, even though he wants this partial good more than he wants God and is regretfully willing to give God up because he so loves his sin.

Properly speaking, one sin is not the penalty for another. Penalty, after all, is something against our will; and sin is essentially a free act. Our sins, like all our acts, are our own; they are not thrown at us by God or by anyone else. they are not the infliction of a superior power but the choice of our own free will. In a way one sin follows another, even naturally speaking, for one sin, like any one human act, leaves its mark behind, blazes a trail, increases an inclination that will make the succeeding act easier, more likely.

From the viewpoint of the supernatural, one sin by destroying grace removes the helps that might have impeded the commission of other sins and so is indirectly the cause of other sins. Certainly the subtraction of grace is a penalty wrapped up with the sin itself; but still the following sins are our very own and not really penalties. However, in the supernatural order the penalty upon which our interest is constantly focused is the eternal punishment of hell. And it is the punishment which to the modern mind seems most ludicrous.

This is not the place to enter into an extended discussion of hell. That is work which is taken up in detail in the fourth volume of this work. But it is essential here that we insist on the absolute certitude of the fact of eternal punishment as far as Catholics are concerned. The fact of eternal punishment is vouched for by the infallible authority of God Himself. It is expressly stated in Scripture;[1] and has been repeated again and again by the Councils of the Church.[2]

It is quite a task, even for our efficient modern world, to laugh God out of existence. The attempt is in fact an insult to human intelligence. Yet to escape the fact of eternal punishment we must either laugh God out of existence or, what is no less insulting both to God and man, we must paint the divinity as a sentimental half-wit. Even without attempting a study of hell, from what we have seen in this book it is evident that a man cannot refuse to have the goal of life and still have it, since that goal depends on his choice; from what we have said in this chapter it is evident a man cannot forbid the entrance of light and at the same time expect the dispelling of darkness. More concretely, sin is a perversion of order, a rebellion against order that demands the resistance of that order; just as long as man insists upon escaping from the light of human and divine reason, just so long does he ask for punishment. When death intervenes, man's ability to return to the

[1] e.g. Mark iii. 29; Matt. xxv. 46, xii. 32; 2 Thess. i. 9.

[2] e.g. IV Lateran Council, chap. 1 (Denzinger, # 429); Council of Trent, Sess. VI, canon 30 (Denzinger, # 840).

paths of reason ceases, for death shuts off the flow of divine grace. Putting it in another way, by sin man steps down from a supernatural plane; as far as his natural powers are concerned he can never again achieve that plane. Unless supernatural help be given, he must for ever remain off that plane; and supernatural help ceases after death. From then on for ever he must remain in the ugly darkness of sin and this is the essential pain of hell.

One of the foundations of our restlessness in the face of this truth is due to our visualizing hell in terms of a spanking given to a child for stealing cakes, while, as a matter of fact, it is like the blindness that follows on plucking out an eye. This latter destroys not only vision but the very power of sight; so sin destroys the very principle of supernatural life and refuses to take the steps that might win back that principle of life which is grace. The sinner refuses to return to God; he deserts God, he is not deserted by God.

The immediate cause, then, of this eternal punishment is a sin that disrupts the divine order, a sin that turns man from the path leading to his goal, i.e. a mortal sin. As long as he stays off that path, as long as that order remains disrupted by his attachment to partial goods in preference to the universal good, so long will that punishment endure.

It has seemed to many men and women that the notion of hell is particularly obnoxious because there is no proportion between the sin and the punishment. An infinite punishment for a moment of sin seems beyond the limits of the most severe justice. The truth is that the proportion is very exact indeed. We might put this proportion clearly and briefly by saying that the duration of the punishment corresponds to the duration of the guilt of sin, the quantity of the punishment responds to the gravity of that sin. In other words, the duration of this punishment is without limit because the sin never ceases, because a man never forsakes the darkness to turn back to the light; the quantity of that punishment is finite because no matter how wholeheartedly we turn to a creature, our embrace of that creature is still a limited, a finite act.

Perhaps it will be clearer to state this in terms of the elements of sin by saying that the duration of the punishment corresponds to the aversion from the goal of life or from God—and so is equal in all men, infinite in the sense of never ending for the double reason that it is a turning away from an infinite good and it is the answer to an eternally enduring choice.

To understand punishment, then, we must go to the root of it, to the first incurring of the obligation to undergo punishment. That starting point is the act of sin. It may be a thing of only a moment; but instantly the beauty of the soul is stained and the necessity of punishment is incurred. The connection between these three is intimate, absolute: as long as the sin endures, as long as the sinner refuses to turn back to God, so long does the stain remain on the soul and so long must he face the fact of punishment. Turning back to God, the sin ceases, the stain on the soul is removed and automatically punishment strictly so called, as an evil unwillingly sustained, ceases. Our renunciation of the sin and our return to the path of reason is itself an acceptance of the penalty for our fault, a willingness to satisfy for what we have done which takes all the sting out of the punishment. It may be only a few Hail Marys that we face so bravely, or it may be a few eons in purgatory; whatever it is, it is no longer punishment but satisfaction, an evil that we willingly accept.[1] A delicate balance, an order, has been upset by our sin; and the equality of justice demands that that balance be restored, either unwillingly through punishment or willingly through satisfaction.

But always punishment or satisfaction must be traced back to sin. We can no more expect someone else to undergo

[1] It is of faith that some debt of punishment (temporal) may remain after the remission of the guilt of sin and the debt of eternal punishment. Council of Trent, Sess. VI, canon 30 (Denzinger, # 840).

the punishment for our personal sins than we can expect to have someone else undergo our operation for appendicitis or our death agony. It is only when that punishment is no longer strictly personal, when it has become the proper matter of a group, that others can enter in. So the bond of charity that binds us to Christ and Christ to us and ourselves to all other members of Christ—makes the satisfaction for the sins of any member of that body of Christ the proper task of everyone joined to Christ. In this way could Christ satisfy for our sins; in this way can we carry on the work of Christ satisfying for the sins of others. The common bond of nature makes nature's sin common to all children of Adam, and the penalties of that sin things to be carried on the shoulders of every child of Adam.

Perhaps we can put this in another way by saying that the spiritual penalties of sin are something that must be born by each man individually and personally; for these spiritual penalties, being the supreme evils to which man is subject, cannot be ordained to a good greater than that of which they deprive man. No one can go to hell as our substitute; no one can lose his sanctifying grace as a protection to our loss of sanctifying grace because of our mortal sins. On the other hand, the physical penalties of sin, depriving man of inferior and morally insignificant perfections, can be endured by others. In fact this is one of the privileges so jealously guarded by the saints; it is a task that at the same time perfects both the sinner and the saint, satisfying for one, elevating the other.

Punishment is always dependent on sin; so that we can know accurately what punishment we deserve by knowing the distinction of sins. Of course, from the point of view of punishment, the most important of these is the distinction between mortal and venial sins. Mortal sin alone carries with it condemnation to the eternal punishment of hell.

It seems strange that the Church was obliged time and time again, particularly since the days of the Reformation, to insist that there were such things as venial sins. Normally we might expect men to be eager to look on sins as less grievous. But then the reformers were not normal. The despair of Luther, the unfounded confidence of Calvin and the narrow pride of Baius continued the work of the Pharisees in putting burdens on the shoulders of men that no man could bear, insisting that every single sin committed by men was a mortal sin. Indeed, to Luther every act placed by men was mortally sinful. Perhaps this is one of the reasons for the modern world's swing to the no less insulting extreme of denial of all sin. Certainly it was the reason for the thundering condemnations of the Council of Trent.[1]

The distinction between mortal and venial sin is the distinction between sickness and death; the one destroys the principle of spiritual life, the other impairs its full healthy operation. Both classes are sins in the sense that both offend God; but that is the only similarity between them. There is no comparison between the sin that turns its back on human and divine reason, abandoning God and defying His law, and the sin that holds fast to the essential direction of human and divine reason, that clings to the love of the Supreme Good above all other things. There is a tremendous gap between empty-headed laughter and murder, between idle, harmless gossip and blasphemous hatred of God, just as there is a great gap between having a cold in the head and having a dozen machine-gun bullets in the heart. It is the gap between the irreparable and the reparable. Mortal sin, as far as the powers of the sinner are concerned, is definitely irreparable; only because Christ has died for us and because God is good can something be done about mortal sin.

This distinction of mortal sin is not merely a question of subjective responsibility. Just as there are some diseases

[1] Sess. VI, chap. 11 (Denzinger, # 804). Confer: Condemnation of errors of Michael Baius by Pius V, condemned props. 25, 35, 67 (Denzinger, # 1025, 1035, 1067).

that are never fatal, so there are some sins that, objectively considered, are never mortal; essentially they are venial sins because the goals to which they are aimed are not contrary to the goal of human life. On the contrary, there are sins whose objective goal is in direct opposition to the goal of human life, sins that are essentially mortal, like murder, adultery and theft. Some of these latter are objectively mortal at all times, as, for example, murder; others are mortal only when the matter is grave, as in the case of theft or anger (*ex toto genere et ex genere*). The simple reason for this is that sometimes the object even of these sins is not in direct opposition to charity and the goal of life.

It is evident then that no matter how many venial sins are piled one on the other, the result will not be a mortal sin. The question is not one of weight or number but of the direction taken by these sinful human acts; and that direction is not reversed by the frequency of venial sin.

If there is to be any metamorphosis of mortal into venial sin it must be effected from the side of the sinner, from the side of deliberate control and not from the side of the object. The essences of these acts, like all other essences, are eternally unchangeable. But because they must be human acts to be sins, they must proceed under our deliberate control. A man who falls to his death from a window is not guilty of sin, whereas another man who kills himself by jumping from a window has committed the sin of suicide. Any defect in that deliberate control which makes an act human is also a defect in the sin; if either the deliberation or the willingness is seriously impaired, the essential morality of the sin is proportionately cut down. To say that there must be sufficient reflection and full consent for mortal sin is no more than saying that this sin must be a complete human act, an act for which we are wholly responsible because it proceeded under our full control to goals of our choice.

In fact the malice of venial sin suffers the same decrease for exactly the same reason.

Of course no amount of concentration is going to make any change in a sin already committed. But I can make a very real change in a sin that would objectively be venial. I can, for example, become so enamoured of bridge or golf that I sacrifice everything else in life to satisfy my passion for bridge or golf. I have placed my final end in these things and stand willing to prefer them to everything else. Really what I have done is to make of bridge or golf an object that is directly opposed to the goal of human life; though certainly in themselves bridge and golf are harmless things. Or again a man can tell a very small lie for a very evil purpose, such as to ruin a man's character or to accomplish a seduction; while a lie in itself is a venial sin, yet here and now its direction is definitely changed, it goes far beyond the goal of mere lying to more tragic goals that are directly opposed to the ultimate end of man. And the lie itself becomes a mortal sin.

The example of the bridge or golf addict is not nearly so absurd as might appear at first glance. A venial sin, like any human act, starts the groove of a habit; it means that the succeeding acts become easier, more pleasant, more like nature itself. After a while these things become second nature to us, the appetite for them is constantly increased so that quite easily we slip into a way of acting that makes the love of play the end of our being rather than a means of refreshing the soul for the real tasks of life. That is one way in which venial sin disposes us to commit mortal sin; it is a psychological consequence founded on the nature of the habits we build into ourselves.

Still another way in which we are prepared for mortal sin by venial sin is by getting ourselves accustomed to offending God. We start out in little things, rebelling in a mild way against the divine order, rubbing elbows with sedition until we have to a great extent destroyed our respect for law. Then we are ready for a full-fledged rebellion that will outlaw us from the courts of heaven. This, as a matter of fact, is true of the overthrow of any order: religious, political, economic. It is rare, indeed, that beginnings are anything but small. It is not often that an expert thief got his start by filching crown jewels; the hardened murderer hardly had the same complete willingness and deliberation for his first murder that he enjoys for his fiftieth. It is as true of vice as it usually is of virtue that we "ease into it".

There is, then, a grave danger in venial sin, the grave danger of slipping bit by bit into mortal sin and so into the eternity of hell's punishment. We can look at venial sin as an offence against God and see that it outstrips any or all physical evils that can come upon the human race, and so is unjustifiable for any reason whatever. We can look at it as a disposition to mortal sin and so as something to be carefully avoided as a serious threat to our eternal happiness. Or we can look upon venial sin in comparison to mortal sin and see only the tremendous gap which separates one from the other and lightly dismiss a small boy's rudeness to his sister as "only a venial sin".

No matter what viewpoint we take, it is difficult to explain the modern attitude towards venial sin. Certainly a world that has denied the existence of God is not worrying about a slight offence against the divinity; an age that has laughed hell and heaven and sin to scorn is not worrying about a disposition to mortal sin. Yet very frequently among the neo-pagans of our age we find a scrupulous avoidance of venial sin. Petty theft, lying, rudeness, idle gossip, wasting of time are all looked on with real horror; even though side by side with this horror is an indifference to contraception, divorce, large-scale theft, unlimited greed, irreligion, and so on. In other words, they seem to have disregarded the absolute essentials of human life while clinging desperately to the things that make for the adornment, the perfection, the integrity of that life.

On the contrary, looking only at the gap between mortal and venial sin, those who are working desperately, courageously to keep intact the essential demands of reason are apt to shrug their shoulders at an unkind word, a white lie or a bit of gossip as "only a venial sin". But venial sin cannot be shrugged off. If a single lie would save the human race from extinction, that lie could not be lawfully told. Not only is venial sin an offence against God and a disposition to mortal sin, it carries with it sufficient evil effects to give us pause just considering the venial sin in itself.

The beauty of the soul does not emerge from contact with venial sin totally disfigured by acid burns or with long gashes dug by a destroying knife; but it does come out with a muddy face. Venial sin does not destroy the lustrous splendour of the soul because it does not turn the soul away from the streaming light of human and divine reason; but it goes far toward preventing that splendour of the soul from shining forth in our acts. It is like a heavy coating of dirt on the windows of a cathedral, blocking out the sunlight; or, more accurately, like a heavy bank of clouds blocking out the light of the sun. For venial sin does operate against acts of virtue, not only in the venial sins themselves, but in their effects—the dispositions they cause to similar acts, the habits they engender, the increase of the appetite for sin, the impediments they place to the graces and movements of the Holy Ghost and to the increase of charity.

We can picture venial sin graphically as the ropes that securely bind the hands and feet of a man; they do no intrinsic injury to man's ability to act, but certainly they hinder his activities. Or venial sin can be likened to a heavy blanket hung between a warm fire and the shivering wretch who is trying to get warm; for while venial sin does not extinguish or even diminish the fire of charity, it does prevent the saving heat of it from spreading out into our actions as it could.

There is one more interesting point to notice about venial sin, namely that it is peculiarly our own. Adam or Eve could not commit venial sin until they had lost their original justice, no angel or devil is capable of venial sin, and no man with original sin on his soul can commit venial sin without having first either freed himself from original sin or committed mortal sin. All of these apparently disparate conclusions follow from the very notion of venial sin as a disorder affecting not the end or goal but the means. Evidently where there is perfect order, even the slight disorder of venial sin is not possible without the destruction of the basis of that absolutely perfect order; Adam and Eve possessed that perfect order which followed from the subjection of the will to God and of the lower powers of man to his reason. The angels, whose knowledge deals not with conclusions but with principles, cannot suffer disorder concerning the conclusions without disorder having first invaded the principles; and in the moral order, the end is the principle, the means to the end—the material of venial sin—are the conclusions. Likewise a man in original sin either has not reached the age of reason and so is incapable of any sin; or having the use of reason, must first make a choice of end or goal before dealing with the means to that end. That first act of choice of a goal will then be either an act of virtue destroying original sin, or an act of vice putting the stain of mortal sin on the soul, for it will be a choice of a right or a wrong goal.

Perhaps we can best sum all this up by going back to our starting-point—to beauty. There have been men from ancient times who maintained that beauty is something completely objective, outside of man; there have been others holding that beauty was entirely subjective, a projection from within man himself. Both schools still have their disciples. Aristotle, and after him Thomas, insisted that beauty was neither entirely objective nor entirely subjective, but the result of the combination of both subject and object. St. Thomas expressed this neatly when he defined beauty as "that which being contemplated, pleases" (*quod visum placet*). In other words, beauty arises from reality plus a relation to a knowing subject.

Looking at the very foundations, we see that reality as merely known constitutes truth; reality as merely desired or possessed is the good; but reality as known and as pleasing because known is the beautiful. For beauty reality must affect the intellect, but not the intellect alone; it must affect the appetite, but in a disinterested fashion, in a fashion that precludes desire and possession, resting serenely in contemplation.

For beauty, then, there is demanded a fullness of reality; an integrity that means not only lack of defect but richness of perfection, a proportion that means the completion of perfect order, and a brilliance or clarity that means the presentation of that perfection and order in a vivid refulgence of the form or principle of perfection and order breaking through the material envelope and bursting upon our intelligence. Beauty is a thing of reality, not of dreams, a thing of full rich reality, a thing of splendid reality that is sought unselfishly, disinterestedly, with a serenity that precludes the clouding of passion.

It is because of the nature of beauty that in the beginning of this chapter it was said that we are not an age in love with beauty. We are not an age in love with reality, but only with that superficial, partial reality that falls under the senses. Our philosophers have chained man down to the sense world, so they have made his taste for the beautiful a taste that destroys the object it feeds upon. If the sense appetite of man is his only appetite, then his search for reality is an acquisitive, grasping, passionate search that can be satisfied only in absorbing the object of its search, that must be constantly immersed in the uproar of passion. And he must end his search in the realization that even the sense beauty available to him always eludes his grasp.

Actually the scale of the beautiful is the scale of being, of actuality, of reality. Our age has insisted that man stay on the lowest rung of the ladder. As we go up step by step through forms dependent on matter to forms independent of matter but in matter, through forms utterly independent of matter to the final pure form or pure act which is God, we are advancing by each step into worlds of ever increasing beauty. As our joy in those worlds becomes more and more disinterested, more and more unselfish, as our contemplation becomes more and more penetrating, more and more pure, this beauty breaks upon us with more and more force until in that last supreme vision we are indeed overwhelmed with beauty.

Of course sin is an attack on beauty, for sin is an attack on reality. It is an attack on the integrity, the perfection, the brilliance of humanity and humanity's acts; sin is a defective human act, a disorderly human act, a rebellious human act which does its utmost to destroy that form of human acts which is reason. There is in fact nothing of beauty in sin. That deliberately invoked ugliness deserves punishment; that deliberate attack on order meets with the prompt resistance of order; that deliberate clouding or destruction of brilliance meets the just deprivation of light and splendour.

Sin is the enemy of beauty, for sin is the enemy of virtue. Virtue is the principle working for greater perfection, for the rich fullness of man's powers under the perfect order of reason; a principle whose climax is the ultimate perfection of man's union with the Supreme Reality which is the goal of his life. Virtue makes for constantly increasing beauty within a man himself, and a constantly more penetrating vision of the beauty outside of himself; it works for greater perfection and at the same time for greater mastery over the lower faculties of man. That serene contemplation demanded for beauty is possible only where passion is under the rule of its master and where love is so great that it is able to be utterly selfless. The virtuous man walks in beauty to the goal of beauty which is at the same time the Supreme Beauty and the source of all that is beautiful. For the virtuous man walks the roads of reason to the mansions of God.

CHAPTER XVIII

(OUTLINE)

THE COMPASS OF HAPPINESS

(Q. 90–94)

1. Law and life:
   (*a*) Motion and its direction.
   (*b*) The goal and the path to the goal.

2. Sources of confusion on law:
   (*a*) Fact of confusion.
   (*b*) Its sources: errors on fundamentals of human life.

3. Essence of law:
   (*a*) A command of reason.
   (*b*) To the common good.
   (*c*) By authority.
   (*d*) Promulgated.

4. Varieties of law in general:
   (*a*) Eternal law.
   (*b*) Natural law.
   (*c*) Human law.
   (*d*) Divine positive law.

5. Effects of law:
   (*a*) Making men good.
   (*b*) Integral acts of law: precept, prohibition, permission and punishment.

6. Eternal Law:
   (*a*) Its nature.
   (*b*) Its universal recognition as truth and law.
   (*c*) Source of all law.
   (*d*) Subjects of the Eternal Law.

7. Natural Law:
   (*a*) Its nature.
   (*b*) Its precepts.

(*c*) Source of virtue.
(*d*) Universality.
(*e*) Incorruptibility and mutability.
(*f*) Its obligation.
(*g*) Its relation to religion.

Conclusion:

1. Life and law:

    (*a*) Life, morality and nature.
    (*b*) Morality and law.

2. Law and liberty.

3. Law and happiness.

CHAPTER XVIII

THE COMPASS OF HAPPINESS

(Q. 90–94)

IF we could borrow several pairs of eyes from small boys in New York and through them look at a police officer patrolling his beat, we would be as surprised as would a primitive man if he could look through a microscope at a drop of water. Both policemen and water are taken for granted. Policemen are just another part of our lives; we hardly consider them for months at a time and then only superficially. But children have a knack of plunging deeper. To some of these children the policeman is a bogey man whose job is to spoil as much fun as he can, a person to be watched out for and to be fled as the supreme evil of a child's life. To others the policeman is nearly a god. He carries a gun, looks fine and brave in his uniform, is the master of the child's little world; the boy hopes that some day he too can find a place among the gods and be a "cop". Still others look on the policeman with that frank, easy familiarity which children give so freely to those who can walk sympathetically on their level. The "cop" is a big, good-natured, easy-going chap whom a boy can approach without fear of condescension or baby-talk.

Of course we have outgrown all this. To us a policeman is just a policeman and we are rather smug about having discovered this great truth. As a matter of fact we have not grown up so very much. We have merely transferred the point of view from the policeman to the law he enforces. To some of us law is a spoil-sport, a barrier limiting our activities, an expression of tyranny to be evaded whenever possible. To others, law is a kind of god; the supreme remedy for every evil is more legislation. To others, law is a friend directing men through the hazards of the traffic of life, a reasonable, human, friendly help to happiness.

We must have some such view of law because law enters too intimately into human life to be overlooked. We must think about life because we must live life; that means that we must think about law. Just what we think of law will depend to a great extent on what we think of life. From our study of human life in this volume, we can picture it as a fairly brief walk toward some goal. The steps by which we approach that goal are our own human actions. More importantly, life is a walk to or away from the right goal, to or away from happiness; it is a motion that sweeps towards a goal of our choosing, a motion, in a word, that is going somewhere.

Putting it briefly, we can say that human life is directed motion which reaches its goal at the moment of death. Saying that, we have stated the nature and work of law. The direction of the motion which is life is precisely the work of law. Law, then, is a friendly thing anxious that we keep to the right road. Its directions are not the impersonal information of the sign-post, nor the uninterested information of the complete stranger, but the friendly direction of one whose interest is great enough to include severity, of one who realizes our feelings of the moment are not nearly so important as the avoidance of personal disaster.

Yet this is not at all the view of our age on law. The output of our legislatures and the content of their laws are vivid testimony of our almost ridiculous faith in law. Our complete surrender of every department and activity of human life to the laboratory gives an inkling of our whole-hearted worship of recently enthroned physical or scientific laws. Yet at the same time we thoroughly resent law, are not adverse to flouting it, demand the release of the individual from the clutches of law, and, as a final absurd touch, we insist upon tossing aside the only foundation upon which law can rest.

All this is another of those modern paradoxes that come from the attempt to deny the humanity of human life and at the same time to live that human life. The strange part of this modern attitude is that we have any regard for law. What we think of life determines what we think of law; and our notion of human life is a sorry thing indeed. Our confusion about the goal or end of human life, or our denial of such a goal, thoroughly robs that motion which is human life of its meaning. Denial of intellect and will robs our actions of their personal character and so effectively freezes that motion which is human life, for the steps by which life moves to its goal are exactly our personal, our human actions, proceeding under the control of reason and will. We do not know where we are going, or indeed if we are going at all. We are sure in any case that we cannot move. Of course we will have fantastic ideas about the direction of human life.

Our work in this chapter is fairly easy because of what we have already accomplished. In the beginning of this volume we established the fundamentals of human activity, the meaning of human life. We are moving towards a goal by our action; law's work is effectively to direct that action in view of the goal. Of course we are not talking here of law as it is filed away for reference in a code nor as it is in the subject whom it obliges, but rather of law as it is in the lawmaker. In that strict sense we can accurately place law by remembering that law is a command, it is a rule of human action.

Law as a command indicates immediately that law in the legislator is an act of the practical reason, for command, as we have seen, is that act of reason which takes charge of the difficult work of making our decisions materialize in spite of the difficulties offered by passing from the internal to the external order. In fact this notion of command clearly shows the elements of will and reason that go into law. It will be remembered that in command there is an element of ordination or direction, of intimation or declaration, and of movement. It is not merely movement, not merely direction, not merely directive movement to which no one pays attention; but effective directive movement. So law as command presupposes movement of the will, direction of that movement by the intellect, and the passing on of that directive movement to the subjects who are being directed. Directing or ordaining and the intimation of that direction are the work of reason; movement comes from the will.

This essential notion of law shows us the movement of the will flowing through the intellect to the subjects of law; the immediate, the eliciting faculty from which law springs is the intellect. This is no mere academic point. Rather it is absolutely fundamental for an understanding of the limitations of government and the protection of human rights. The will of the superior, his whims and caprices, cannot be imposed on a community simply because he is the superior. His subjects are to be directed, not played with. His orders, to be law at all, must be reasonable, must be directions of reason to the goal of reason or they have no binding force.

This truth is tremendously important. Yet, like so many important truths, it is obvious. Take law as a rule of human action—and certainly no one will question that—immediately we remember that the rule of human action is reason and so of course law is a thing of reason. Our actions are human in so far as they are reasonable, reason is the rule by which we judge of their humanity; the form that gives them humanity, that breathes the breath of human life into their cold clay is our reason controlling, directing them along paths we have chosen. We can put this even more concretely by saying that law is an act of prudence, of that intellectual virtue whose work is to stamp the brand of reason on the actions that proceed from man. Like prudence, law does not select the goal or give orders concerning its establishment, it must take the goal as it finds it, for the material of prudence is the steps to that goal, the actions which are called forth by the attractiveness of that goal.

Law, then, is not the produce of a legislator's indigestion or the nagging of his wife. It is a product of reason. Laws do not pop out of the legislature because the congress is in the mood for legislation or because there is nothing more exciting to do. Like all acts of reason they are themselves for a goal or they are not laws at all, not reasonable at all, not human at all. And the goal at which all law aims is usually called "the common good".

The phrase "common good" may sound a bit vague. Certainly it has been tossed back and forth carelessly enough to have the life shaken out of it. But quite simply it means the attainment of the end for which a society exists. If the society itself and the rule or law of that society do not go steadily in that direction, that society is an impostor in the social order. Let us take that phrase "common good" more concretely, in the sense of the common good of the state. The immediate common good of the state might be summed up in the one word "peace", or in the phrase "the preservation of unity". It is an end constituted by the assurance of the necessities of life to the subjects, by the establishment of internal harmony through just distribution of rewards and penalties and by giving security against external enemies. The ultimate common good of the state has been summed up by Thomas and Aristotle as "the life of virtue" or the life of reason for the whole community. In plain language it means no more than the assurance to all the subjects of the opportunity to follow the law of reason to individual perfection, the opportunity to live a successful human life.

Turning to the little kingdom which is the individual, we find the immediate end of the individual precisely the living of that human life, the steady progress to the goal for which he was made. The ultimate end for each individual is the attainment of that goal, the full perfection of human nature, the peak of human hopes realized in the eternal vision of God. Let us put it frankly and say the measure of the extent of civil government is the need of the individual. The state exists for the individual as a man; the subject, as subject, is a part of the state and as such exists for the state. But he is a subject only in so far as he needs help, and the very ends of the state for which, as a subject he must work, are ordained to his life as an individual.

This is a harsh saying indeed for the ears of the modern world. But why should it sound so harsh? Why should the insistence that law aims always at the goal of presenting the individual with a chance to live a full human life sound like an insult to constituted authority and the majesty of the state? Who, after all, has the right to make these laws, who has the right to order this man or that man about, to tell him what he can or cannot do? Certainly no other individual has that right. A dictator may be strong enough to enforce his will or a politician corrupt enough to turn the state to his own ends and subtle enough to fool the people into following him. In either case the regulations made are not law but tyranny; these men are giving not government but injustice; it is not a state they are heading but a group of men and women beaten by force or intrigue into slavery.

"Stick to your last" is more than a proverb. We do not call in a psychoanalyst to care for a broken leg, nor do we expect the broad muscles of the back to decide a delicate question of political policy. Direction to an end belongs to the one for whom that end is a goal, to whom that end belongs; and the end of the state is not the property of any individual but of the community. The making of laws is the work of the community or of someone to whom that community power has been delegated, to someone who has care of that community. But whether the community is acting directly or through an individual, the goal of law must always be the same—the common good.

There is one more point to be considered for the essential notion of law, namely its promulgation. Promulgation is not a part of the essence of law, it is merely law's application. If a law is to be obeyed it must at the very least be so published that the citizens or subjects can know the direction their actions are expected to take. The classic definition of law, then, a definition containing just the four elements we have explained thus far, is: law is an ordination of reason for the common good by him who has care of the community—and an ordination promulgated.

For some reason or other, humanity often misses the obvious. We do not see the wood for the trees; it is a common human experience to overlook love because of its steady stream of unobtrusive thoughtfulness. Somewhat the same thing is happening to-day: the multitude of human and scientific laws are the trees that hide the forest, the bustling expressions of profounder government that itself goes unnoticed or is denied. The variety of law is not summed up in these two. The universe is very carefully governed (as we saw in the first volume of this work) and government or direction to an end is the effect of law. The universe is governed by a divine Governor, ordered by the dictate of the reason of God, ordered for the common good, the ultimate end of that universe, and that direction, that ordering, like everything in the mind of God, is eternal. Putting it in another way, the world is governed by God and a detailed plan of that government, which we call providence, exists in the mind of God; the root of that providence and government, the universal principles from which providence proceeds to its detailed conclusions and to the execution of those conclusions, we call the Eternal Law.

In God that law is the Eternal Law; the same law as it is found in creatures is called the Natural Law. Natural Law is, then, nothing more than a participation of the Eternal Law by creatures. We find a purely passive participation common to all creatures in the form of natural inclinations to proper goals; or, again as passive but proper to men alone, in the light of reason naturally, intuitively knowing first principles; and, finally, in its only active form, we find this participation in the natural dictate of human reason by which man regulates both himself and other creatures.

What this really means is simply that this law is natural, that God, having established nature, respected His own creation. For this means that every single thing in the universe is governed or directed by God but each single thing according to its nature. The truth is so obvious that we take it for granted but still overlook it. We would be totally astonished to see a squirrel developing like a tree or shrinking under spring rains like a cheap suit of clothes; and our astonishment would have this profound truth as its basis. Man, like every other creature, is a part of nature and, like every other creature, is governed according to his nature; that nature is a moral or free nature, master of its own acts. As far as he has animal and vegetable nature we find man subject to the same necessary physical laws, or passive participations of Eternal Law, which govern the rest of creation; but in so far as he is man, he cannot be other than his own director, he must somehow direct himself, he cannot be necessarily pushed this way and that and still remain free. His natural law must be a moral not a physical law.

Only in that active participation of the Eternal Law in man do we find Natural Law in the strict sense, i.e., as an active principle, a dictate of reason in the legislator.

In every other case we are dealing with law not as it is in the legislator but as it is in the subject of that law. But man is in a sense a legislator for himself. For the complete statement of natural law in man, then, we must include his natural inclinations, the recognition of those inclinations by reason and the dictate of reason which follows naturally from this recognition. We shall look into all of these later on in this chapter. It is worth pointing out from just this silhouette of the Natural Moral Law that it is neither imposed from the outside upon man nor does it depend on the will but rather on the reason of almighty God.

Eternal Law is the universal principle from which providence proceeds to the detailed plan of world government. Natural Law is, in its own way, a declaration of universal principles from which men proceed to the government of human life. Of course these in themselves are not sufficient ; universal principles never are. It was all very well for St. Paul to say that "charity fulfils the law"; theologians and confessors have been kept busy ever since trying to point out to men and women what here and now answers the description of charity. These universal principles not only need application, they need further determination. We know the pedestrian's life must be protected and there are several ways of protecting that life: we might destroy all automobiles, drive at five miles an hour or follow a system of traffic lights. Which shall be adopted? That is the work of human law and its reason for existence, namely further to determine the universal principles of Natural Moral Law. Human law was not meant to supplant Natural Moral Law or to change it but to supplement it by more definite determinations.

In fact even these three are not sufficient for the important work of guiding man to his end. Over and above Eternal Law, Natural Moral Law and human law, a divine positive law is absolutely essential to fill in the gaps left by the others. Natural Moral Law does very well as the universal principle of guidance for man's natural life; but he has a supernatural life to lead. Even in the natural order, as we get further from the universal principles and closer to particular actions more and more mistakes creep in; and this guidance of man in successful living allows of no mistakes, since every error takes on the tragic aspect of personal calamity. As far as human law is concerned—well, even if detectives had the intellectual acumen of the highest of angels, they could not uncover a man's internal actions, the precise actions that are virtuous or sinful, the actions that determine the success or failure in human life. Human law deals only with externals and not too successfully as a glance around any large city in America will amply prove. Certainly law should punish evil; human law can take care of only a very little of the external evil that men commit.

When human law does try to punish all evil the result is confusion and often comedy. We have had a prohibition law, a law closing an international bridge at an early hour to prevent Americans from gambling in a foreign country, and a law banning sweepstakes tickets from the mails. These go beyond the prohibition or punishment of evil. Many other laws go further in the same direction; so far, in fact, as to reach a point of hilarious absurdity and furnish the material for a regular cartoon feature in one of our monthly magazines. Behind all this is, perhaps, the notion that since law's purpose is to guide men rightly the purpose of law is to make men good. That notion is true enough as far as it goes; but not a step farther. Certainly every law tends to make men good citizens; but just as certainly no law which stops at the outer walls of man's citadel, which cannot reach in to guide the intellect and will of man, can hope to make men good in the full and absolute sense of the term. A good man is distinguished from a bad man precisely because the will of the first is straining eagerly to the goal of human life, while the will of the other is slinking away from that goal.

Within its own field law aims at the limited goodness its guidance can confer. Sometimes it works to this end by stern command, again by frowning prohibition, at another time by suave permission or, frequently enough, by a punishment calculated to bring the offender to his senses, to teach a salutary lesson to others or to restore the upset balance of justice. Not that every law must do all four of these things; but there is no law that does not place one or another of these integral acts of law. In mentioning these integral acts of law St. Thomas makes no mention of obligation. He takes that for granted because obligation flows from the essential notion of law as an effective dictate of practical reason. The very nature of man which makes moral not physical guidance a necessity indicates that the force of such guidance cannot be physical force but rather the moral force which we call obligation. We shall see more of obligation later on in this chapter but this will suffice to close our general examination of law and its varieties.

Plunging into an examination of the Eternal Law means no less than fixing our attention on an act of the mind of God Himself. And we go at it rather nonchalantly, as a boy back from college wanders unconcernedly through the house with the complete assurance of one at home. Our attitude is a part of that "slavery of dogma" which sets us free to wander through all eternity and even to plunge into infinity itself. We belong there, we are at home. So we do not hesitate to apply strictly our essential notion of law to the eternal act of the reason of God which is the foundation of the orderly direction of the universe. Like all law this is an act of the practical reason of the Governor of the community which is the universe. Like all law, it directs that community to its common good which is God Himself. Like all law, it deals only with the means to that goal. And like all law, it is promulgated—on the part of God from all eternity, on the part of the subjects, in time.

All this St. Thomas has packed into his concise definition of the Eternal Law: "the type of divine wisdom which directs all actions and motions."

In itself the Eternal Law is one of the secrets of divinity to be unfolded to us when we see God face to face. Just now that law is known directly only by the angels and saints in heaven; only God Himself will ever fully comprehend it, for only the infinite can grasp the infinite and everything in God is without limit. We can know it only through its effects. As a matter of fact every man does know something of the Eternal Law.

An industrial captain who could so efficiently organize his industry that the mark of efficient organization was apparent in every least employee would be a bit of a genius. If the office boy's attack on his lunch or the stenographer's stroke in powdering her nose reflected something of that organization and character, we would readily grant that the industrialist had extraordinary genius and extraordinary power. That is something like what we are stumbling over in the universe all the time. Every smallest particle of truth uncovered is an unveiling of the beauty of the Eternal Law; a lover of truth is a lover of law and the searcher for truth is constantly discovering the beauties of the Eternal Law. Putting it more simply, the universe has somewhat the same relation to the mind of God that a house has to the architect's plan of that house. The intellect of God is the measure of the perfection of things, as the architect's plan is the measure of the perfection of the house; to us as onlookers, the house and the universe are the measures of the perfection of our knowledge of them. The mind of God measures the truth of things, and things measure the truth of our minds; and reason, as the rule or measure of things, is law. Every truth has its origin in the Eternal Law of God; every defect of truth is a falling away from that infinite measure of things as they are. Every man knows something of the Eternal Law, for even the humblest of us knows something of truth—at the very least, the first principles of thought and action which come to us naturally with the use of reason.

This is not, it is true, a knowledge of the Eternal Law as law. But even under this formal aspect of law as law, the Eternal Law is known in its effects by every man. Even granting, for the sake of argument, that there is someone who is ignorant of the smooth order of the universe or some part of that order, some physical law, some relation of cause and effect, there is no man or woman who does not know the Eternal Law in its effect within themselves, ruling them, directing them. That is a statement which will be seriously challenged to-day. But it can be questioned only at the price of denying to men a knowledge of those first practical principles of human action, "do good, avoid evil"; or, putting it in another way, only by denying that men know they must act for a goal if their actions are to be human. Such a denial must proceed against all the evidence, as we have seen in the first chapter of this book. Even more simply, we can say that the denial of a knowledge of the Eternal Law as moral law operating within ourselves is a denial of the Natural Moral Law, for the Eternal Law as participated by men is the Natural Moral Law. Such a denial not only violates all the evidence, it goes to the absurd extreme of making man the freak of the universe, the only creature without a proper natural law. As a brief summary of all this, we can say that in man there is a double participation of the Eternal Law, one under the aspect of truth, the other under the aspect of law; and under both aspects the Eternal Law is universally known by all men.

If we refer back to our essential notion of law as an effective directive motion and apply that notion to the Eternal Law we are brought face to face with a profound and significant truth. Eternal Law is not only an effective directive motion, it is the first of such motions, the beginnings of all government; consequently it is the source of all other such movements, of all other laws. This is clear when we stop to realize that every other directive movement will do no more than carry out some detail of that government of actions and motions which is the field of the Eternal Law.

We can rigidly prove the primacy of Eternal Law by St. Thomas' first argument for the existence of God, the argument of the first mover upon whom all motion depends. All other laws are linked to this first law like railroad coaches to the locomotive; no matter how far down the train we may go, each coach depends for its movement on the motion of the engine. In the concrete this is evident. No human law can violate the Natural Moral Law and still claim to be a law, because it cannot still pretend to aim at the ends of nature, the common good of the state and the individual. So every human law is a law only in so far as it is in harmony with Natural Moral Law, and Natural Moral Law is nothing more than Eternal Law from the side of man. The truth is so obvious that we find it difficult to see it clearly. Every law is an ordination of reason; and every operation of reason is derived from that which is according to nature, from the first principles naturally known, which of course are merely another bit of the Eternal Law as it is in man.

The sweep of Eternal Law has the magnificence of infinity about it. It rules over the kingdom of the universe and embraces as its subjects absolutely every created thing, action and motion. Its magnificence is deeper than we ordinarily realize, for it not only includes the extent of the universe, it includes the depths of every created thing. Contingency, necessity, and freedom are products of this divine guidance which, unlike the guidance of human law, does not rest content with a subject's knowledge of its ordinations but imprints those ordinations in the depths of every created nature. Just as necessity in the physical order finds its explanation in the Eternal Law, so freedom in the moral order is not an exception to but rather an indication of the all-including embrace of God's eternal guidance of His creatures to Himself.

There seems to be no serious difficulty about the *de facto* ordering of the physical universe. The difficulty for our times comes in the ordering of the moral universe or, more technically, in the participation of the Eternal Law by the rational creature that is man. What is this Natural Moral Law which we insist is the guiding principle of man's human activity? Nature has the right to feel a very much insulted old lady for all the actions of man that have been blamed on her lately, for all the unflattering descriptions, for the out-and-out favouritism she has been accused of showing to the physical universe.

Acquaintance with her is not at all difficult. She attempts no superior or inferior airs when she steps into the higher world of rational life. She is her old, plain, dependable self. Of course man is guided by natural law—he is an integral part of nature. Of course he is guided by natural law in accordance with, not in violation of, his nature. He is then guided to his end by a Natural Moral Law, for his nature is moral, free, rational, gifted with the ability to control his own actions, to pick his own path, to go to his end or away from it.

There has been a tremendous amount of vagueness attached to the notion of Natural Moral Law, a kind of dense fog clinging to it to give it an air of mystery, eeriness, unreality. It should not be at all mysterious. Like all other animals, man has natural inclinations; unlike all others he has the faculty of reason which recognizes these natural inclinations naturally; and the result of these two is a natural dictate or command of reason. There is no more to Natural Moral Law than just this: a passive participation of Eternal Law in common with all creatures; a passive participation proper to his nature; and an active participation of Eternal Law again proper to his rational nature.

In this last, the dictate or proposition of practical reason, precisely consists the essence of the Natural Moral Law, answering to all the essential notions of law we have exposed in the beginning of this chapter. But this dictate of reason is unintelligible as *natural* law without the preceding inclinations and light of reason. Put it this way. Separately the inclinations of man or the light of reason do not at all answer to the description of *law;* separately the dictate of reason does not answer to the qualifications of the *natural*, for it is not born in us. With the three elements taken together all difficulties about the Natural Moral Law vanish. This dictate is natural, necessary as flowing immediately and inevitably from the two preceding elements, dependent upon them.

Stated plainly, this dictate of reason robs the Natural Moral Law of all its vagueness. This first necessary and natural dictate of practical reason is: do good, avoid evil. The "good" here is that which is according to natural inclinations, the "evil" that which is against those inclinations; for the whole purpose of man's natural inclinations, as natural, is to indicate what nature needs for its perfection.

Let us compare the practical reason, which produces law, to the speculative reason of man. After all, they are not two faculties, but one; so the speculative and practical operations will proceed in the same manner. In the speculative order, dealing with truth for its own sake, the first principle is founded on "being"—the object of the intellect—and is: "what is, is", the principle of identity. In the practical order, which deals with actions, the first principle is founded on the object of appetite, the root of desire and action— on "good"—and is: "good is to be done, evil is to be avoided". In other words the goal or end, the object of desire, is at the root of all action, is indeed the sole explanation of intelligent action; this first principle demands that man act for his end.

But what is good? That is easy. Good is what is in accordance with the natural inclinations of man. The natural inclinations guide the practical reason to good; then the practical reason guides the appetites of man and their inclinations to the attainment of that good. Nor is this a vicious circle. The inclinations of man's appetite are his guide to truth relative to the end or goal; for the means by which that end is to be attained, reason takes the lead and points out the path. This is only to say again that law does not establish an end, or point it out, but rather, as an act of the virtue of prudence, guides our steps to that end.

This is the first and fundamental command of the Natural Moral Law in man. From it, by way of conclusion, immediately follow the secondary precepts of the Natural Moral Law which are restated in the ten commandments, then the more remote but none the less direct conclusions.

The first is known immediately by all men; everyone can easily know the secondary precepts by taking the rational step down from the principle to these immediate conclusions. The remote precepts are known only by the wise and then with difficulty and with a frequent admixture of error. For always as we get further away from the principles we run greater risks of mistakes.

Another way of classifying these precepts would be by comparison with the rest of nature. Some proceed from the natural inclinations we have in common with all creatures, such as those commanding the conservation of life; others proceed from the natural inclinations we have in common with all the animals, such as the command to generate and educate children; still others proceed from the natural inclinations proper to human nature, such as the precepts to know truth, to live in society, and so on. All of them are moral precepts because the acts they command proceed under the controlled direction of a moral or free agent. We cannot excuse any of our actions by pointing to parallel action in the animals and saying "it is natural". For us an action is natural only in so far as it harmonizes with the law of reason. This agreement with reason is not only the mark of naturalness, of humanity, it is the stamp of virtue; our actions are virtuous or good exactly in so far as they harmonize with the commands of reason, or, in other words, precisely in so far as they follow the directions of reason and move towards the goal of man. In one sense it is very true that all virtue comes from the Natural Moral Law, that is in the sense that all virtue is in complete harmony with Natural Moral Law; but of course there are many acts of virtue which are not demanded by nature. In fact Natural Moral Law deals primarily with those things which are essential for the living of human life.

On the face of it, Natural Moral Law should be universal. It flows from the very principles of nature itself and human nature does not change, however much we may coddle and embellish it. As a matter of fact the law *is* universal, the same for all men and in all men. There is no difficulty about the natural inclinations and the light of reason; these innate elements of Natural Moral Law are found in each and every man. As to the dictate of reason, the precise element of Natural Moral Law, we must distinguish very carefully between the different classes of precepts. The first and fundamental precept, "do good and avoid evil", is absolutely universal; always men act for good, every goal of action must wear at least the appearance of goodness. The secondary precepts, or ten commandments, are morally universal, i.e. they are known by the overwhelming majority of men because the overwhelming majority of men can see a conclusion that immediately follows from a first principle. Among the minority, some of these precepts may be unknown by reason of corrupt appetites, bad habits, education, tradition. And this is of considerable importance in view of our materialistic education in America to-day.

Actually the universality demanded by St. Thomas for the ten commandments amounts to this: none of these commandments have dropped out of the minds of all men; all nations or groups know the majority of these ten commandments. This type of moral universality seems to be experimentally vouched for by the findings of modern anthropology, as far as these findings allow conclusions to be drawn. The more remote commands of the Natural Moral Law can be, and frequently are, lost sight of for much the same reasons as militate against knowledge of the ten commandments, with the added reason of difficulty in tracing the connection of these remote commands with the first principles of Natural Moral Law.

In other words, the Natural Moral Law is in one sense immutable; in another it is subject to change. Whatever change there is in Natural Moral Law will fall on the secondary and remote commands of that law; and that change can either be a real subjective change in the form of ignorance of those commands, or the apparent objective change involved in the mutation of the material with which a command deals. If a man leaves a knife with me for safe-keeping, I am bound in natural justice to return it to him on demand; but if he returns roaring drunk, not only am I not obliged to return the knife, I am forbidden to do so. The material of the precept has changed.

From what we have said so far, it must be evident that the Natural Moral Law in man is a completely intrinsic law, not a law imposed from the outside. It does not demand a knowledge of a legislator or an external promulgation; the natural inclinations, the light of reason recognizing those inclinations and the resulting natural dictate of reason all flow necessarily, naturally, from nature itself. But what of the obligation of natural Moral Law? How can man oblige himself morally? Or how can the principles of his nature oblige him? Is not obligation after all the imposition of the will of the superior upon an inferior? That is exactly the point. Obligation is no such thing. Law is a thing of reason, not will; and its obligation is established by reason, not by will. God Himself can no more change or dispense from the Natural Moral Law than He can change the essences of things, than He can change the eternal truth within Himself.

The whole difficulty has arisen from our misinterpretation of obligation. Moral obligation is a result of a double necessity: the necessity of an act in relation to a necessary end. It is necessary for me to go to Europe, so I am obliged to take a boat. My goal is necessarily fixed by nature, so I am obliged to place this act of justice which necessarily leads me to this end; I am obliged to refrain from this act of murder which necessarily leads me away from that goal. In other words, this necessary relation of act to end binds the will but does not destroy the liberty of the will, leaving intact the power of acting or not acting. The will is bound in as much as the goal is its object and the intellect proposes both end and necessary means to the will, but there is no question of direct coercion, of physical necessity imposed on the will.

The picture of obligation as a whip wielded by a tyrant according to his whims is altogether wrong. In the natural order, the command of natural reason, "do good and avoid evil", is no more than the command "act for your end", for "good" here means conducive to the end and "evil" means that which is leading away from the end. The will of man is a faculty whose object is the rational good, the end of man. Consequently it is essentially ordained to its act, which act is in turn essentially ordained to the determined effect—the rational good of man. So that this rational appetite or will which is capable of willing the goal of man and is, moreover, essentially ordained to this act and object, cannot refuse to will this end of man without losing the very reason of its existence, without going contrary to the essential order of things, without losing its conformity to right reason.

Putting it quite simply, the essential order of things, more particularly the rational good of man, is the proximate source of the obligation of the Natural Moral Law. It is a secondary but true cause in the moral order, producing a true effect, a true obligation.

The obligation of the Natural Moral Law no more demands a knowledge of God as legislator for its efficacy than do the first principles of the speculative order for their validity. This obligation follows from a first principle, the principle of finality, which like the other first principles has ontological value. The discovery, if it has been made, of a tribe keeping roughly to the ten commandments and at the same time possessed of no knowledge of a supreme legislator is not a contradiction in terms. This law is intrinsic, a natural law, a law that flows from nature; and obligation is an essential part of the notion of law or command. Law, of course, is primarily a rule of order; but it is an effective rule of order which therefore includes in its very notion the idea of obligation.

That the Natural Moral Law does not demand an idea of God for its efficacy does not mean that God is a superfluity in the moral order. I do not need a knowledge of God to fry eggs; but without God there would not only be no frying done, there would be no eggs and no cook. The efficacy of the second cause does not exclude dependence on the first cause. If the first cause should cease to exist, the second cause would lose all causality; it is only in reducing the undoubted causality of the second cause to the first cause that this secondary causality is entirely explicable and intelligible. The proximate source of the obligation of the natural Moral Law is indeed the essential order of things as understood by natural reason and proposed to the will of man; but the supreme and first cause of this obligation is the Eternal Law and its author, God.

The Natural Moral Law is in the fullest sense a natural law, an intrinsic, efficacious rule by which man partakes actively in his own guidance to the goal of human life. Religion is not a cause of the morality inculcated by the Natural Moral Law; it is rather an effect of that law, one of the commands issued by that law. A primitive people who had no religion but had a morality embracing most of the ten commandments would be a people in whom the Natural Moral Law was operating effectively though not perfectly. Supernatural religion, of course, adds much to the motives and sanctions of the morality established by the natural Moral Law. But it is important that we stress that note of independence: the Natural Moral Law makes no suppositions, presupposes no mysteriously natural goodness or evil, it supposes only the existence of the first cause and then in its own right it establishes morality.

We can sum this up briefly by saying that law is a compass of life. It is much more a part of a man living a human life than the compass is of the navigator sailing the seven seas. We cannot live life without law; we cannot even pretend to go through the motions of living. We must have law and we must have definite notions about the nature of law, because we must live life and we cannot do that without having some notions as to what life is and means.

Life and law are as closely intertwined as motion and its direction to a goal. Stating the nature of life in saying that it is a motion to a goal, we have also stated the nature and purpose of law; for law is exactly the direction of the motion which is life to the goal of life. It deals only with the direction of life; it does not constitute life, nor does it establish the end of life. There are limits to the powers of legislation, even of divine legislation.

The identification of human life and moral life is an immediate indication of the close connection of law and morality. Indeed morality is nothing more than conformity with the rule which regulates human life—the rule of reason or law.

Human life is reasonable life; morality is accord with the rule of reason, and law to establish that morality and rule that reasonable life must be the product of reason. It is not the result of caprice, even of divine caprice; it is not the decree of a superior will. The power of command is a power of the reason and not of the will. It is an ordination, a direction of motion, an effective directive motion; so it is an act proceeding immediately from the intellect on the presupposition of the movement of the will.

It is a foregone conclusion that our view of life will determine our view of law. If life is a motion to a goal and law the direction of that motion, of course our view on the goal of life will determine our view on both life and law. This, then, is the whole explanation of our muddled views on law to-day, of our absurd faith in law, of our complete surrender of all departments of life to law, and paradoxically of our resentment of and contempt for law: our views on life and the goal of life are hopelessly confused. We have reached the point of seriously doubting or openly denying a goal to human life, a meaning to human action, a personal freedom that would alone make those actions human.

Yet we go on producing laws on a mass-production scale, we go on uncovering details of scientific or physical laws until we have swamped ourselves in detail, we have hidden the forest in a profusion of trees. We have missed the obvious and essential, the law behind all laws, the government at the root of all order, the Eternal Law which is the source of all law and of all truth. It was not hard, then, for us to miss the participation of that Eternal Law in man, the Natural Moral Law; nor to misinterpret the whole purpose of those determinations of the Natural Moral Law which are called human positive law.

In fact we have lost ourselves in a maze of contradictions. While bending down before the power, majesty and order of nature, we have insisted on making man the one exception to that power, majesty and order, the sole freak in the universe, the sole creature escaping the government of natural law. In a way this contradiction was necessary to wipe morality and human responsibility from the minds of men, for it is quite impossible to include man in the natural order, to have him governed, as everything in the universe is governed, by a law that does not violate but perfects his nature, and at the same time to escape morality. Man's nature is free; his actions cannot be the result of physical force, physical necessity, and be human actions. The only law that can govern this moral nature without violence to it is a moral law.

This Natural Moral Law in man, as natural, is an intrinsic law, a law flowing immediately from man's nature with all the equipment necessary for the essential notion of law. Like all nature and all law, it depends on the source of nature and law, on God, for its very existence but it does not demand a knowledge of God for its effectiveness or for its binding power. It is not the product of religion but of nature; rather of itself it will immediately produce religion. Like human nature, it is universally found in man proceeding from the principles of that human nature. Like the Eternal Law, it is a thing of reason; as must also be all positive human law which is founded upon it.

Law is necessary for human life because human life is free life, moral life, and law is the protection of liberty. Its moral character is an open evidence of God's great respect for the liberty He has given man; its purpose is a plain statement of the high things God expects of that human liberty. Its operation and limitation when it proceeds from human authority is a constant defence of man's position at the peak of the universe, above things, plants, animals, parties, states, nations.

As life exists because of the goal of life which is human happiness, as morality is nothing but a statement of man's progress towards and share in that goal of life, so law is the official guide of man to his final happiness, to his final goal. Law exists for no other reason than that men should find their way home. The enemy of law is an enemy of life, an enemy of morality, an enemy of society, an enemy of God and, to reach the depths of despair, he is an enemy of himself.

CHAPTER XIX

(OUTLINE)

SIGNPOSTS OF HAPPINESS

(Q. 95–108)

1. Positive law and man:
    - (*a*) A privilege of his perfection.
    - (*b*) A necessity of his insufficiency.

2. Division of positive law:
    - (*a*) Human and divine positive law.
    - (*b*) Their common ground—essence of law.

3. Human positive law:
    - (*a*) Its utility.
    - (*b*) Its general characteristics:
        - (1) Rational—derived from natural law.
        - (2) In harmony with religion—divine law.
        - (3) In harmony with discipline—natural law.
        - (4) Contributing to welfare—common good.

4. Powers of human law:
    - (*a*) Universal, not particular.
    - (*b*) Not extending to all vices nor to all virtues.
    - (*c*) Obliging in conscience:
        - (1) Just laws.
        - (2) Unjust laws—contrary to human and divine good.
    - (*d*) Subjects and letter of the law.
    - (*e*) Its immutability:
        - (1) Custom and law.
        - (2) Dispensation.

5. Divine positive law of the Old Testament:
    - (*a*) In general:
        - (1) Its purpose, origin and subjects.
        - (2) Its precepts: moral, ceremonial and judicial.
        - (3) Its promises and threats.
    - (*b*) In particular: moral precepts and natural law.

6. Divine positive law of the New Testament:
   (*a*) In itself.
   (*b*) In comparison with the Old Law.
   (*c*) Its contents:
      (1) External acts.
      (2) Internal acts.
      (3) Counsels.

Conclusion:

1. The beginnings of law.
2. The progress of law.
3. The ends of law.

CHAPTER XIX

SIGNPOSTS OF HAPPINESS

(Q. 95-108)

WE have come a long way in our investigation of human happiness. Perhaps the last few miles will seem hard and long, as they usually do; but a glance over our shoulder at the long, long road already covered will give us new vigour for the last effort of these final chapters. So far we have seen just two things: the goal or end of man in whose attainment happiness consists; and the means or steps by which man can reach that goal—his own human actions. In fact we have not quite seen all of his human actions. We have analyzed these actions in themselves, looked at their intrinsic principles—the passions and the habits, both good and bad, which we have called sins and virtues. There still remain to be examined the two extrinsic principles of human actions: law by which we are instructed and grace by which we are helped. We have seen something of Natural Moral Law, above all its intrinsic character; in this chapter we will examine that law which is extrinsic to man. In the final chapter of Thomistic exposition we will study grace.

For years people have been standing before the cages in the zoo and remarking of this or that animal: "How very human it is." To-day the trend seems to be to invert that remark and say: "How very animal we are", and to take the remark so seriously as to end up by saying; "How exactly and wholly animal we are." Of course we are also animals. But people used to notice that while there were always signs on the cages instructing us what we should or should not feed the animals, forbidding us to tease them or get too familiar with them, there were no directions at all telling the animals how they should treat us. All the signs face just one way—towards a human mind.

That fact is significant of the gap that stretches between the spiritual and the material. We can place an animal under a physical necessity of following orders by cracking a whip or the equivalent of a whip; actually it follows not the orders but its own instinct driving it away from the evil or driving it to the good. Only when we reach the level of spirituality, where intellectual knowledge makes free choice possible, can there be a question of a necessity which is not physical but moral, a necessity that leaves the appetite free to obey or disobey. Only when we come to the spiritual level can there be any question of law and its obligation.

Law (of course we are speaking of moral law) belongs to us because we stand at the peak of creation, above the level of the brutes though touching on it. Yet at the same time law is a necessity for us because we are still engaged in the work of developing, perfecting ourselves; we are still on the road to ultimate perfection, to happiness, and we need the direction and instruction offered by law until such a time as we arrive at that goal. Positive law is a necessity for us because we stand on the lowest rung of the ladder of intellectuality. We must hobble down, on the crutches of rational thought, from the height of principles to the lower levels of conclusions; as we come down, the chances of falling, of taking the wrong road, increase as we get farther and farther from the clear bright atmosphere of the heights. Natural Moral Law with its principles is not enough for us, as it is for the angels; there are gaps to be filled in, further determinations to be made, because we do not rush in one magnificent plunge to all that a principle contains, but rather stumble slowly along, more puzzled, more confused as we get closer to the concrete details of action.

The difference of the authority which fills in those gaps

of the Natural Moral Law gives us the fundamental division of all positive law, for that authority is either human or divine. Positive law is either divine or human, but whether it comes directly from God or from lawfully constituted human authority, always it must answer to the essential notion of law: a dictate of practical reason for the common good, by him who has care of the community, and promulgated. In other words, both human and divine positive laws are laws in the strictest sense of the term. It is on this common ground of law that we shall examine both of them in this chapter.

A momentary consideration of what happened some years ago in Boston during a police strike or, more recently, what has happened in some Spanish cities when a mob usurped the power of the government, will immediately bring this discussion of the necessity and utility of human law down to the level of the vividly real. There are always some men who can appreciate no force but physical force. They can understand the threat of a jail sentence, a noose or an electric chair, but they have no regard for an obligation in conscience. The work of government is to give peace, to give its subjects a chance to lead individual lives of fuller and fuller perfection; and its proper act is law. These evil men must be curbed, for the others must have peace if the state is to have any reason for existence.

Actually the curbing of criminals by the force of law does more than guarantee peace to orderly citizens. A child often starts off in life brushing its teeth, practising on the piano and eating spinach simply because there is no escape from these things. What it learned under duress, later on in life it does voluntarily, even eagerly. Not infrequently, the same thing is true of the lawbreaker. After all, what the law demands of the criminal is most fully in accord with his nature, i.e. action for his end, movement towards instead of away from his goal; and what is natural to man has in itself a mighty appeal.

Still, granted the utility of law, there seems to be an alternative. Why could not the government select some wise, prudent men, equip them with means of transportation and turn them loose on the community with instructions to use their common sense and guide the citizens to that peace and life of virtue which are the ends of the state? Well, in the first place, it is not too easy to find enough wise, prudent men to judge every single case solely by their own wisdom. In fact it is quite impossible. On the other hand it is comparatively easy to gather the few prudent men necessary to frame laws to be universally applied to the community. Then, too, it is one thing to attempt the settlement of a case that has risen suddenly and must be disposed of here and now; and quite another leisurely to consider all possible angles with a view to solving future cases of one type. Even a judge would find it hard to mete out impartial justice solely on his own reasoning after a bad night's sleep, a week or two of poor fare, or on a day that leaves him hot, dusty, irritated. All in all, concludes St. Thomas, it is a good thing to leave few things to the judgment of men.

We simply must have human law if we are to move surely to the goal of reason. Of course, as we saw in the last chapter, if this human law is to be law at all it must be derived from the Natural Moral Law; in fact its whole purpose is to supplement that law, fill in its gaps, make further determinations of it. Over and above this fundamental character of human law, what are its other qualities? How can we recognize a real human law when we see one? What are its family characteristics?

These characteristics have been recorded in some detail from the earliest days of Roman Law. Their very detail often leads to confusion though really there is no need of our being confused in this matter. If we are looking for the family characteristics of law, we have simply to look back to the family tree of law, to trace it back step by step through its progenitors—the community, nature and God. This order we are trying to identify must have the qualities demanded from such a lineage. We can put this in another way by saying briefly that human law must be in harmony with religion, with discipline or order, and contribute to welfare; or, even more simply, it must be in harmony with divine law, with the Natural Moral Law, and be to the common good.

In reference to the first of these, the identification of law is absurdly easy. A human law which flatly contradicts divine law is no law at all because it cuts itself off from the first source of all law and aims at goals opposed to the goal of all law. From the point of view of nature, human law will be reasonable and the reasonable thing in the material of human law is the just thing. It will be within the powers of the subjects and fitting to the time, place and customs of the country for which it is framed. All that is no more than saying it will be reasonable from the side of the matter, the subject and the circumstances; a demand for harmony with man's nature is always a demand for the reasonable. An unreasonable human law has the same place in the family of laws as an unreasonable action of man has in the family of human acts; the legislator should feel the same way about it that the pipe-smoker feels about throwing his pipe out of the window and putting the match in his mouth. It is not something to be defended, insisted on or gloated over; but rather something to cause embarrassment, mild astonishment, confusion and even shame. It is out of its class.

Serving the common good, a human law will serve the ends of necessity in acting for the removal of evil, the ends of utility in moving to the attainment of good, and the ends of caution in forestalling any injury from the law itself. In other words, it will be proportionate to human utility. Otherwise it will be as malicious in its own order as an Alpine guide with a homicidal mania.

Before going into the wide range of human law it might be well here to set to one side a type of law that, while human, is not framed by any government nor dependent on the sanction of any state. This law has been known for thousands of years as "the law of nations" (*jus gentium*). It is not international law, but rather a law common to all men; it is not natural law, for it is dependent upon a set of contingent facts, it does not spring immediately from man's nature. It is rather a determination of the Natural Moral Law made by human reason without the intervention of any institution whatever. An example of it is the necessity of private property. Starting from a principle of Natural Moral Law—social life demands that in their use of external goods men avoid confusion, neglect and discord—it comes upon the contingent fact that men, not as they could be or should be, but as they are, are not industrious, orderly and peaceful in their use of external goods commonly owned; and so concludes to the necessity of private property. A universal principle of Natural Moral Law, placed by human reason beside a universal but contingent fact, forces reason immediately to conclude to a dictate of "the law of nations".

To get back to human positive law in its ordinary sense, I think most of us have felt, at one time or another, unsatisfied with law. The root of that dissatisfaction is that law never seems to fit the individual case perfectly. The man who has just purchased a ready-made suit, having once known the perfection of the tailor-made product, has a taste of much the same dissatisfaction. The manufacturer of the ready-made suit does not know, cannot know, all the individual eccentricities—stoop-shoulders, hollow chests, short arms—of everyone who will buy his suits. He strikes a fair average that enables any tailor to bring the suit down to individual requirements. The legislator also strikes an average so accurate that an ordinary judge can bring the law down to the individual case. It would be more pleasant if everyone could have tailor-made suits. But it would be an impossible situation if everyone could have tailor-made laws. Law must be universal, not particular. It is made for many persons, in fact for the whole community, for many different periods, for many different circumstances, for many different actions. In fact it is made for succeeding generations of citizens, it is intended to be perpetual and of course cannot be tailored to any one individual.

Up to this time the majority of citizens of any state have not been saints; probably they never will be. This fact gives us the clue to the proper interpretation of the universality of law. That universality does not mean that human law should prohibit all vices nor that it should command all virtues; it is framed for the whole community and should be suited to the ordinary condition of its subjects. Some vices it must forbid, certainly those that threaten the very survival of society; some virtues it must command, certainly those which either directly or indirectly can be ordained by human means to the common good. But its aim is not to make men saints but to give them peace and a chance to work out their own individual perfection, their individual sanctity. Sanctity will always remain an individual affair.

This does not mean, of course, that human law is divorced from morality. In fact its chief efficacy lies precisely in the moral obligation, an obligation in conscience, which it imposes. Indeed it must impose such an obligation to live up to the essential notion of law, to be law at all. As we saw in the preceding chapter, law as the command or dictate of practical reason necessarily implies an obligation, a connection of some necessity between the act commanded and the end for which that act is commanded. The same truth is brought out when we remember that human law is derived from Natural Moral Law, or that it is derived from Eternal Law; either way it is traced back to the essential order of things and ultimately to the mind of God as the supreme source of truth and law. From St. Thomas's point of view, a law that does not oblige in conscience is, strictly speaking, not a law.

The obligation of human law is of its very nature limited to laws that are really laws, that is, to just laws. Since obligation follows from the very essence of law, a statute lacking that legal essence has no basis for obliging the citizens of a state. When is a law just? Well, really there is no other kind that deserves the name of law. Consequently a just law is one that answers to St. Thomas's definition of law as a dictate of reason for the common good by him who has care of the community.

In more detail, a just law is one that is framed for the common good by legitimate authority and which imposes burdens on the citizens in proportion both to the powers of the different citizens and the needs of the common good. This will perhaps be clearer if viewed from the other side. A law is unjust when it is contrary to human or divine good. Again, contrariety to the divine good is easy to see and immediately precludes any possibility of ever complying with the particular law. A law is contrary to human good because of its end, its author or its form; that is, because it is ordained to the cupidity or glory of the ruler instead of to the common good, because it exceeds the powers of the legislator, or because its distribution of burdens is unequal, not proportionate either to the citizens or to the common good. It is possible for such a law, contrary to human good, to oblige in conscience, not because of its innate character as law, but because of some accidental consequence of its disobedience, like scandal or rioting. More simply, even our disobedience as citizens must be ordained to the common good of the community.

It has long been recognized that disrespect for law is a serious threat to government. What is not recognized to-day is that disrespect for law is a serious threat to freedom.

If the citizen feels that his will is being coerced by just laws, then there is something the matter with his will. If he thinks that just laws are a threat to his liberty, he has forgotten what liberty is. His will, if it is good, should be moving towards precisely the ends of just laws; the whole purpose of just laws is to give the individual citizen an opportunity to exercise his liberty in the perfection of himself. A burglar or a murderer is right in thinking of law as a coercive power directed against his operations; it is and it should be. Even the stupidest of burglars would hardly make the mistake of basing his defence on a plea of justice and liberty. It is only the criminals who are subject to law in the sense of being coerced by law; the rest of the citizens are really free of law in this sense, for the demands of law are demands that are in accord with their wills.

While law and good will are in harmony, law has much greater stability about it than has the individual will. There is a comfort in stability which is not found in change. I remember once seeing a burly individual aggressively approach a swinging door. It struck me watching him that someone had done excellent work cleaning the glass panel of that door to give it such crystal clearness and transparency. As he reached the door he stretched out his arm to give it that insolent sort of shove which seems to expect a door to jump off its hinges and stand to one side at attention. He pushed right at the glass—but there was no glass there; as he hung half in and half out the door, like a sack of flour thrown over a horse's back, I am sure he was disconcerted. We expect things to be as they are. Imagine someone enjoying a siesta under a shady tree only to have the tree turn around and bite or walk off and leave the sleeper under the sun's glare. There are things we expect to find always the same, things like God, nature and the goals of humanity. Because law has its roots in God and nature and its hopes in the goals of man, there is an immutable character to all law.

Not that law is absolutely unchangeable. It seems evident that the laws regulating the hitching of horses along Twenty-third Street in New York half a century ago would not be of much help in handling modern New York traffic. It is as least conceivable that a better system of traffic regulation will be devised in the future. Conditions can and do change, better laws can be framed; for these two reasons law can be changed.

But a change in law is something to be gone about slowly, cautiously, almost regretfully, for there is always a real loss in a change of law, a loss of the force of custom behind that law. Law is not to be changed every time something better comes up, but only on condition that the good effect obtained by the change of law sufficiently compensates the common good for the loss incurred by the change of law. It is possible that, considered in the abstract, the English way of having traffic move on the left is superior to ours; but if the English "look right" were painted on all the streets to-morrow as warning that the superior system had been installed, half the pedestrians of New York would be dead by noontime.

Custom is a mighty force. It can obtain the full force of law, can abolish and interpret laws. After all, the right reason of a community can be as effectively declared by actions as by words. That basic source of the power of custom—the declaration of right reason by the community—brings out clearly the difference between the power of custom among different people. In a free people custom and consent of the people actually have more power than the ruler or his words, for the ruler's power is really only a vicarious power of the people. In a people who are not free, custom has the power of law in so far as its toleration is an implicit approval on the part of the ruler; and of course there must have been considerable toleration for a practice to develop the full strength of custom.

However, we will make a mistake if we think of custom and law as opponents glaring at each other across the ring. Often custom precedes law and law is really its crystallization. Usually custom is not against law but rather over and above it, supplying the deficiences of law, or, in a case of real opposition, showing the uselessness of that law. If, as a matter of fact, the reason for the law still exists and it is therefore still useful for the common good, a contrary custom springing up does not conquer the law but is rather conquered by it; unless, of course, the custom is of such long standing that the law is *de facto* useless, because unenforceable in the face of the custom of the country. It is not an easy thing to change the customs of a people. Indeed it is so drastic a task that only the greatest necessity justifies the attempt, like a curfew or regulations on the showing of lights in time of war.

Running all through this discussion of law, its nature, its extent and obligation, there has been a fundamental consideration for the common good. Granted the legitimacy of the legislator, that will always be the prime consideration. So it is not surprising to find St. Thomas agreeing that when the letter of the law here and now would militate against the common good, the law is not to be followed, for that would be to act against the intention of the legislator. However, unless the emergency has arisen so suddenly and must be settled so quickly that recourse is impossible, the interpretation or absolution from the law in this particular case must be made by the legislator himself. Not only has he the power to declare in the name of the common good that this law does not bind in this case, he can when the common good does not suffer, dispense in a particular case from a law. It is quite possible that a law which in general works to the good of the people, in this particular case works a hardship on the individual; if there is good reason for the dispensation and the common good does not suffer, then he who framed the law can dispense from it.

So much for human positive law. When we come to the divine positive law, we find it clearly divided into the New and the Old Law, the preparation and the fulfilment, the imperfect and the perfect. The Old Law was exactly a preparation of one race for the coming of Christ; imperfect, like all preparations, doing the work of divine law in drawing men to the friendship of God, but not doing the whole work because sanctification, as St. Paul insisted, was not by the law but by faith in the coming Redeemer.

While the New Law was given directly by the son of God Himself, the Old Law came to men through the ministry of angels and men, following the universal order of divine providence by which the inferiors are led to perfection by their superiors. Unlike the New Law, the Old Law was not given to all men nor for all men; it was given to a single race, the Jews, for their special sanctification. Nor was this a case of favouritism on the part of God. Favouritism implies an injury to justice, an overlooking of merit; and this whole law was gratuitously given. Merit did not enter into the question. It was given to the Jews, for they above all other peoples needed sanctification, since it was from them that the Son of God was to be born. Consequently the Old Law, except in so far as it contained precepts of the Natural Moral Law, did not oblige any other people but the Jews themselves. It was, strictly speaking, their law, and theirs alone.

The law governing a whole people has always been a complex affair. It has to be for so great a task. The Old Law was no exception to this general rule. If we glance hastily through the first five books of the Bible we will get something like the same sense of bewilderment that settles upon the layman who has wandered by mistake into the legal section of a modern library. The Old Law is not to be summed up in terms of the ten commandments; those commandments are only one part of the law, the moral part. Actually the law was divided into three classes of precepts: moral, ceremonial and judicial.

As a general description of these three we might say that the moral precepts were merely a restatement of the secondary precepts of the Natural Moral Law; the ceremonial precepts, proceeding from the Natural Moral Law's command to worship God, made further determinations as to the time, place and manner of this worship; the judicial precepts, proceeding from the natural precept of justice, made further determinations as to how this justice was to be observed among men. All three typs of precepts were enforced by temporal threats and temporal promises—a long life, peace, many children, the blotting of the family name from the earth, and so on. This is just another mark of the imperfection of the Old Law. The perfection of man is the spurning of temporal things to cling to the spiritual; the imperfection, to desire the temporal in preference to the spiritual; the perversion, to desire the temporal above all others. The Old Law led men by the imperfect way, inducing them by temporal promises and threats to start the practice of virtue to the end that they might continue and perfect that practice for the ends of virtue itself, much as we might start a child on a good habit with a promise of toys, sure that long after the toys are forgotten the habit will endure.

Examining the moral precepts more closely we see many things commanded that are not immediately evident from the Natural Moral Law itself; a more accurate way of stating these precepts would be to say that they are all reducible to the ten commandments or to the secondary precepts of the Natural Moral Law. There is, for example, such a precept as that commanding reverence for the old —a precept that, while following immediately from the Natural Moral Law as a conclusion from a principle, nevertheless demands wise consideration and study before its connection with the Natural Moral Law is seen. There are others which demanded divine instruction for the knowledge of their connection with the secondary precepts of Natural Moral Law, for example, the prohibition of sculpture to a people completely surrounded by the unnatural practice of idolatry. In these latter precepts the divine character of this positive law shines out clearly; human positive law proposes only those precepts that deal with justice, the divine goes beyond that to the material of other virtues, commanding under the obligation of precept those things without which the order of reason (not the social order) cannot be maintained, advocating under the admonishment of counsel those things that pertain to the perfection of reason and virtue.

In this treatise on the ten commandments, St. Thomas handles the Decalogue as a connoisseur would handle a very rare, very precious jewel. He turns it slowly in his hands, looking at it now from this angle, now from that; he holds it up to the light, puts it against rich, dark backgrounds, savouring its full beauty and exquisite perfection.

For example: of these ten commandments, three deal with God, seven with our neighbour; the first three against pride of life that would puff us up above God, two against the concupiscence of the flesh, defending the sanctity of marriage, the rest against the concupiscence of the eyes—dealing with the things of others. Or considering them from the viewpoint of social life with its two essentials of ruler and subjects, we find the first three commandments regulating harmonious relationship with the ruler by demanding fidelity, reverence and properly restrained familiarity; the other seven, regulating relations between fellow citizens, demand rendering of what is due to parents as having the supreme claim, and the avoiding of injury to all citizens in their persons or possessions by thought, word or work. Or, again, putting the ten commandments against the more sombre background of moral gravity, we find that the very order in which they are stated is the order of gravity—most easily and immediately seen by men: first, the three commandments driving men's minds to God their goal, the three whose contraries are the gravest of evils; then the seven commandments dealing with our neighbour, first in reference to parents to whom we have greater obligation and, following this in quick logical order, the commands forbidding offence by deed, word or thought with most emphasis on offences in actual deed where a cloak of protection is thrown around life, the family and external possessions by the prohibition of murder, adultery and theft.

Before passing on to the New Law, it might be well here to note that, with the exception of the element of Natural Moral Law it contained, the Old Law ceased with Christ. St. Augustine, speaking of the ceremonial precepts, puts this pithily when he distinguishes three stages: the first before the passion of Christ in which these precepts were neither dead nor deadly; the second from the passion of Christ until the spreading of the gospel when they were dead but not deadly; the third, after the spread of the gospel, when they were both dead and deadly. The judicial precepts died with Christ also, but since in themselves they were not figurative or prophetic of the future coming of Christ, their observance after Christ did not contain that same element of propagation of error.

With Christ the Old Law died and the New Law was born; or, better, the Old Law was fulfilled by this New Law which was not merely a written law but a law written in the hearts of the faithful. It was necessary by word and writing to instruct men about the things to be believed and the things to be done, but over and above that was the grace of the Holy Spirit in the hearts of the followers of Christ. It was this internal element of the New Law which did what the Old Law could never do, justify men.

This is indeed a divine law, divine in the depths of our nature which it touches, divine in its endurance to the end of time and divine in the wisdom of its coming which gave men plenty of time to realize how badly they needed the grace of God for the living of human life.

The Old Law was really a teacher of fundamentals for children; the New, a teacher of perfection. So the multitude of commands necessary for children are done away with in the New Law. As far as exterior observances go, this New Law is much lighter, much easier; but because it is no longer for children, the internal demands it makes are much harder, as hard, indeed, as perfection. Or putting this in another way, the external work to be done is easier in the New Law, but the way in which it must be done is much harder, the way, namely, of charity.

Yet for all the limitation of externals, the New Law is not sketchy and unsatisfactory in this regard. Evidently some external acts had to be commanded, specifically those whose contraries opposed the constitution of internal grace and its proper use. All else was left to the determination of superiors and individuals as befits a law of liberty. In other words, the New Law had to insist upon the sacraments and the moral precepts; and these two were sufficient, for by them, grace is established and properly used.

We find the same brief sufficiency and strong emphasis in the New Law's regulation of the internal life of man. St. Augustine says this is sufficiently shown forth in the Sermon on the Mount where our Lord handled briefly man's own internal life, his relations with his neighbours and the manner of fulfilling both classes of works. For his own regulation man is ordered to avoid evil not merely in its external manifestations, but in his own thoughts and desires, even to avoid the occasions from which evil springs; and at the same time to do good not for human glory, not for human riches, but to the end that he might be perfect, might one day be with God. In his dealings with his neighbours even his judgments must not be rash nor smack of injustice. This New Law that is given to him is not merely to be heard, he is not merely to confess the faith, but he is to ask the divine help he needs, then very humbly and courageously set about the work of keeping the ten commandments.

Over and above that which is strictly necessary for the successful living of life, for the bare attainment of the goal which will spell eternal happiness, there is the rich material of perfection which is the subject-matter of the counsels given by Christ. Man is in the middle between things of the spirit and things of the world. The more he holds to one, the more he must recede from the other. His calamitous failure consists in embracing temporal things and receding entirely from the spiritual; he meets the bare requirements of success by adhering to temporal things, using them, but always in view of the spiritual goal for which he was made; but he reaches that same goal more expeditiously, lives his life more fully, participates more heartily in that perfection of God by totally receding from temporal things. It is to this supreme peak of human perfection that the New Law points, not harshly, not threateningly, but with that gracious respect for the freedom of man shown by the counsels—"*qui potest capere, capiat*".

Perhaps the best summary of these chapters on law could be made by pointing to the beginnings of law. Law takes its rise from the eternal mind of God Himself, from the imprint of that Eternal Law on and in nature itself, from the intrinsic principles of man's own nature. Always law has something of that stability of God and nature and human nature about it, always it has the force of a direction that comes from nature, transmuted into that delicately respectful moral force as the movement of God passes through the moral nature of man. As it progresses law comes closer and closer to individual lives, to individual actions, determining the sweepingly universal dictates of nature to fit the exact circumstances of everyday life. It comes down from the absolutely essential to the less necessary, to the fitting and finally, in that complete perfection of divine law, to the heroic details which make a man as perfect as he can well be in this life.

It was part of God's great tact and respect for human nature that made of Natural Moral Law an utterly intrinsic thing, that made man in a very real sense his own legislator. It was that same divine thoughtfulness and generosity which gave to human institutions a part in the government of the world, leaving to the state the further determinations of Natural Moral Law necessary for the living of human life. But because the whole direction of life which is law is so completely from God, it is not surprising that God should step in with explicit directions where the mind and institutions of men had fallen short or begun to fail. It is not surprising that God, Who had offered His only begotten Son for men, should specially prepare the people from whom that Son was to be born; not surprising that God, Whose whole purpose in framing law was to bring men to Himself, should take upon Himself the office of Lawgiver of positive law that men might reach Him more surely, more expeditiously, more perfectly.

God, nature, human nature—these are the sources of law. Their ends are the ends of law. Law exists that it might guide men, not in any direction, not to any goal, but to the right goal, to the goal whose attainment means happiness for man. Eternal Law, Natural Moral Law, divine positive law, all aim directly at this goal of human life, for all are directly from God and God is the goal of life. Human positive law, because it is of man, approaches that goal more humbly, stopping somewhat short of the goal, feeling that it is treading on holy ground. It is satisfied to give to men peace and an opportunity to work their individual way to that supreme goal of human life, to give them the means by which they can live "the life of virtue". Law is intimately linked up with human life. Man alone needs law, for man alone can fail. Man alone, of all the creatures on earth, can have law, for only man can succeed, for only man has for a goal attainable by his own actions, the eternal vision of God.

CHAPTER XX

(OUTLINE)

HEIGHTS OF HAPPINESS

(Q. 109–114)

1. Meaning of human life:
    - (*a*) Key to human activity—desire and happiness.
    - (*b*) The natural and happiness.
    - (*c*) The supernatural and happiness.

2. Grace and meaning of human life.

3. Grace considered in itself:
    - (*a*) Necessity of grace:
        - (1) For man without grace.
        - (2) For man in the state of grace.
    - (*b*) Nature of grace:
        - (1) A supernatural quality.
        - (2) In the essence of the soul.
    - (*c*) Division of grace:
        - (1) Given for the salvation of others.
        - (2) Given for personal sanctification:
            - *a*. Habitual.
            - *b*. Actual: sufficient and efficacious.

4. Causes of grace:
    - (*a*) God's part in grace.
    - (*b*) Man's part in grace.

5. Effects of grace:
    - (*a*) Justification:
        - (1) Nature.
        - (2) Production.
        - (3) Excellence.
    - (*b*) Merit:
        - (1) Nature and existence.
        - (2) Principle and conditions of merit.
        - (3) Manner.

(4) Objects:

a. First grace for self and others.
b. Increase of grace.
c. Final perseverance.
d. Temporal goods.

Conclusion:

1. Grace and the natural world.

2. Grace and the natural man.

3. Grace and human action.

4. Grace and human happiness.

Appendix: Revealed doctrine pertaining to grace.

CHAPTER XX

THE HEIGHTS OF HAPPINESS

(Q. 109–114)

THE little boy who is just tasting the first delicious morsels of independence, his curls gone, wearing a real shirt with his own tie and a pair of trousers with a real belt, looks down the long dreams of youth to great goals, great ends, to the time when he will be a man. The old man with death's door almost within reach of his fingers, turns his head and looks back regretfully, dreamingly, smilingly, at the beginnings of life, to the days when he was a boy. It is the natural thing to do, for if there are to be any beginnings of human life, of human action, there must be a goal, an end; and if we are to understand the end we must look back to the beginning.

In the beginning of this book we considered the end, the goal of human life. Now approaching the end of this volume, to understand it all we must look to the beginning, which is also the end. At the start of this long study we saw that the key to the ceaseless activity of men and women was desire. Because the object of desire is attainable but not yet attained, we act; and in that action, progressing toward the object of desire, we have a foretaste of the happiness that the attainment of that object of desire will bring. All men act for one thing—to obtain the object of desire, to be happy.

Human life is accurately stated as a search for happiness. But because the objects men have desired have so seldom brought them happiness, it has become the attitude of our age to emphasize the quest and shudder at the thought of attaining the goal. Men are happy in a way while the hunt for happiness is going on. When they stand with the quarry at bay, with sensible pleasure, riches, power or fame in their hands, then there is not happiness but disillusionment, disgust, despair at such an ending to human life, to human action. Really to-day the friend of the neo-pagan is he who wishes him not success but failure, for success is the end of the quest and only in the quest is happiness found. The reason for this is that the quest has been limited to the world around or beneath man, to the world within man, the world of his body or his soul, but never extended to the world above man, to the infinite world of divine perfection. However great the goods of these worlds of nature, they are puny substitutes to an intellect thirsting for supreme truth, to an appetite that only the universal good will ever satisfy.

In the beginning of this study we determined the goal which alone would bring men happiness, a goal no less than the eternal vision of God Himself. It is an impossible goal if we look only at the powers of man's nature, as San Francisco is out of the range of our ears if we forget the radio or the telephone which makes it possible to hear a voice across the continent. Without help we cannot possibly hear someone speaking so far away; without help man cannot possibly attain the one goal that will give him happiness. And the help by which God is brought within range of the hands of men, the help by which the actions of men can lift those same men up to the vision of God, is called grace—the subject of our present chapter.

As the bridge spanning the gap between the supernatural and the natural, grace is all-important to the individual man, for it is only by bridging this gap that happiness is possible. Grace should have an eminent place among the great Catholic truths. It has. Indeed just a glance at its relation to the great truths of our Faith is sufficient to bring out even more clearly its tremendous importance in human life. It was grace that was lost by original sin. Grace was the immediate fruit of the Incarnation and

Redemption. It is the means of the justification of the sinner, the immediate fruit of the sacraments and the purpose of the whole sacramental system which continues the work of Christ in supplying the souls of men with this life-giving gift. The priesthood exists for the Mass and the sacraments and so for grace. Progress in grace is spiritual progress, perfection. With grace comes the whole supernatural equipment of virtues and gifts of the Holy Ghost; with the loss of grace most of this equipment is lost. Mortal sin is the destruction of grace and the death of the soul. The subject of grace enters deeply into our Mariology, particularly to-day when Mary's position as co-Redemptrix and channel of all grace is being brought out more clearly. Grace is the means by which we live a divine life, yet the understanding of grace makes impossible the absurdities of pantheism; it is grace which lifts us to the heights of God, lets us live the life of God, yet leaves God God and man man.

There is no end to this. Yet St. Thomas treated this enormous subject adequately, scientifically, with profound beauty in just six questions of his *Summa Theologica*, one of the shortest of his tracts.

A man in perfect health has little thought for or appreciation of his splendid health. A short tour through a hospital will awaken him to his fortunate condition. So a statement of the importance of grace wins our agreement, but it does not drive that importance deep into our souls as does a momentary consideration of man's condition without grace. Physical sickness makes apparent the value of health; spiritual sickness makes vividly evident the necessity of grace.

Let us put to one side that purely hypothetical state of humanity—the state of pure nature in which man would have had all that nature demands but would never have known anything of the supernatural or preternatural gifts. Our interest is with man as he is to-day and that means with man in the state of fallen nature, the state of man with the sickness of sin on his soul and his nature injured by being stripped of the preternatural gifts by which God had supplied the defects inherent in the very elements of which man is made. What is the condition of man in this state without grace?

What is such a man like? If we desire to know this man, or any man, the intelligent way to go about the investigation is not to ask what does he look like, how does he part his hair or what kind of a smile has he, but rather to get down to essentially human activities. What does he know? What does he aim at, what does he will? What can he do? If we can answer these questions we know a man thoroughly.

The answers to all these questions about a man in the state of fallen nature are extremely easy. Without grace in the sense of supernatural help, certainly he cannot know supernatural truth. A cat has no knowledge of mental hygiene and no one is in the least surprised; such things are above the nature of the cat. Much less can a man of his own natural powers know supernatural truths, for these are not only above his nature, they are above all nature. Since reason is the guide holding the hand of appetite and steering its blind steps, appetite stops at the wall of the supernatural along with its guide, reason. If a man cannot know supernatural things, of course he cannot aim at them, cannot desire them. Much less can he do any supernatural work, for his work contains no more than flows into it from the principles of all human work, the intellect and will.

All in all, fallen man without grace is much more helpless in the supernatural order than is the infant crying for the moon and refusing to be satisfied with anything less than the moon. Man cannot be satisfied with any goal less than the supernatural, yet, left to himself, he cannot even know of his supernatural goal; he can know only his own restless discontent. As we look into this more closely, the helplessness of man becomes more and more apparent. He cannot produce the smallest act meritorious of eternal life, for there is less proportion between his natural acts and eternal life than between the child's high-chair and the fiftieth story of a modern skyscraper. Without that supernatural help of God which is actual grace he cannot even prepare himself for the grace that will establish some proportion between his acts and eternal life, any more than the child not yet conceived can prepare itself for life.

While apparently very comforting, it would actually be disastrous if we could turn from this picture of our helplessness in the supernatural order to a picture of easy efficiency and perfection in the natural order. This latter is the picture our modern world is trying so hard to bring to life by breathing a steady flow of words upon it. But it remains a figment of our imagination. Even in the natural order of things we make a sorry job of human life without grace. Look what we do with the ten commandments. True enough there is no one of them that cannot be observed; but to observe all of them, taken collectively, is too much. That is a work for a healthy nature. Fallen nature is not healthy, it is sick with the sickness of sin, naked with the loss of the preternatural gifts. A sick man cannot do the day's work measured out by an efficiency expert for a healthy man, nor can he eat the meal designed by the expert chef for a healthy appetite; no more can a sick nature keep the commandments that were carefully proportioned to a healthy nature. Granted that there is no mortal sin that cannot be avoided, that fallen man can avoid all mortal sins for a time—this much is demanded by the very nature of sin—still it is impossible for him to escape mortal sin for any length of time.

Look at the case dispassionately for a moment. This man is sick and his sickness has not been healed by grace. Consequently his will is not totally subject to God. We have within ourselves a parallel to this in the sense appetite which is not totally subject to reason. How long can we go without some movement of that sense appetite contrary to reason? The fact is that such a man's heart is not firmly fixed on God and where sudden action is demanded that action will be moulded by the end that is firmly fixed in his heart.

Without grace, then, even those precepts of the Natural Moral Law which are the ten commandments are going to be violated. And without grace fallen man in the state of mortal sin has slipped, or rather plunged, into a smooth-sided well. He can do nothing to raise himself from the depths of sin if he remains unaided by the grace of God. What has he done by his sin? He has destroyed the splendid lustre of the soul, perverted the order of nature by averting his will from God, and incurred a debt of punishment by his offence against God. Auto-suggestion, will power, legislative action or scientific research can be of no aid to him here. That splendid lustre of the soul, the effect of the streaming light of human and divine reason, came to him by grace; only through grace can it be restored. It was by grace that he could turn his will to God, his supernatural goal; it is only by grace that he can now turn back to that same goal. It is God Who has been offended and Who is the judge of men, only God can do anything about the punishment due to sin.

Turning from these gloomy wards of the spiritual hospital, we wonder how men can be so intent upon getting along without God and His grace. A turn about the ward of the convalescents, while decidedly more cheerful, only brings the importance of grace home to us more keenly. Here we have men with that same sick nature but partially healed by the grace that has removed sin from their souls, though they still bear the infirmities consequent on the loss of the gifts first given to human nature. In other words here we find ourselves. We are supernaturally alive by the habitual or sanctifying grace in our souls, we have all the infused virtues, so we know supernatural truths, we aim at the supernatural goal, we love God for Himself above all things. With no more than this, what do we get done supernaturally? The answer is: nothing at all.

Habitual grace gives us life, the remote principle of action, but not action itself; it does not overcome the difficulties in the way of getting things done, it is not a licence freeing us from constant dependence on the first mover. It brings us into the world of the living, but if we are to get things done, if we are to take steps towards the goal of eternal happiness, we must have yet more grace—the grace of action or actual grace. If we are to do good, if we are to avoid sin, if we are to persevere in the friendship of God to the end of life, then we must have actual supernatural help from God.

All this sounds difficult, perhaps even a little harsh, somehow a reflection on the dignity and independence of man. It seems so only because we know so little about man and so very little about God; or rather because the truths that we know so certainly have not been allowed to penetrate into the depths of our being where their full meaning would become an integral part of us. We could tell this whole story of man's utter dependence on God in the supernatural order by simply pointing to that same dependence in the natural order. Both could be summed up by saying that it is a contradiction in terms to suppose that man or any other creature can for a moment, in the least of his actions, escape from the causality of the first cause.

In the natural order we do not give life to ourselves; that life must be traced to the source of all life, to the source of all being, to the first cause. In the natural order we actually get things done, we eat meals, we take walks, we think and love. But we do not do any of these things alone. True enough they are our actions; but we are the secondary causes. Along with us, step by step, moves the first cause upon which not only the actions but our very ability to cause those actions depend at every instant. More simply, there is only one utterly independent being and that being is God. To escape from our dependence on Him means the annihilation of that action because from Him alone is everything of reality. That dependence on God is not a reflection on the dignity, the independence, the personal responsibility of man. Rather that dependence is the sole explanation of man's dignity, of his mastery over his own actions.

Exactly the same is true in the supernatural order. We do not give ourselves supernatural life; that life must come from the Author of all life. Our supernatural actions are not ours alone; we depend on God here as we do in the natural order. Grace is nothing more than the action of the first cause in the supernatural order, the help by which it is possible for men to be and to operate in the order that is proper to God alone.

If we keep that parallel with the natural order in mind we have an exact notion of the nature of grace. We have already seen the natural dependence of man several times in the course of this work: in the first volume, in treating of the will of God, of the will of man and of the government of the world by God; in this volume in treating of the acts of the intellect and will. It is a fundamental dependence that in its simplest terms is an insistence on the self-evident truth that a realization of potentialities is not brought about by the unaided subject of that realization. Or, even more simply, a man does not give himself perfections which he does not possess.

Grace is that supernatural help by which it is possible for a man to realize his potentialities for life and action on a supernatural plane. If we look first at the grace which brings supernatural life to man, we see it most accurately in terms of God's love for us. There is a vast difference between human and divine love. With us it is a case of stumbling along until we find goodness to attract and hold our love; we are merely discoverers of the goodness we love, not its creators. With God, where outside of Himself can He find goodness that has not its source in

Himself? His love must create the goodness which He loves. So in the natural order we find the effect of His divine love always a positive goodness; concretely the effect of that divine love is the individual nature of every creature existing with all that belongs to that creature. So in the supernatural order, that same divine love does not discover goodness, it produces it; first supernatural life, then all the supernatural equipment of virtues and helps which makes the fulfilment of that supernatural life possible. That supernatural life, the effect of divine love in the supernatural order, is grace; and that grace is not an outburst of poetry, a figment of imagination, an idle hope, but a reality, a positive good, a good as positive as life itself, for that is precisely what it is—a participation of an infinite life.

God, of course, is the only supernatural substance, the only substance that is above and totally beyond the natural order. Everything else supernatural belongs to what the philosophers call the class of "accidents". That is, grace does not walk the streets or loll in an easy chair; like colour in a child's cheeks, or a smile on a man's face, it cannot exist alone, it must exist in something else. It is an "accident" modifying, qualifying the very principle of life within us, the very essence of the soul; qualifying it to such an extent as to make that same soul the principle by which we move and live on the level of divinity. Unlike the virtues which enable us to operate on that level, grace gives the much more fundamental requirement of life itself. Grace is not a virtue, not to be confused with the virtues, but rather the foundation and source of the supernatural virtues much as the soul itself is the foundation and source of life, of our faculties, of our operations in the natural order.

That is the type of grace which we call habitual or sanctifying, the grace without which the soul is supernaturally dead. It is a very personal gift whose direct object is to bring life to this individual, to make this man holy and pleasing to God. Before continuing with this personal angle of grace, it might be well to point out, passingly, another class of graces given not primarily for the sanctification of the one receiving them but for the sanctification of others.

Rather than personal graces, these are apostolic in their character, effecting the things most necessary to apostolic activity: a full knowledge of divine things, a confirmation of this divine doctrine through deeds that only God can do or knowledge that only God could have, and finally a fitting proposal of these truths to others. Among such graces are the gifts of tongues, of prophecy, of miracles, and so on. In other words, the apostle as such is an instrument of God bringing salvation to others; if the greatness of his works tempts him to pride, a momentary consideration of the other instruments God has used in this work—the high priest who prophesied in moving form the death of Christ and the talking ass of Balaam—will bring home the realization that these works are God's works done through him not primarily because of his great goodness but because of God's great love for souls.

To get back to the personal angle of grace, it is evidently not sufficient that we exist. We have work to do, things to get done, steps to take, for in the supernatural as well as in the natural order it is equally true that we carve out our own destiny with the tools of our own human actions. In the natural order, the smooth motion of God is the cause not only of the note that pours from the throat of a bird, but also of the sweetness of that note, of the necessity with which it springs from the bird's instincts. The same divine motion is the cause of the note that pours from the human singer's throat, and at the same time is the cause of the sweetness of the note and the freedom with which it is produced. In a word, that divine motion is the cause of whatever reality there is in action. In the supernatural order the divine motion preparing us for action, moving us to action, producing the action with us, is called actual grace.

This divine movement which is actual grace is not to be understood in terms of extrinsic assistance, like an extra oarsman furnishing just enough more power to give the boat headway, or an extra horse whose help makes possible the pulling of a load too heavy for one alone. It is more far-reaching than that. It is an intrinsic movement in the order of first cause which, in its own order, is the cause of the action yet leaves our causality intact, indeed produces or makes possible our causality.

It is a movement, then, that flows into our very faculties and through our faculties into the effect, the actual action. If this divine movement gives us the proximate dispositions for action, bringing us to the point where action is immediately possible to us, it is called sufficient actual grace; it is the grace given to every man born into the world and the grace that is found at the root of every supernatural action. Over and above this, a distinct divine movement bringing about the realization of this proximate power of action, bridging the gap between the power to act and action itself, must be had for every supernatural action. That distinct divine movement is called efficacious actual grace. Both intrinsically affect the faculties themselves, both are complete and efficient in their own order—the one in the order of potentiality, the other in the order of actuality—both, like all divine motion properly affecting men, leave intact, indeed guarantee and cause, the ability and freedom of man to produce his own actions.

Perhaps this seems a little abstract; but with a moment's thought the practical consequences of these abstract truths assume tremendous importance. Thus it is immediately evident that grace is not something to be nonchalantly tossed away like a half-smoked cigarette when there is a full pack in our pocket. It is not something that can be ordered by telephone, purchased in a shop or imported at our commands; it is not to be found, stumbled over, grown in a garden or inherited. It is not the result of industry, a quick wit or ready speech. Rather it is something that can come from God alone—it is a gift of God that once lost can be regained only by another outburst of generosity on the part of the divine Donor. Grace is supernatural; it exceeds the power of all nature, even the combined powers of everything in nature. It can come only from the Author of the natural and the supernatural.

Our part in grace is enough to set us towering above all other creatures in the world and yet is humble enough to keep us very close to God. We can prepare ourselves for habitual or sanctifying grace, we can increase that grace in our souls; we do both by our own actions, yet can do neither one nor the other without the help of actual grace, without the movement of God. In this case, as in every action of man, there are two sides to the story, two truths to be taken into account, two angles, both strictly accurate, both rigidly true, but neither able to be considered alone without distorting the truth. It is strictly true that we love, learn, talk, and so on; it is we who are doing these things, these are our actions, proceeding under our control, and for them we are wholly responsible. It is equally true that God causes our loving, our learning, our talking and the rest. If we look only at our part in all this, we are looking only at the activity of the secondary causes which is totally inexplicable considered in itself. If we look only at God's part in all this, we are neglecting half the truth, even neglecting part of the truth of God's activity, namely the causality of the secondary causes and their freedom.

In the supernatural order we prepare ourselves for grace by our own actions proceeding from our free will, under our control. They are ours. But we are only seeing half the truth if we do not see that these actions are also God's, that behind our causality is the causality of the first cause, necessary for every instant of our causality. Looked at from our side, we prepare ourselves for grace; looked at from God's side, God prepares us for grace. Both sides are true. A statement of only one side, whichever it be, is only a half-truth with all the falseness of a half-truth.

Putting the same thing briefly, we can say that even in our preparation for sanctifying grace we are men and God is God. Because we are men and not God, every step of that preparation depends not only on our free will but on the divine supernatural movement that is actual grace. Bringing it down to the concrete, a man has committed mortal sin and so lost sanctifying grace; by his acts of sorrow for sin and of love for God, his determinations to make amends and seek forgiveness, he is preparing himself for sanctifying grace. But these very acts of preparation spring not only from the free will of the sinner but also from the supernatural movement of God which is actual grace.

We need grace badly, in fact our dependence on it is complete. That is saying no more than that our dependence on God is complete, a dependence that does not stop at the natural order but is equally true of the supernatural. Of course we cannot produce grace, in fact nothing in nature can. Grace must always remain a completely free gift of a generous God. The fact that the love of God for us has driven Him to incredible generosity which, coupled with the infinite merits of a God-man's death, has put grace practically at our convenience in no way changes the gratuitous character of this gift. True enough Christ established the sacraments as channels down which pour the graces His death has won for us, true enough we have only to stoop and drink, true enough it is easier to get grace now than it is to get bread or water; but the supreme truth behind all this is that only an extravagant divine love could have devised so precious a gift and only the uttermost limits of that divine extravagance could have put that gift within reach of the hand of the stuttering child, the doddering old man at the point of death, the rich and the poor, the learned and ignorant, the sick and the healthy.

Each can prepare himself for sanctifying grace, can increase that grace in his soul. To each God gives grace in proportion to the preparation made by the help of that divine movement. It is strictly true that to a man doing his best, doing what is in him, God does not deny grace; the very doing of his best is already an evidence of the rain of grace falling on the soil of his soul. As one's preparation is more intense, greater than another's, so is the sanctifying grace in the soul of one greater than the sanctifying grace in the soul of another, even though all sanctifying grace has the same great goal of sanctifying men, uniting them to God, bringing them to their goal.

The angle at which we hold our heads, the beatific look on our faces or the grave majesty of our steps is not proof of our possession of grace. Such things might be due to rheumatism, falling in love, or tight shoes. There is no proof of our possession of grace. Always we must work out our salvation in fear and trembling. Short of a special revelation of God we cannot be absolutely certain of having sanctifying grace. But we can be fairly sure from such signs as our refusal to give temporal things preference over divine things when a choice is necessary, from our not being conscious of mortal sin, from our joy in the things of God.

When we come to the effects of grace within us we step into the field of drama. The fulfilment of the age-old dream of men, the dream of becoming like God, could not be otherwise than dramatic. Whether we look at this first effect of grace—justification of the sinner—as a soaring to divine heights, a turning to the streaming light of divine wisdom, a revulsion from the ugliness of sin and a swift flight back to God, or as the declaration of peace and reconciliation between God and the rebel sinner, we have drama. It is the drama of impossible accomplishment plucking down the stars, the drama of sunrise conquering night, of escape from darkness and slavery into freedom and light, the drama of the prodigal son and his father's unquestioning pardon. The infusion of grace and the forgiveness of sin are two sides of the same picture, like the coming of light and the dispelling of darkness. It is a motion from sin and to God in which our free will plays an enormous part. Looked at from God's side there is the infusion of grace, the turning away from sin, the turning to God and finally the remission of sin; from our side there is the remission of sin, the turning away from sin, the turning to God and the infusion of grace. Actually it is one and the same motion looked at from different angles, a motion which takes place in an instant though its preparation may be fast or slow.

However we look at it, the justification of man must always stand out as one of the greatest works of God. Indeed from the side of the thing actually done—giving men a participation in the divine life of God—it is the greatest work of God. It is, in a very real sense, even greater than the glorification of man in heaven, for there is much less proportion between the life of grace and the sinner to whom it is given than between the life of glory in heaven and the saint who has earned that glory. Even creation, the greatest work of God considering the manner in which it was accomplished, i.e. because it was a work produced from nothing, had as its final effect only the world of nature. Grace has as its effect the supernatural, exceeding the natural and any combination of the natural by the distance between the things that are proper to God and the things that are proper to His creatures.

Yet this greatest work of God, this work which can be produced by God alone, which lifts men up to the heights of God fulfilling their wildest hopes, has by the mercy of

God become so ordinary, so much the usual thing, the common way in which God's providence works, that it cannot be classed as a miraculous work. This is a tremendous truth. Raising the dead, curing the sick, giving sight to the blind—all these are miracles and all are child's play in comparison with the forgiveness of sin. But they are extraordinary, outside the usual run of the providence of God. This, the greatest work, is become an ordinary thing which, please God, we shall never take for granted.

The second effect of grace is hardly less astonishing, the effect of merit. By it we can actually earn the increase of grace and the reward of heaven by our own actions. By it we have a right in justice to the things of God. It is almost as though a father were solemnly to engage his five-year-old son as his secretary, putting his name on the pay-roll and each week give the boy wages with a completely serious face. But this is no game. This is solemn fact. Of course there can be no strict justice between God and ourselves, for strict justice demands equality; but there is a real justice established by the ordination of God Himself by which our childish works through grace are turned into works which demand full payment from God. We work according to our nature extolled by grace, and God rewards us according to His nature. He goes even further and allows us to merit where we have not this claim in justice, where our claim is based only on friendship, on His generosity, on the fittingness of the request we make.

Whether we merit in justice (*ex condigno*) or from the generosity of God (*ex congruo*), the two elements of merit must always be present: the grace of God which is the principle of merit and our human actions, the actions proceeding under our control to our goals. This merited reward, in other words, is ours. Though we receive the principle by which we can merit from God as a starting-point, it must be our actions that complete the work of meriting, it is by our own tools that we carve out even our supernatural destiny. When we speak of grace here, it is of course sanctifying or habitual grace that we mean. The sinner who has lost this grace, praying here and now by the help of actual grace, merits only in a very, very wide sense, a sense so wide as to mean that what is given to him will be entirely from the extravagant love of God.

Grace is the mysterious alchemy by which the base metal of our actions is turned into gold. With that gold, in our own right, we purchase the kingdom of heaven. We can merit eternal life in real justice. We can merit the end or goal of our supernatural life here on earth, but of course we cannot merit the beginning of that life any more than a man can give birth to himself, for that beginning is grace itself, the principle of merit. We might, by the help of actual grace, put in some claim on the mercy of God for this grace for ourselves; in possession of habitual grace, we can put a more serious claim on the friendship of God for this first beginning of grace for others. But our strict meriting, our meriting in justice, is done only for ourselves and we must have habitual grace before we can so merit.

If we can merit the end of supernatural life, of course we can merit the means to that end; that is, we can and do merit a constant increase in grace, charity and the virtues, we can and do merit temporal goods to the extent in which they are necessary to the task of saving our souls. But we cannot merit that special gift which is called final perseverance, a gift which extends from the beginning to the end of life, taking in the whole sweep of our activities from the first instant of grace to the culmination of grace in glory. It is something too big for any one act or any series of acts in the order of grace, for it embraces the whole of that order; something so big, in other words, that it must come wholly from the one Being Who is responsible for the whole of his order of grace, as He is for the whole of the order of nature.

Perhaps we can put all this more clearly by contrasting

it again with natural things. Irrational creation does the will of God, but does not merit; the result of its necessary fulfilment of the natural physical law is its own perfection. Men without grace obeying the Natural Moral Law merit some reward, for their obedience was free, personal, their very own; but they do not merit supernatural reward by purely natural actions. Man in the state of grace fulfilling the will of God, because of the double principle of grace and free will merits eternal life with God and the means to that life by his own actions.

In the attempt to sum up this doctrine of grace briefly we can do no better than continue the contrast with nature. The smallest degree of grace is infinitely more precious than all the beauty, order and riches of nature, indeed than all of nature thrown together; it is a gift above nature, a gift belonging to the supernatural, exceeding by its very essence the whole of the natural order. Consequently it is a gift that can come only from God. It is the bridge by which man steps from the world of nature into the supernatural world; so it is a gift transforming the world of nature for man. In the light of this gift, it is much more evident to man that nature is his servant, his tool, not something to fall in love with, to attempt to be satisfied with, to which he is chained or dedicated. Nature is a stepping-stone into the realms of the divine.

In the light of this gift all of human life, all of human action, takes on new meaning, tremendous significance. There is no poverty, drabness, failure, misery or despair in human existence that can compare with the poverty, drabness, failure, misery and despair of sin, for sin means the loss of grace. Anything short of sin is incapable of robbing human life of its high romance, its tense drama, its high hopes. With grace there is no insignificant human action; nothing can be insignificant that echoes in eternity. There is no unimportant human being. There is no meaningless human life.

With grace there is no place for slavery, for irresponsibility, for brutish plunging into the sensible in an attempt to escape humanity. By grace man reaches his supreme dignity, a participation of the life of God; not a confusion with divinity, not a loss of his personal existence, personal activity, personal possibilities, but rather a full realization of all these that here and now gives a foretaste of that happiness which will be had fully when grace reaches its climax in glory, in the glory of the vision of God. This is the end which was the beginning and which is an eternal beginning, the beginning of a supreme act that never reaches its termination.

Appendix to Chapter XX

REVEALED DOCTRINE PERTAINING TO GRACE

I

1. Man does not need grace to know natural truth. Council of Vatican, Session III, chapter 2, canon 1 (Denziger, ♯ 1806).

2. To know supernatural truth man needs grace. II Council of Orange, canon 7 (Denz., ♯ 180). Council of Vatican, Sess. III, chapter 2 (Denz., ♯ 1786). Council of Trent, Sess. VI, canon 3 (Denz., ♯ 813).

3. Without grace there can be no work valid for salvation. II Council of Orange, canon 7 (Denz., ♯ 180). Council of Trent, Sess. VI, canon 2 (Denz., ♯ 812).

4. Without grace man cannot begin work for salvation. II Council of Orange, canons 5 and 7 (Denz., ♯ 178, 180).

5. Not all the works of the just are sins. Council of Trent, Sess. VI, chapter 11 (Denz., ♯ 804) and canon 31 (Denz., ♯ 841).

6. Works are not always evil if they are done without perfect charity. Council of Trent, Sess. XIV, canon 5 (Denz., ♯ 915) and Sess. VI, canon 7 (Denz., ♯ 817).

7. Not all the works of infidels are sins. Council of Trent, Sess. VI, canon 7 (Denz., ♯ 817).

II

1. Without grace man cannot keep any supernatural precept as to the substance of the work. II Council of Mileve, canon 5 (Denz., ♯ 105). Council of Trent, Sess. VI, canon 2 (Denz., ♯ 812).

2. Nor can man keep any natural precept according to the mode of charity without grace. Council of Trent, ibid., canon 3 (Denz., # 813). II Council of Orange, canons 6 and 7 (Denz., # 179, 180).

3. Without grace man cannot merit eternal life. Council of Trent, Sess. VI, canon 2 (Denz., # 812).

4. Actual grace is necessary to attain habitual grace. II Council of Orange, canons 3 and 6 (Denz., # 176, 179). Council of Trent, Sess. VI, chapter 5 (Denz., # 797) and canon 3 (Denz., # 813).

5. Man cannot rise from sin without grace. II Council of Orange, canons 4 and 5 (Denz., # 177, 178). Council of Trent, Sess. VI, canon 3 (Denz., # 813).

6. Man in the state of fallen nature, healed by habitual grace, can avoid single venial sins, but not all venial sins unless by special privilege. II Council of Mileve, canon 6 (Denz., # 106). Council of Trent, Sess. VI, canon 23 (Denz., # 833).

7. Man in this state, not healed by habitual grace, cannot long remain without mortal sin. II Council of Mileve, canon 3 (Denz., # 103). Coelestine I, "Indiculus" (Denz., # 132).

III

1. Man needs actual grace to perform a supernaturally good work. II Council of Orange, canon 9 (Denz., # 182). Council of Trent, Sess. VI, chapter 16 (Denz., # 809).

2. For final perseverance man needs a special divine help directing and protecting him against temptation. II Council of Orange, canon 10 (Denz., # 183). Council of Trent, Sess. VI, canons 16 and 22 (Denz., # 826, 832).

3. Grace is something created and infused in the soul, inhering there by way of habit. Council of Vienna (*contra errores Joannes Olivi*) (Denz., # 483). Council of Trent, Sess. VI, canon 11 (Denz., # 821).

4. God is the first and universal cause and His knowledge is universal and infallible, depending on no one or nothing else. IV Lateran Council, chapter 1 (Denz., # 428). Vatican Council, Sess. III, chapter 1 (Denz., # 1782–1784).

5. The will of man is free in its action, even its supernatural action. Council of Trent, Sess. VI, chapter 5 (Denz., # 797, 798, 799) and canons 4, 5, 6 (Denz., # 814–816).

6. God is the only principal efficient cause of grace. II Council of Orange, canons 7 and 20 (Denz., # 180, 193). Council of Trent, Sess. VI, chapter 7 (Denz., # 799).

IV

1. Some preparation is necessary for habitual grace. Council of Trent, Sess. VI, canons 3 and 9 (Denz., # 813, 819).

2. Man prepares himself for grace by good movements of his free will. Ibid., canons 4 and 9 (Denz., # 814, 819).

3. All the just are given grace sufficient to observe all precepts. II Council of Orange, canon 25 (Denz., # 199,200). Council of Trent, Sess. VI, chapter 11 (Denz., # 804).

4. To all sinners among the faithful, even obdurate and blinded, God gives grace truly sufficient for repentance and avoidance of new sins. IV Lateran Council, chapter 1 (Denz., # 430). Council of Trent, Sess. VI, canons 17 and 29 (Denz., # 827, 839).

5. Grace sufficient for salvation is given to all infidels, even negative infidels, according to time and place. Propositions of Jansenists condemned by Alex. VIII, prop. 5 (Denz., # 1295). II Council of Orange, canons 23, 25 (Denz., # 196, 200). Coelestine I, "Indiculus" (Denz., # 139). Council of Trent, Sess. VI, canon 17 (Denz., # 827).

V

1. Sanctifying grace can be increased and is not equal in all. Council of Trent, Sess. VI, chapter 7 and canon 24 (Denz., # 799, 834).

2. Without a revelation, man cannot know certainly that he has grace. Council of Trent, Sess. VI, chapter 9 and canons 13, 14, 16 (Denz., # 802, 823, 824, 826).

3. Movement of free will is necessary for the justification of the sinner. Ibid., chapter 6 and canon 4 (Denz., # 798, 814).

4. For justification of a sinner a movement of faith is required. Ibid., chapter 6 (Denz., # 798).

5. For justification of a sinner movement of will against sin is necessary. Ibid.

6. Remission of sin is to be enumerated among the things required for justification. Ibid., chapter 7 (Denz., # 799).

1. The just truly merit. IV Lateran Council, chapter 1 (Denz., # 429). Council of Trent, Sess. VI, chapter 16 and canon 24 (Denz., # 809, 834).

2. The power of meriting is from the mercy of God and the merit of Christ. Council of Trent, Sess. VI, chapter 16 and canon 26 (Denz., # 809, 836).

3. Our merits give us a true right to reward. II Council of Orange, canon 18 (Denz., # 191). Council of Trent, ibid., canon 32 (Denz., # 842).

4. No one can merit for himself the first actual grace. II Council of Orange, canons 3 and 5 (Denz., # 176, 178). Council of Trent, Sess. VI, chapter 6 (Denz., # 798), chapter 5 (Denz., # 797).

5. No one can merit the first habitual grace *de condigno*. Council of Trent, Sess. VI, chapter 16, chapter 8, canon 32 (Denz., # 809,801,842).

6. Man cannot merit reparation after a future fall. Ibid., chapter 8 (Denz., # 801).

7. Man can merit an increase in grace and charity. Ibid., canons 24 and 32 (Denz., # 834, 842).

8. Man can merit eternal life. Ibid., chapter 16 and canon 32 (Denz., # 809, 842.)

CHAPTER XXI

AN ANALYSIS OF MODERN ETHICAL OPINION

CHAPTER XXI

AN ANALYSIS OF MODERN ETHICAL OPINION

THIS present and final chapter needs some justification. Its place in a work dedicated to the exposition of the *Theological Summa* of St. Thomas is not obvious unless we remember how profoundly St. Thomas knew his own age, how profoundly he treated its problems and how timeless are the principles upon which he based the solutions of those problems. Surely after such a study as we have made of the principles of Thomas the evaluation of the problems and opinions of our time can be made with much more accuracy and profundity.

There were other reasons which made this present chapter a necessity. Chapter by chapter throughout this volume analyses of modern thought have been given. Rigidly to document those analyses would have been to over-balance a book occupied with the well-nigh impossible task of crowding the already concise thought of a full part of the *Summa* into the covers of one volume. The whole aim of the book would have been defeated had the thought of Thomas not been adequately exposed; the profusion of notes necessary for an accurate documentation of modern ethical thought would definitely prohibit such an adequate exposition.

The tremendous variety in modern ethical thought is a solemn fact. It is "impressing", "an apparent babel", even though it is but the current rendering of thought-traditions which have been developing through the centuries.[1] The full confusion of this babel is appreciated if we remember that "naturally no present-day representative

[1] H. N. Wieman and B. E. Meland, *American Philosophies of Religion* (Chicago: Willet, Clark & Co., 1936), p. 5.

is consistent with the tradition which he continues".[1] This great variety of opinion is an admitted fact, a fact that is not surprising or unwelcome, but rather decidedly encouraging. Professor Brightman assures us that such differences of opinion will continue; creative differences after all are more valuable than reductions to any "common faith" that sacrifices individual creative energy.[2]

Actually this great variety of ethical opinion is the most important, and most disastrous fact in modern ethical thought. As we shall see, this variety furnishes us with the key to the weaknesses and defects of modern ethics and gives us the rational background of the calamitous consequences of our present-day ethical theory.

We can understand the fact of this variety of modern opinion if we grasp the fact that ethics has come to be identified with an age. There is no doubt about such an identification. It is agreed that "our generation faces new events, new ideas bound to support, destroy, modify current beliefs about right and wrong".[3] Philosophy of religion is a phase of the current cultural revolution. To remain it must continue as an integrated intellectual expression of the times.[4] Religion is being materially influenced by changes in American culture, and more than any other element in that culture.[5] If religious faith is to be adequate its foundation must be in the world of observation and social experience.[6]

This identification of ethics with an age is quite universal and accompanied by an almost panicky insistence on our need for reorientation, for catching up with the times, for

[1] H. N. Wieman, and B. E. Meland, *American Philosophies of Religon* (Chicago; Willet, Clarke & Co., 1936), p. viii.

[2] In *American Philosophies of Religion*, p. 325.

[3] R. C. Cabot, *The Meaning of Right and Wrong* (New York: Macmillan, 1936), pp. 1 and 3.

[4] *American Philosophies of Religion*, p. 311.

[5] H. B. Jefferson, "The Role of Religion In a Changing Culture", *The Journal of Religion*, Vol. XVI (1936), p. 57.

[6] G. K. Robertson, "Ethics, Cosmology, and Religious Faith", *The Journal of Religion*, Vol. XVI (1936), p. 56.

change.[1] This viewpoint reaches an extreme when a modern writer on ethics solemnly asures us that he renounces the past and makes no attempt to defend any past opinion.[2] Even Traditional Supernaturalism, we are assured, has been forced in self-defence to develop a contemporary philosophy of religion in order to ascertain if its presuppositions are consistent with the total cultural organization of life which prevails.[3] Indeed this cult of the contemporary is taken so seriously that it unconsciously furnishes amusement to the mere spectator by flinging the charge of "reactionary" at the very champions of the cult.[4]

In the concrete this modern attitude towards ethics means that ethics is affected by the varying currents of the age. We should expect to find modern authors ferreting out these factors in ethical change; and we do. In fact the multitude of factors discovered is enough to make us despair of the future of ethics. W. E. Hocking, for example, finds that Christianity is being affected by the notion of relativity, the criterion of naturalness, the change in the conception of salvation, the new sense of the necessity of an historic root of religion and a sense of shame for the division and lack of co-operation among Christians.[5] Shirley Jackson Case says the three significant influences in the transformation of religious heritages are modern scientific thinking, social maladjustments resulting from applied science and the

[1] Innumerable authors could be cited in substantiation of this statement. A few examples will suffice. W. H. Bernhardt, "The Significance of the Changing Function of Religion", *The Journal of Religion*, Vol. XII (1932), pp. 556, 558. E. E. Aubrey, *Present Theological Tendencies* (New York: Harper & Bros., 1936), pp. 4, 28, 54, 229, etc. Wieman and Meland, *American Philosophies of Religion*, p. 341.

[2] John Laird, *An Enquiry into Moral Notions* (New York: Columbia University Press, 1936), p. 10.

[3] *American Philosophies of Religion*, p. 62.

[4] Thus Dr. R. C. Cabot, *The Meaning of Right and Wrong*, includes among those who preach a "Gospel of Standpat" psychiatrists, bureaucrats, those entrenched behind scientific expertness and champions of hygienic behaviour (pp. 326, 327).

[5] "Christianity and Intercultural Contacts", *The Journal of Religion*, Vol. XIV (1934), pp. 127–138.

interpenetration of cultures.[1] Historical factors, such as the reaction against supernaturalism in medieval thought, against subjection of philosophy to science, the conflict between religion of authority and religion of spirit and the protest against reason as sole arbiter in religious thought, are all currently expressed in the different schools of ethical thought.[2] Then, too, there are the cultural problems of our age: wealth and poverty together with the impossibility of enjoying our great wealth because of our system of loyalties and ideals, the increase in the power of our achievement with no cause sufficiently dominant to draw all this power into its service, the increase of material and opportunities for happiness without adequate standards of choice and appreciation, the increase of interdependence without integrating loyalties, habits and sentiments, the drift towards collectivism.[3]

C. S. Patton has this strange medley to offer: the decay of old doctrines, strengthening sway of natural science, rise of naturalism and realism and other anti-idealistic philosophies, the enthronement of fate, unreason and cruelty by the World War, Biblical criticism and the doctrine of evolution as applied to the Bible, to God and to moral and spiritual life.[4] On the other hand we are told that idealism is a dominant factor in modern thought.[5] Science is profoundly influencing ethical thought;[6] on the contrary, science is producing confusion and discouragement;[7] psychoanalysis, behavourism and Bergson's theory especially have led to determinism, fatalism and irrationalism.[8]

[1] Editor's note, *The Journal of Religion,* Vol. XIV (1934), p. 2.

[2] *American Philosophies of Religion,* pp. 12 and 13. [3] Ibid., p. 23.

[4] "The American Theological Scene", *The Journal of Religion,* Vol. XVI (1936), p. 460.

[5] *Present Theological Tendencies,* p. 62. C. E. M. Joad, *A Guide To Modern Thought* (London: Faber and Faber), p. 119. *American Philosophies of Religion,* p. 319 (Prof. Brightman).

[6] E. S. Ames, "Christianity and Scientific Thinking", *The Journal of Religion,* Vol. XIV (1934), pp. 4–12. B. E. Meland, "A Present-Day Evaluation of Christian Ethics", ibid., Vol. X (1930), pp. 378 ff. *Present Theological Tendencies,* pp. 24, 13.

[7] *A Guide to Modern Thought,* pp. 23, 60.

[8] Ibid., pp. 26, 60, 216.

Both collectivism[1] and individualism[2] take a mighty part in the moulding of modern ethics. In fact there is little that does not go into that discouraging process. Of course summaries of these factors have been made; but even the summaries offer a confusing variety.[3]

Such a great variety of opinion makes classification almost an impossibility. Recently two attempts have been made to accomplish some classification, earnest, scholarly attempts.[4] But their success has been at best vague. In fact we are assured at the outset that no two interpreters can hope to arrange the thought of their contemporaries in systematic form so as to satisfy all concerned; philosophies of religion are too organic in content and too flexible in method for rigid classification. Any scheme is inadequate because thought, organic and mobile, overruns mechanical categories.[5] As concrete evidence of this impossibility, the editors of *American Philosophies of Religion*, after having reduced modern thought to the four root-traditions of supernaturalism, idealism, romanticism and naturalism, show clearly that these currents of thought tend to intermingle more and more.[6] Some fifty-seven modern authors are grouped under these four schools of thought; and among members of the same school there are extreme differences on such fundamentals of moral thought as the notion of God.[7]

Granted the extreme difficulty of classification of modern ethical opinion, it should not be difficult to detect the changes brought about in ethical thought by the identification of ethics with an age and the consequent subjection of ethics

[1] *Present Theological Tendencies*, p. 216.
[2] Ibid., p. 213.
[3] K. S. Latourette, "Have We Passed the Age of Religion?" *The Journal of Religion*, Vol. XVI (1936), pp. 419 ff. *Present Theological Tendencies*, pp. 4–8, 13, 191, 212, 221. *A Guide To Modern Thought*, p. 216. *American Philosophies of Religion*, pp. 21, 49, 309.
[4] *American Philosophies of Religion* and *Present Theological Tendencies*.
[5] *American Philosophies of Religion*, pp. 5 and 11.
[6] Ibid., pp. 7 and 341.
[7] e.g. ibid., p. 136. Brightman (idealist) holds for a finite God.

to steady bombardment by the currents of the age. It could reasonably be expected that ethics under such circumstances would change as much as a house that is subjected to rifle, machine-gun and artillery fire with a rain of aerial bombs thrown in for good measure. Modern authors assure us that just such a change as might have been expected has actually taken place.

Our age is an age of transformation so great in the religious world as to be, if not an abandonment of religion, at least (from the viewpoint of orthodoxy) a betrayal of fundamentals. The groups in each religion might be classified as fundamentalists, mystics, institutionalists, modernists, liberals and radicals.[1] Except for the belief in God, and a vigorous but somewhat changed attitude toward Jesus, we have little, almost nothing, left of the orthodoxy with which we started out fifty years ago. The Trinity, the Incarnation, miracles, fall of man, atonement, heaven and hell have dropped out of the discussion. Theism, belief in God, the Character of God, the relation of God to man and the universe, the concept of God, something about God, furnishes their (theologians') central and almost only theme.[2] We shall see shortly how poverty-stricken our age is when we examine the modern notion of God.

The destruction has been nearly complete. None of these historical absolutes (God, Eternal Patterns, Reason, Nature) has been able to remain changeless and at the same time continue to serve as a standard. In fact it is better so, for ethics will make greater progress by seeking stability, meeting the growing needs of changing man and changing society than in the search for changeless essences. A standard for ethics in a changing world must be capable of change if it is to continue as a standard.[3] The modernist

[1] Editor's note in *The Journal of Religion*, Vol. XIV (1934), p. 1 (the editor is Shirley Jackson Case).

[2] C. S. Patton, "The American Theological Scene", *The Journal of Religion*, Vol. XVI (1936), pp. 459 and 460.

[3] J. H. Tufts, "The Institution as Agency of Stability and Readjustment in Ethics", *The Philosophical Review*, Vol. XLIV (1935), pp. 138, 140, 142.

shares with other theologians a method of theology rather than stressing differences of conclusions; he cares less for his own conclusions than for the method.[1] In fact we are told that the humanists can be divided into theists and atheists; both groups have difficulty identifying themselves with Christianity and it is even questionable whether the word "religion" should be used in reference to their teaching.[2] The transformation of the processes of living has been so rapid that it has run away from forms, standards, ideals, affections, loyalties, objectives.[3] The social change has, indeed, been so great that the individual is clearly conscious of the shift in major objectives within a lifetime. If he develops a satisfactory way of living in youth and clings to it, he finds himself in an alien world in old age.[4]

Seen thus at a distance and in a general way, the havoc wrought on ethics by the cult of the contemporary seems nearly complete. If we descend into the wreckage the full horror is brought home to us unforgettably. Take the very fundamental moral notions of the goal of human life, God, man and morality. How are they faring under the sweeping attack of the champions of change?

A consideration of the goal of human life is not an arbitrary procedure. As we have seen, the whole essence of morality is man's approach to or recession from his goal. Among the moderns themselves, psychiatrists recognize that disintegration of personality comes where no dominant purpose controls individual life.[5] The intelligentsia of China, India and Russia have abandoned religion as worship of gods or God; but in each country there is an object of devotion approaching

[1] *Present Theological Tendencies*, p. 28.
[2] E. S. Ames, "Christianity and Scientific Thinking", *The Journal of Religion*, pp. 7 ff.
[3] *American Philosophies of Religion*, pp. 18 and 19.
[4] Ibid., p. 20.
[5] *Present Theological Tendencies*, p. 232.

religious worship in its intensity—Sun-Yat-Sen, Gandhi, Lenin.[1] Man must have a goal at which his actions are aimed.

In a general way, it is the ascription of personality to the object of worship at which modern naturalism or humanism takes offence and for which it seeks a substitute. The religions of the past are outworn; science and humanitarian interest and effort must be the bases of religion.[2] Religious humanism, with its background of Feuerbach's recognition of divine qualities as human experiences and Comte's sublimation of the worship of a supernatural deity in the worship of humanity, frankly advocates a social idealism whose end is to control sub-human forces both in society and the world of nature and release the potential spiritual forces in man himself.[3] It is openly anthropocentric, i.e. humanity is the goal of man.[4]

The cosmic theists put some cosmic process or order in the place of humanity as the supreme guide and sovereign of human life.[5] Aesthetic naturalism is an appreciative response to reality; religion is the art of finding our emotional relationship to the world conceived as a whole, thus tending toward a quiescence that ignores the moral imperatives.[6] An empirical theist like Shailer Matthews declares that the ultimate basis of morality must be placed in the basic activity of the total process in which men are involved.[7] To the personalists the aim of the universe is not absorption in the Infinite nor mere assertion of personal liberty but free and moral co-operation with God. This is the essence of religion and religious salvation and if there is a good

[1] A. E. Garvie, "Religion Without God", *Journal of Philosophical Studies*, Vol. V (1930), p. 208.

[2] Garvie, "Religion Without God", ibid.

[3] *American Philosophies of Religion*, p. 253.

[4] Ibid., p. 253. Confer: *Present Theological Tendencies*, pp. 39 ff., 167, 258; *American Philosophies of Religion*, p. 229.

[5] *American Philosophies of Religion*, l.c.

[6] Ibid., p. 180.

[7] Shailer Matthews, "The Religious Basis of Ethics", *The Journal of Religion*, Vol. X (1930), pp. 222 ff. Confer: "Doctrines as Social Patterns", ibid. ab eodem, pp. 1 ff.

in future life it must be moral and rational, developing, a good of work and service.[1] The neo-supernaturalists criticize the moderns for losing the end in the means and then losing the meaning of the means, for finding the end of human life in man himself, exalting human personalities thus losing humility and a sense of humour.[2] For themselves, they see that the natural life of man is condemned by God as evil,[3] and that what men must live for completely is an absolute obedience to the will of God, though this obedience does not indicate what is right and wrong but leaves us free to discover right and wrong by the best standards available. No standards are God-given. It does not seem to make much difference what happens to the individuals or the world, by the very fact of this obedience life is triumphant.[4]

There you have the modern goal of man: humanity or some social ideal; a cosmic process or order; a tuning of emotions to the world; a constant co-operation with a finite, struggling God, maybe an eternal co-operation of work and service; or a fatalistic obedience which holds out no personal end to be attained beyond that obedience. For one of these man must direct every action, for one of these goals man must live his life, some one of these will be the supreme victory won by living life.

The notion of God has suffered even more. According to one analysis there are four types of opinion on God: supernaturalism looks on God as Being; idealism and romanticism hold God is Mind; naturalistic theism describes God as Process; to humanistic theism and aesthetic naturalism God is Symbol.[5] A more comprehensive view of modern opinion classifies the views on God as: denial of God;

[1] *American Philosophies of Religion*, pp. 144–145.
[2] *Present Theological Tendencies*, p. 191.
[3] *American Philosophies of Religion*, pp. 82, 87, 89.
[4] Ibid., pp. 78, 80, 82.
[5] *American Philosophies of Religion*, p. 10.

God is a man-made ideal; God can not be known through science but only directly by feeling or faith; God can be known by reason as an explanation or interpretation of some phase of the universe or of reality in its totality.[1] Still another assures us there is a fourfold modern attitude to God: the attitude of those who affirm the existence of God, an attitude that is still powerful and numerically strong; the agnostic attitude, proper to a lesser group; the atheistic attitude which clearly and openly denies God, an attitude that is steadily increasing; and finally the attitude of the equivocators—men who for the most part belong to the atheistic group but who keep the old words, redefining them until they have lost all meaning. To this last group belong Whitehead, Lake, Alexander, J. Huxley, Drake, J. H. Holmes, Wieman, Randall, Eddington, Jeans, Millikan and Conklin.[2]

Such a flight away from the Christian idea of God is quite understandable to some modern minds; in fact a self-respecting scientist or moralist feels himself not only justified but compelled to seek satisfaction for such needs as he may feel elsewhere than in God.[3] God seems unnecessary in an age which has mastered physical environment to such an extent that food, clothing, comforts, and luxuries are obtainable by other than religious means. We look to a machine, an economic or a political system rather than to a temple.[4] In fact the God-concept is entirely secondary in humanists' thinking; among those carrying the humanistic principle to its extreme conclusion, the God-concept is excluded.[5] It is not surprising, then, that in our colleges students tend in the direction of the agnostic or atheistic

[1] Gertrude C. Bussey, "Religion and Truth", *The Journal of Religion*, Vol. XI (1931), p. 80.

[2] Corliss Lamont, "Equivocation on Religious Issues", *The Journal of Religion*, Vol. XIV (1934), pp. 412 ff.

[3] A. E. Garvie, "Religion Without God", *The Journal of Philosophical Studies*, Vol. V (1930), p. 207.

[4] K. S. Latourette, "Have We Passed the Age of Religion?", *The Journal of Religion*, Vol. XVI (1936), p. 424.

[5] *American Philosophies of Religion*, p. 252.

position;[1] and that we hear moderns seriously speak of "God in the making".[2] It is no wonder that fatalism is a fact of present-day life.[3]

Taken school by school, the philosophers of our age present us with a strange assortment of gods. All mysticism and idealism, so of course the personalists, posit an absolute being; yet the personalist god is strangely intermingled with the physical world—which is the will of God organizing His own experience and communicating it to us. He is a developing god and though everything in nature is His work, nature is not wholly controlled by Him.[4] The God of the neo-supernaturalists is neither purely transcendant nor entirely immanent, he is both. He is world-seeking[5] yet stands as judge and condemner of the world, having nothing to do with the standards of right and wrong, unknowable by reason and apparently not very careful about what becomes of men.[6] Romantic liberalism readily identifies God's will with the point of view and social cause dominating at any particular time and place.[7] Humanism makes a god out of the growing ideal of man, or out of a social ideal.[8] The naturalistic school, identifying God with process, offers an unlimited variety of God-concepts.[9]

If there is little room for divinity in the Christian sense among modern theorists, there is still less room for humanity. Man, in the cult of the contemporary, may be almost anything else but he is not a rational animal. He is made a

[1] A. C. Wakenden, "The Effect of the College Experience Upon Students' Concepts of God", *The Journal of Religion*, Vol. XII (1932), p. 266.
[2] W. M. Urban, "Modernism in Science and Philosophy", *Journal of Philosophical Studies*, Vol. V (1930), p. 230.
[3] C. E. M. Joad, *A Guide to Modern Thought*, p. 220.
[4] *American Philosophies of Religion*, pp. 115, 136, 138.
[5] *Present Theological Tendencies*, p. 203.
[6] *American Philosophies of Religion*, pp. 78, 80, 82, 86, 87, 89.
[7] *American Philosophies of Religion*, p. 83.
[8] Ibid., pp. 229, 258. *Present Theological Tendencies*, p. 167.
[9] e.g. Those offered by Bergson, L. Morgan, S. Alexander, Wieman, Whitehead, Ames, Dewey, Matthews. Confer: *Present Theological Tendencies*, pp., 174, 182. A. S. Woodburne, "The Goal of Religion", *The Journal of Religion*, Vol. XII (1932), p. 214. *American Philosophies of Religion*, pp. 274, 295. Shailer Matthews (*supra*, note 7, p. 448) and A. E. Garvie (*supra*, note 3, p. 450).

god by the humanists (*supra*, note 8, p. 451). To the naturalists he is merely part of a process; he has been produced by the natural universe and through healthful relations with the environing process he can fulfil his life.[1] He has, of course, no substantial spiritual soul, no ideas or mental states[2] and is wholly committed to a naturalistic world.[3] To the personalists man is a personality; but personalism rejects soul-psychology, i.e. the psychology which says that the true self is found in some transcendant entity of substance that underlies and supports consciousness. To the personalist it is enough to know that self is "a whole of conscious experience".[4] To the aesthetic naturalist, man is an emotional creature occupied in the one all-important work of tuning his emotions to the world conceived as a whole.[5] The neo-supernaturalists conceive man as a creature moving in a world that is under the judgment of God, his every act infected with evil, obeying moral standards that have nothing to do with God and obliged for a totally unexplained reason to give absolute obedience to a will of God which can be known in no rational way.[6] To the psychologists (Freudians and Behaviourists) turned philosophers man is a machine at the mercy of stimuli or surgings of the unconscious, without power to mould his own life, a complete automaton.[7]

With the old notions of the goal of life, of God and of man out of the way, there is no difficulty in disposing of the old morality. Of course the notion of sin is gone and with it, logically, the old notion of virtue. An action, after all, is moral in so far as it proceeds under our control to goals

[1] *American Philosophies of Religion*, p. 272.
[2] D. F. Ehlman, "Correcting Subjectivism In Religion", *The Journal of Religion*, Vol. XIV (1934), pp. 273 ff.
[3] B. E. Meland, "A Present-Day Evaluation of Christian Ethics", *The Journal of Religion*, Vol. X (1930), p. 384.
[4] *American Philosophies of Religion*, p. 140.
[5] Ibid., p. 180.
[6] *American Philosophies of Religion*, pp. 87 and 89. Confer *supra*, pp. 10 and 11.
[7] *A Guide To Modern Thought*, pp. 60, 219, 220. Cf. J. B. Watson, "The Behaviourist Looks at Instincts", *Harper's Magazine*, Vol. 155 (July, 1927), p. 228. "The Myth of the Unconscious", ibid. ab eodem (Sept., 1927), p. 502.

of our choosing; take away that control or change the supreme goal and of course morality is destroyed or changed. Probably all that need be said about modern ideas of morality was said when it was declared that the new spirit and new ideology of the world was characterized by relativity, resulting in a new intellectual and moral climate.[1] That fundamental notion of relativity, of variability, of change is universal among modern ethical thinkers, as has been abundantly shown.

It is precisely this notion of relativity, of variability, of change that is of paramount importance for an understanding of modern ethical opinion. Indeed with that notion of variability well understood, all the other characteristics of modern ethics follow as symptoms follow on the contraction of a disease or as conclusions follow from a principle.

Obviously this relative character of ethics and ethical fundamentals means that the anchor of the unchangeable, the eternally enduring, the absolute, has been lost; and cheerfully, even eagerly, lost. That loss is the rock-bottom truth of modern ethics. From it some startling, even terrifying, conclusions follow, conclusions which have been noted, even gloated over by modern thinkers. We can sum up these conclusions which are characteristics of modern ethics this way:

1. With the loss of the unchangeable, the absolute, modern ethics is cut off from God, from a spiritual soul, from the supernatural—indeed from everything that is above the transient change of the material world.[2]
   (*a*) Consequently there is a growing emphasis on the material (not necessarily in the sense of

[1] *Present Theological Tendencies*, pp. 9–12.

[2] Confer *supra*, p. 446 ff. See also: Corliss Lamont, "Equivocation on Religious Issues", *The Journal of Religion*, Vol. XIV (1934), pp. 412–421. *American Philosophies of Religion*, pp. 62, 83, 229, 314. *Present Theological*

mechanistic materialism but in the sense of a self-sufficient universe) with changed or abandoned notions of virtue, sin, merit, blame, sanction.[1]

(*b*) Consequently there is a glorification of changeable knowledge, of the scientific method; where this method has been attacked, the conclusion drawn from its unsatisfactory character has not been that there is some other method of rational investigation but that reason cannot lead us to knowledge.[2]

(*c*) So there has been a thorough discrediting of the intellectual processes to the exaltation of feeling, intuition, faith and religious experience as sources of knowledge.[3]

2. Divorced from the unchangeable, modern ethics has been inextricably bound up with the elements of human life that do change: scientific, political, economic and social organization.[4]
3. Hence the end of ethics and morality (guidance to a goal) is no longer the personal, absolute, immutable goal of individual salvation, but the collective, relative, fluctuating goals of economic, scientific, political or social good.[5]

Tendencies, pp. 156, 167, 174, note. E. S. Ames, "Christianity and Scientific Thinking", *The Journal of Religion*, pp. 4–12. B. E. Meland, "A Present-Day Evaluation of Christian Ethics", *The Journal of Religion*, pp. 378–393. D. F. Ehlman, "Correcting Subjectivisms in Religion", *The Journal of Religion*, pp. 273, 285. A. E. Garvie, "Religion Without God", *Journal of Philosophical Studies*, pp. 208 ff. A. E. Haydon, "Mr. Dewey On Religion and God", *The Journal of Religion*, Vol. XV. (1936), pp. 22–25. John B. Watson, *Psychology From the Standpoint of a Behaviourist* (Philadelphia: J. B. Lippincott), p. 355.

[1] *Supra*, p. 446 ff. C. E. M. Joad, *A Guide to Modern Thought*, pp. 216, 220. *Present Theological Tendencies*, p. 24. W. H. Bernhardt, "The Significance of the Changing Function of Religion", *The Journal of Religion*, pp. 556 ff. *American Philosophies of Religion*, pp. 55, 248, 253, 312. G. K. Robertson, "Ethics, Cosmology, and Religious Faith", *The Journal of Religion*, p. 47–56 .

[2] The attitude towards the scientific method and intellectual processes is interesting. First there is the exaltation of the scientific method: *Present Theological Tendencies*, pp. 13, 30–33. *American Philosophies of Religion*, pp.

From this welter of modern ethical opinion, four characteristics stand out as commonly shared, namely:

1. Materialism in the sense of a self-sufficient natural order with its concomitant emphasis on scientific method and empirical findings. Only the neo-supernaturalists escape this characteristic.
2. Totalitarian or holistic ideals to the constantly decreasing importance of the individual. The neo-supernaturalists would seem to share at least in the universal disregard of the individual's happiness.
3. As an inevitable consequence there is pessimism; and here the neo-supernaturalists take the lead. Others will stoutly deny pessimism while naïvely championing materialism and totalitarian ideals.
4. Finally relativity or variability. And in this last all others are contained.

These characteristics are not odious marks that must be proved to be present. They are shouted from the housetops and thus can easily be substantiated from almost any modern author picked at random. The one characteristic which no modern author will allow to stand in doubt for an instant is that of variability. By that variability

228–229. Then an uneasiness from the results of the sciences themselves leading to scepticism and the allowance for non-scientific knowledge: *Present Theological Tendencies*, p. 188. Joad, *A Guide To Modern Thought*, pp. 71, 86, 192, 217. Finally the open attack which uncovers the weaknesses and limitations of this scientific method and despairs of rational knowledge: *Present-Day Theological Tendencies*, pp. 46–53, 73, 89 ff, 158. *American Philosophies of Religion*, pp. 81, 314.

[3] This discrediting of intellectual processes is unequivocably declared and lamented by W. M. Urban, "Modernism in Science and Philosophy", *Journal of Philosophical Studies*, Vol. V (1930), pp. 230–245. It is clear from some of the modern definitions of truth cited by E. G. Spaulding, *A World of Chance* (New York: Macmillan, 1936), p. 109. It is unblushingly stated in *American Philosophies of Religion*, pp. 13, 69. For the growth of the subjective and emotional sources of knowledge cf. ibid, pp. 120, 136, 175.

[4] *Supra*, p. 446. *American Philosophies of Religion*, pp. 4, 251, 285, 309, 319; *Present Theological Tendencies*, pp. 24, 103, 216, 221. R. C. Cabot, *The Meaning of Right and Wrong*, p. 328.

[5] Ibid.

modern ethics demands that it be judged. Perhaps the nature of that judgment will be clearer if in one sentence we contrast Christian ethics as exposed by St. Thomas to modern ethical opinion. That contrast can be thus briefly stated: the former rests on the immutable mind of God, is absolute, rational, objective and personal; the latter, with no unchanging foundation, is relative, irrational, subjective and collective.

INDEX

S